WINNIPEG
WN
D0565399

Being a Dog Is
a Full-Time Job

Being a Dog Is a Full-Time Job

A Peanuts® Collection.

by Charles M. Schulz

Andrews McMeel Publishing®

Kansas City • Sydney • London

Peanuts © is distributed internationally by Universal Uclick.

Being a Dog Is a Full-Time Job copyright © 1994 by Peanuts Worldwide, Inc. All rights reserved. PEANUTS Comic Strips © 1989 Peanuts Worldwide, Inc. Printed in China. No part of this book may be used or reproduced in any manner whatsoever without written permission except in the case of reprints in the context of reviews.

Andrews McMeel Publishing
an Andrews McMeel Universal company
1130 Walnut Street, Kansas City, Missouri 64106

www.andrewsmcmeel.com

ISBN: 978-0-8362-1746-9

Library of Congress Catalog Card Number: 93-74270

14 15 16 17 18 SDB 28 27 26 25 24 23

──── **ATTENTION: SCHOOLS AND BUSINESSES** ────

Andrews McMeel books are available at quantity discounts with bulk purchase for educational, business, or sales promotional use. For information, please e-mail the Andrews McMeel Publishing Special Sales Department:
specialsales@amuniversal.com

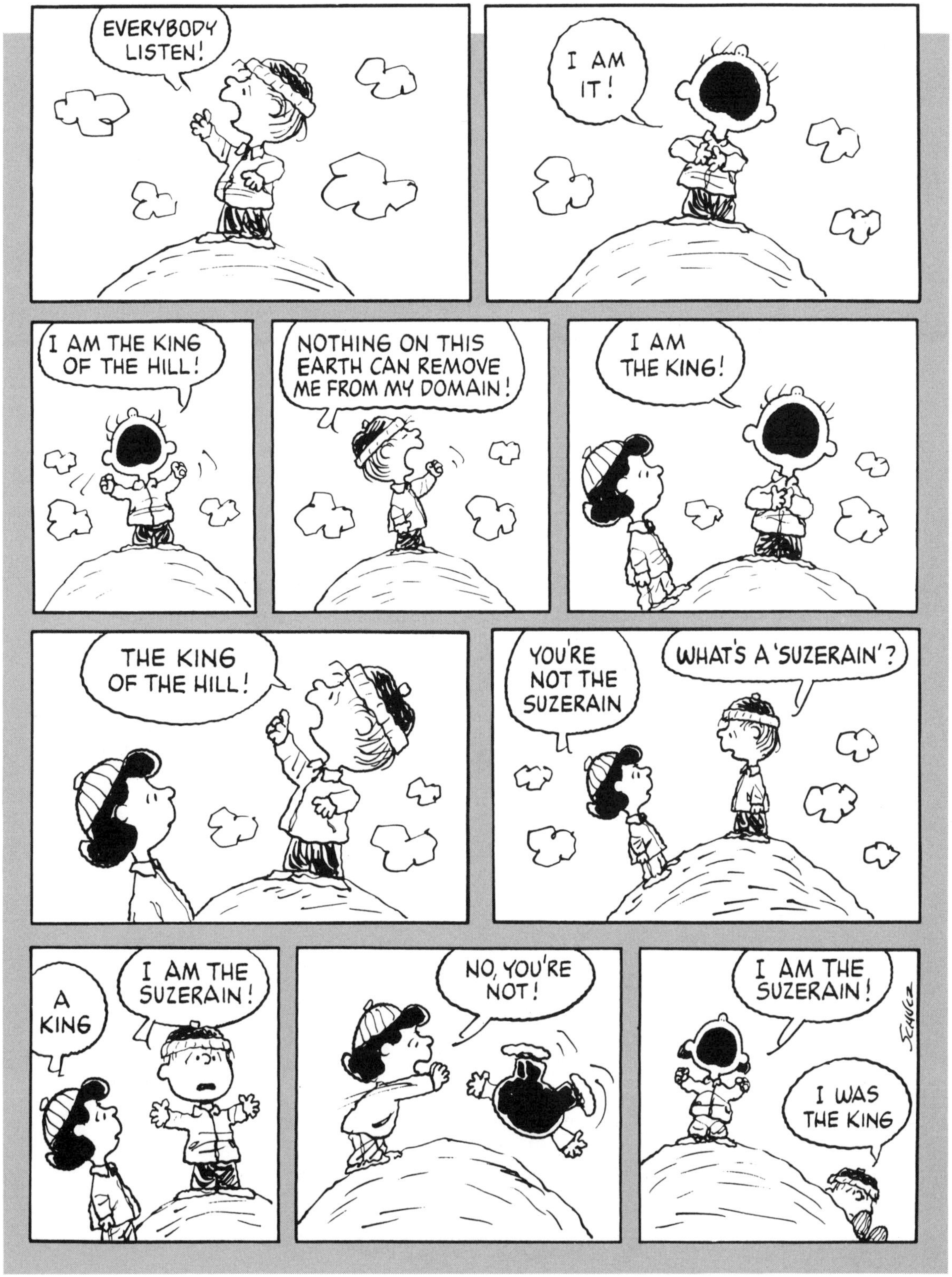
EVERYBODY LISTEN!
I AM IT!
I AM THE KING OF THE HILL!
NOTHING ON THIS EARTH CAN REMOVE ME FROM MY DOMAIN!
I AM THE KING!
THE KING OF THE HILL!
YOU'RE NOT THE SUZERAIN
WHAT'S A 'SUZERAIN'?
A KING
I AM THE SUZERAIN!
NO, YOU'RE NOT!
I AM THE SUZERAIN!
I WAS THE KING
SCHULZ

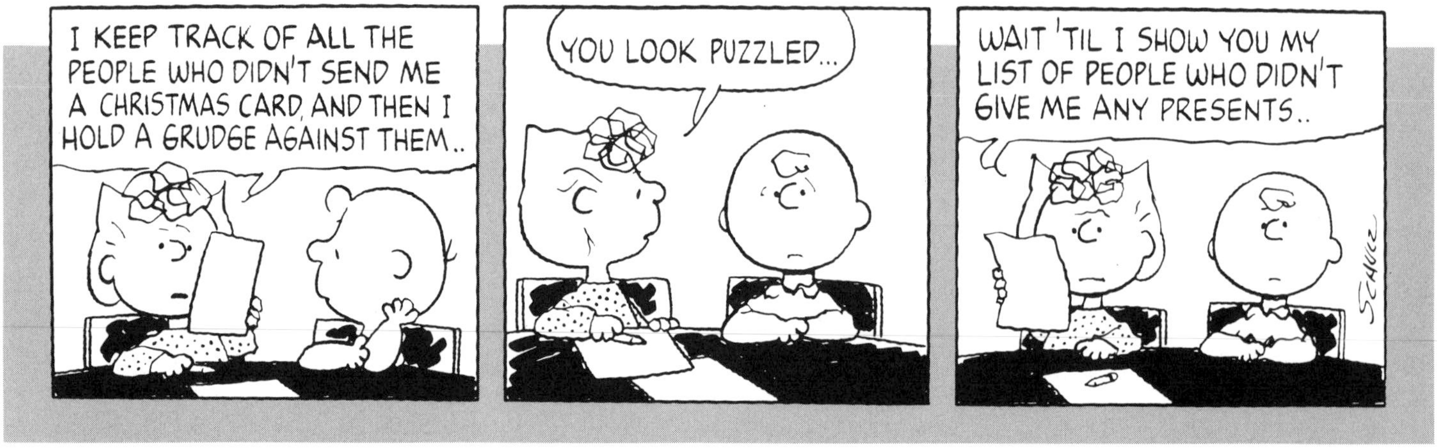
I KEEP TRACK OF ALL THE PEOPLE WHO DIDN'T SEND ME A CHRISTMAS CARD, AND THEN I HOLD A GRUDGE AGAINST THEM..
YOU LOOK PUZZLED...
WAIT 'TIL I SHOW YOU MY LIST OF PEOPLE WHO DIDN'T GIVE ME ANY PRESENTS..

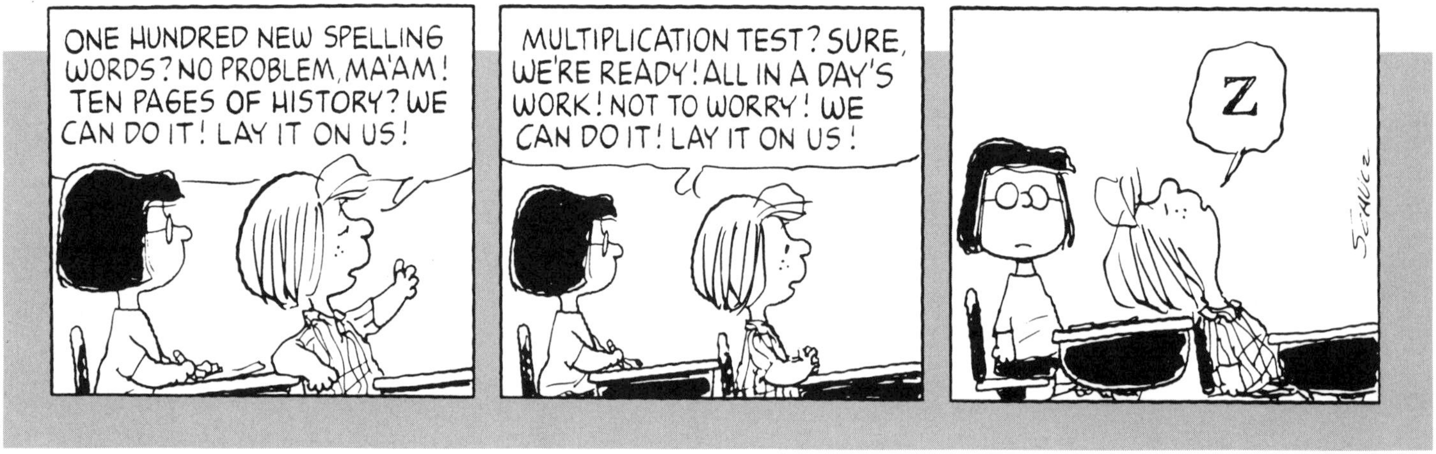
ONE HUNDRED NEW SPELLING WORDS? NO PROBLEM, MA'AM! TEN PAGES OF HISTORY? WE CAN DO IT! LAY IT ON US!
MULTIPLICATION TEST? SURE, WE'RE READY! ALL IN A DAY'S WORK! NOT TO WORRY! WE CAN DO IT! LAY IT ON US!
Z

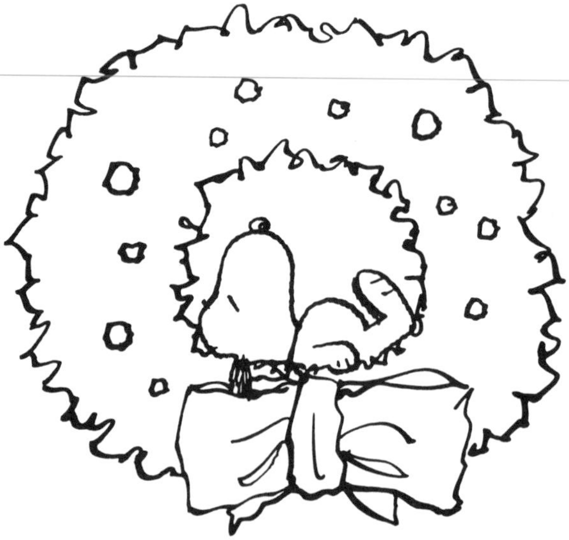

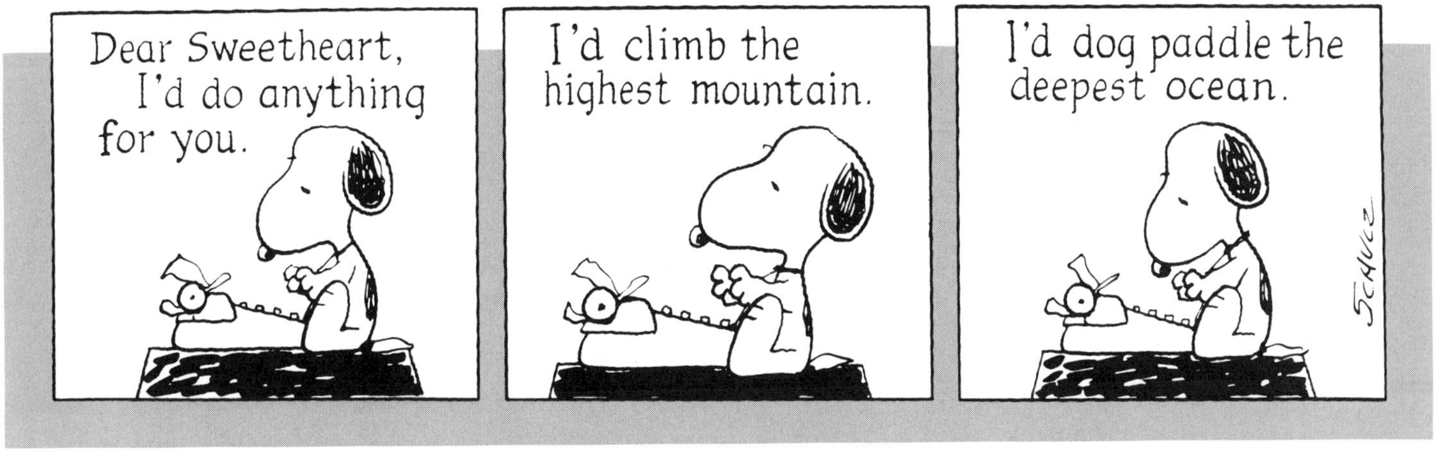
Dear Sweetheart,
I'd do anything for you.
I'd climb the highest mountain.
I'd dog paddle the deepest ocean.
SCHULZ

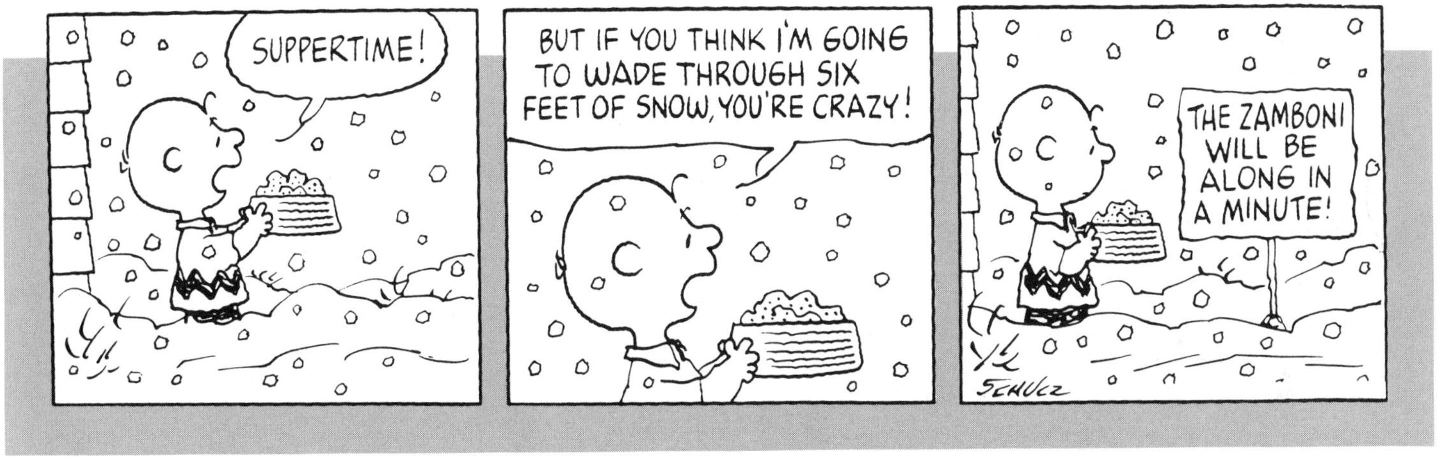
SUPPERTIME!
BUT IF YOU THINK I'M GOING TO WADE THROUGH SIX FEET OF SNOW, YOU'RE CRAZY!
THE ZAMBONI WILL BE ALONG IN A MINUTE!
SCHULZ

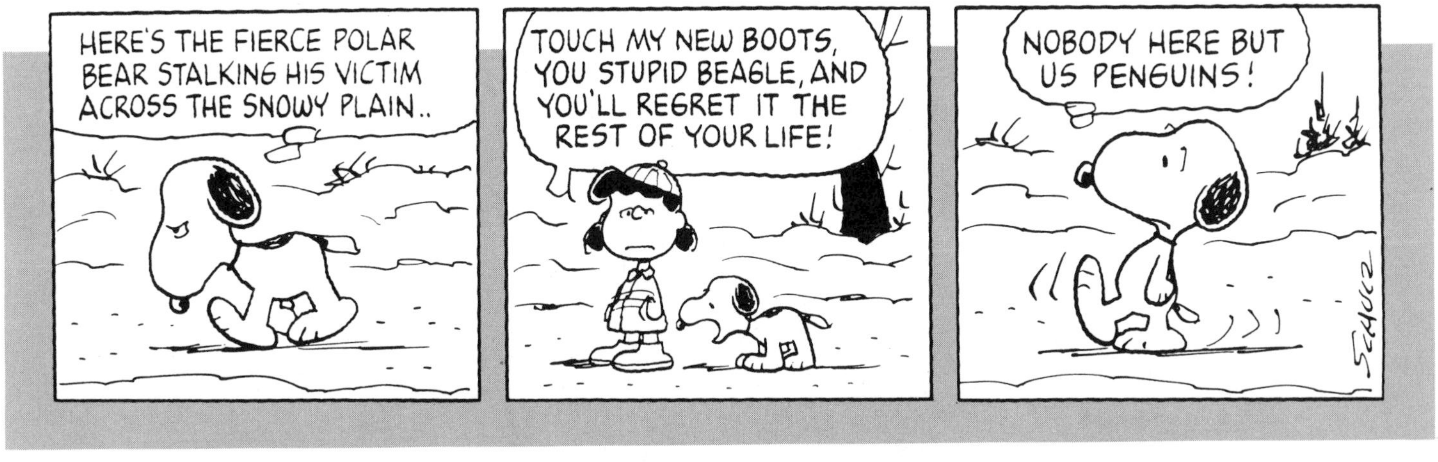
HERE'S THE FIERCE POLAR BEAR STALKING HIS VICTIM ACROSS THE SNOWY PLAIN..
TOUCH MY NEW BOOTS, YOU STUPID BEAGLE, AND YOU'LL REGRET IT THE REST OF YOUR LIFE!
NOBODY HERE BUT US PENGUINS!
SCHULZ

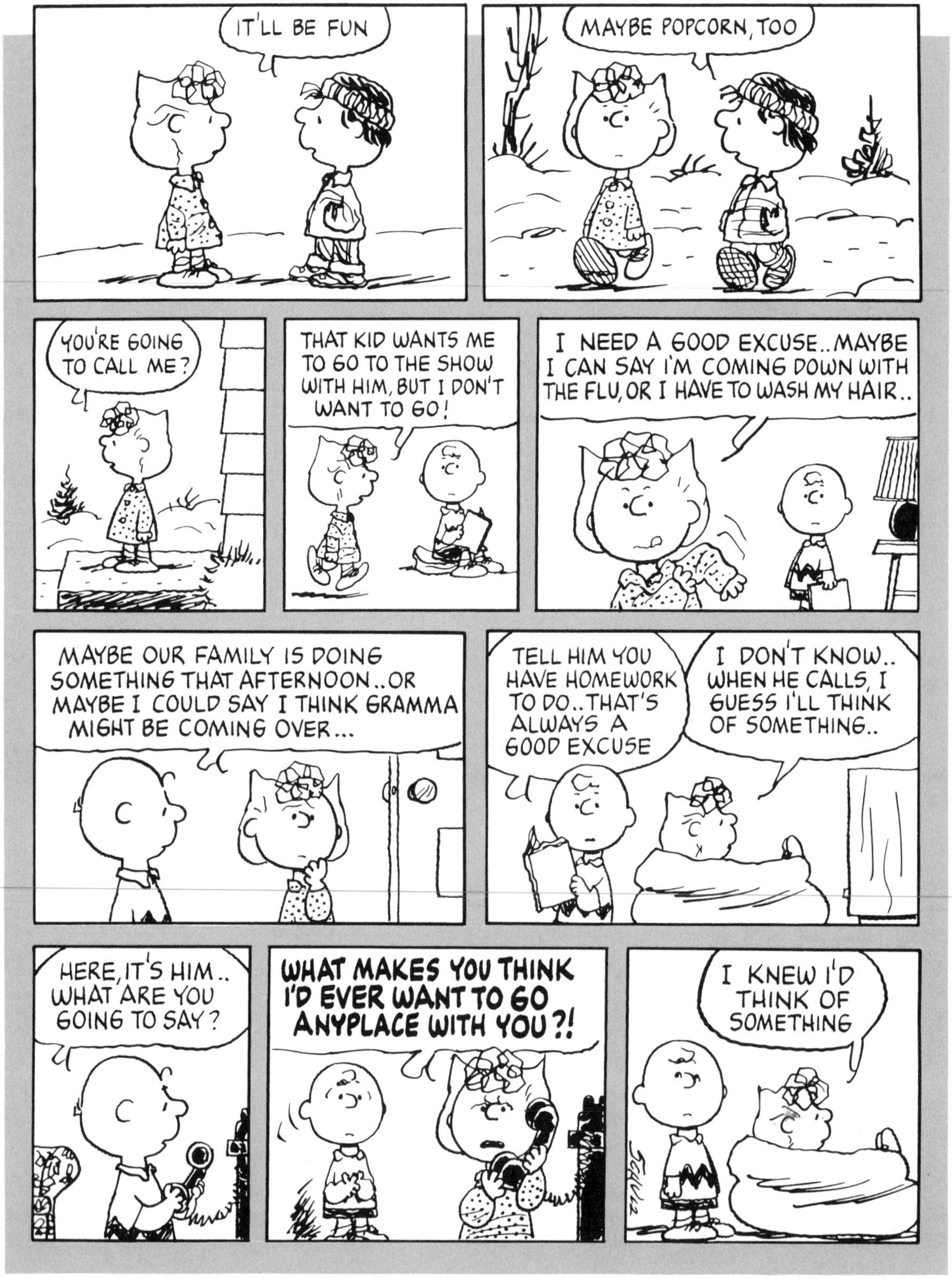
IT'LL BE FUN
MAYBE POPCORN, TOO
YOU'RE GOING TO CALL ME?
THAT KID WANTS ME TO GO TO THE SHOW WITH HIM, BUT I DON'T WANT TO GO!
I NEED A GOOD EXCUSE..MAYBE I CAN SAY I'M COMING DOWN WITH THE FLU, OR I HAVE TO WASH MY HAIR..
MAYBE OUR FAMILY IS DOING SOMETHING THAT AFTERNOON..OR MAYBE I COULD SAY I THINK GRAMMA MIGHT BE COMING OVER...
TELL HIM YOU HAVE HOMEWORK TO DO..THAT'S ALWAYS A GOOD EXCUSE
I DON'T KNOW.. WHEN HE CALLS, I GUESS I'LL THINK OF SOMETHING..
HERE, IT'S HIM.. WHAT ARE YOU GOING TO SAY?
WHAT MAKES YOU THINK I'D EVER WANT TO GO ANYPLACE WITH YOU?!
I KNEW I'D THINK OF SOMETHING

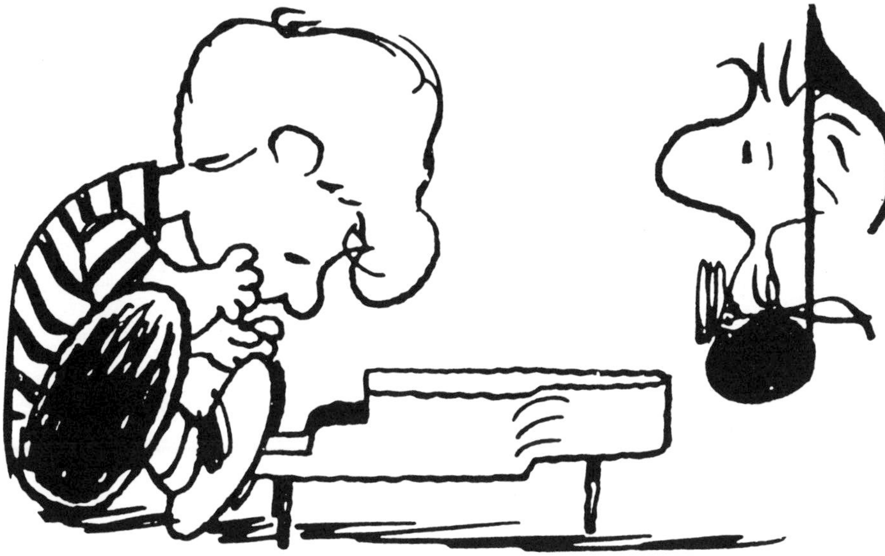

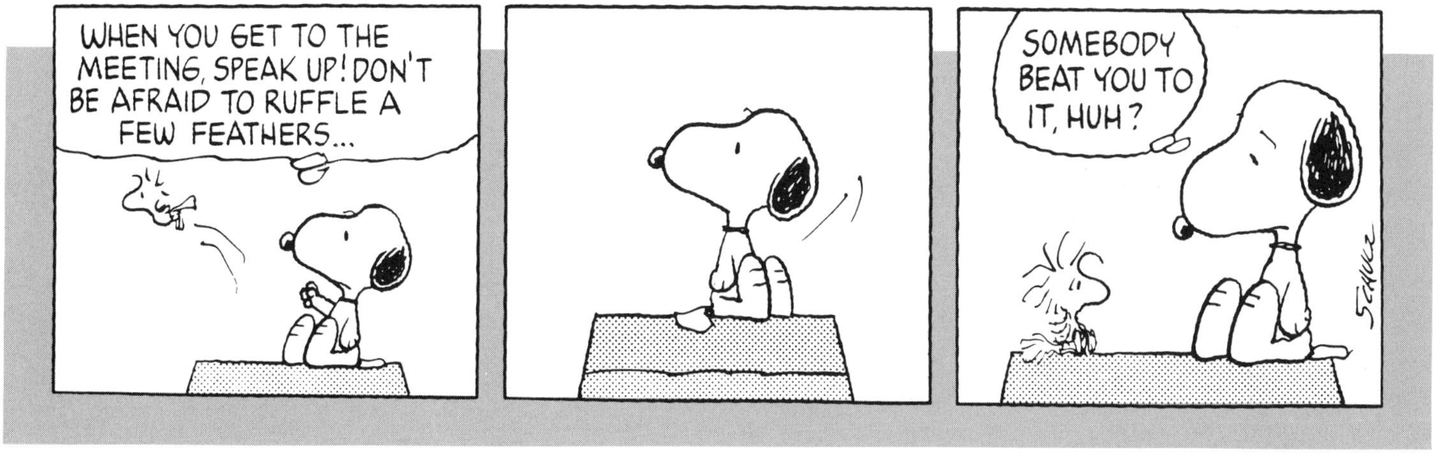

WHEN YOU GET TO THE MEETING, SPEAK UP! DON'T BE AFRAID TO RUFFLE A FEW FEATHERS...
SOMEBODY BEAT YOU TO IT, HUH?
SCHULZ

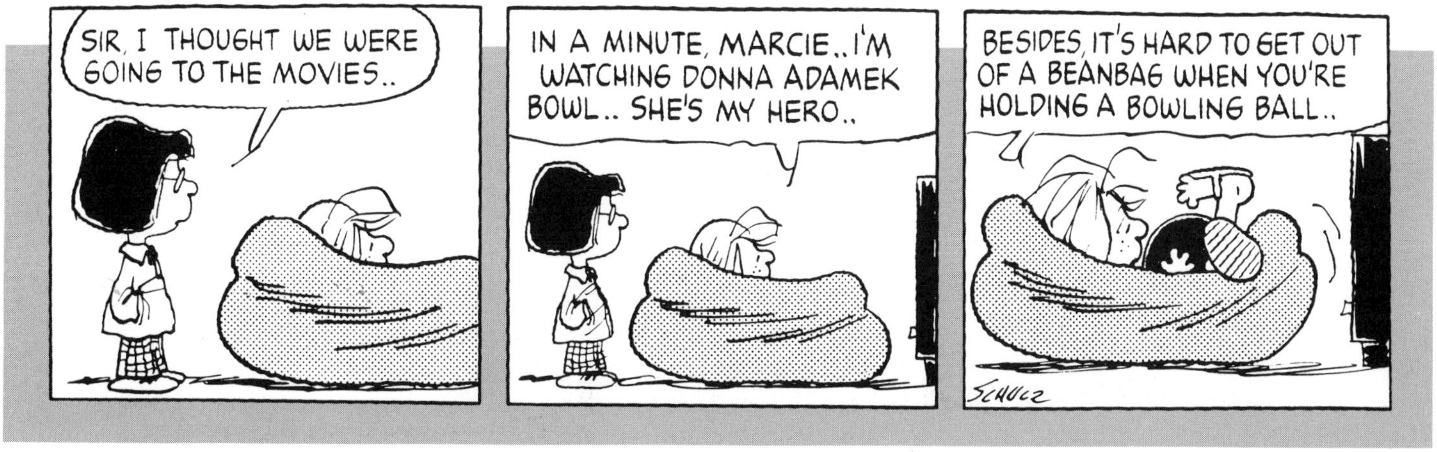

SIR, I THOUGHT WE WERE GOING TO THE MOVIES..
IN A MINUTE, MARCIE.. I'M WATCHING DONNA ADAMEK BOWL.. SHE'S MY HERO..
BESIDES, IT'S HARD TO GET OUT OF A BEANBAG WHEN YOU'RE HOLDING A BOWLING BALL..
SCHULZ

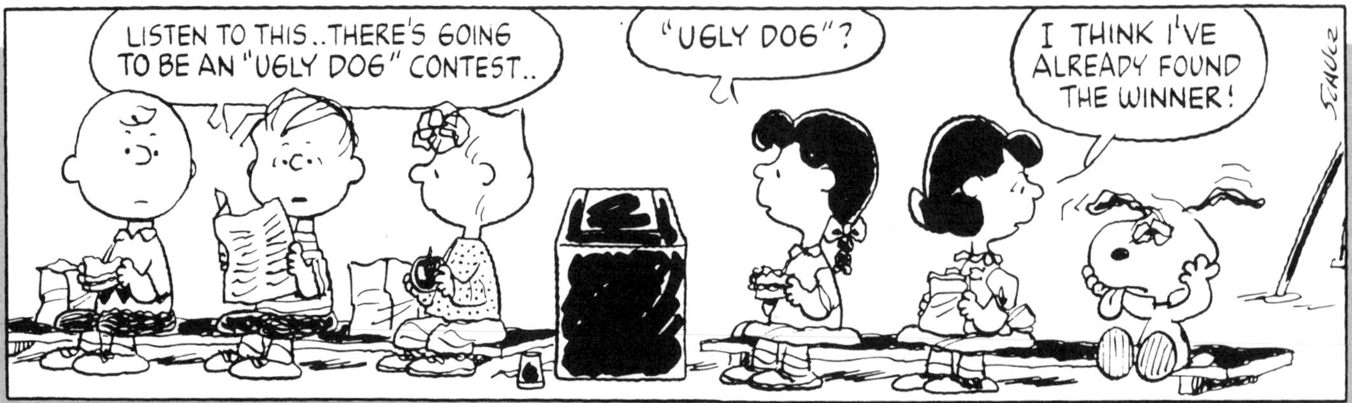
LISTEN TO THIS..THERE'S GOING TO BE AN "UGLY DOG" CONTEST..
"UGLY DOG"?
I THINK I'VE ALREADY FOUND THE WINNER!

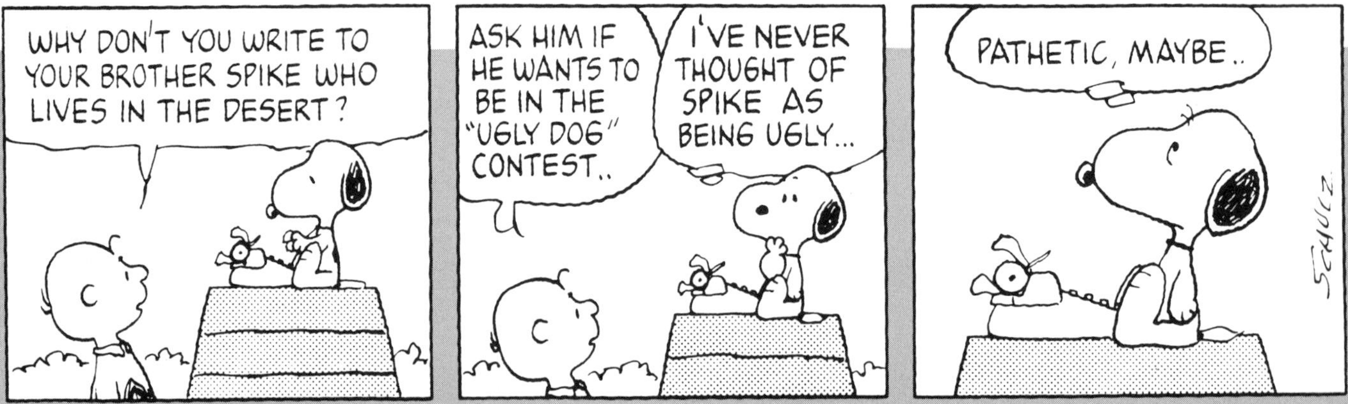
WHY DON'T YOU WRITE TO YOUR BROTHER SPIKE WHO LIVES IN THE DESERT?
ASK HIM IF HE WANTS TO BE IN THE "UGLY DOG" CONTEST..
I'VE NEVER THOUGHT OF SPIKE AS BEING UGLY...
PATHETIC, MAYBE..

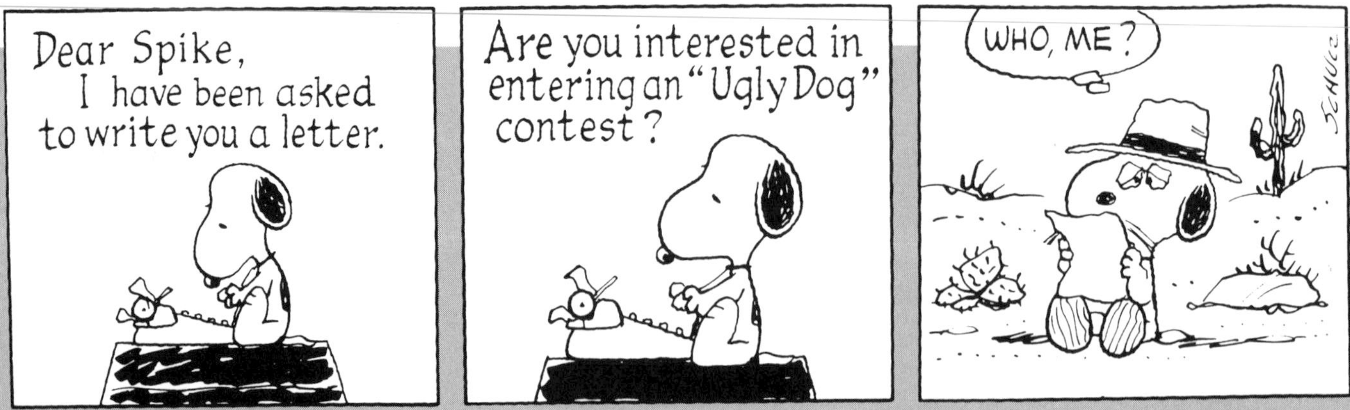
Dear Spike,
I have been asked to write you a letter.
Are you interested in entering an "Ugly Dog" contest?
WHO, ME?

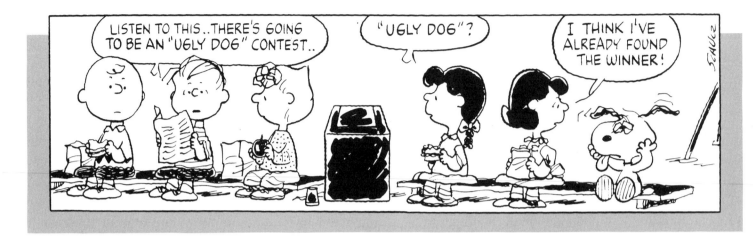

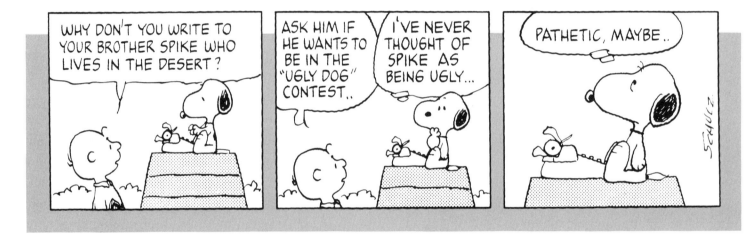

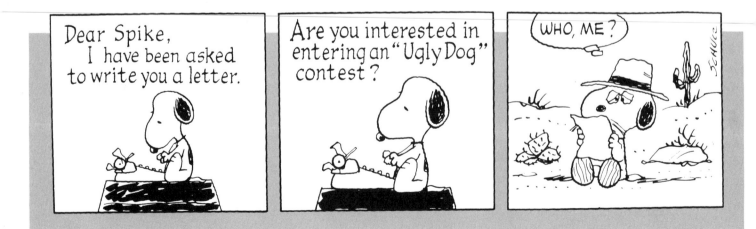

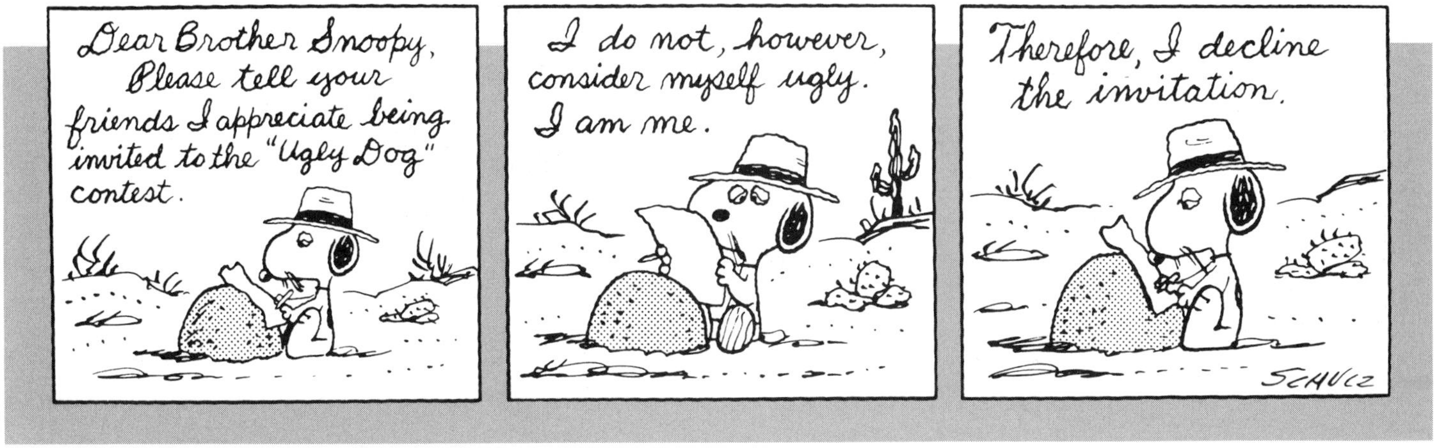
Dear Brother Snoopy,
Please tell your friends I appreciate being invited to the "Ugly Dog" contest.
I do not, however, consider myself ugly. I am me.
Therefore, I decline the invitation.
SCHULZ

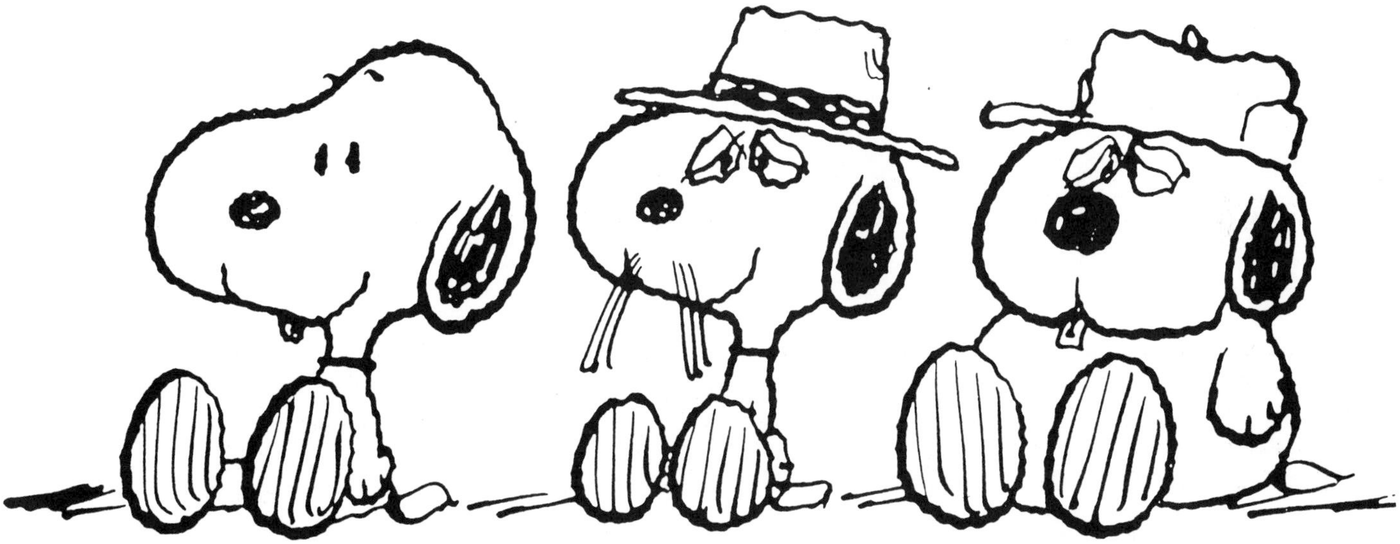

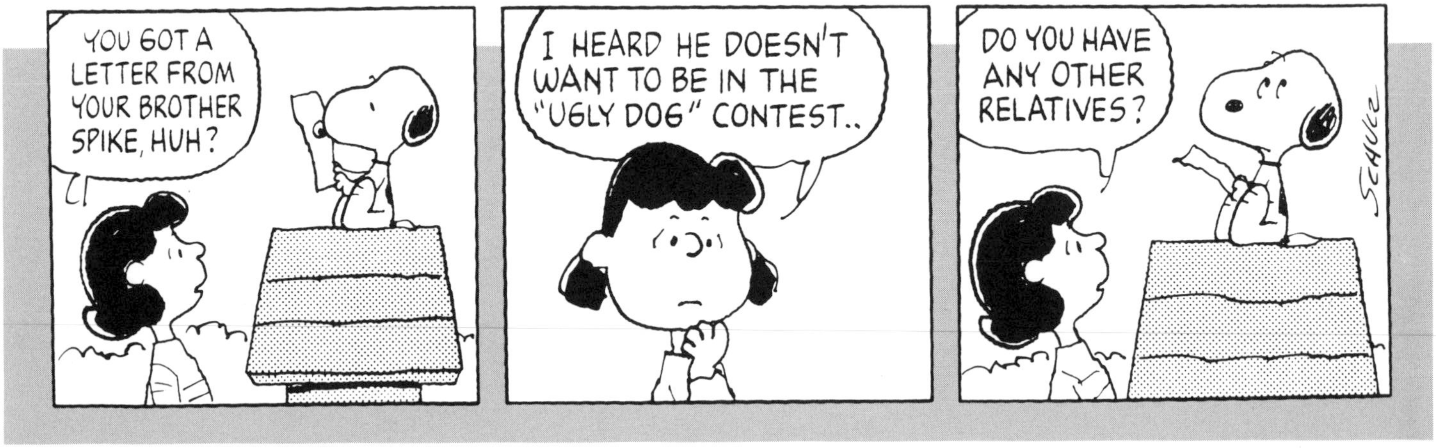
YOU GOT A LETTER FROM YOUR BROTHER SPIKE, HUH?
I HEARD HE DOESN'T WANT TO BE IN THE "UGLY DOG" CONTEST..
DO YOU HAVE ANY OTHER RELATIVES?
SCHULZ

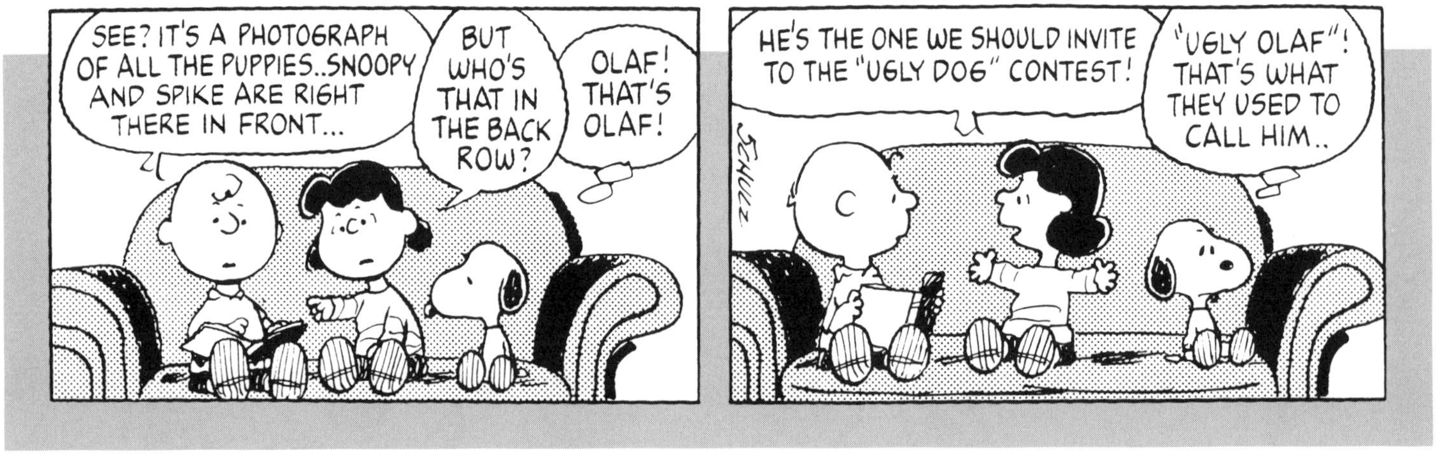
SEE? IT'S A PHOTOGRAPH OF ALL THE PUPPIES..SNOOPY AND SPIKE ARE RIGHT THERE IN FRONT...
BUT WHO'S THAT IN THE BACK ROW?
OLAF! THAT'S OLAF!
SCHULZ
HE'S THE ONE WE SHOULD INVITE TO THE "UGLY DOG" CONTEST!
"UGLY OLAF"! THAT'S WHAT THEY USED TO CALL HIM..

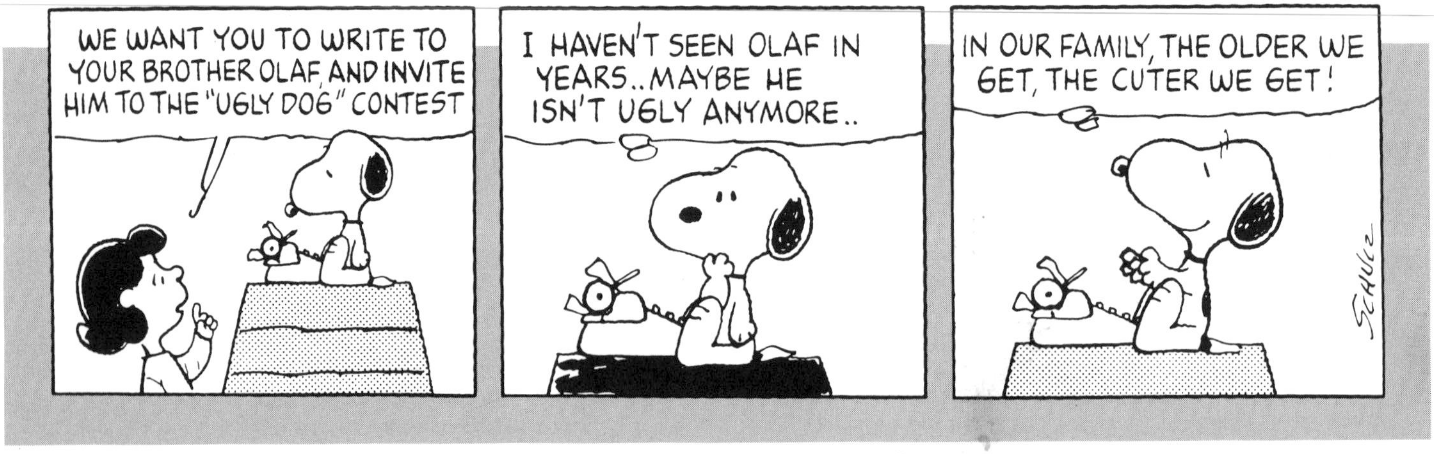
WE WANT YOU TO WRITE TO YOUR BROTHER OLAF, AND INVITE HIM TO THE "UGLY DOG" CONTEST
I HAVEN'T SEEN OLAF IN YEARS..MAYBE HE ISN'T UGLY ANYMORE..
IN OUR FAMILY, THE OLDER WE GET, THE CUTER WE GET!
SCHULZ

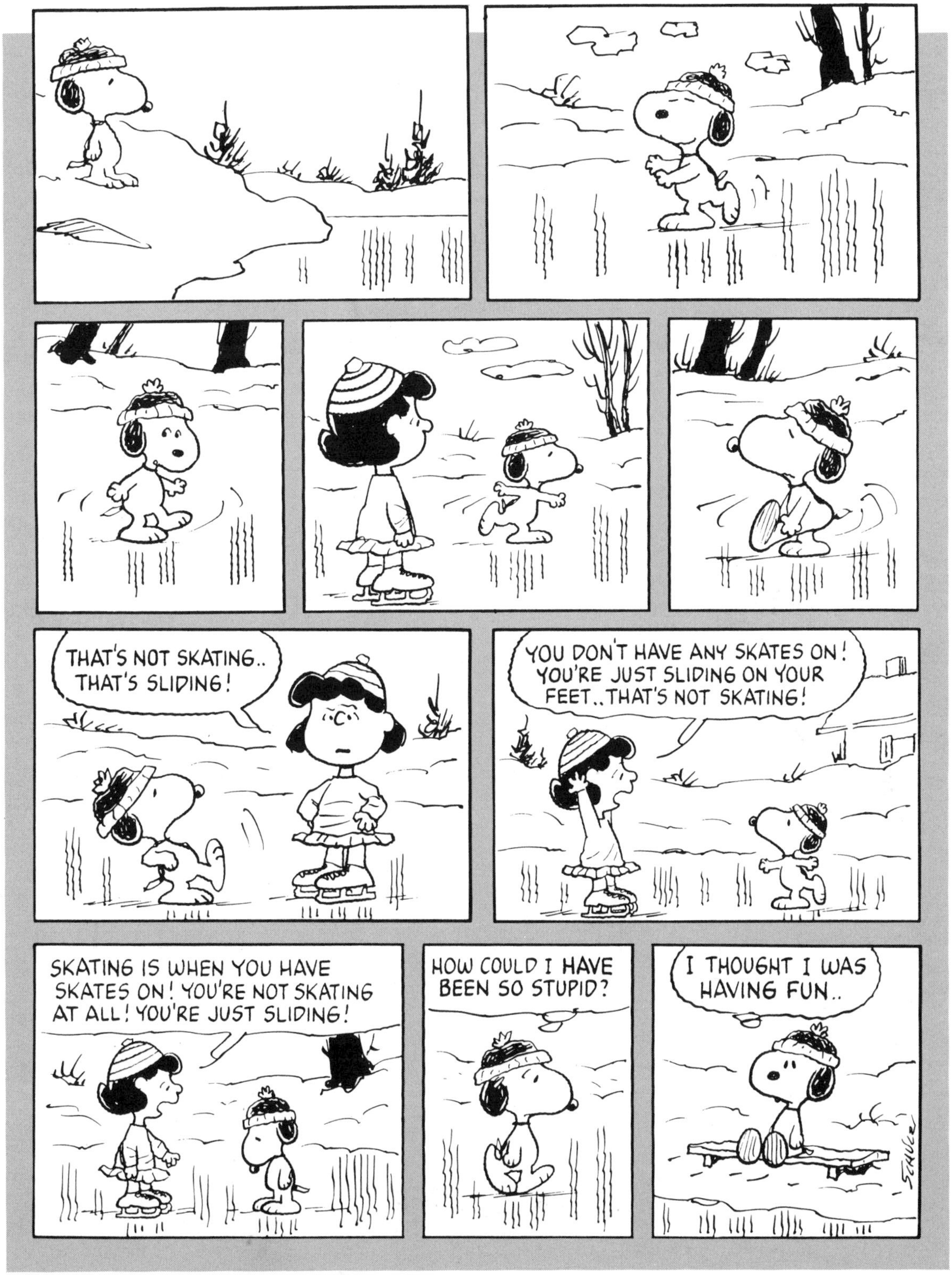
THAT'S NOT SKATING..
THAT'S SLIDING!
YOU DON'T HAVE ANY SKATES ON! YOU'RE JUST SLIDING ON YOUR FEET..THAT'S NOT SKATING!
SKATING IS WHEN YOU HAVE SKATES ON! YOU'RE NOT SKATING AT ALL! YOU'RE JUST SLIDING!
HOW COULD I HAVE BEEN SO STUPID?
I THOUGHT I WAS HAVING FUN..
SCHULZ

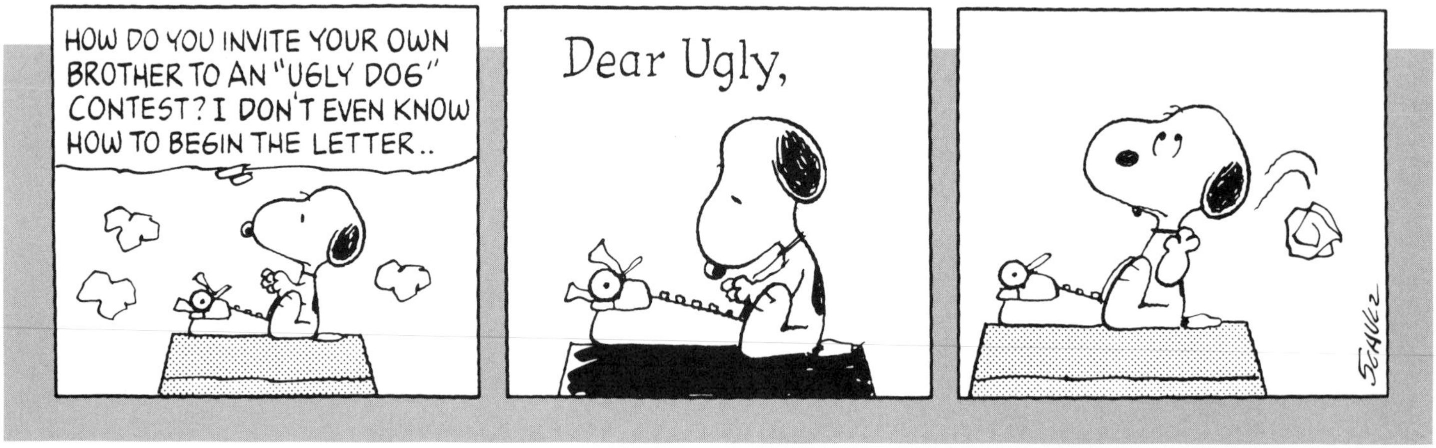
HOW DO YOU INVITE YOUR OWN BROTHER TO AN "UGLY DOG" CONTEST? I DON'T EVEN KNOW HOW TO BEGIN THE LETTER..
Dear Ugly,
SCHULZ

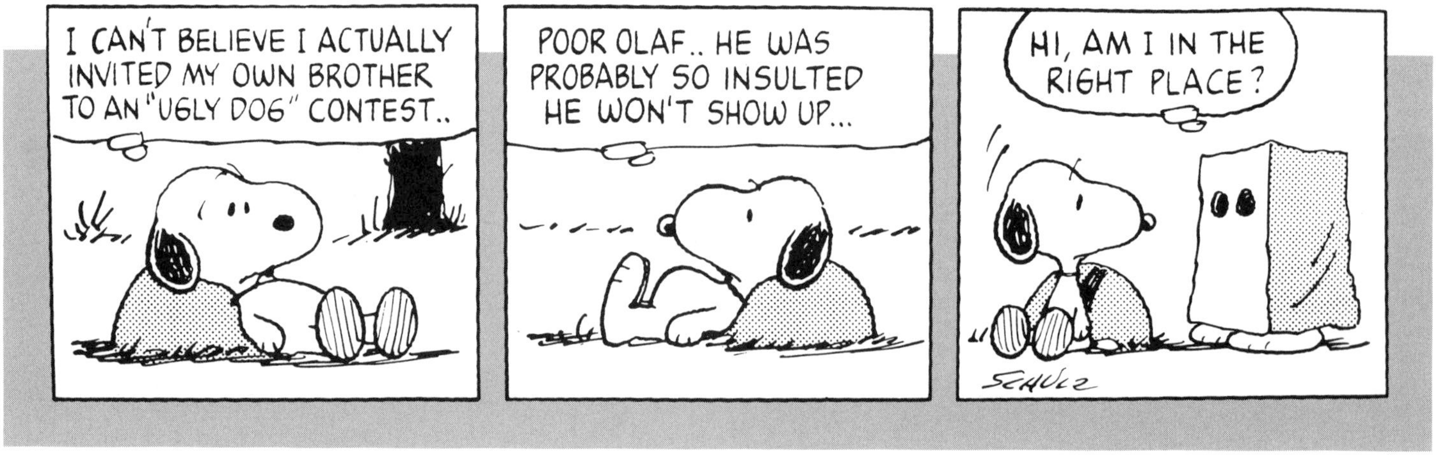
I CAN'T BELIEVE I ACTUALLY INVITED MY OWN BROTHER TO AN "UGLY DOG" CONTEST..
POOR OLAF.. HE WAS PROBABLY SO INSULTED HE WON'T SHOW UP...
HI, AM I IN THE RIGHT PLACE?
SCHULZ

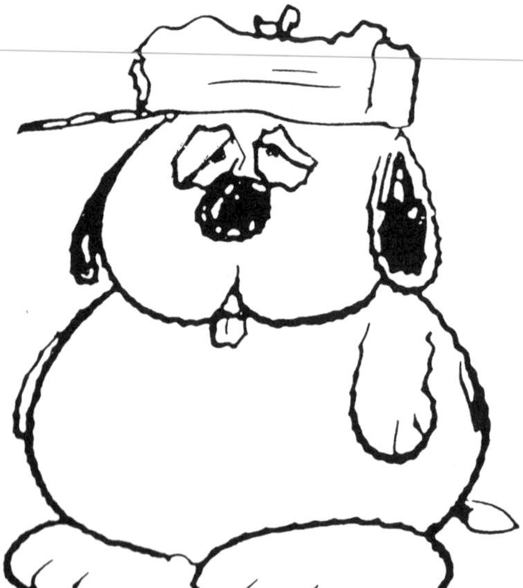

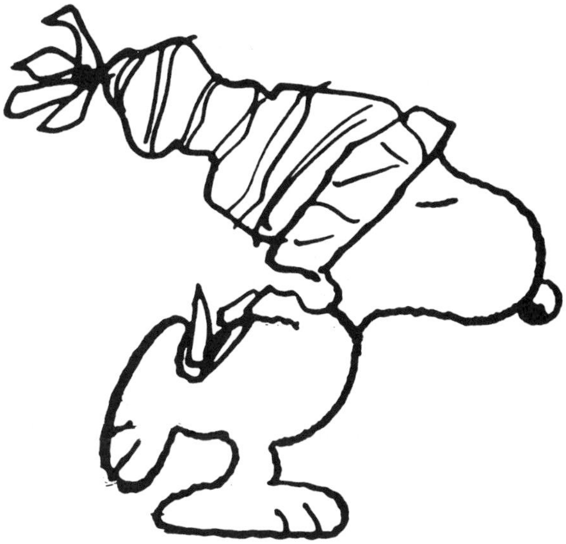

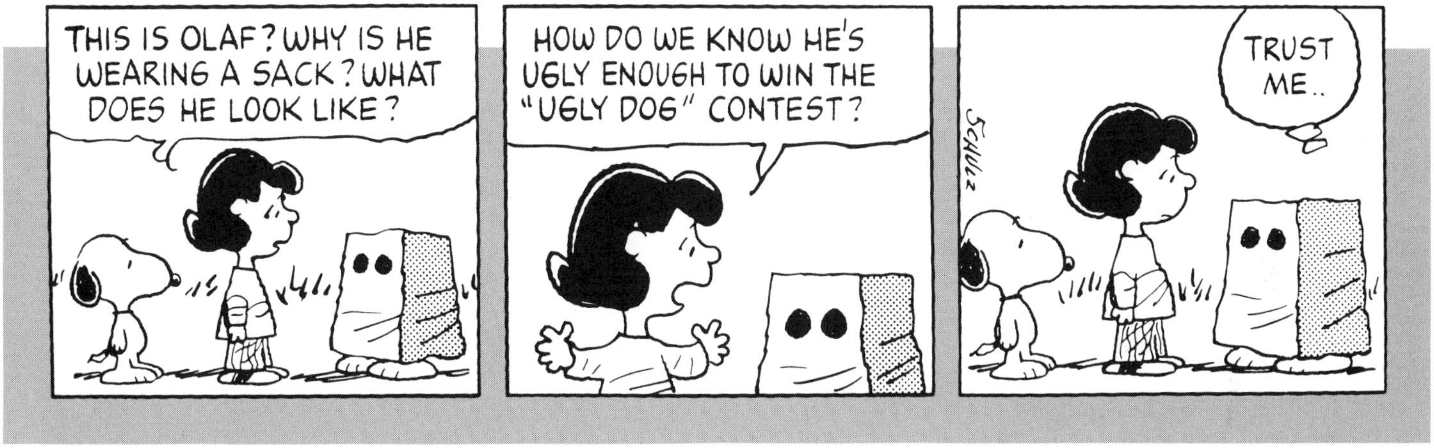
THIS IS OLAF? WHY IS HE WEARING A SACK? WHAT DOES HE LOOK LIKE?
HOW DO WE KNOW HE'S UGLY ENOUGH TO WIN THE "UGLY DOG" CONTEST?
TRUST ME..

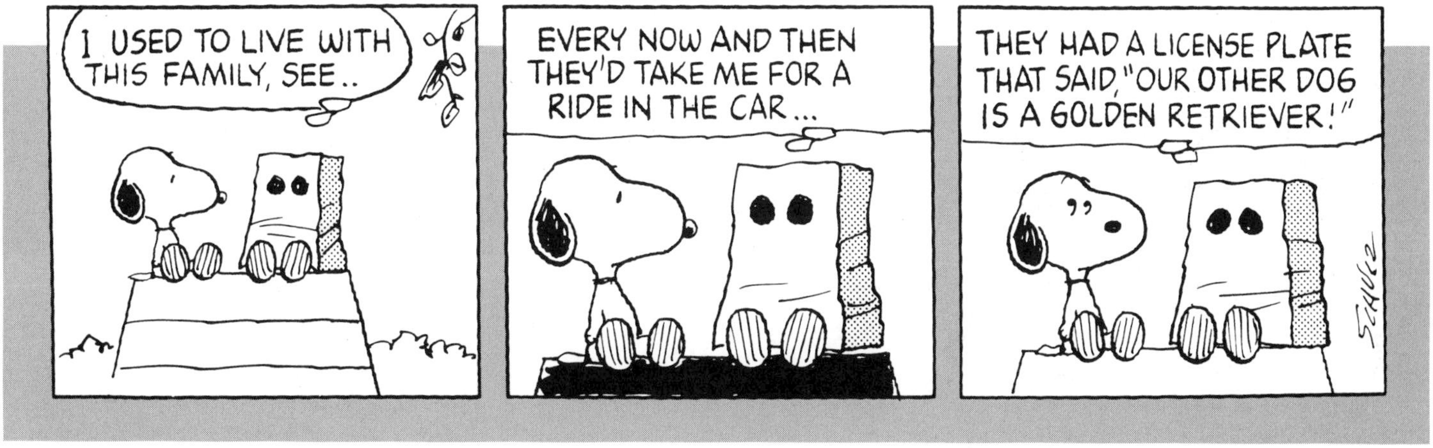
I USED TO LIVE WITH THIS FAMILY, SEE..
EVERY NOW AND THEN THEY'D TAKE ME FOR A RIDE IN THE CAR...
THEY HAD A LICENSE PLATE THAT SAID, "OUR OTHER DOG IS A GOLDEN RETRIEVER!"

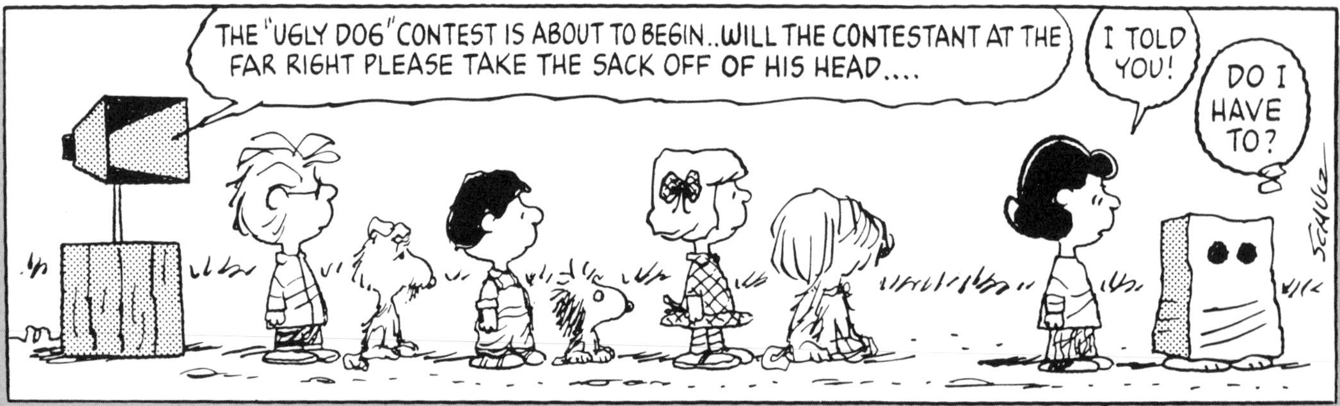
THE "UGLY DOG" CONTEST IS ABOUT TO BEGIN..WILL THE CONTESTANT AT THE FAR RIGHT PLEASE TAKE THE SACK OFF OF HIS HEAD....
I TOLD YOU!
DO I HAVE TO?

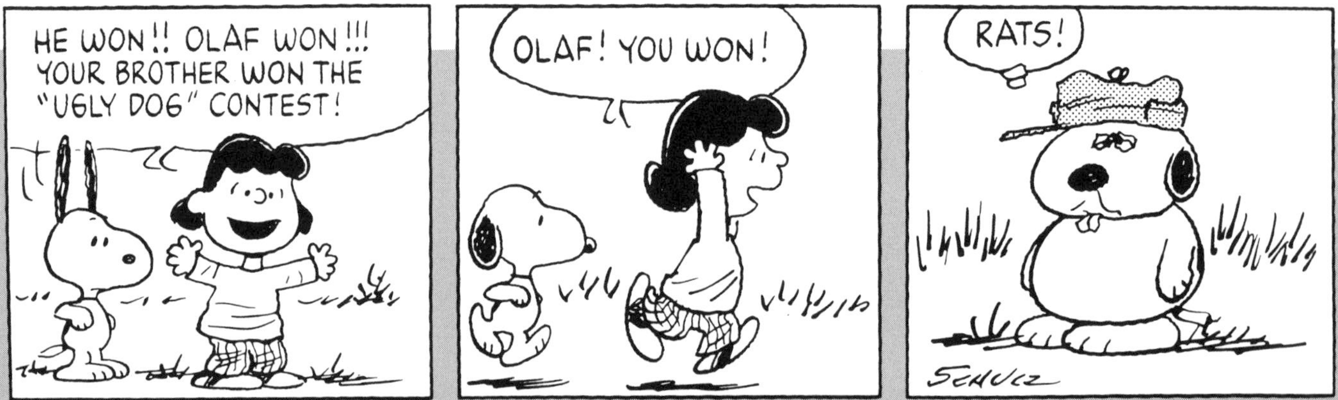
HE WON!! OLAF WON!!! YOUR BROTHER WON THE "UGLY DOG" CONTEST!
OLAF! YOU WON!
RATS!

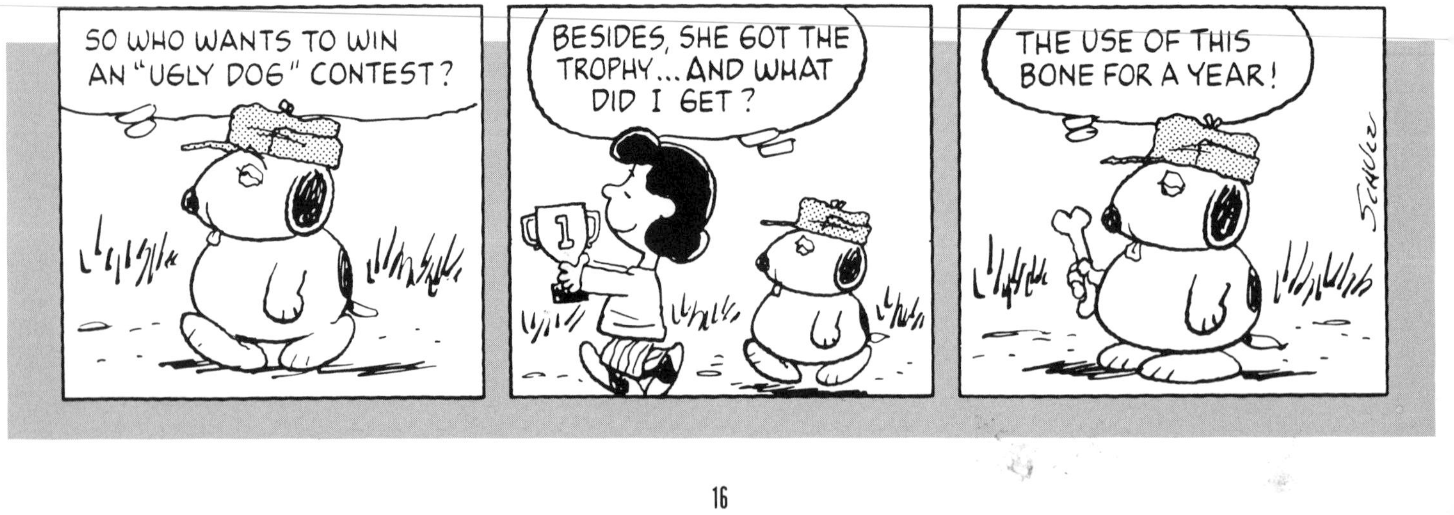
SO WHO WANTS TO WIN AN "UGLY DOG" CONTEST?
BESIDES, SHE GOT THE TROPHY...AND WHAT DID I GET?
THE USE OF THIS BONE FOR A YEAR!

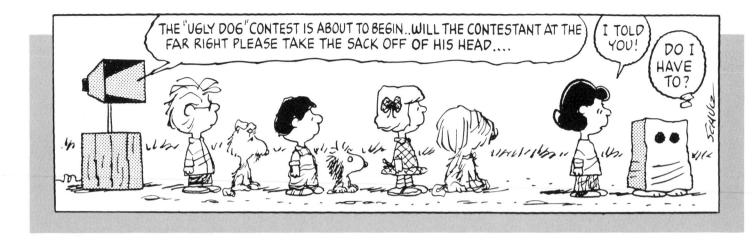

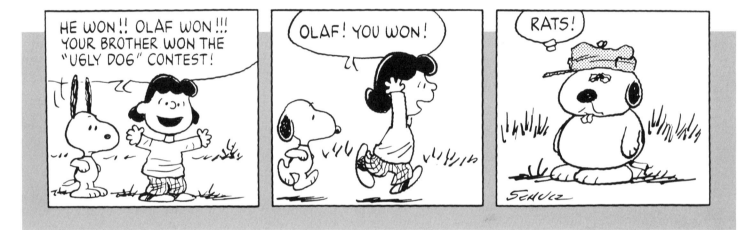

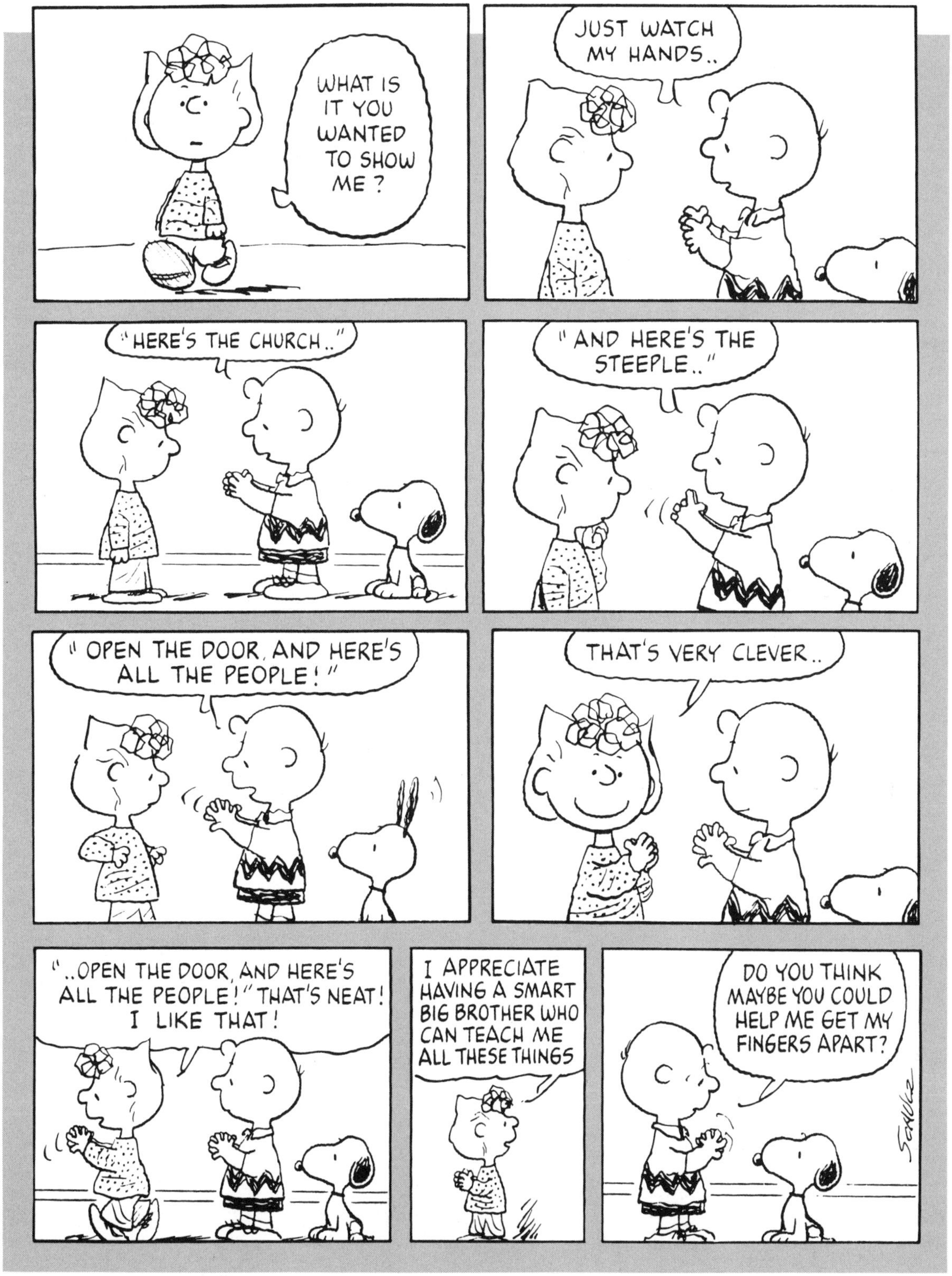

WHAT IS IT YOU WANTED TO SHOW ME ?
JUST WATCH MY HANDS..
"HERE'S THE CHURCH.."
"AND HERE'S THE STEEPLE.."
"OPEN THE DOOR, AND HERE'S ALL THE PEOPLE!"
THAT'S VERY CLEVER..
"..OPEN THE DOOR, AND HERE'S ALL THE PEOPLE!" THAT'S NEAT! I LIKE THAT!
I APPRECIATE HAVING A SMART BIG BROTHER WHO CAN TEACH ME ALL THESE THINGS
DO YOU THINK MAYBE YOU COULD HELP ME GET MY FINGERS APART?
SCHULZ

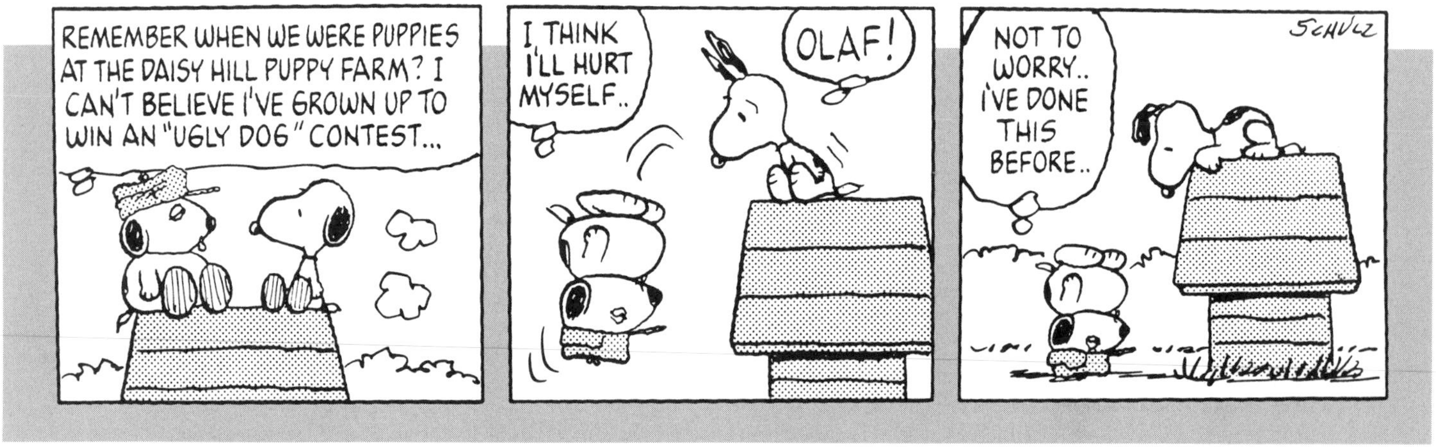
REMEMBER WHEN WE WERE PUPPIES AT THE DAISY HILL PUPPY FARM? I CAN'T BELIEVE I'VE GROWN UP TO WIN AN "UGLY DOG" CONTEST...
I THINK I'LL HURT MYSELF..
OLAF!
NOT TO WORRY.. I'VE DONE THIS BEFORE..
SCHULZ

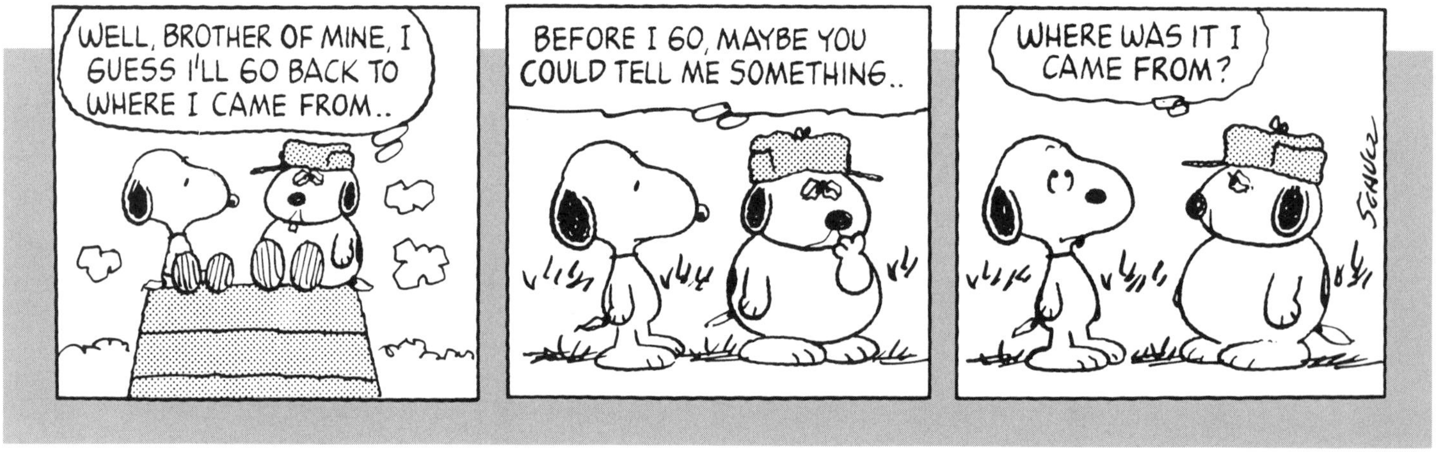
WELL, BROTHER OF MINE, I GUESS I'LL GO BACK TO WHERE I CAME FROM..
BEFORE I GO, MAYBE YOU COULD TELL ME SOMETHING..
WHERE WAS IT I CAME FROM?
SCHULZ

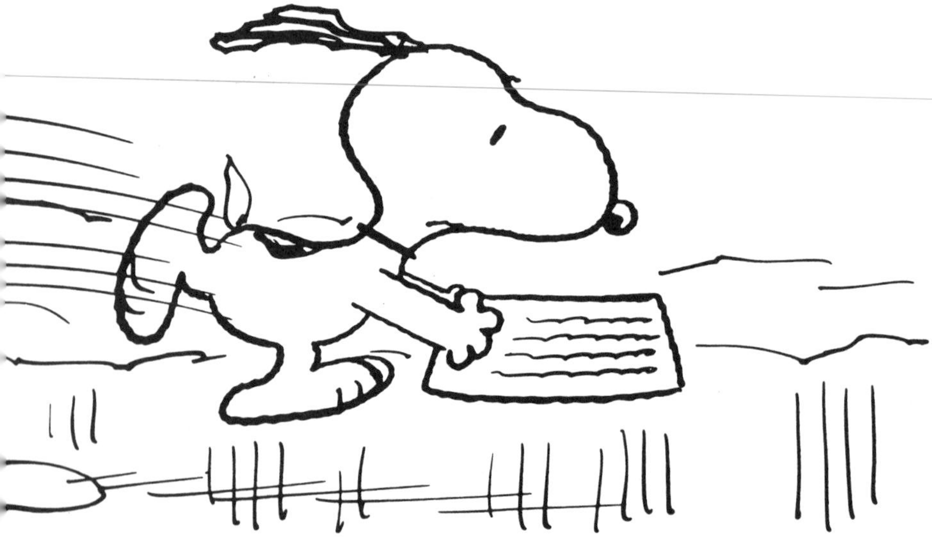

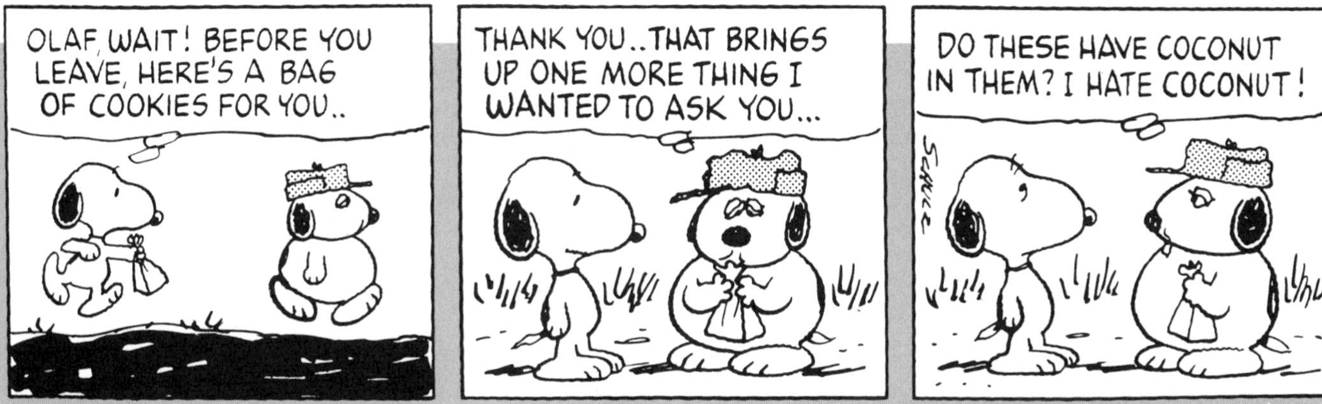
OLAF, WAIT! BEFORE YOU LEAVE, HERE'S A BAG OF COOKIES FOR YOU..
THANK YOU..THAT BRINGS UP ONE MORE THING I WANTED TO ASK YOU...
DO THESE HAVE COCONUT IN THEM? I HATE COCONUT!

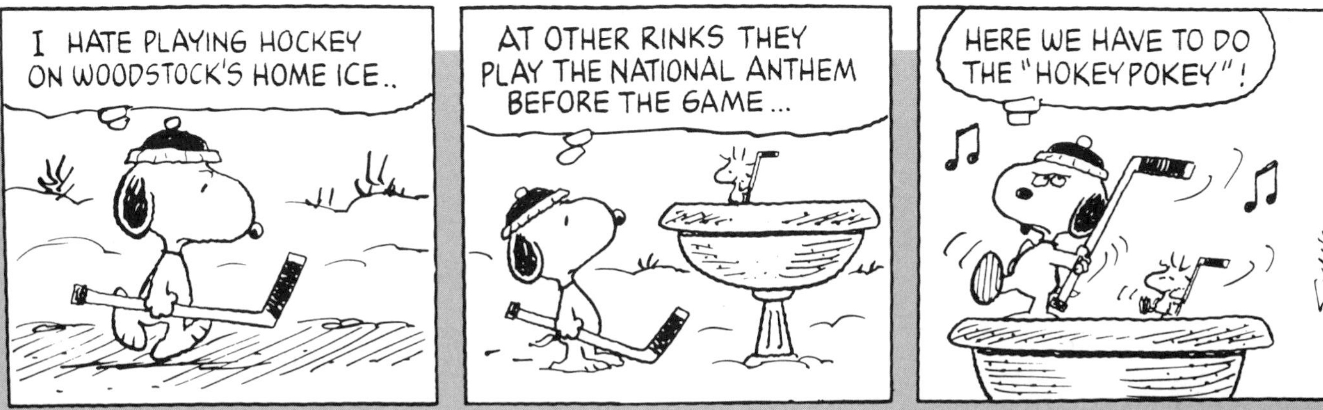
I HATE PLAYING HOCKEY ON WOODSTOCK'S HOME ICE..
AT OTHER RINKS THEY PLAY THE NATIONAL ANTHEM BEFORE THE GAME...
HERE WE HAVE TO DO THE "HOKEYPOKEY"!

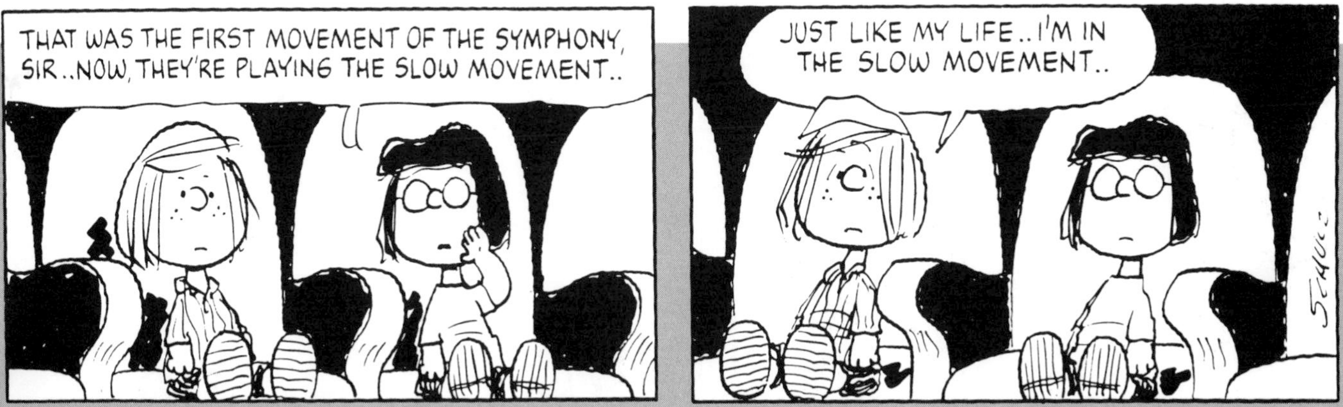
THAT WAS THE FIRST MOVEMENT OF THE SYMPHONY, SIR..NOW, THEY'RE PLAYING THE SLOW MOVEMENT..
JUST LIKE MY LIFE..I'M IN THE SLOW MOVEMENT..

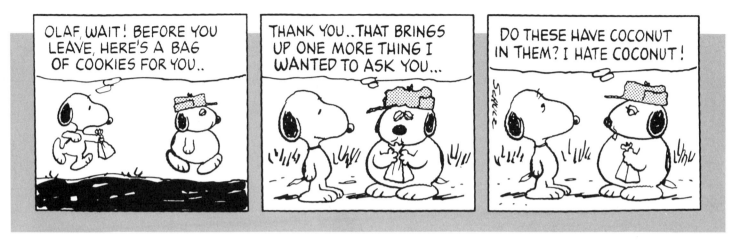

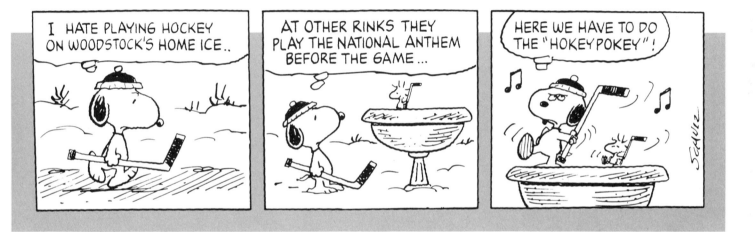

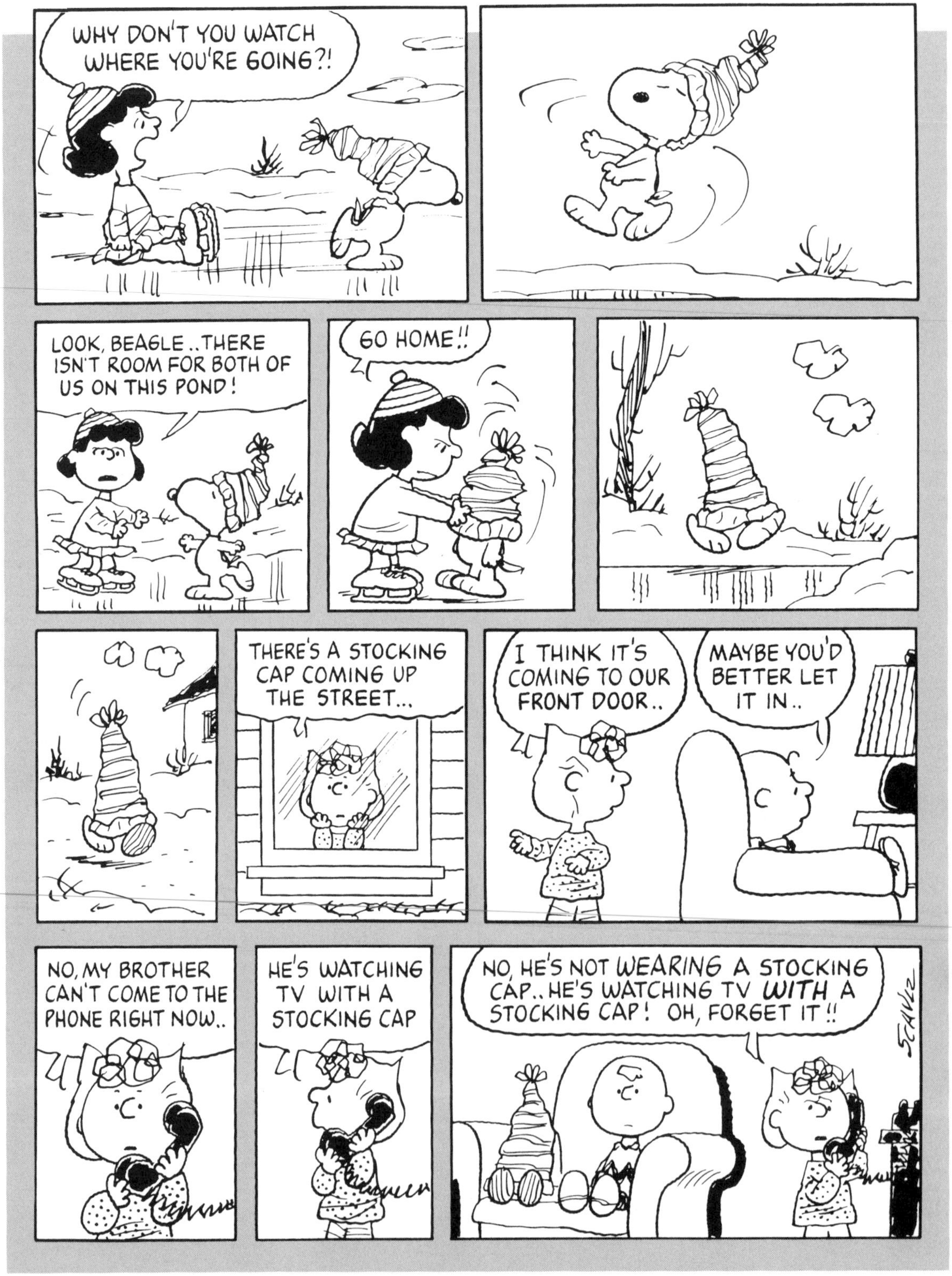
WHY DON'T YOU WATCH WHERE YOU'RE GOING?!
LOOK, BEAGLE..THERE ISN'T ROOM FOR BOTH OF US ON THIS POND!
GO HOME!!
THERE'S A STOCKING CAP COMING UP THE STREET...
I THINK IT'S COMING TO OUR FRONT DOOR..
MAYBE YOU'D BETTER LET IT IN..
NO, MY BROTHER CAN'T COME TO THE PHONE RIGHT NOW..
HE'S WATCHING TV WITH A STOCKING CAP
NO, HE'S NOT WEARING A STOCKING CAP.. HE'S WATCHING TV WITH A STOCKING CAP! OH, FORGET IT!!
SCHULZ

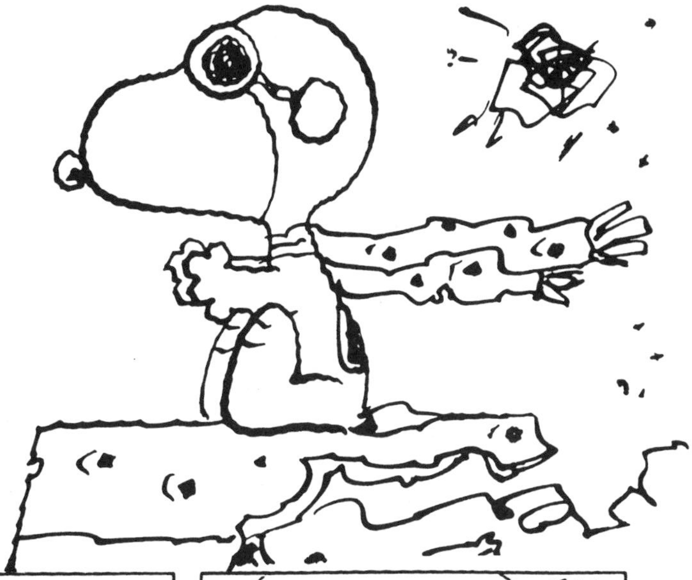

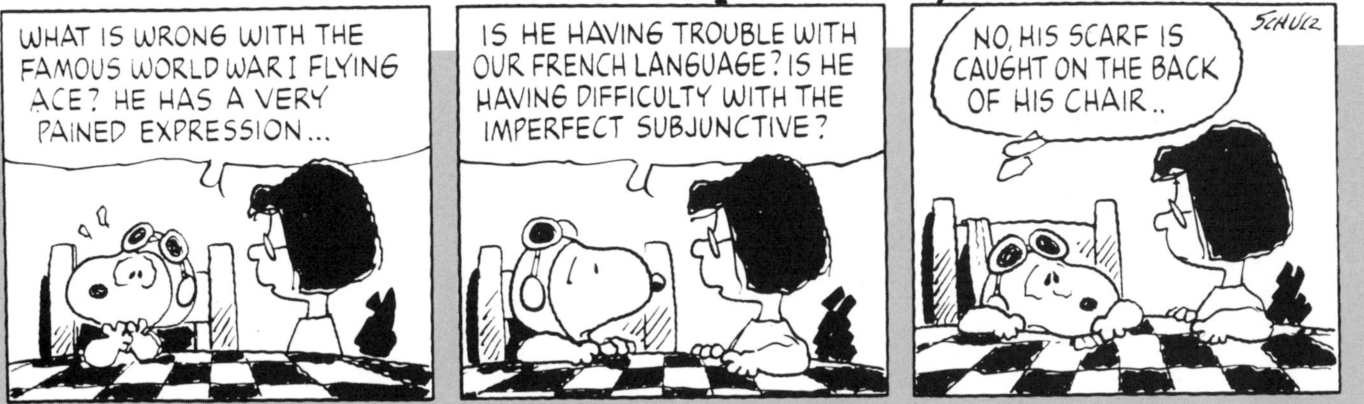
WHAT IS WRONG WITH THE FAMOUS WORLD WAR I FLYING ACE? HE HAS A VERY PAINED EXPRESSION...
IS HE HAVING TROUBLE WITH OUR FRENCH LANGUAGE? IS HE HAVING DIFFICULTY WITH THE IMPERFECT SUBJUNCTIVE?
NO, HIS SCARF IS CAUGHT ON THE BACK OF HIS CHAIR..
SCHULZ

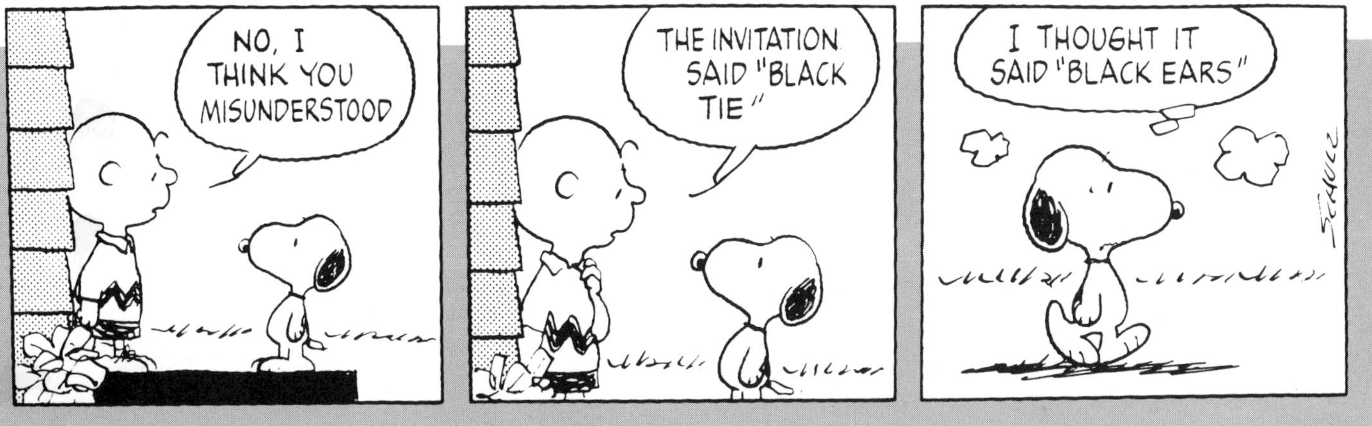
NO, I THINK YOU MISUNDERSTOOD
THE INVITATION SAID "BLACK TIE"
I THOUGHT IT SAID "BLACK EARS"
SCHULZ

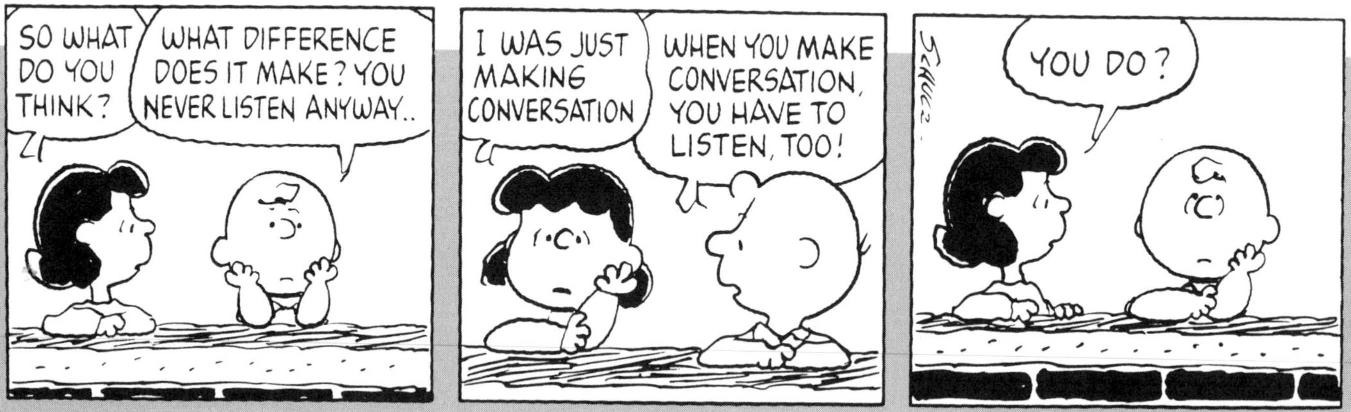
SO WHAT DO YOU THINK?
WHAT DIFFERENCE DOES IT MAKE? YOU NEVER LISTEN ANYWAY..
I WAS JUST MAKING CONVERSATION
WHEN YOU MAKE CONVERSATION, YOU HAVE TO LISTEN, TOO!
YOU DO?

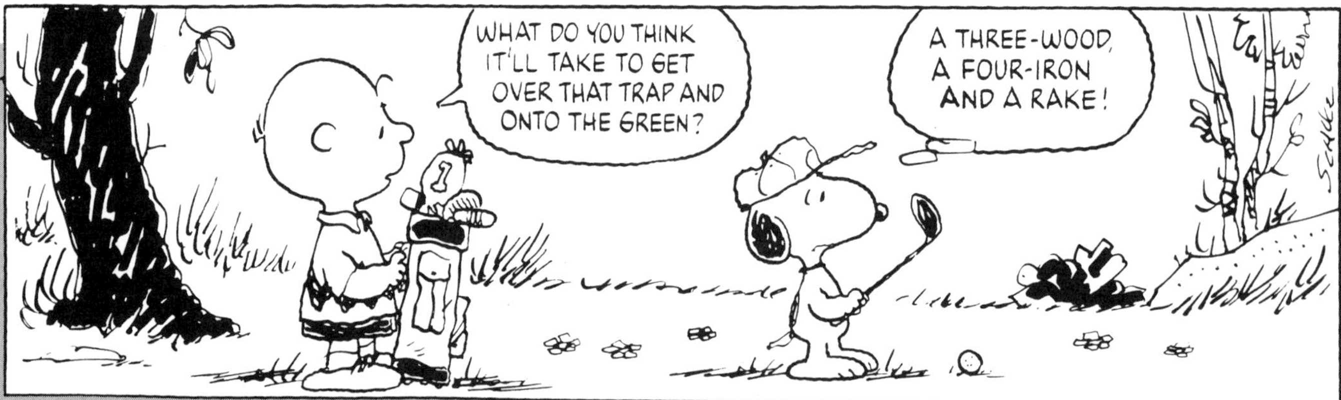
WHAT DO YOU THINK IT'LL TAKE TO GET OVER THAT TRAP AND ONTO THE GREEN?
A THREE-WOOD, A FOUR-IRON AND A RAKE!

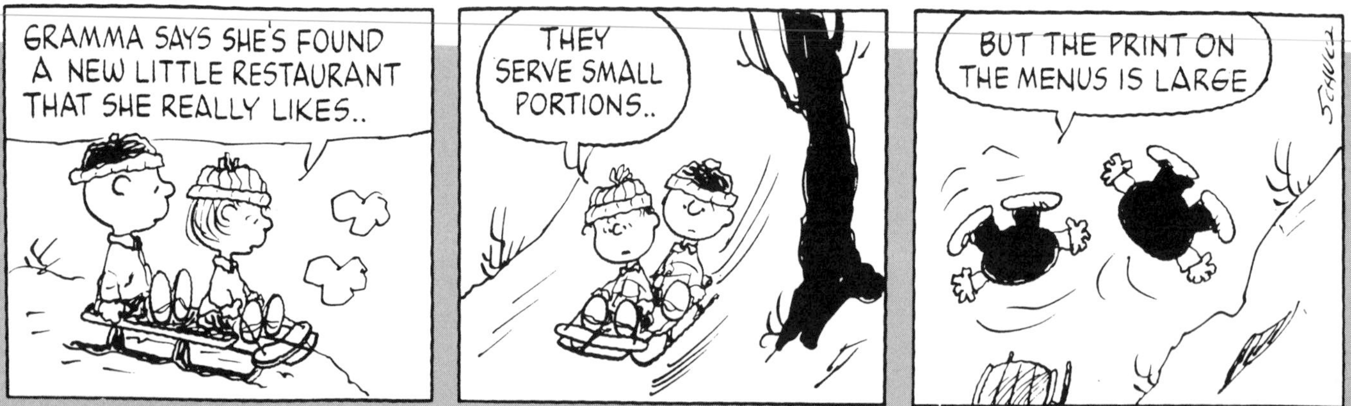
GRAMMA SAYS SHE'S FOUND A NEW LITTLE RESTAURANT THAT SHE REALLY LIKES..
THEY SERVE SMALL PORTIONS..
BUT THE PRINT ON THE MENUS IS LARGE

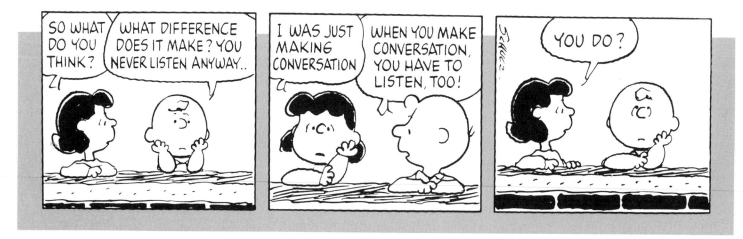

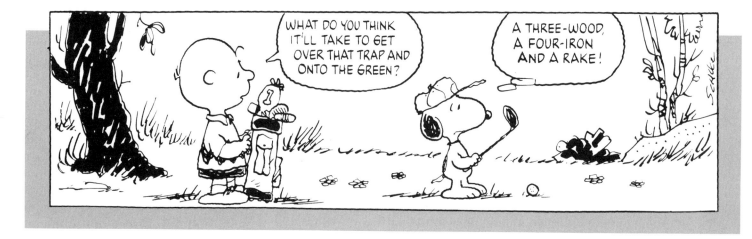

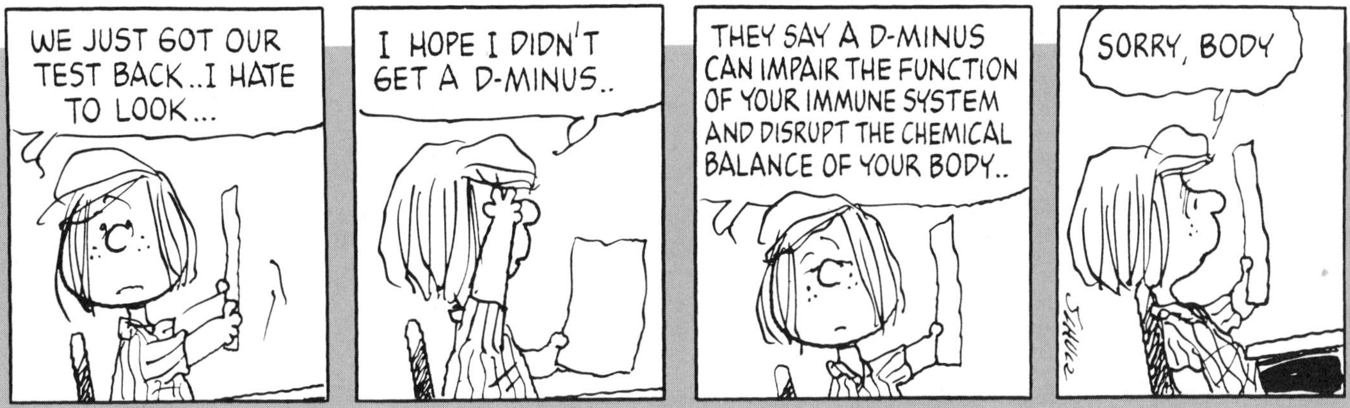
WE JUST GOT OUR TEST BACK..I HATE TO LOOK...
I HOPE I DIDN'T GET A D-MINUS..
THEY SAY A D-MINUS CAN IMPAIR THE FUNCTION OF YOUR IMMUNE SYSTEM AND DISRUPT THE CHEMICAL BALANCE OF YOUR BODY..
SORRY, BODY

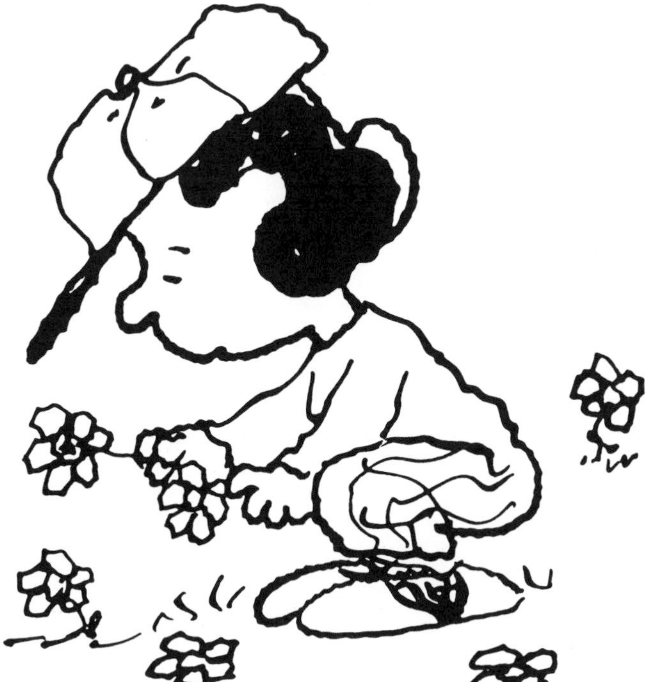

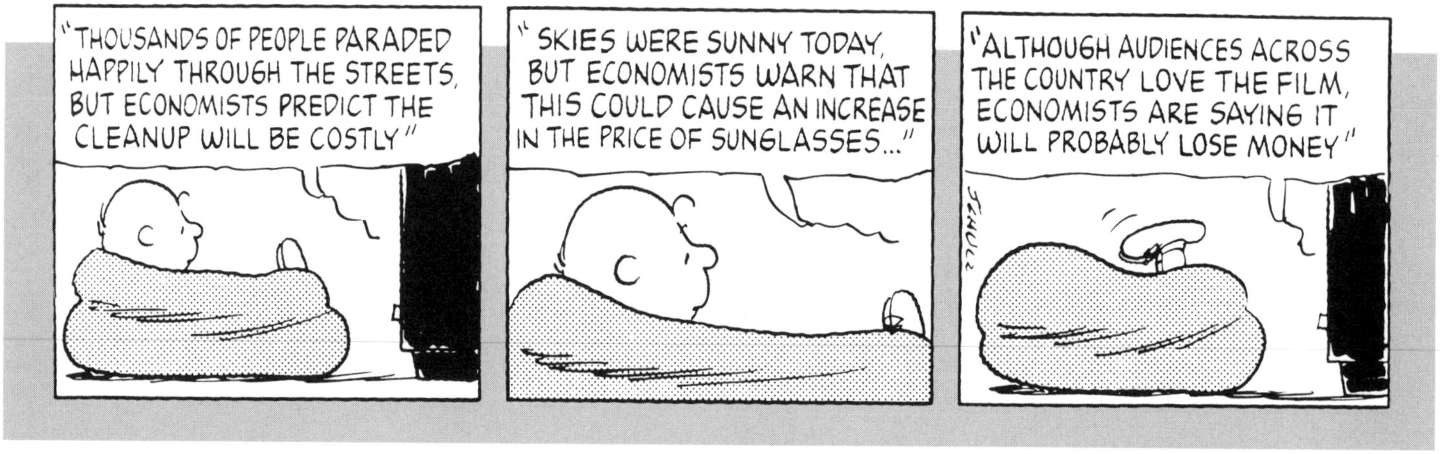
"THOUSANDS OF PEOPLE PARADED HAPPILY THROUGH THE STREETS, BUT ECONOMISTS PREDICT THE CLEANUP WILL BE COSTLY"
" SKIES WERE SUNNY TODAY, BUT ECONOMISTS WARN THAT THIS COULD CAUSE AN INCREASE IN THE PRICE OF SUNGLASSES..."
"ALTHOUGH AUDIENCES ACROSS THE COUNTRY LOVE THE FILM, ECONOMISTS ARE SAYING IT WILL PROBABLY LOSE MONEY"
SCHULZ

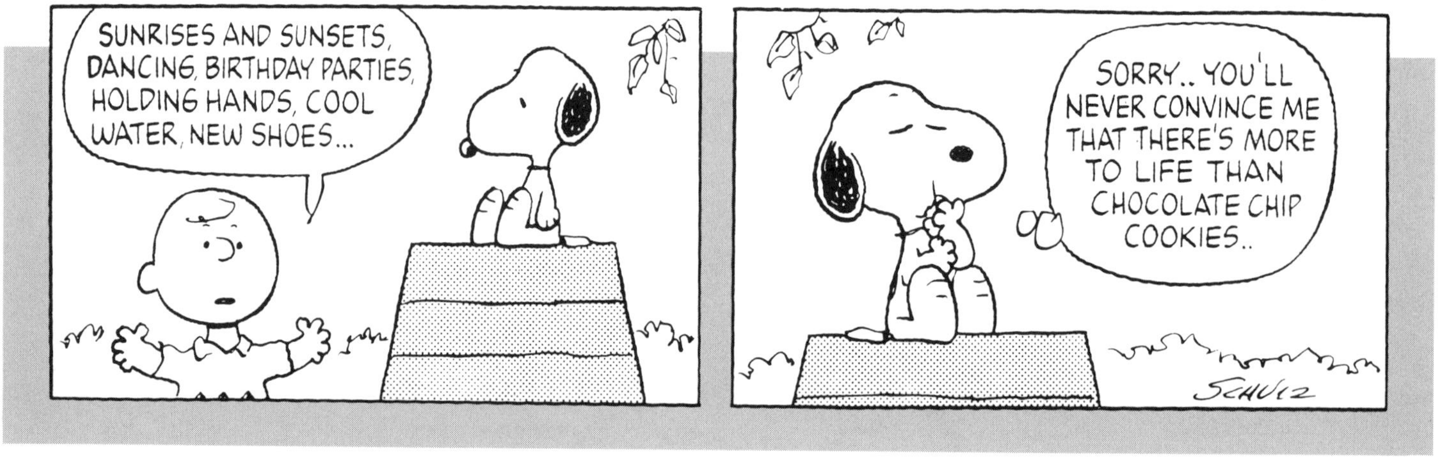
SUNRISES AND SUNSETS, DANCING, BIRTHDAY PARTIES, HOLDING HANDS, COOL WATER, NEW SHOES...
SORRY.. YOU'LL NEVER CONVINCE ME THAT THERE'S MORE TO LIFE THAN CHOCOLATE CHIP COOKIES..
SCHULZ

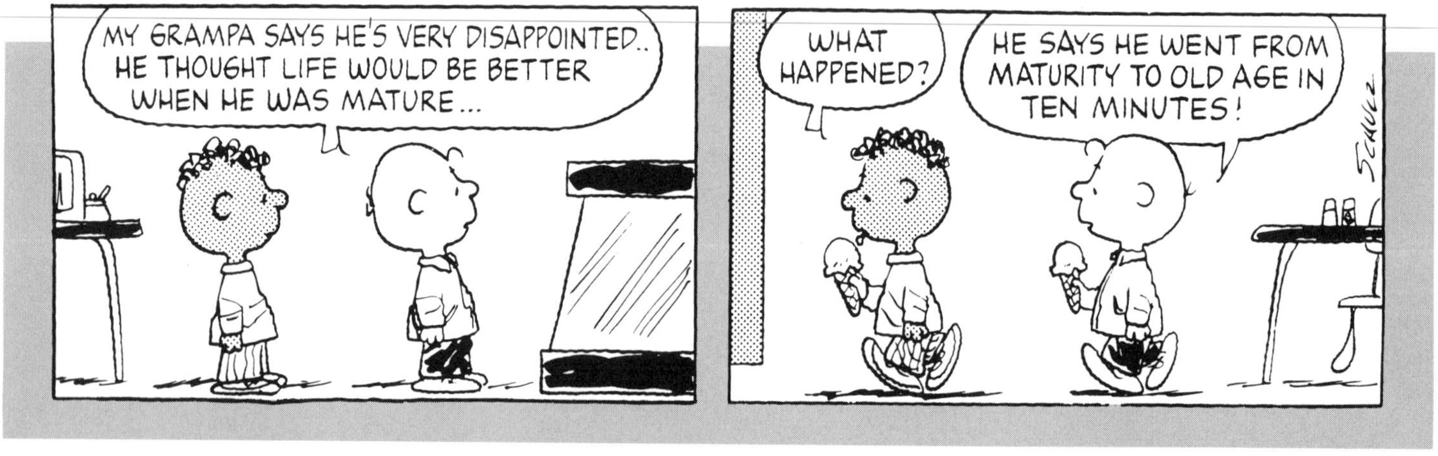
MY GRAMPA SAYS HE'S VERY DISAPPOINTED.. HE THOUGHT LIFE WOULD BE BETTER WHEN HE WAS MATURE...
WHAT HAPPENED?
HE SAYS HE WENT FROM MATURITY TO OLD AGE IN TEN MINUTES!
SCHULZ

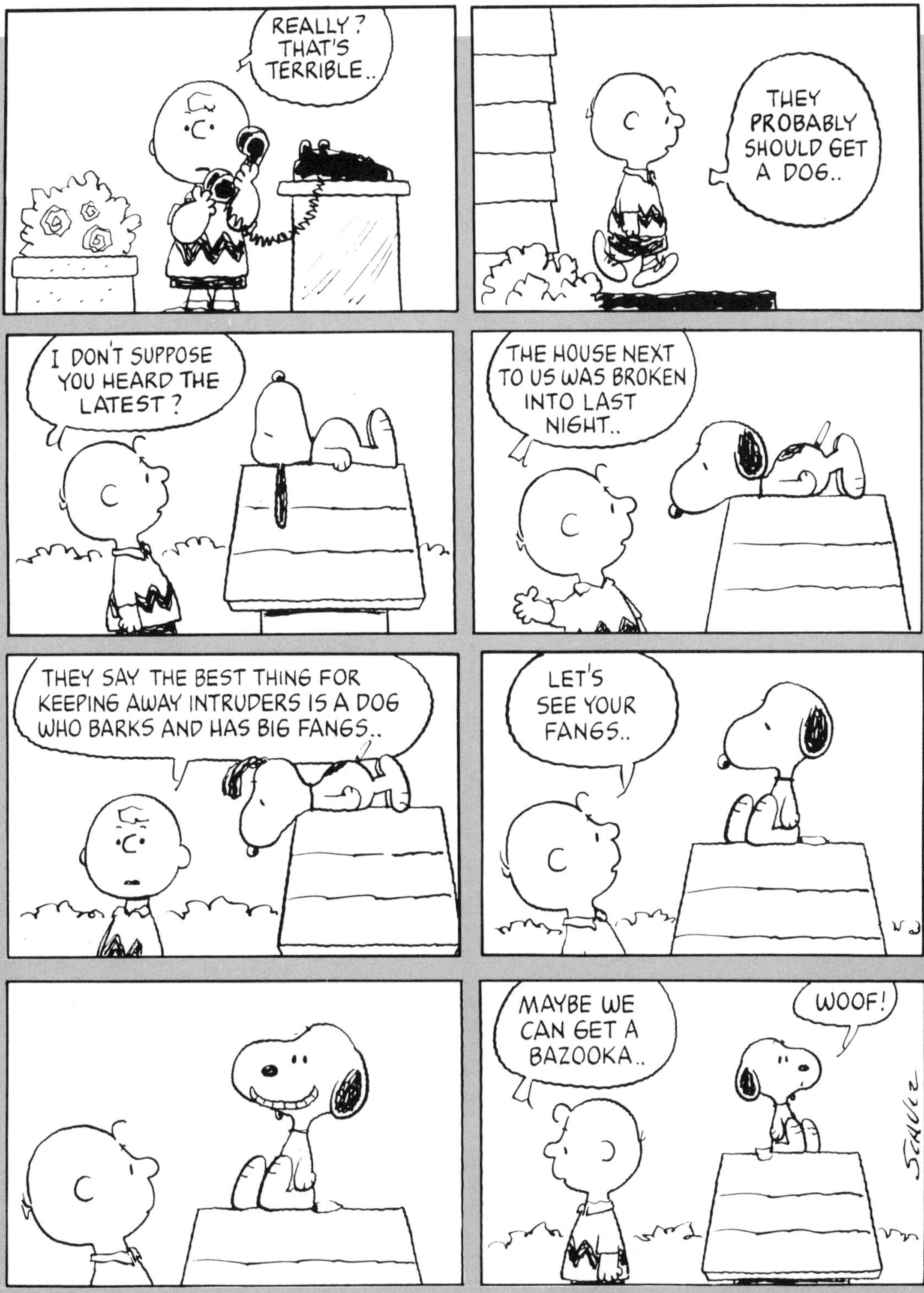
REALLY? THAT'S TERRIBLE..
THEY PROBABLY SHOULD GET A DOG..
I DON'T SUPPOSE YOU HEARD THE LATEST?
THE HOUSE NEXT TO US WAS BROKEN INTO LAST NIGHT..
THEY SAY THE BEST THING FOR KEEPING AWAY INTRUDERS IS A DOG WHO BARKS AND HAS BIG FANGS..
LET'S SEE YOUR FANGS..
MAYBE WE CAN GET A BAZOOKA..
WOOF!
SCHULZ

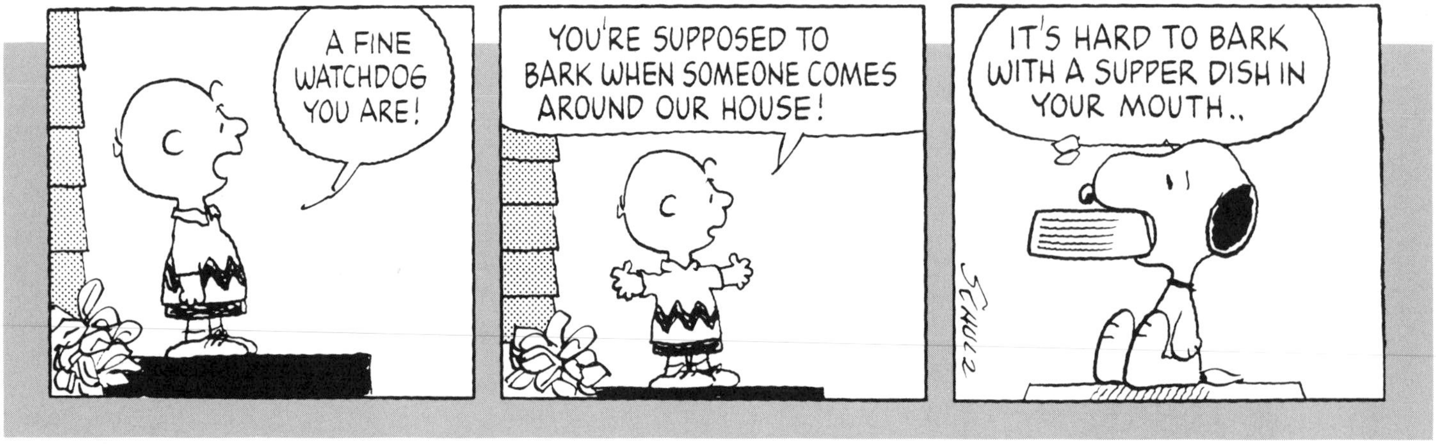
A FINE WATCHDOG YOU ARE!
YOU'RE SUPPOSED TO BARK WHEN SOMEONE COMES AROUND OUR HOUSE!
IT'S HARD TO BARK WITH A SUPPER DISH IN YOUR MOUTH..
SCHULZ

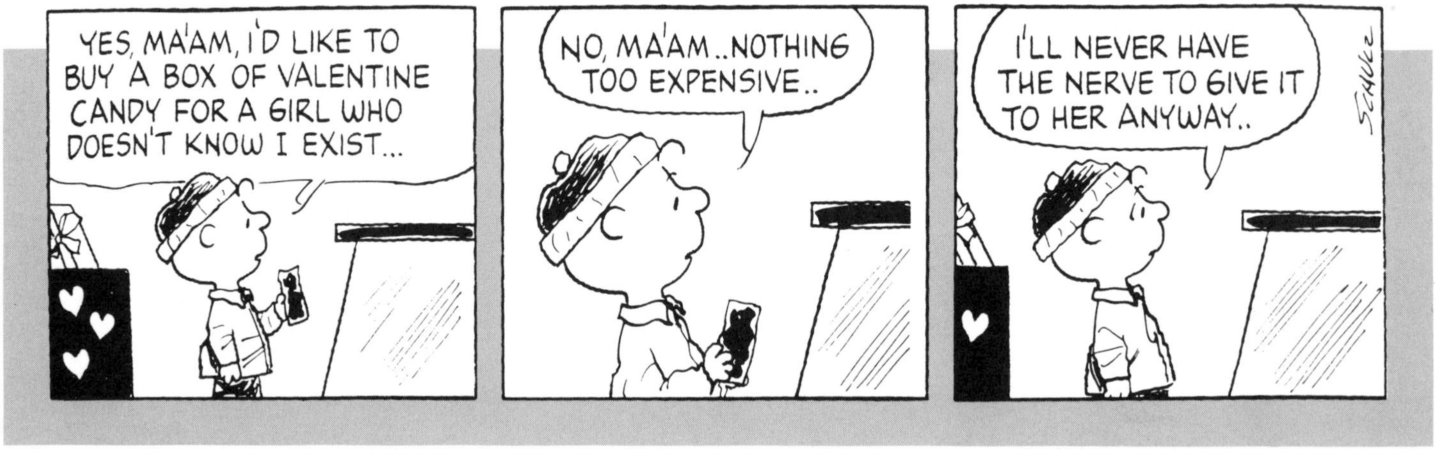
YES, MA'AM, I'D LIKE TO BUY A BOX OF VALENTINE CANDY FOR A GIRL WHO DOESN'T KNOW I EXIST...
NO, MA'AM..NOTHING TOO EXPENSIVE..
I'LL NEVER HAVE THE NERVE TO GIVE IT TO HER ANYWAY..
SCHULZ

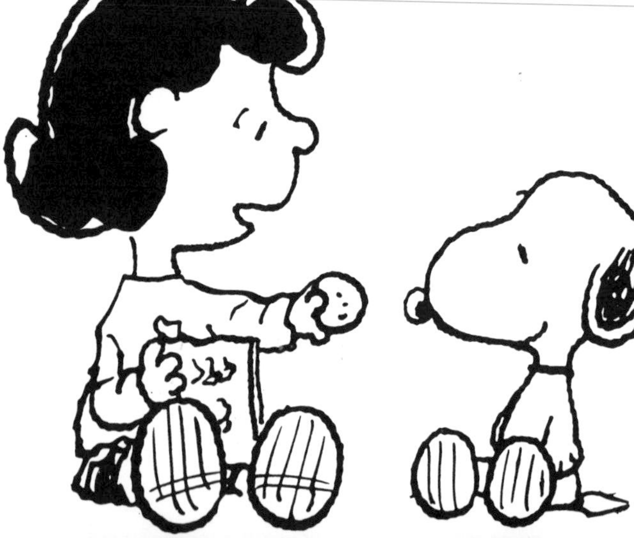

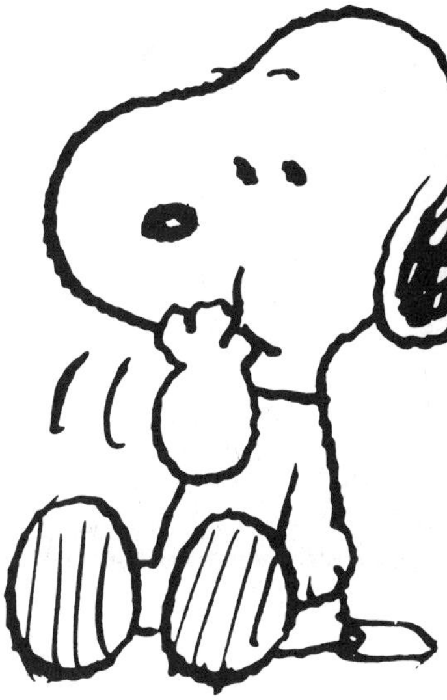

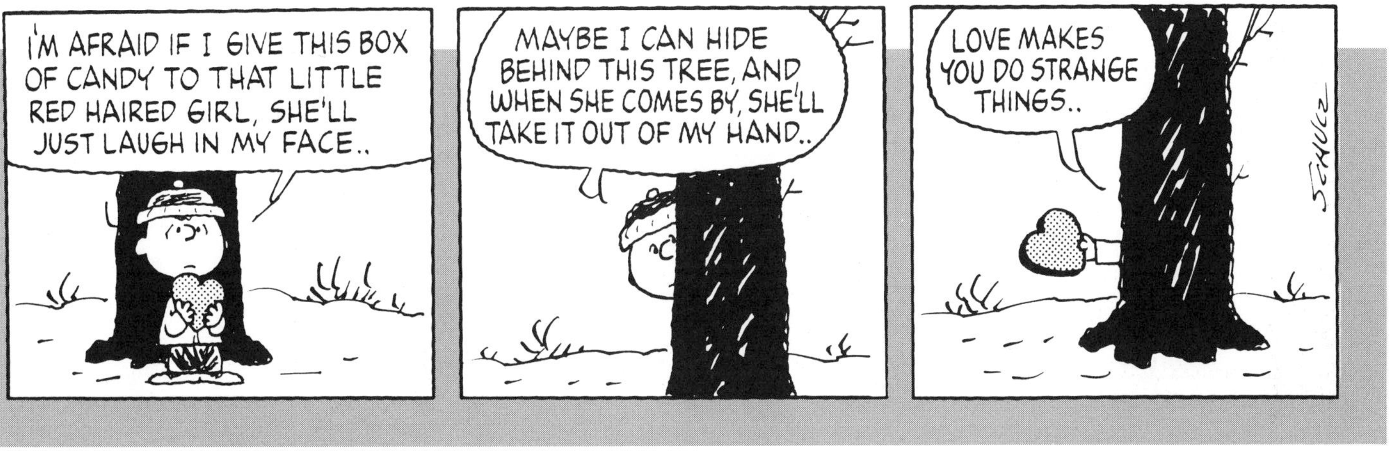

I'M AFRAID IF I GIVE THIS BOX OF CANDY TO THAT LITTLE RED HAIRED GIRL, SHE'LL JUST LAUGH IN MY FACE..
MAYBE I CAN HIDE BEHIND THIS TREE, AND WHEN SHE COMES BY, SHE'LL TAKE IT OUT OF MY HAND..
LOVE MAKES YOU DO STRANGE THINGS..
SCHULZ

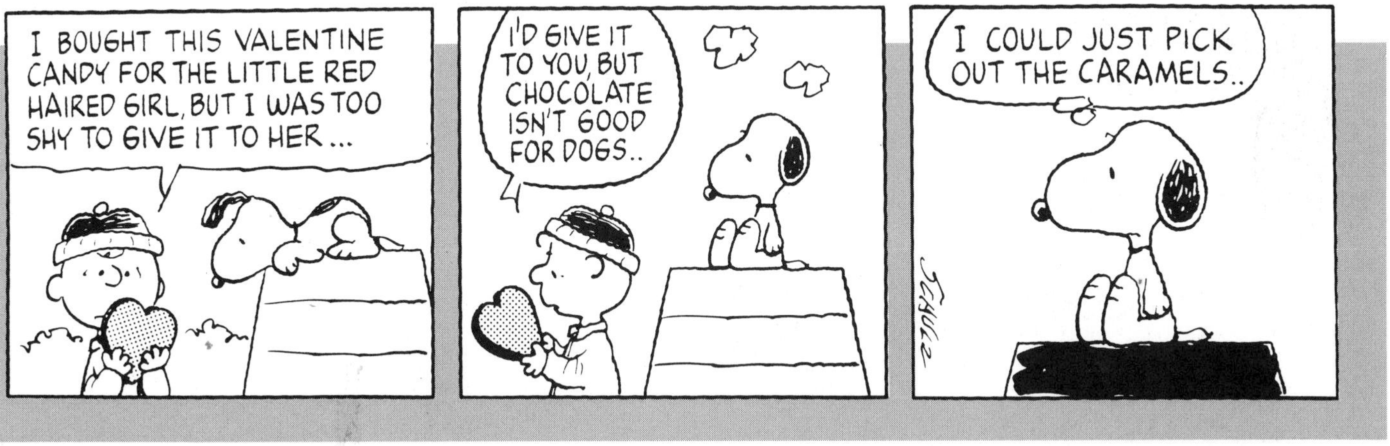

I BOUGHT THIS VALENTINE CANDY FOR THE LITTLE RED HAIRED GIRL, BUT I WAS TOO SHY TO GIVE IT TO HER...
I'D GIVE IT TO YOU, BUT CHOCOLATE ISN'T GOOD FOR DOGS..
SCHULZ
I COULD JUST PICK OUT THE CARAMELS..

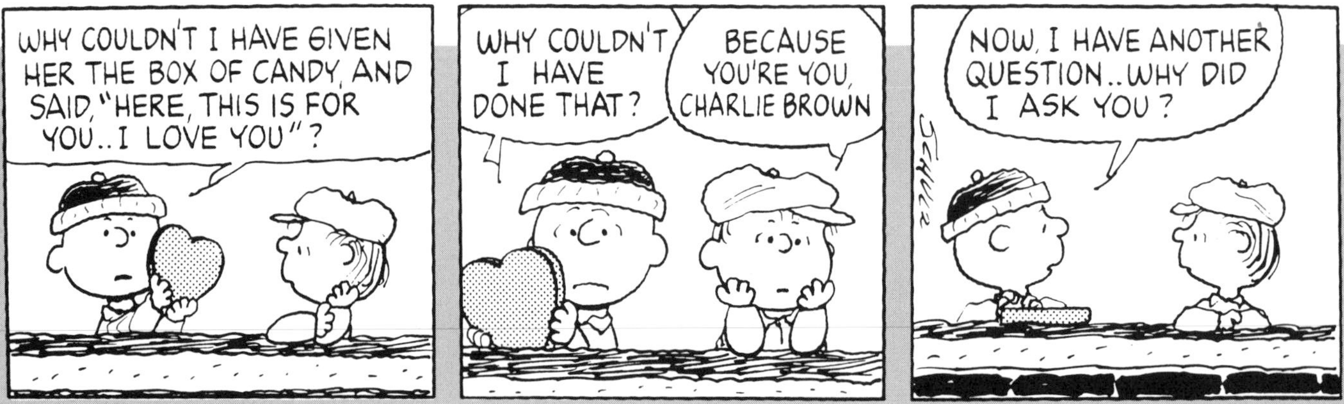
WHY COULDN'T I HAVE GIVEN HER THE BOX OF CANDY, AND SAID, "HERE, THIS IS FOR YOU..I LOVE YOU"?
WHY COULDN'T I HAVE DONE THAT?
BECAUSE YOU'RE YOU, CHARLIE BROWN
NOW, I HAVE ANOTHER QUESTION..WHY DID I ASK YOU?
SCHULZ

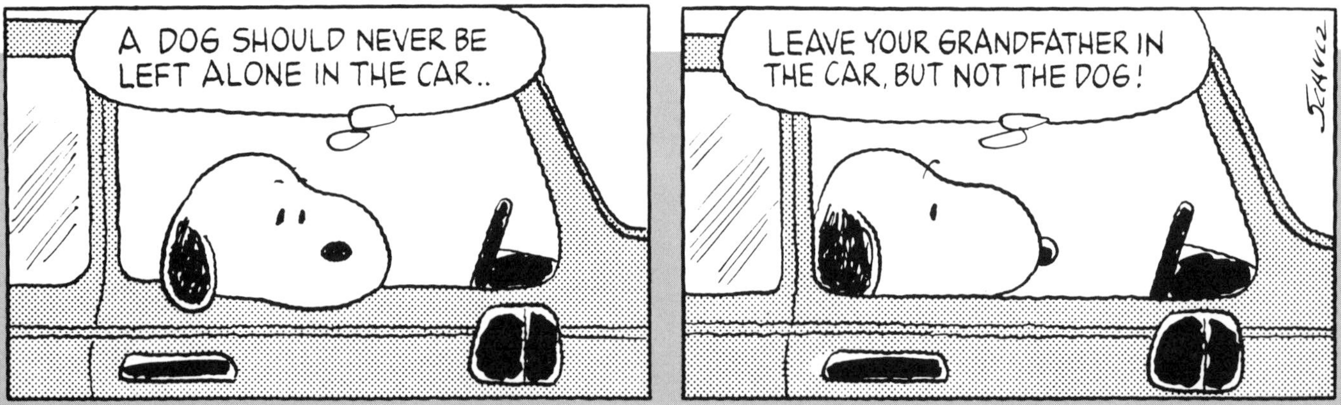
A DOG SHOULD NEVER BE LEFT ALONE IN THE CAR..
LEAVE YOUR GRANDFATHER IN THE CAR, BUT NOT THE DOG!
SCHULZ

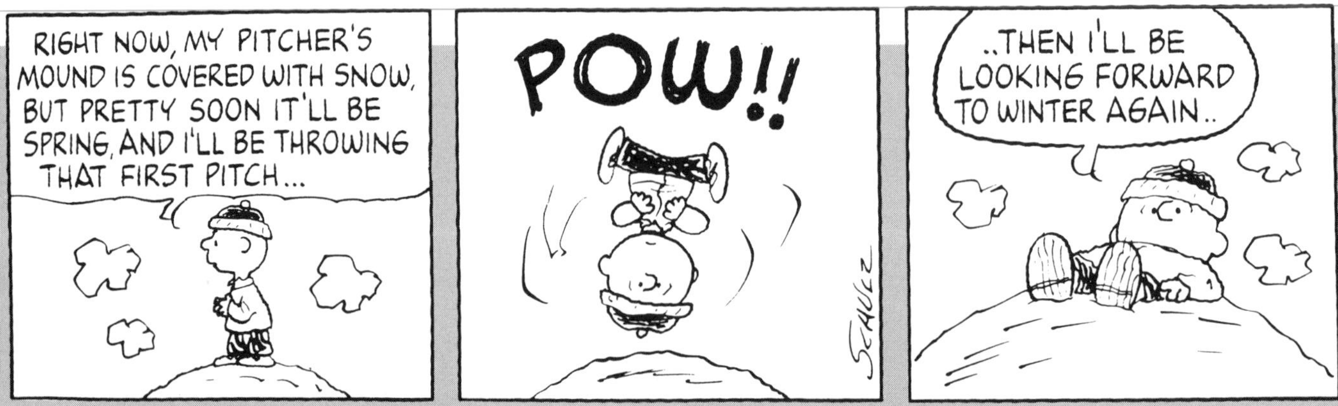
RIGHT NOW, MY PITCHER'S MOUND IS COVERED WITH SNOW, BUT PRETTY SOON IT'LL BE SPRING, AND I'LL BE THROWING THAT FIRST PITCH...
POW!!
SCHULZ
..THEN I'LL BE LOOKING FORWARD TO WINTER AGAIN..

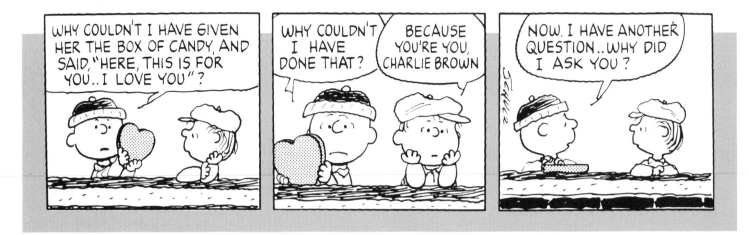

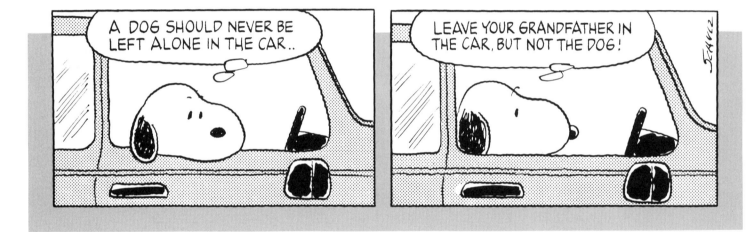

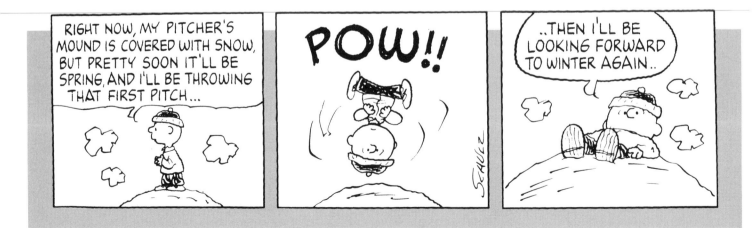

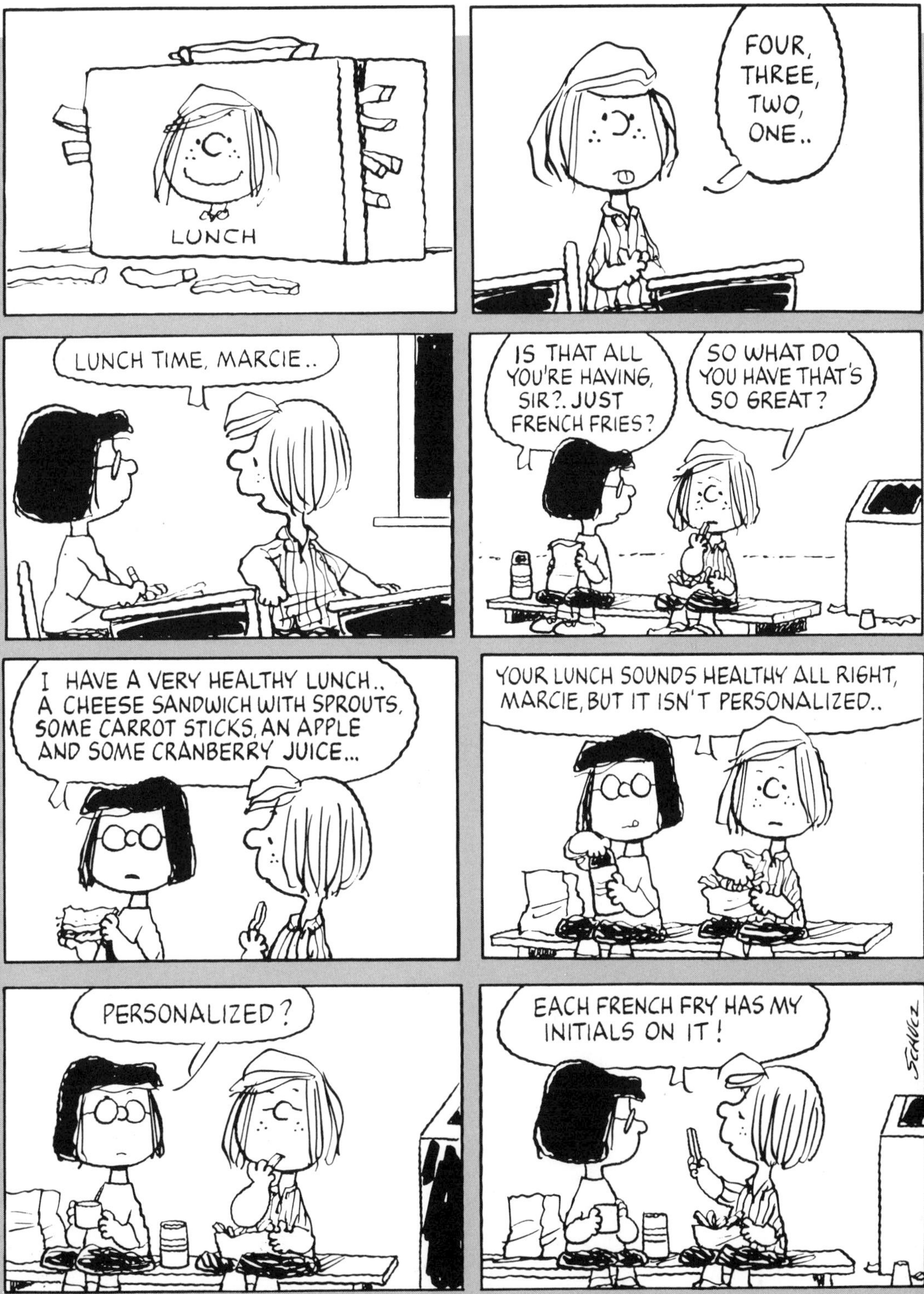
LUNCH
FOUR, THREE, TWO, ONE..
LUNCH TIME, MARCIE..
IS THAT ALL YOU'RE HAVING, SIR?. JUST FRENCH FRIES?
SO WHAT DO YOU HAVE THAT'S SO GREAT?
I HAVE A VERY HEALTHY LUNCH.. A CHEESE SANDWICH WITH SPROUTS, SOME CARROT STICKS, AN APPLE AND SOME CRANBERRY JUICE...
YOUR LUNCH SOUNDS HEALTHY ALL RIGHT, MARCIE, BUT IT ISN'T PERSONALIZED..
PERSONALIZED?
EACH FRENCH FRY HAS MY INITIALS ON IT!
SCHULZ

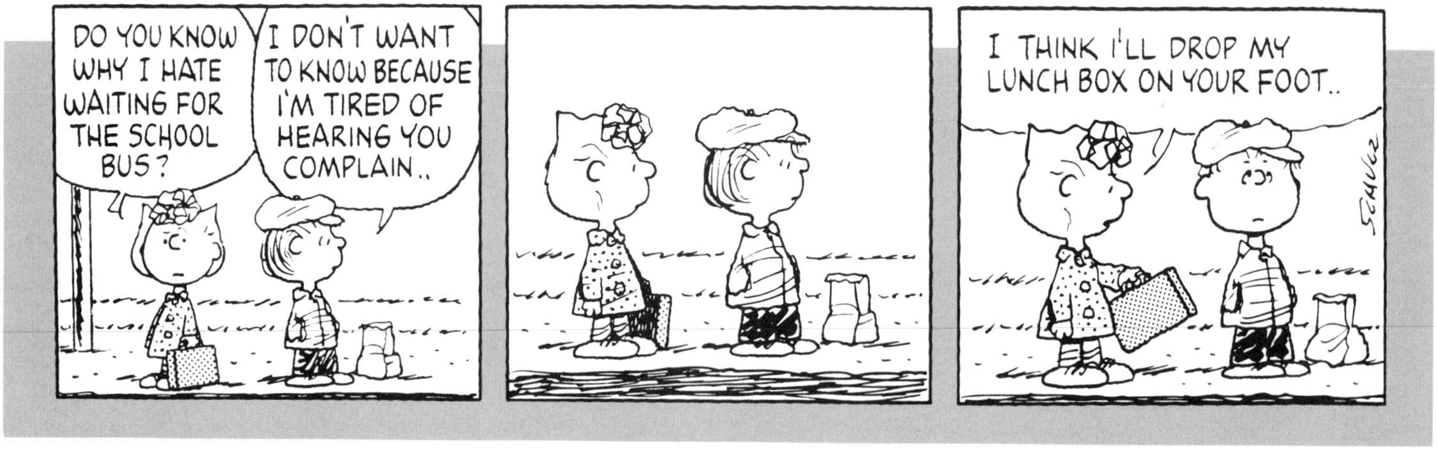
DO YOU KNOW WHY I HATE WAITING FOR THE SCHOOL BUS?
I DON'T WANT TO KNOW BECAUSE I'M TIRED OF HEARING YOU COMPLAIN..
I THINK I'LL DROP MY LUNCH BOX ON YOUR FOOT..
SCHULZ

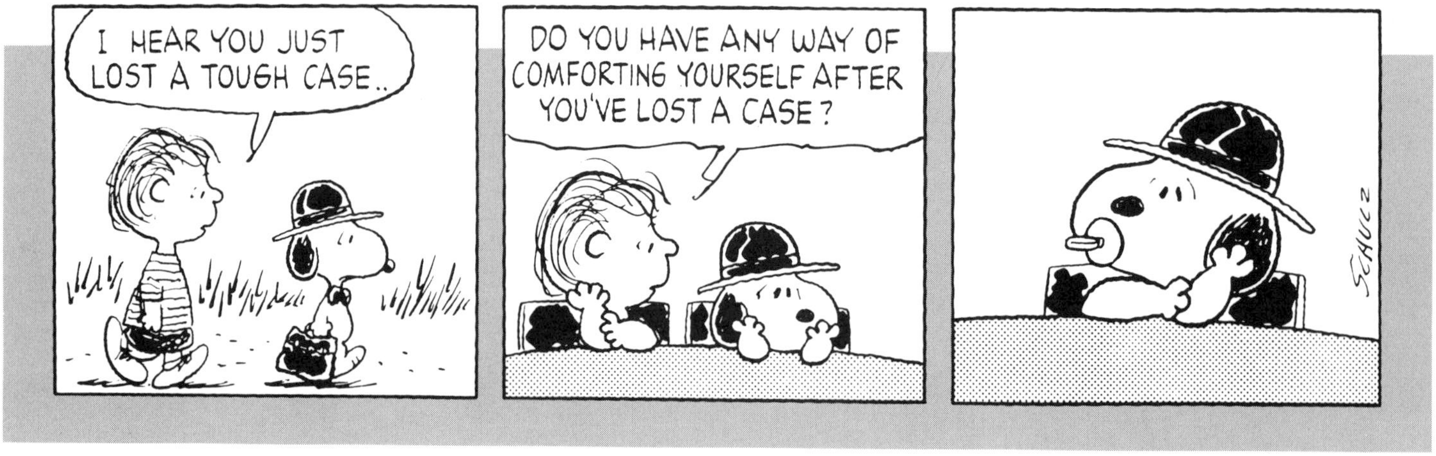
I HEAR YOU JUST LOST A TOUGH CASE..
DO YOU HAVE ANY WAY OF COMFORTING YOURSELF AFTER YOU'VE LOST A CASE?
SCHULZ

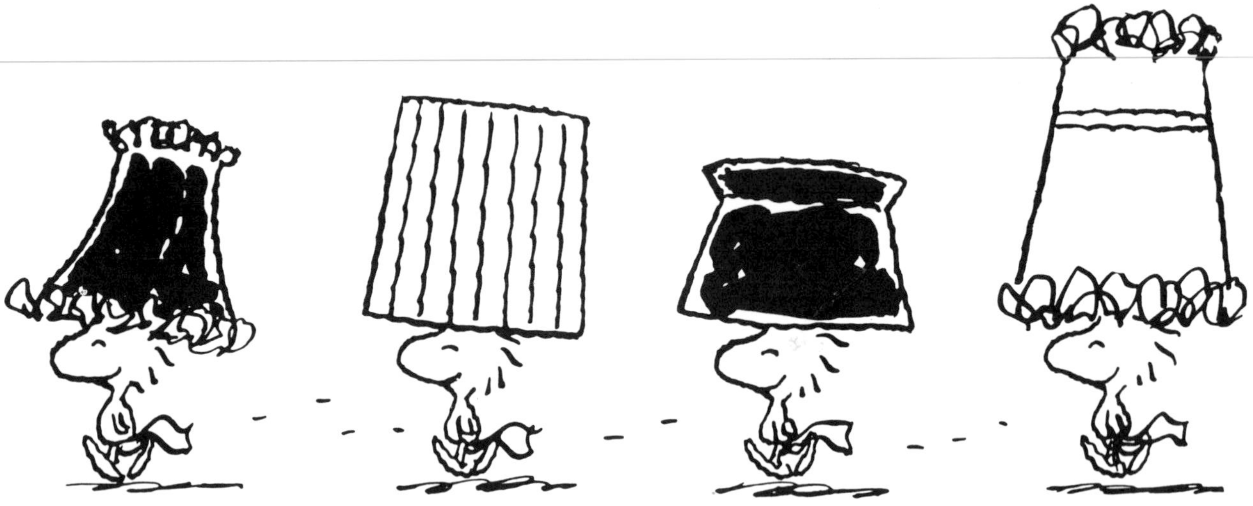

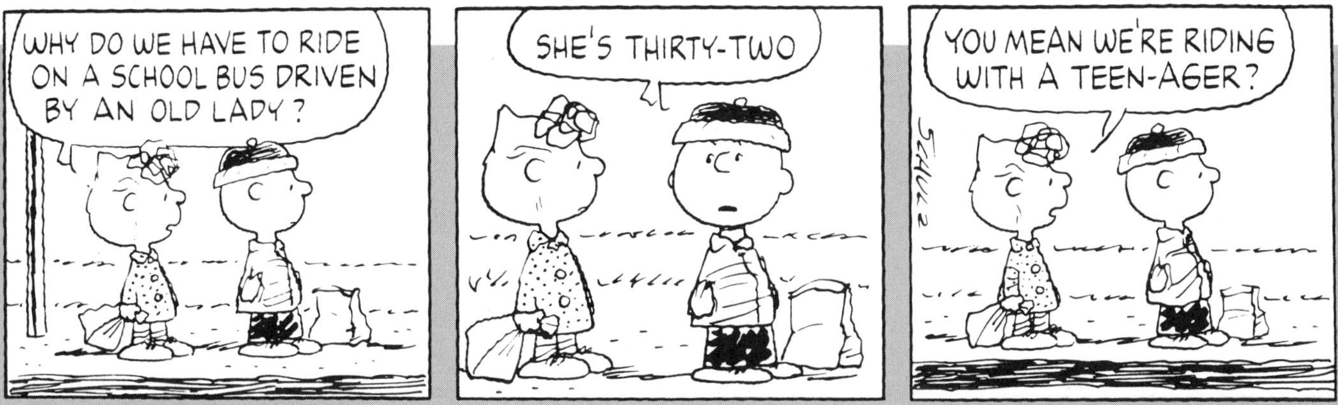
WHY DO WE HAVE TO RIDE ON A SCHOOL BUS DRIVEN BY AN OLD LADY?
SHE'S THIRTY-TWO
YOU MEAN WE'RE RIDING WITH A TEEN-AGER?

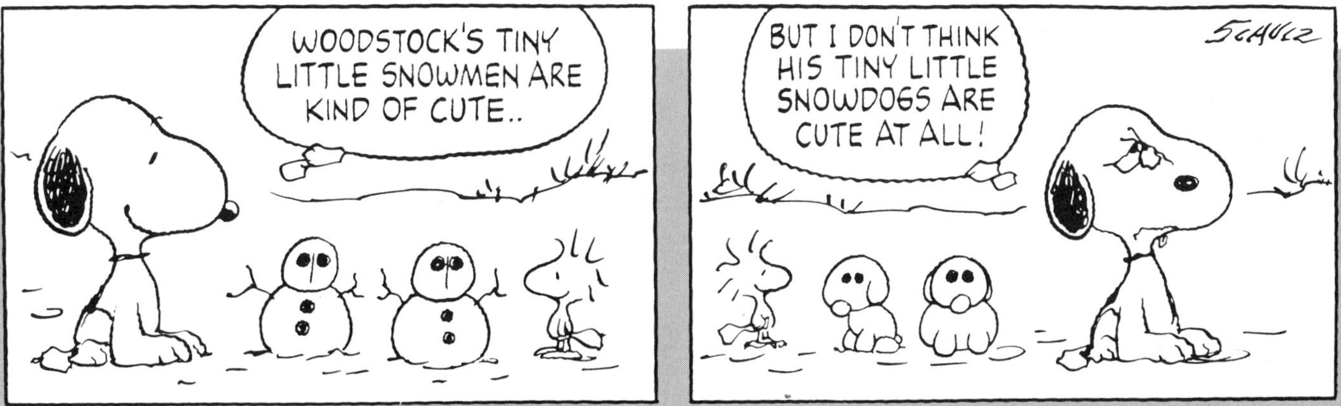
WOODSTOCK'S TINY LITTLE SNOWMEN ARE KIND OF CUTE..
BUT I DON'T THINK HIS TINY LITTLE SNOWDOGS ARE CUTE AT ALL!

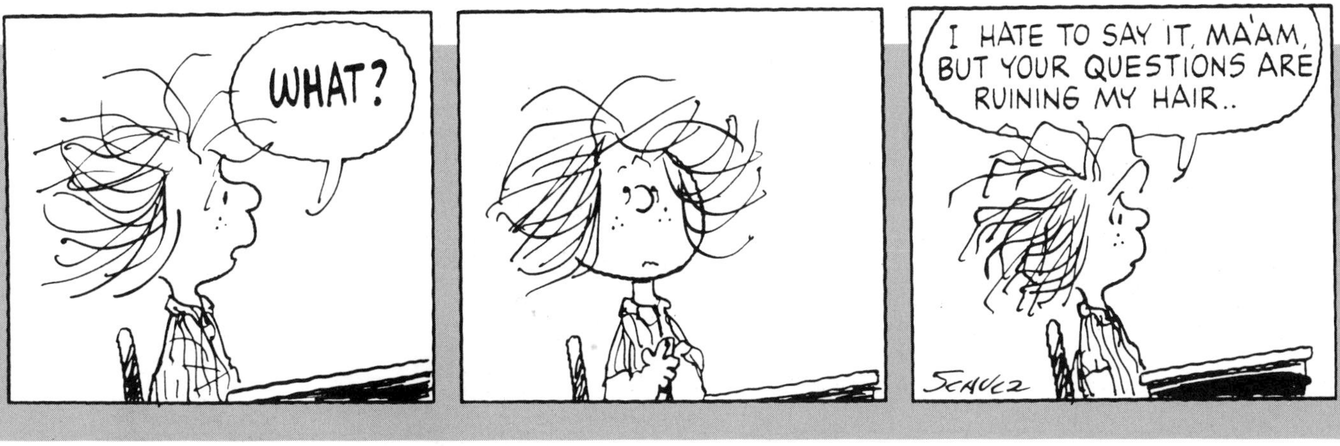
WHAT?
I HATE TO SAY IT, MA'AM, BUT YOUR QUESTIONS ARE RUINING MY HAIR..

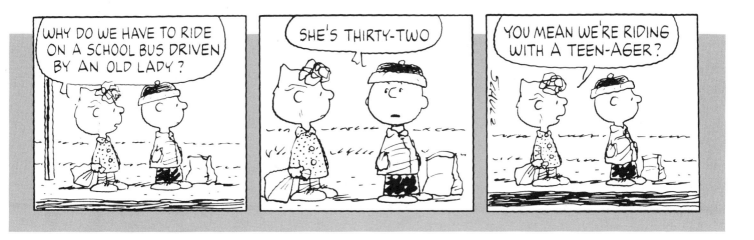

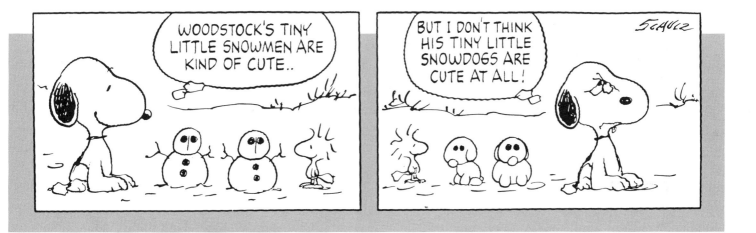

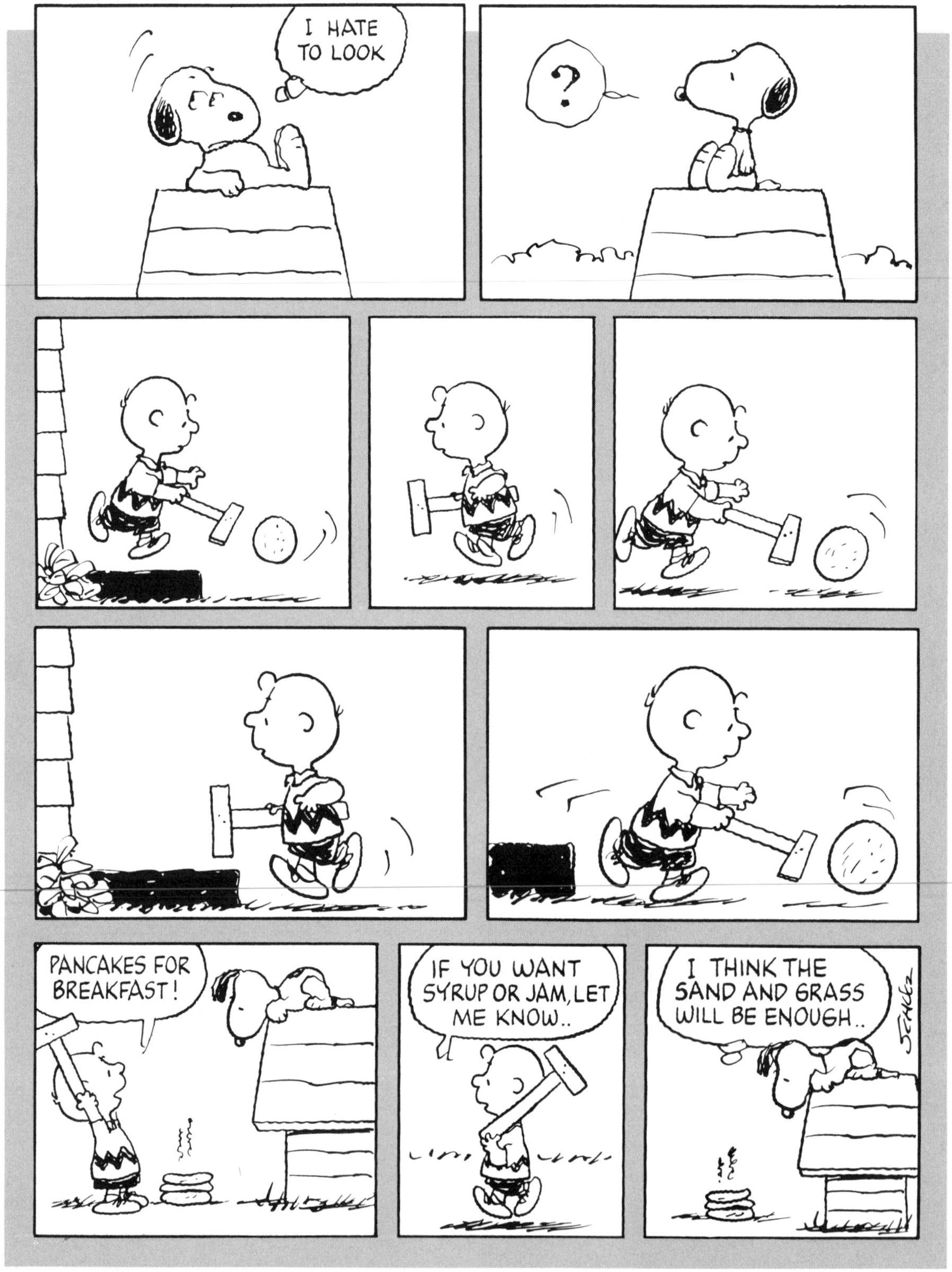
I HATE TO LOOK
?
PANCAKES FOR BREAKFAST!
IF YOU WANT SYRUP OR JAM, LET ME KNOW..
I THINK THE SAND AND GRASS WILL BE ENOUGH..

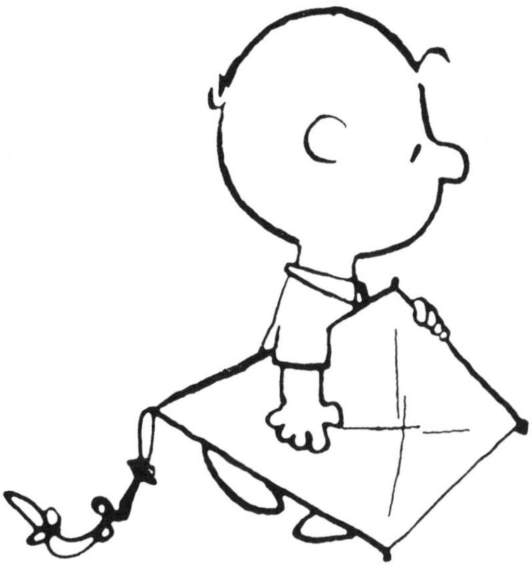

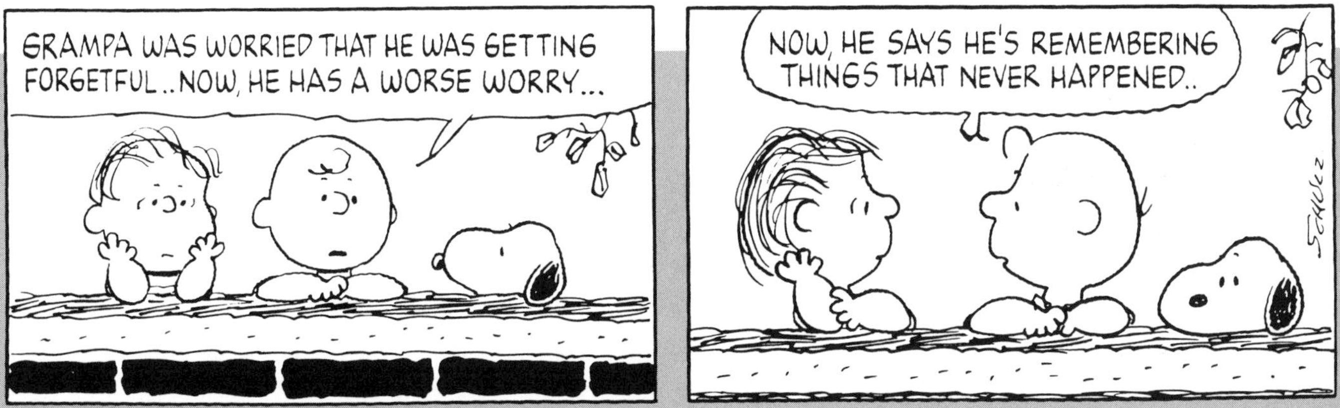
GRAMPA WAS WORRIED THAT HE WAS GETTING FORGETFUL..NOW, HE HAS A WORSE WORRY...
NOW, HE SAYS HE'S REMEMBERING THINGS THAT NEVER HAPPENED..
SCHULZ

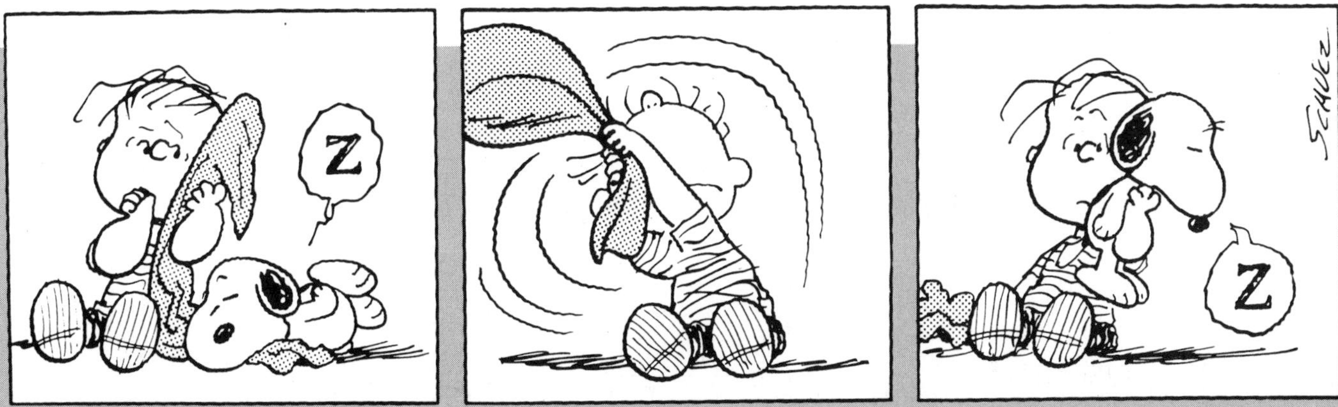
Z
Z
SCHULZ

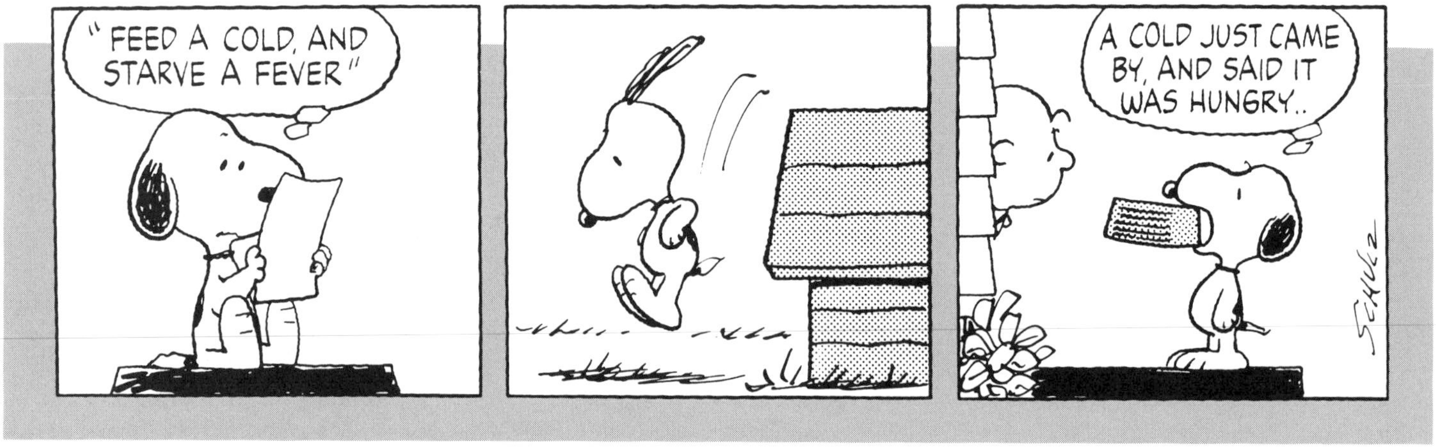
" FEED A COLD, AND STARVE A FEVER"
A COLD JUST CAME BY, AND SAID IT WAS HUNGRY..
SCHULZ

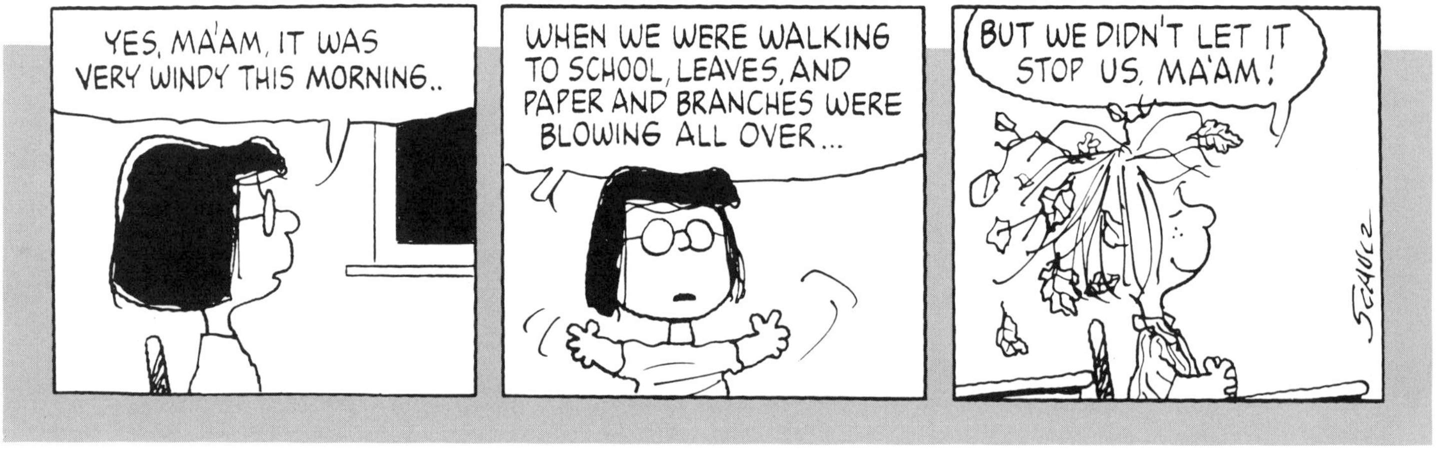
YES, MA'AM, IT WAS VERY WINDY THIS MORNING..
WHEN WE WERE WALKING TO SCHOOL, LEAVES, AND PAPER AND BRANCHES WERE BLOWING ALL OVER...
BUT WE DIDN'T LET IT STOP US, MA'AM!
SCHULZ

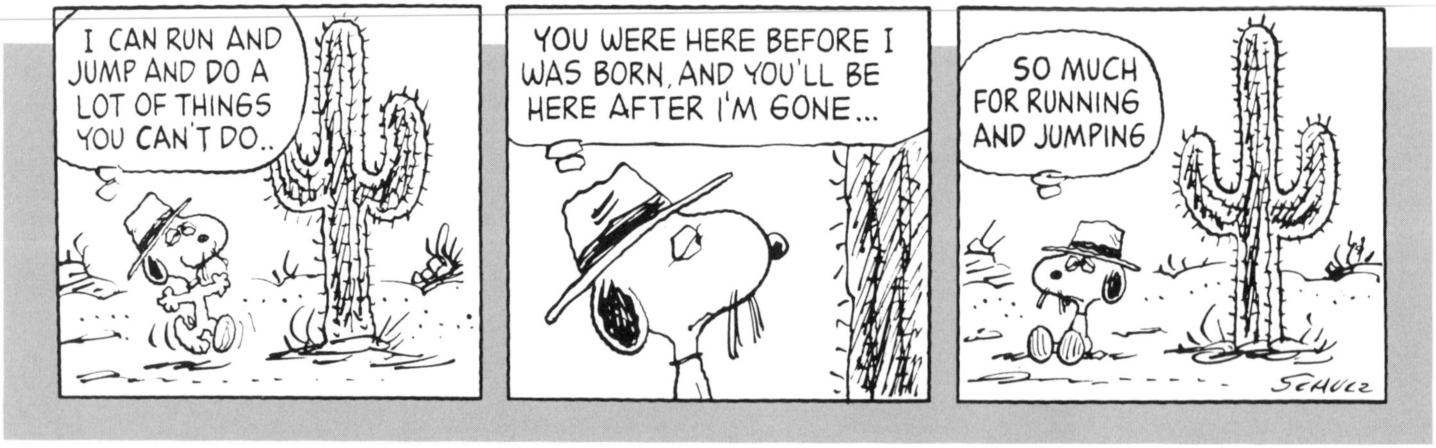
I CAN RUN AND JUMP AND DO A LOT OF THINGS YOU CAN'T DO..
YOU WERE HERE BEFORE I WAS BORN, AND YOU'LL BE HERE AFTER I'M GONE...
SO MUCH FOR RUNNING AND JUMPING
SCHULZ

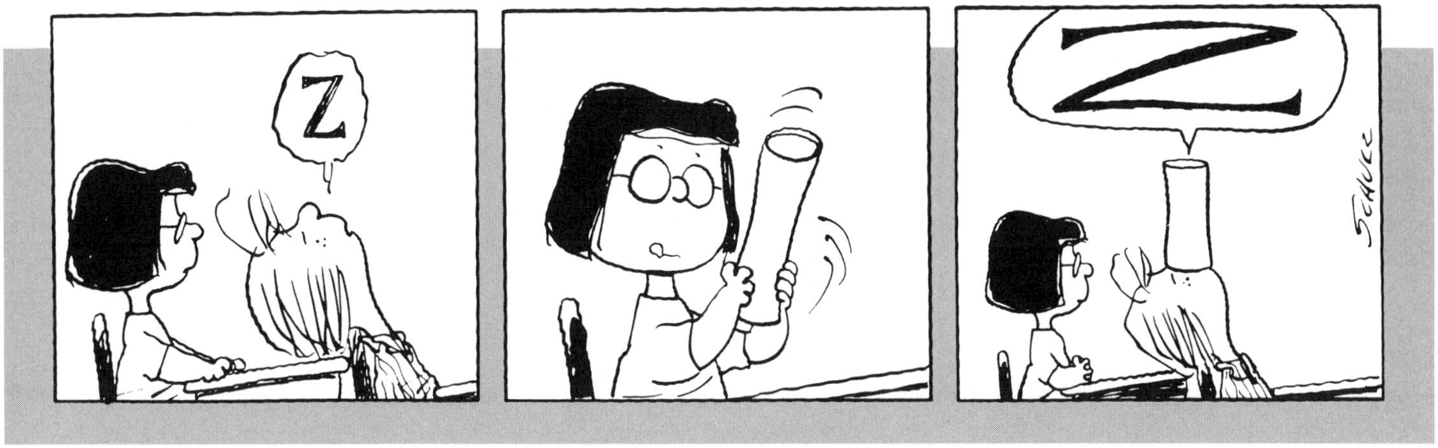
Z
Z
SCHULZ

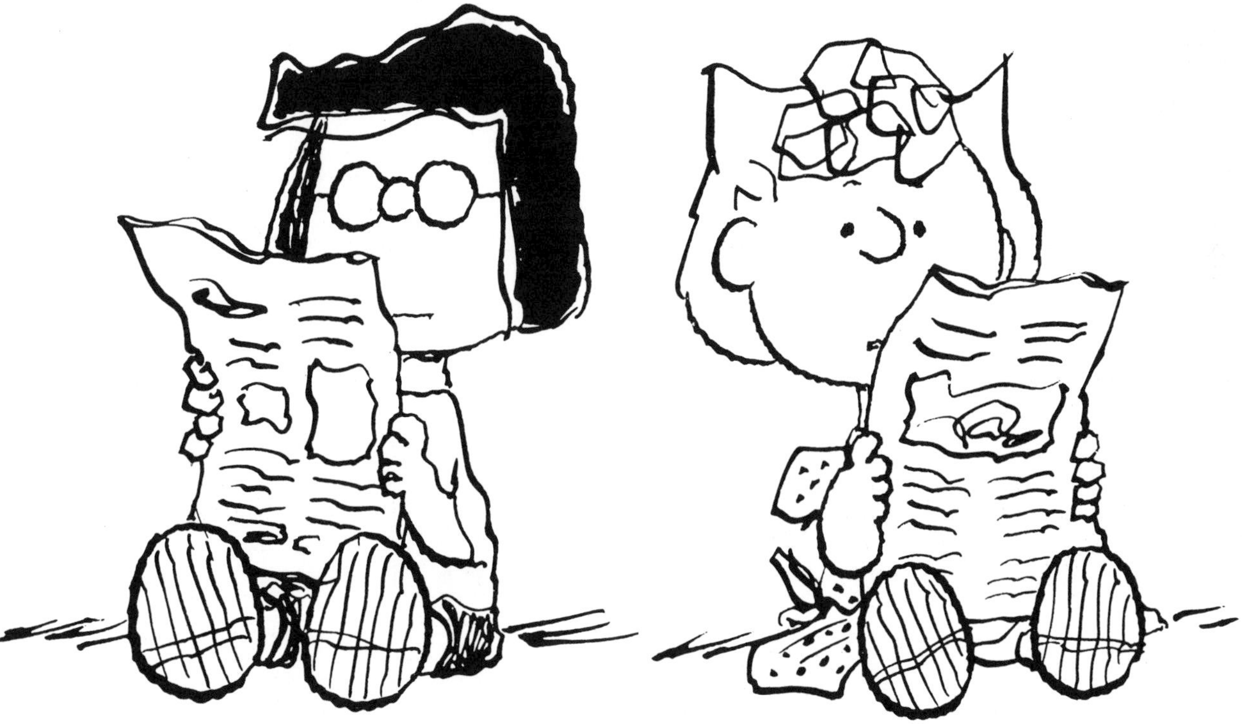

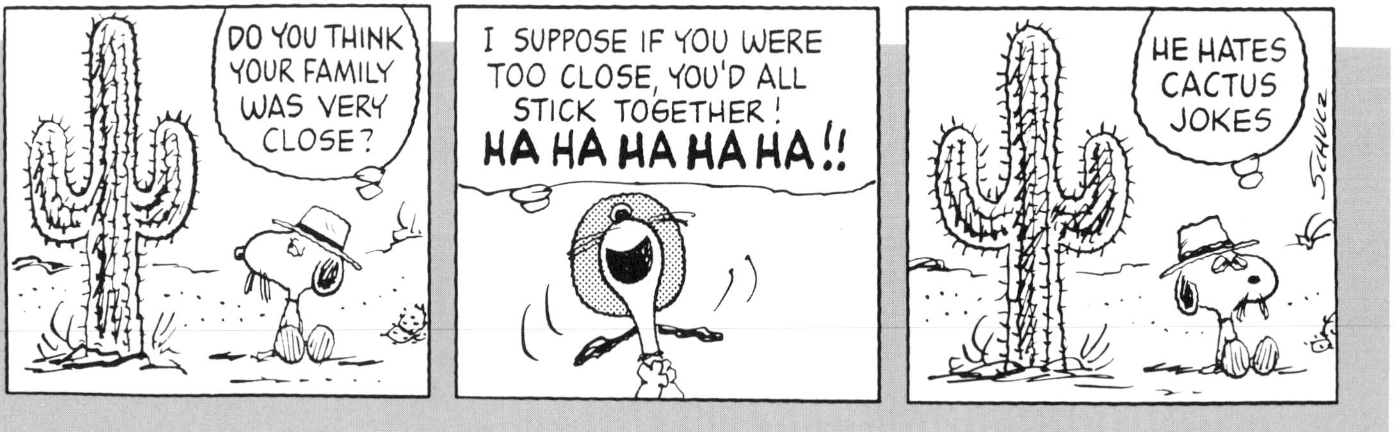
DO YOU THINK YOUR FAMILY WAS VERY CLOSE?
I SUPPOSE IF YOU WERE TOO CLOSE, YOU'D ALL STICK TOGETHER!
HA HA HA HA HA!!
HE HATES CACTUS JOKES

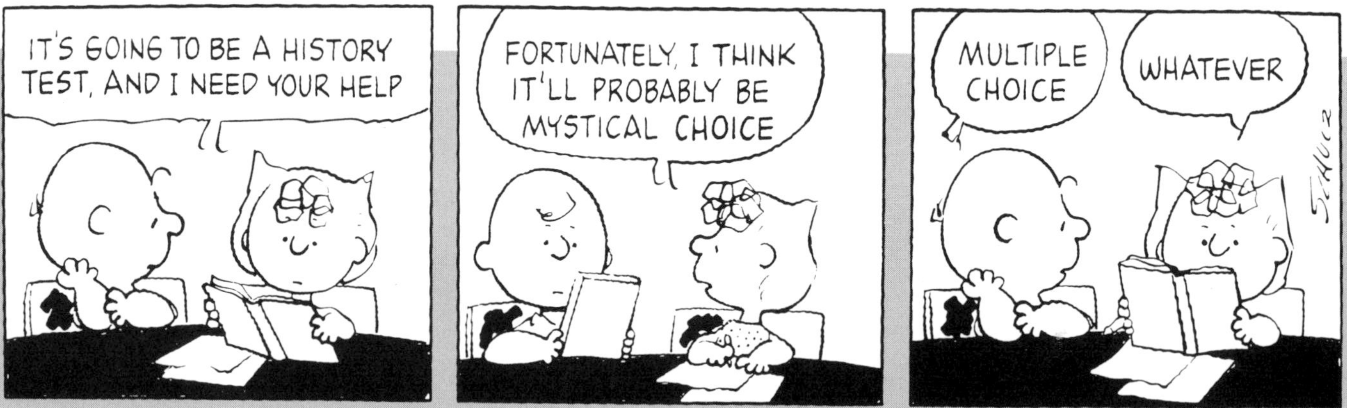
IT'S GOING TO BE A HISTORY TEST, AND I NEED YOUR HELP
FORTUNATELY, I THINK IT'LL PROBABLY BE MYSTICAL CHOICE
MULTIPLE CHOICE
WHATEVER

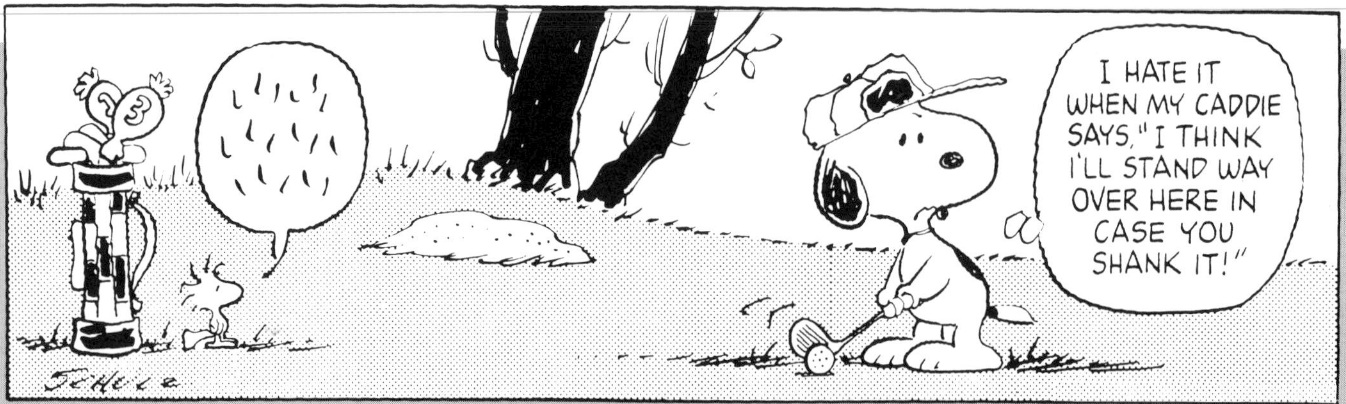
I HATE IT WHEN MY CADDIE SAYS, "I THINK I'LL STAND WAY OVER HERE IN CASE YOU SHANK IT!"

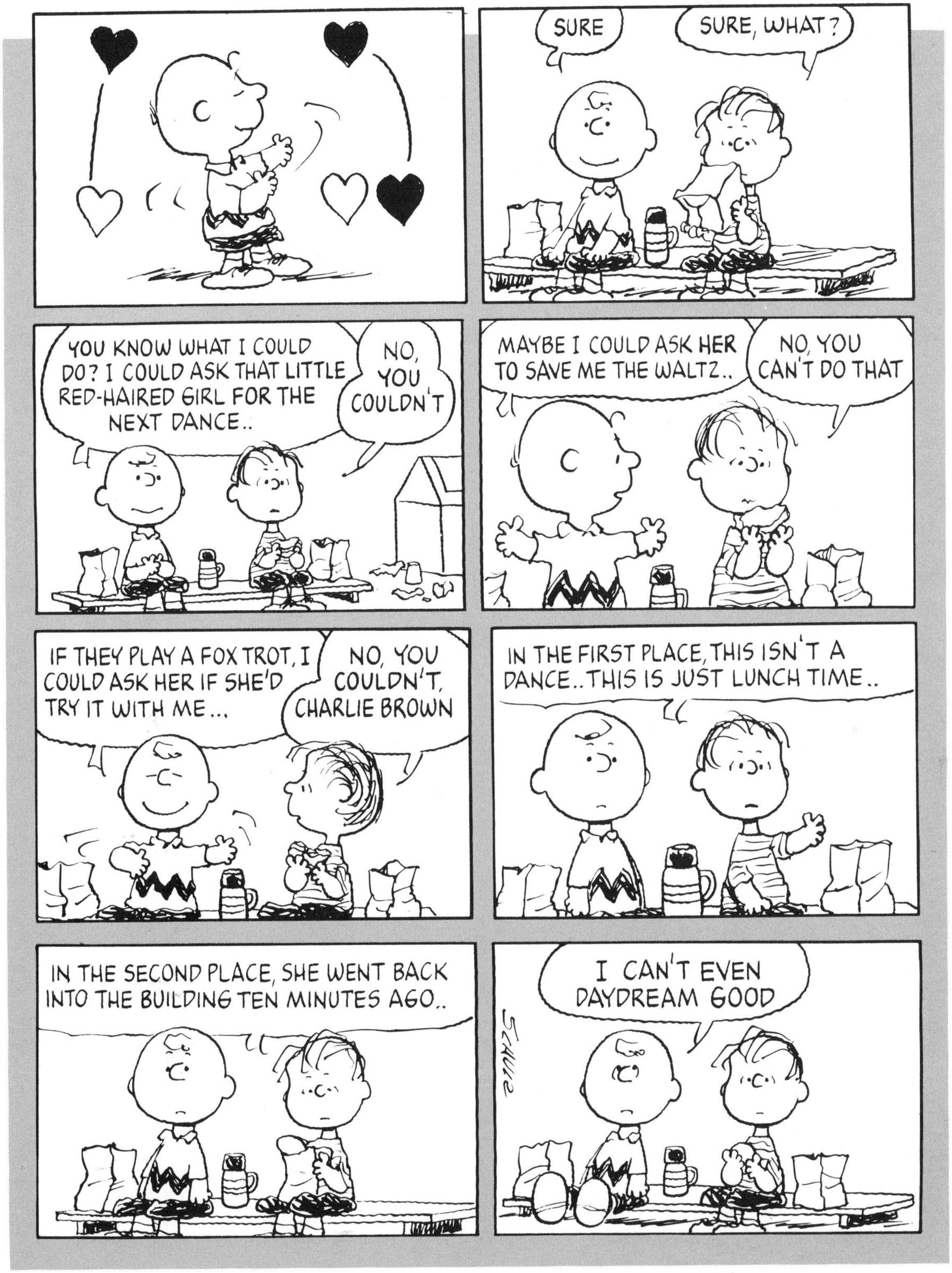
SURE
SURE, WHAT?
YOU KNOW WHAT I COULD DO? I COULD ASK THAT LITTLE RED-HAIRED GIRL FOR THE NEXT DANCE..
NO, YOU COULDN'T
MAYBE I COULD ASK HER TO SAVE ME THE WALTZ..
NO, YOU CAN'T DO THAT
IF THEY PLAY A FOX TROT, I COULD ASK HER IF SHE'D TRY IT WITH ME...
NO, YOU COULDN'T, CHARLIE BROWN
IN THE FIRST PLACE, THIS ISN'T A DANCE..THIS IS JUST LUNCH TIME..
IN THE SECOND PLACE, SHE WENT BACK INTO THE BUILDING TEN MINUTES AGO..
SCHULZ
I CAN'T EVEN DAYDREAM GOOD

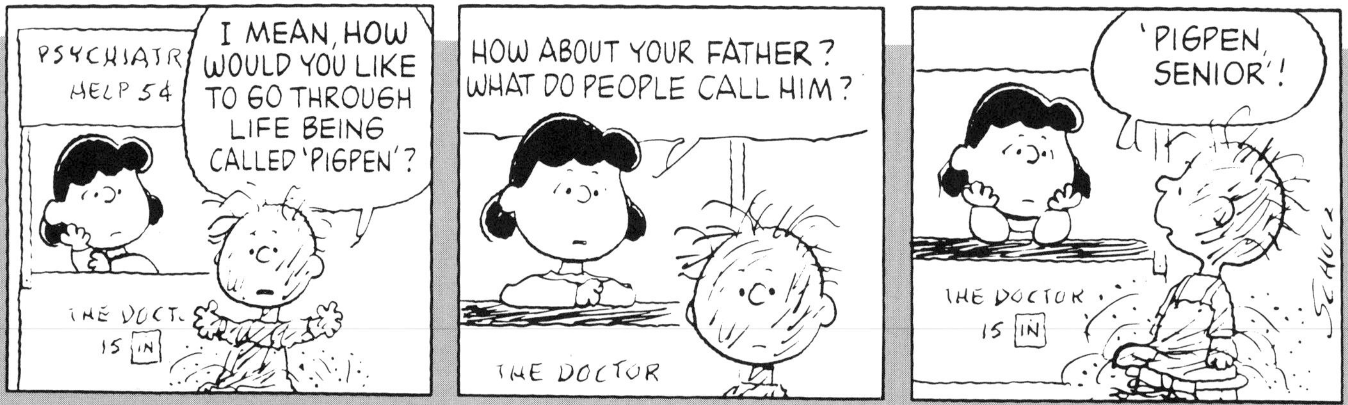
PSYCHIATR
HELP 5¢
I MEAN, HOW WOULD YOU LIKE TO GO THROUGH LIFE BEING CALLED 'PIGPEN'?
THE DOCT.
IS IN
HOW ABOUT YOUR FATHER? WHAT DO PEOPLE CALL HIM?
THE DOCTOR
'PIGPEN, SENIOR'!
THE DOCTOR
IS IN
SCHULZ

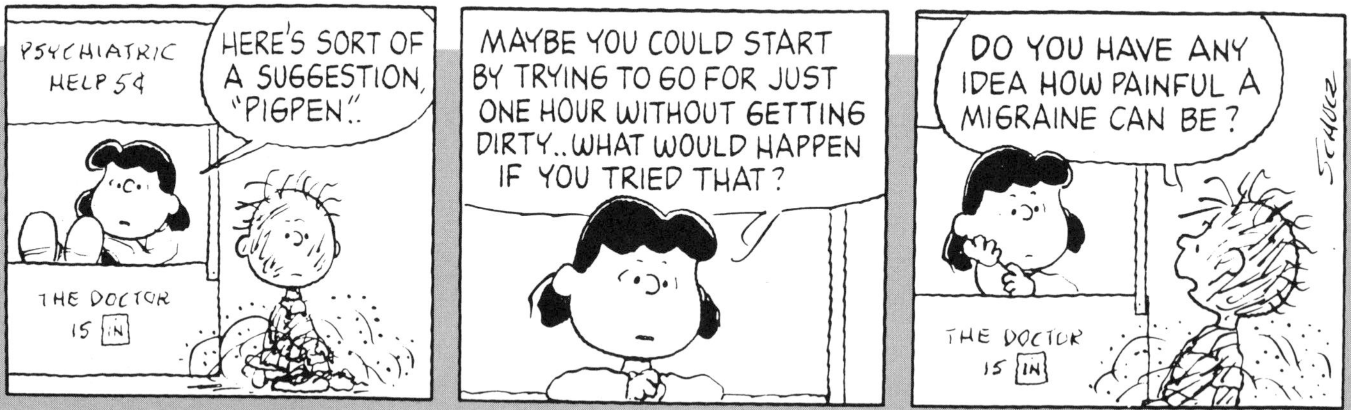
PSYCHIATRIC
HELP 5¢
HERE'S SORT OF A SUGGESTION, "PIGPEN"..
THE DOCTOR
IS IN
MAYBE YOU COULD START BY TRYING TO GO FOR JUST ONE HOUR WITHOUT GETTING DIRTY..WHAT WOULD HAPPEN IF YOU TRIED THAT?
DO YOU HAVE ANY IDEA HOW PAINFUL A MIGRAINE CAN BE?
THE DOCTOR
IS IN
SCHULZ

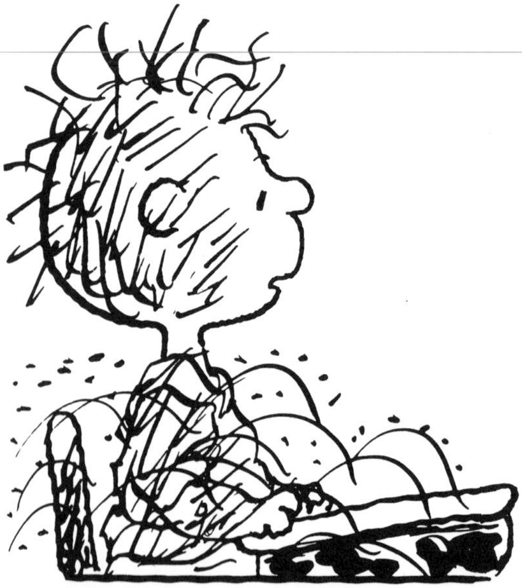

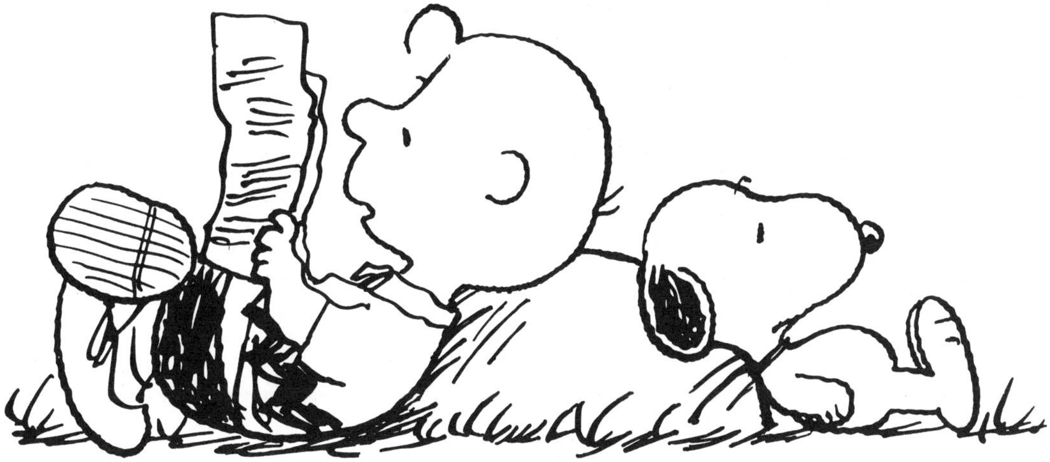

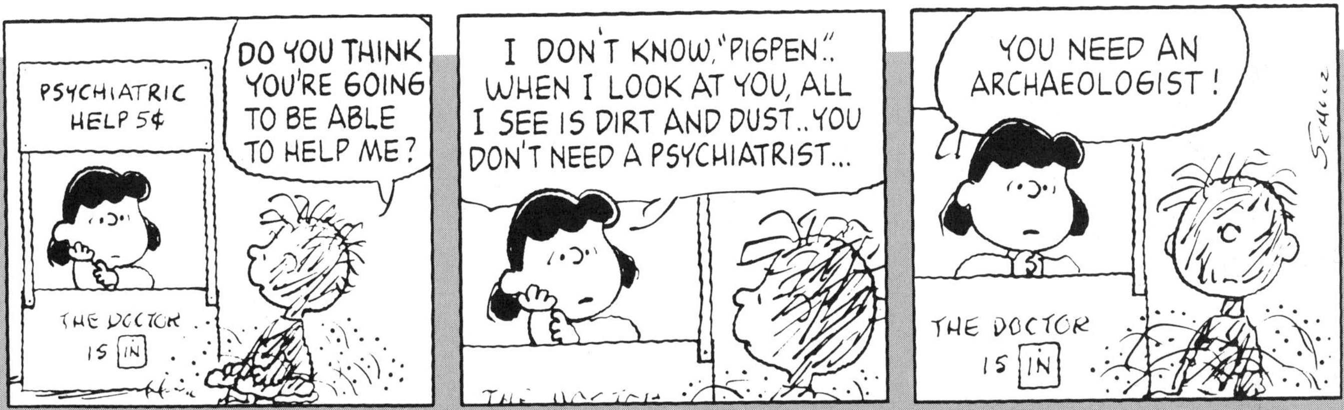
PSYCHIATRIC HELP 5¢
THE DOCTOR IS IN
DO YOU THINK YOU'RE GOING TO BE ABLE TO HELP ME?
I DON'T KNOW, "PIGPEN".. WHEN I LOOK AT YOU, ALL I SEE IS DIRT AND DUST..YOU DON'T NEED A PSYCHIATRIST...
YOU NEED AN ARCHAEOLOGIST!
THE DOCTOR IS IN

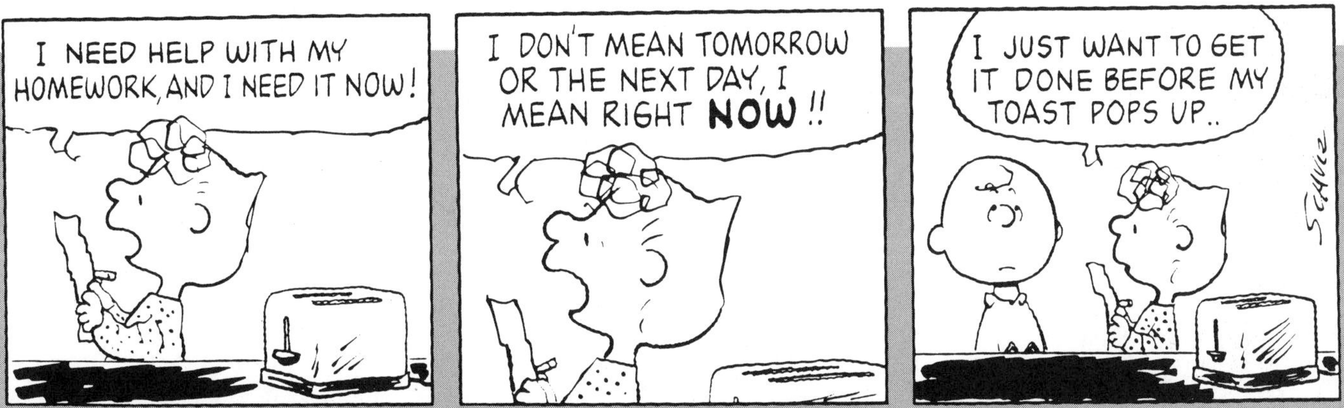
I NEED HELP WITH MY HOMEWORK, AND I NEED IT NOW!
I DON'T MEAN TOMORROW OR THE NEXT DAY, I MEAN RIGHT NOW!!
I JUST WANT TO GET IT DONE BEFORE MY TOAST POPS UP..

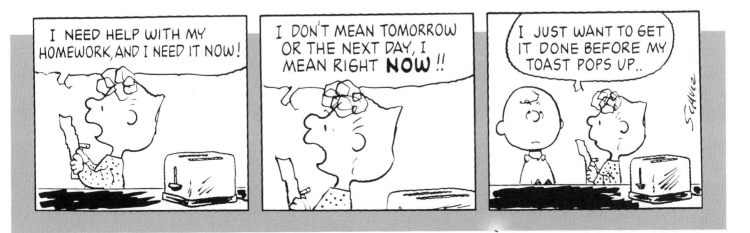

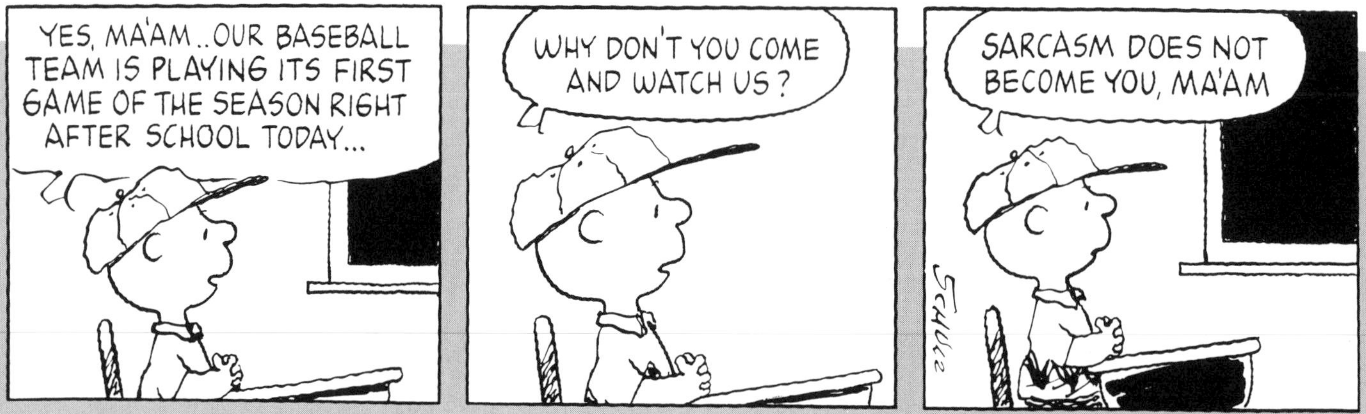
YES, MA'AM..OUR BASEBALL TEAM IS PLAYING ITS FIRST GAME OF THE SEASON RIGHT AFTER SCHOOL TODAY...
WHY DON'T YOU COME AND WATCH US?
SARCASM DOES NOT BECOME YOU, MA'AM
SCHULZ

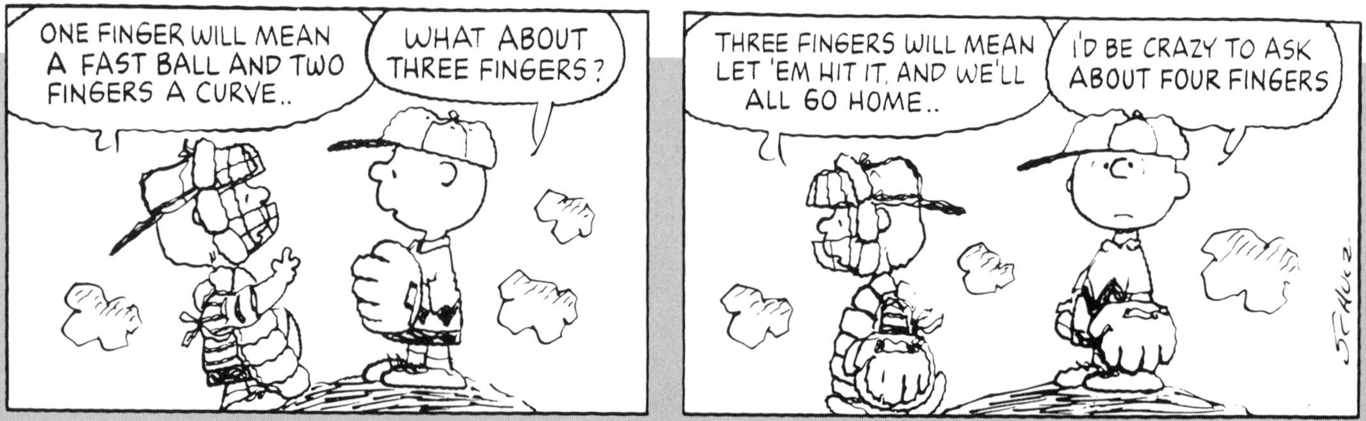
ONE FINGER WILL MEAN A FAST BALL AND TWO FINGERS A CURVE..
WHAT ABOUT THREE FINGERS?
THREE FINGERS WILL MEAN LET 'EM HIT IT, AND WE'LL ALL GO HOME..
I'D BE CRAZY TO ASK ABOUT FOUR FINGERS
SCHULZ

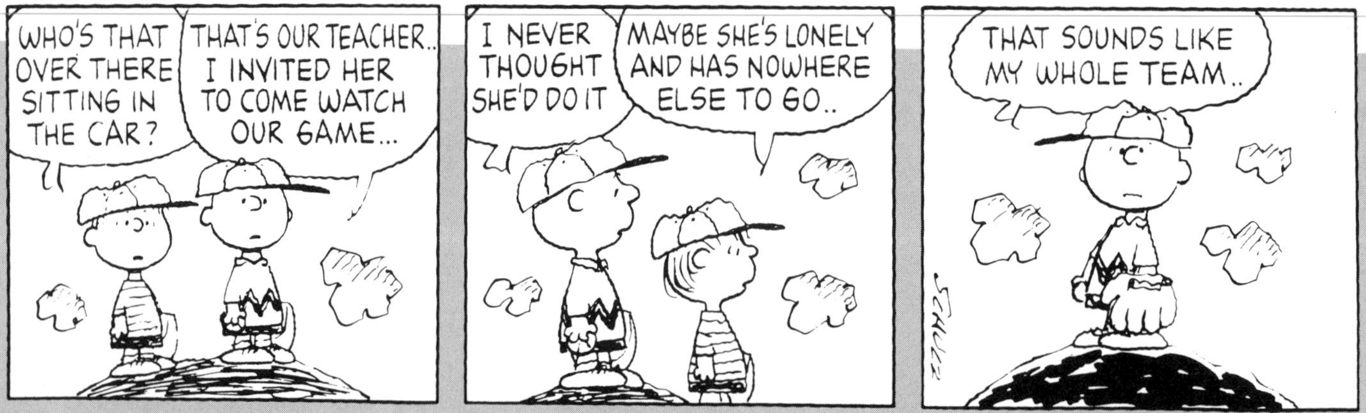
WHO'S THAT OVER THERE SITTING IN THE CAR?
THAT'S OUR TEACHER.. I INVITED HER TO COME WATCH OUR GAME...
I NEVER THOUGHT SHE'D DO IT
MAYBE SHE'S LONELY AND HAS NOWHERE ELSE TO GO..
THAT SOUNDS LIKE MY WHOLE TEAM..
SCHULZ

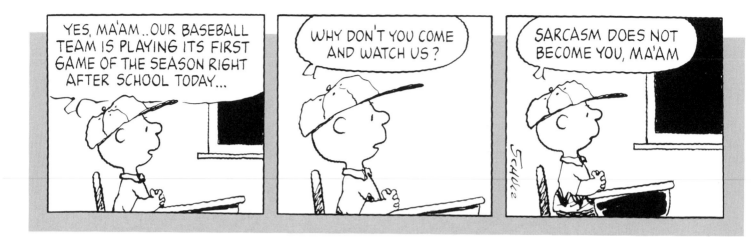

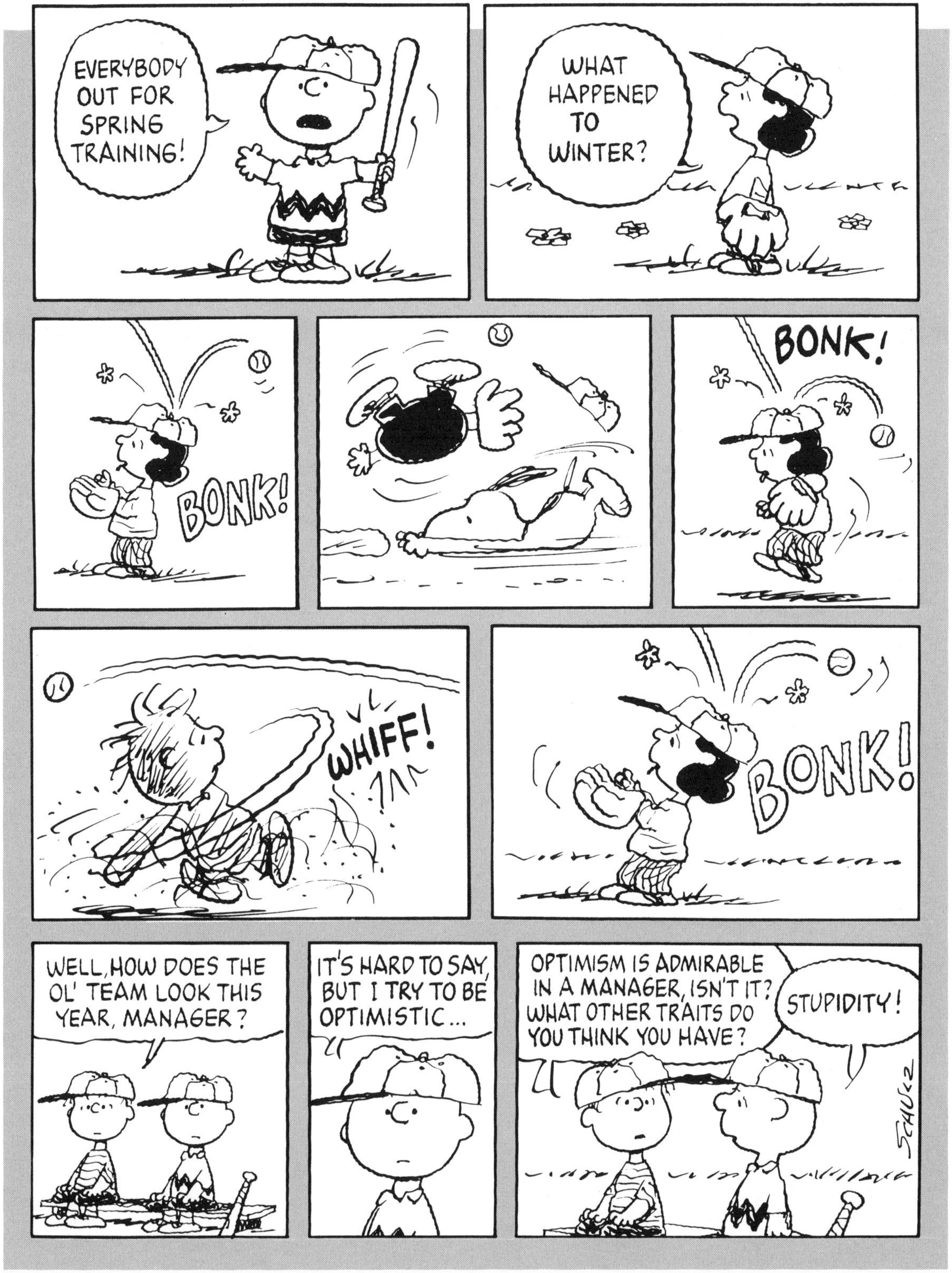
EVERYBODY OUT FOR SPRING TRAINING!
WHAT HAPPENED TO WINTER?
BONK!
BONK!
WHIFF!
BONK!
WELL, HOW DOES THE OL' TEAM LOOK THIS YEAR, MANAGER?
IT'S HARD TO SAY, BUT I TRY TO BE OPTIMISTIC...
OPTIMISM IS ADMIRABLE IN A MANAGER, ISN'T IT? WHAT OTHER TRAITS DO YOU THINK YOU HAVE?
STUPIDITY!
SCHULZ

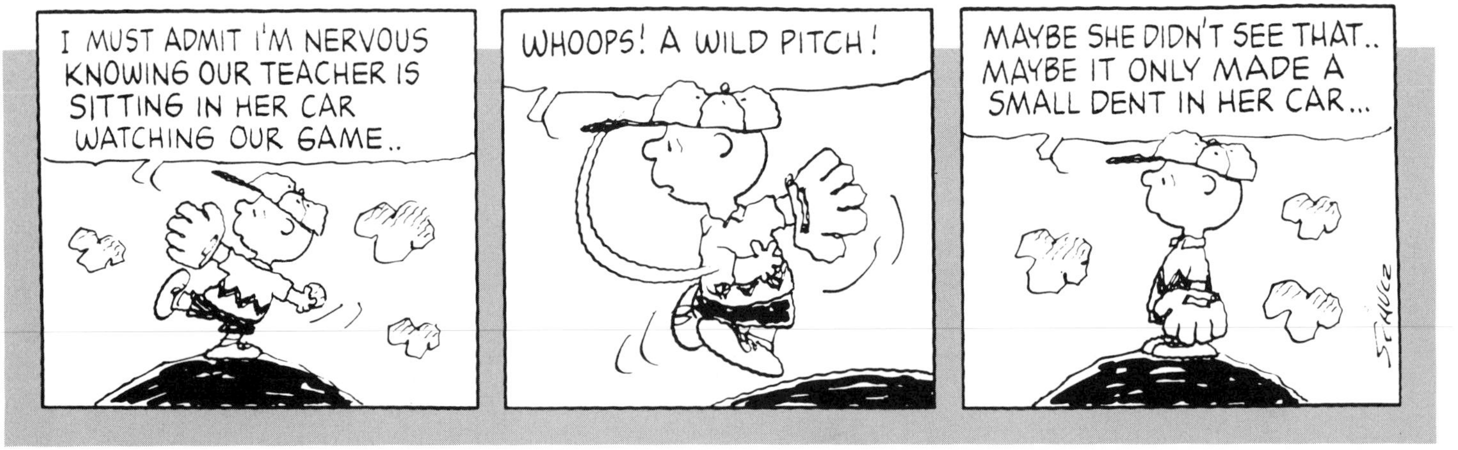
I MUST ADMIT I'M NERVOUS KNOWING OUR TEACHER IS SITTING IN HER CAR WATCHING OUR GAME..
WHOOPS! A WILD PITCH!
MAYBE SHE DIDN'T SEE THAT.. MAYBE IT ONLY MADE A SMALL DENT IN HER CAR...
SCHULZ

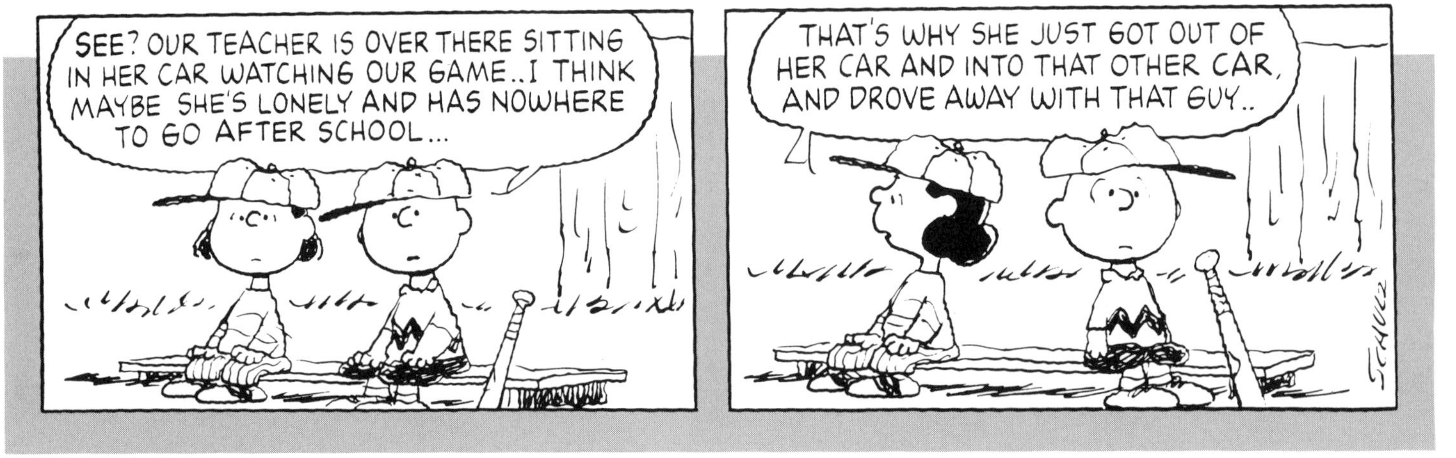
SEE? OUR TEACHER IS OVER THERE SITTING IN HER CAR WATCHING OUR GAME..I THINK MAYBE SHE'S LONELY AND HAS NOWHERE TO GO AFTER SCHOOL...
THAT'S WHY SHE JUST GOT OUT OF HER CAR AND INTO THAT OTHER CAR, AND DROVE AWAY WITH THAT GUY..
SCHULZ

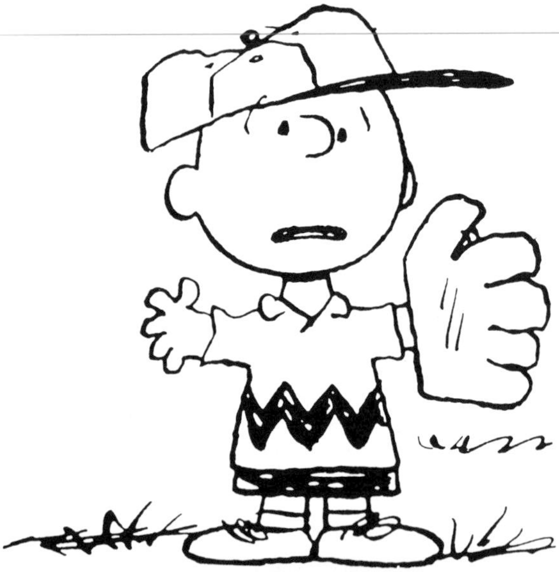

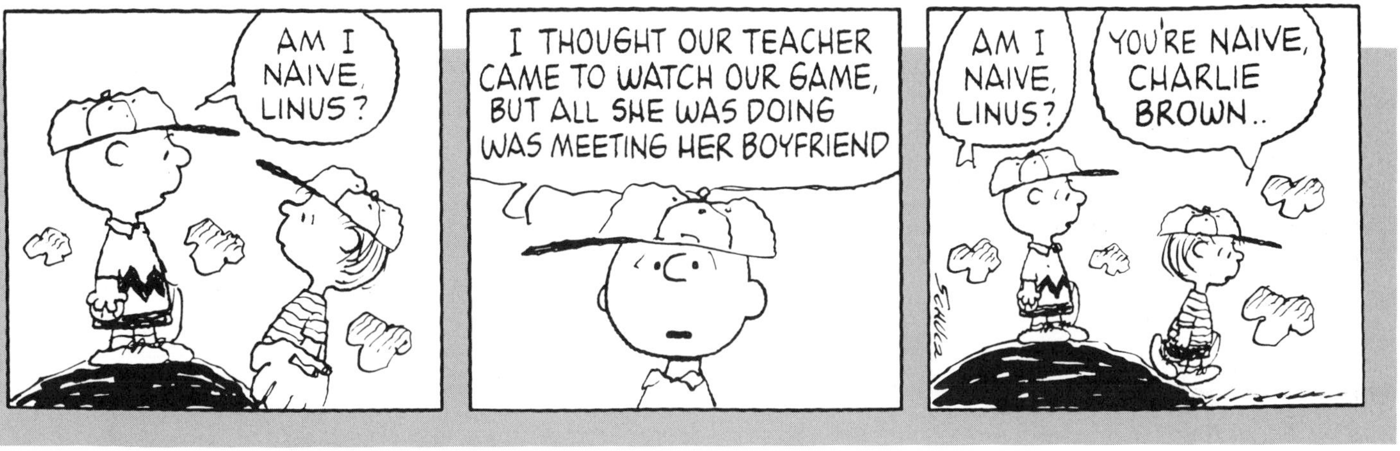
AM I NAIVE, LINUS?
I THOUGHT OUR TEACHER CAME TO WATCH OUR GAME, BUT ALL SHE WAS DOING WAS MEETING HER BOYFRIEND
AM I NAIVE, LINUS?
YOU'RE NAIVE, CHARLIE BROWN..

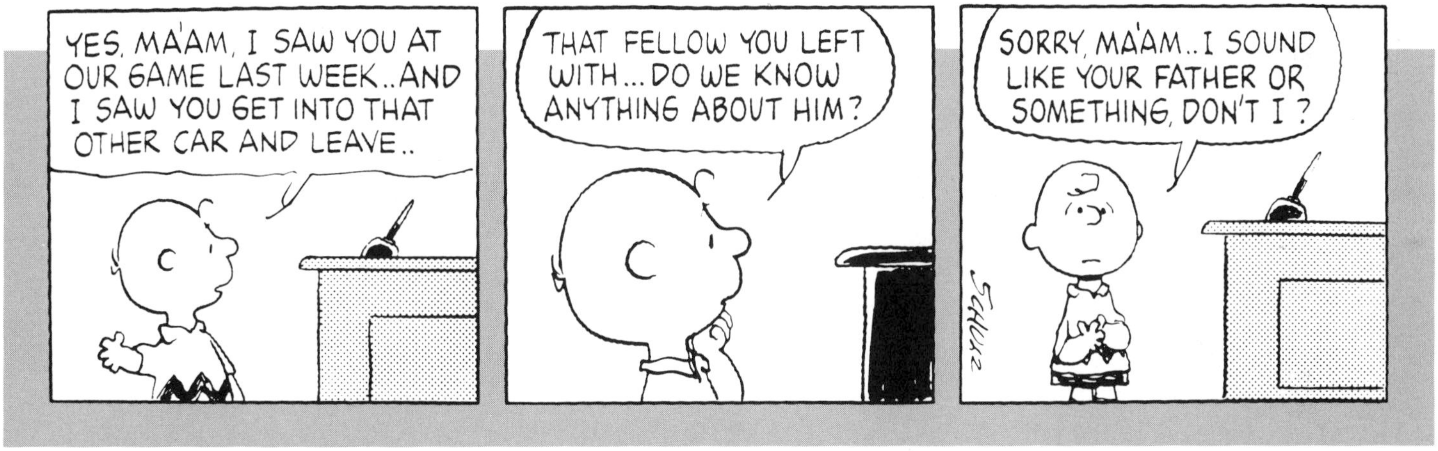
YES, MA'AM, I SAW YOU AT OUR GAME LAST WEEK..AND I SAW YOU GET INTO THAT OTHER CAR AND LEAVE..
THAT FELLOW YOU LEFT WITH...DO WE KNOW ANYTHING ABOUT HIM?
SORRY, MA'AM..I SOUND LIKE YOUR FATHER OR SOMETHING, DON'T I?

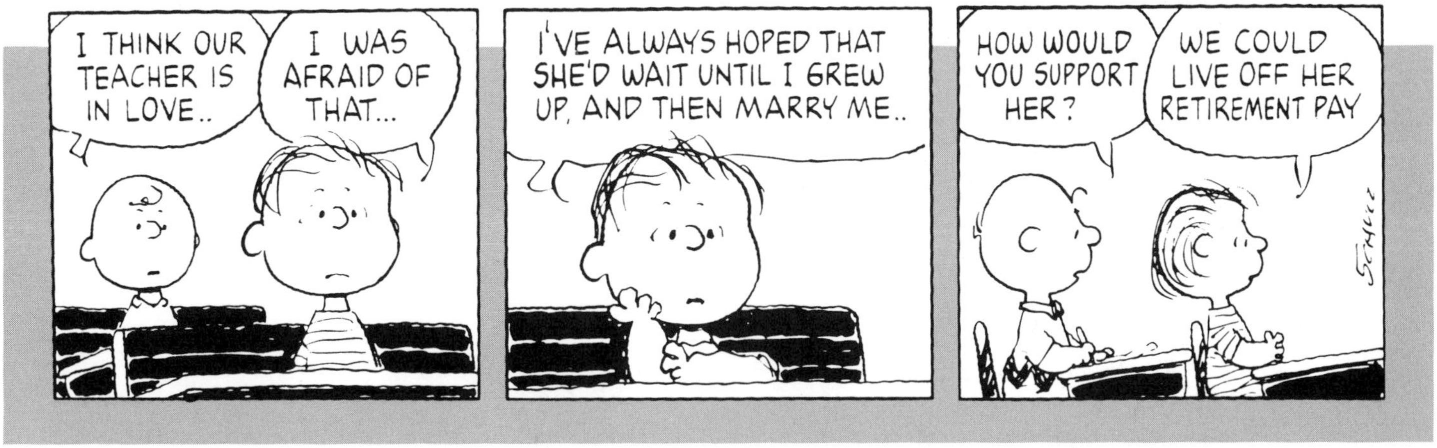
I THINK OUR TEACHER IS IN LOVE..
I WAS AFRAID OF THAT...
I'VE ALWAYS HOPED THAT SHE'D WAIT UNTIL I GREW UP, AND THEN MARRY ME..
HOW WOULD YOU SUPPORT HER?
WE COULD LIVE OFF HER RETIREMENT PAY

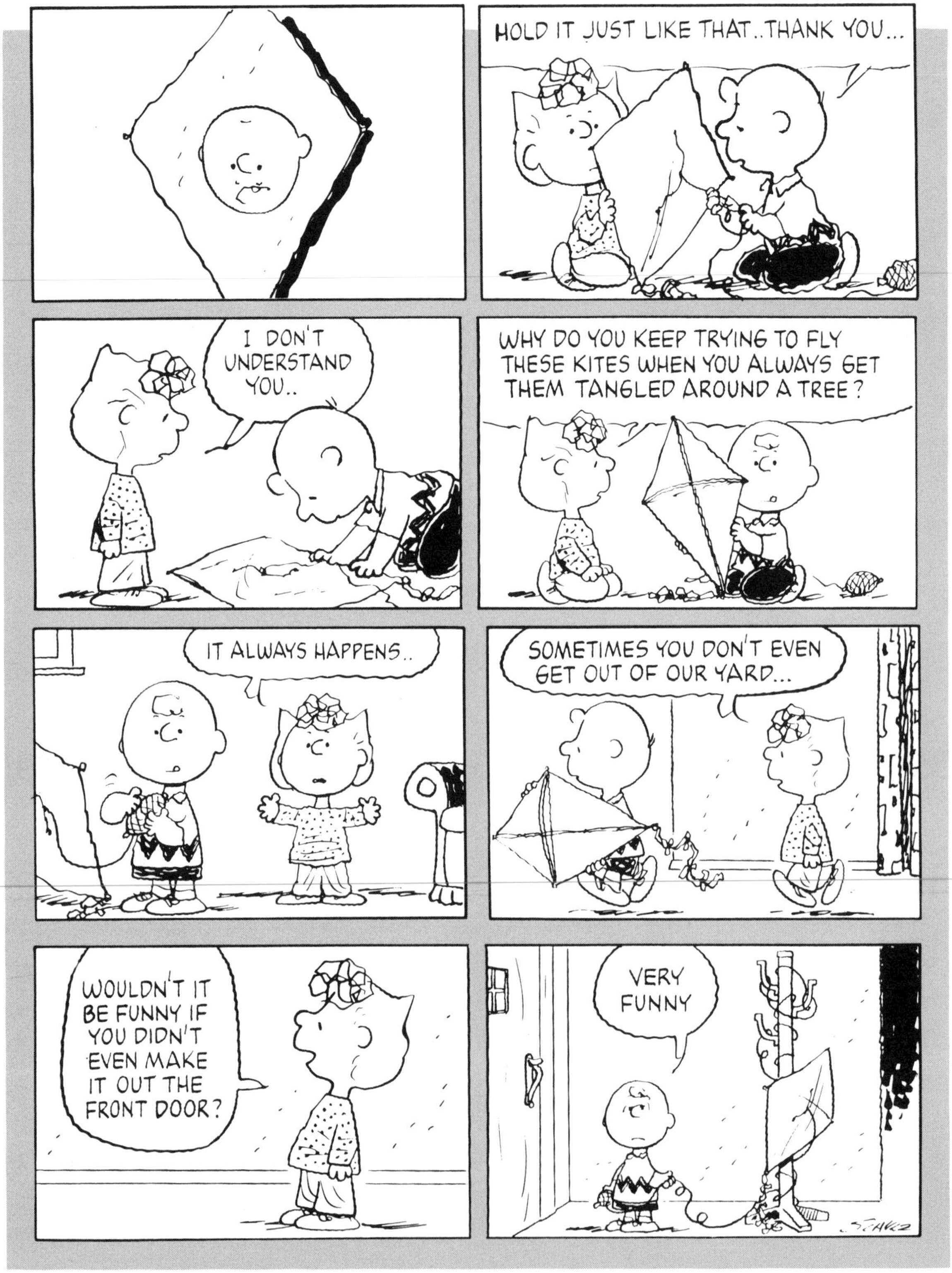
HOLD IT JUST LIKE THAT..THANK YOU...
I DON'T UNDERSTAND YOU..
WHY DO YOU KEEP TRYING TO FLY THESE KITES WHEN YOU ALWAYS GET THEM TANGLED AROUND A TREE?
IT ALWAYS HAPPENS..
SOMETIMES YOU DON'T EVEN GET OUT OF OUR YARD...
WOULDN'T IT BE FUNNY IF YOU DIDN'T EVEN MAKE IT OUT THE FRONT DOOR?
VERY FUNNY
SCHULZ

HEY, MANAGER, I THOUGHT IT MIGHT INCREASE ATTENDANCE IF WE HAD A "MASKED MARVEL" ON OUR TEAM..
BONK!
I CAN SEE THE "MASKED," BUT WHAT ABOUT THE "MARVEL"?!

LOOK, DID YOU SEE THAT ? OUR TEACHER WAS WAITING IN HER CAR, AND HER BOYFRIEND DIDN'T SHOW UP...
SEE? SHE'S DRIVING AWAY ALONE...
SHANE! COME BACK, SHANE!
HER NAME ISN'T "SHANE"!

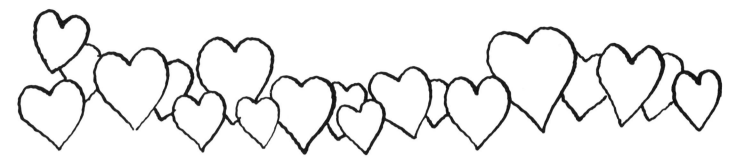

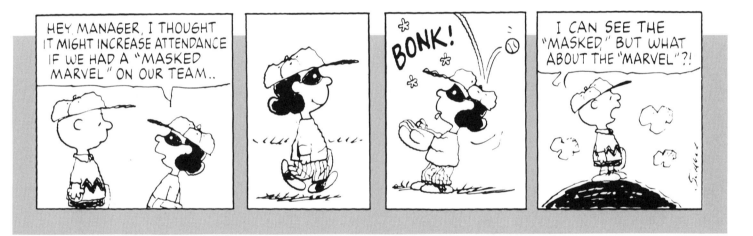

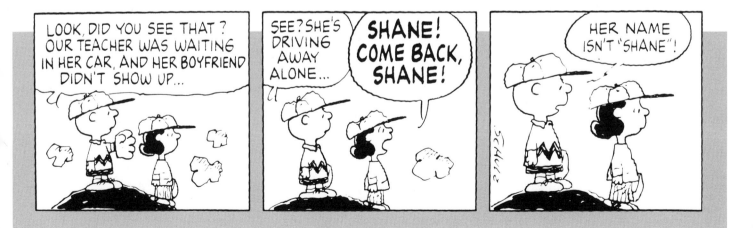

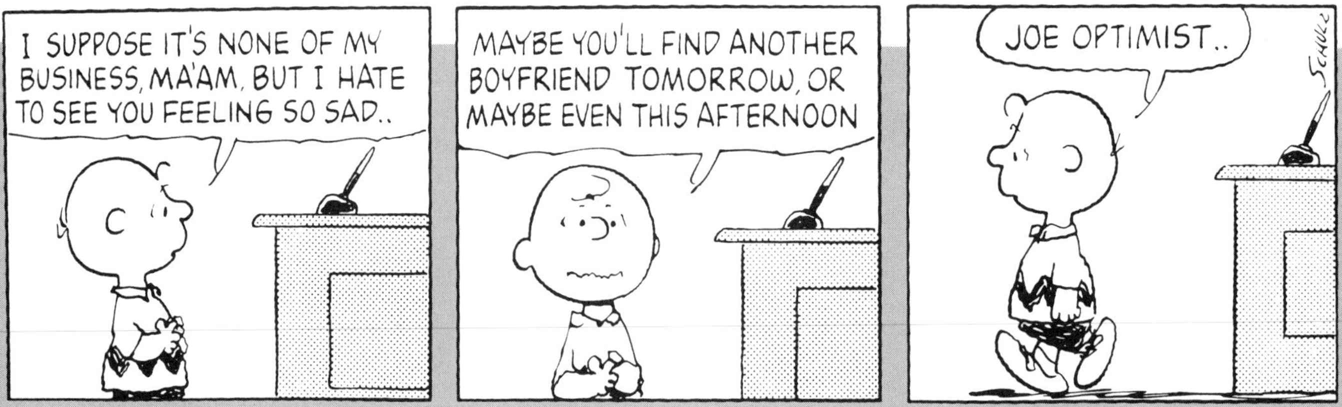
I SUPPOSE IT'S NONE OF MY BUSINESS, MA'AM, BUT I HATE TO SEE YOU FEELING SO SAD..
MAYBE YOU'LL FIND ANOTHER BOYFRIEND TOMORROW, OR MAYBE EVEN THIS AFTERNOON
JOE OPTIMIST..
SCHULZ

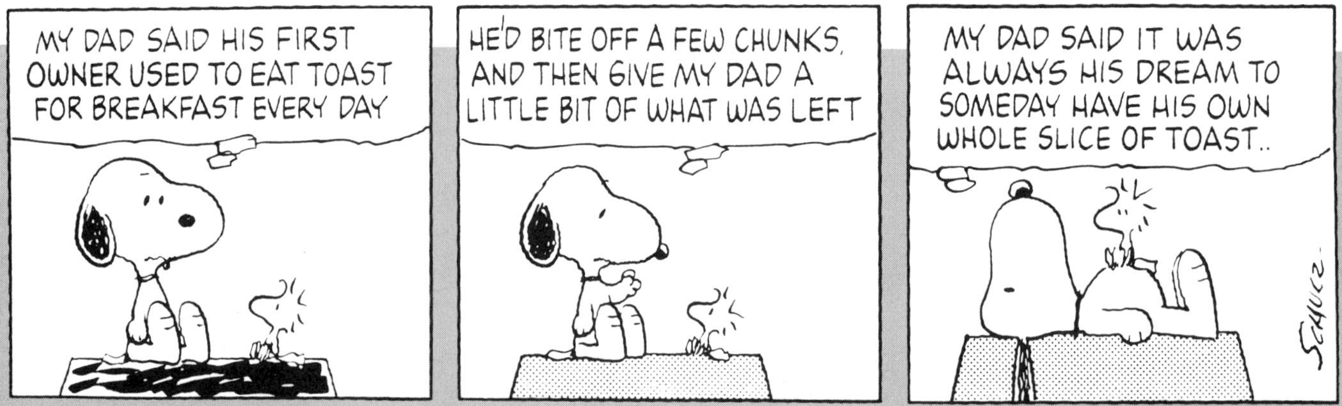
MY DAD SAID HIS FIRST OWNER USED TO EAT TOAST FOR BREAKFAST EVERY DAY
HE'D BITE OFF A FEW CHUNKS, AND THEN GIVE MY DAD A LITTLE BIT OF WHAT WAS LEFT
MY DAD SAID IT WAS ALWAYS HIS DREAM TO SOMEDAY HAVE HIS OWN WHOLE SLICE OF TOAST..
SCHULZ

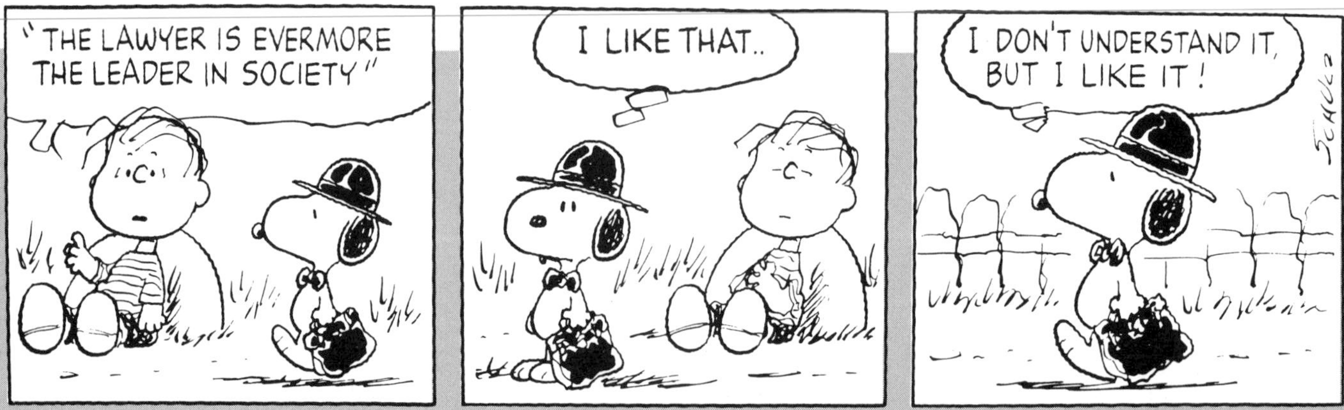
"THE LAWYER IS EVERMORE THE LEADER IN SOCIETY"
I LIKE THAT..
I DON'T UNDERSTAND IT, BUT I LIKE IT!
SCHULZ

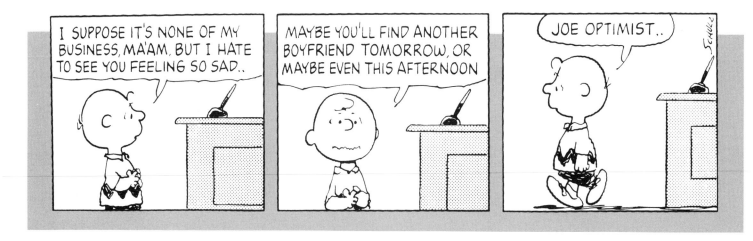

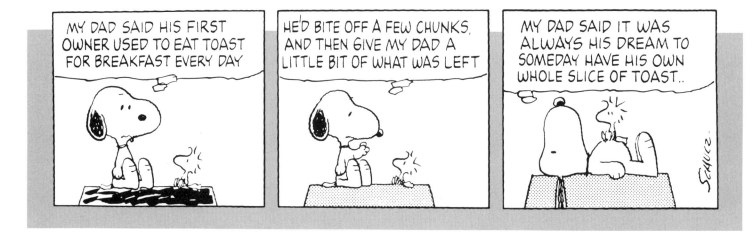

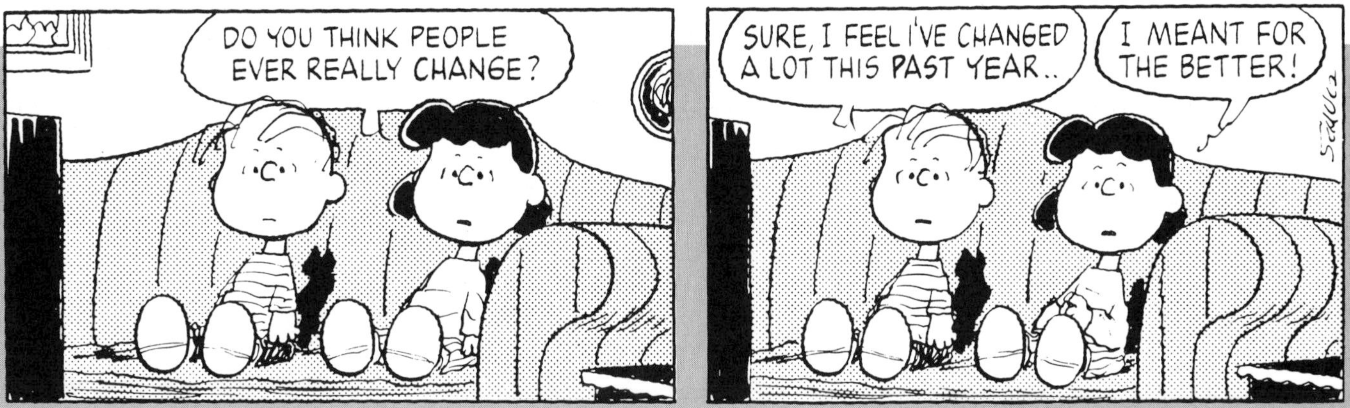
DO YOU THINK PEOPLE EVER REALLY CHANGE?
SURE, I FEEL I'VE CHANGED A LOT THIS PAST YEAR..
I MEANT FOR THE BETTER!

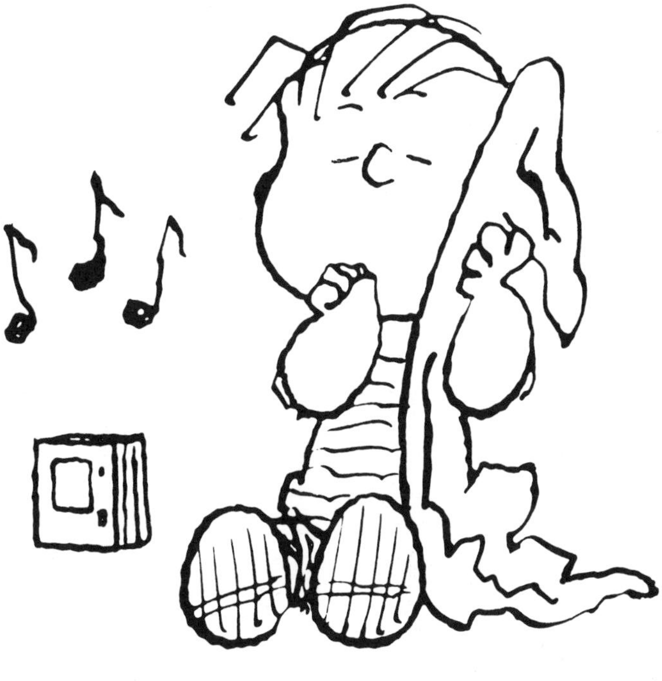

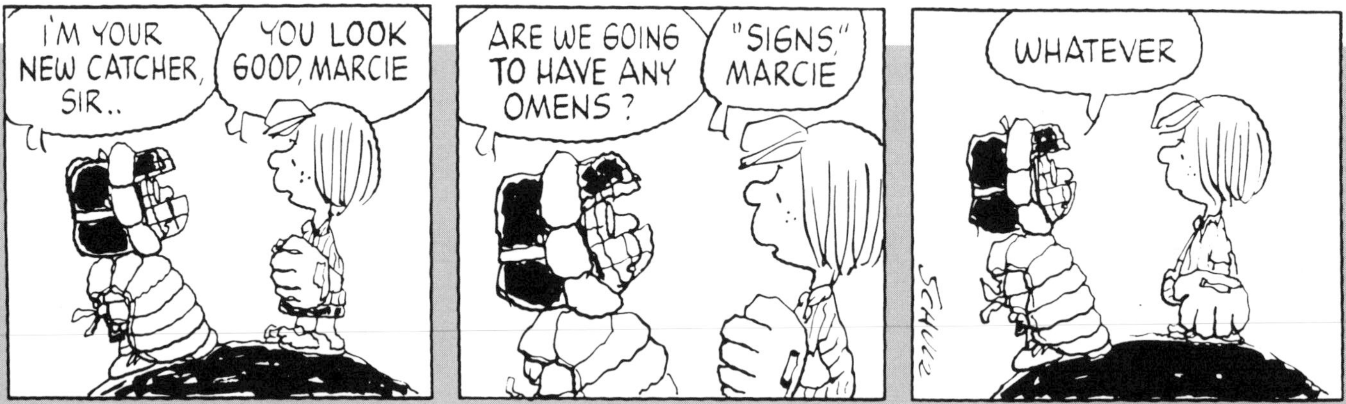
I'M YOUR NEW CATCHER, SIR..
YOU LOOK GOOD, MARCIE
ARE WE GOING TO HAVE ANY OMENS ?
"SIGNS," MARCIE
WHATEVER
SCHULZ

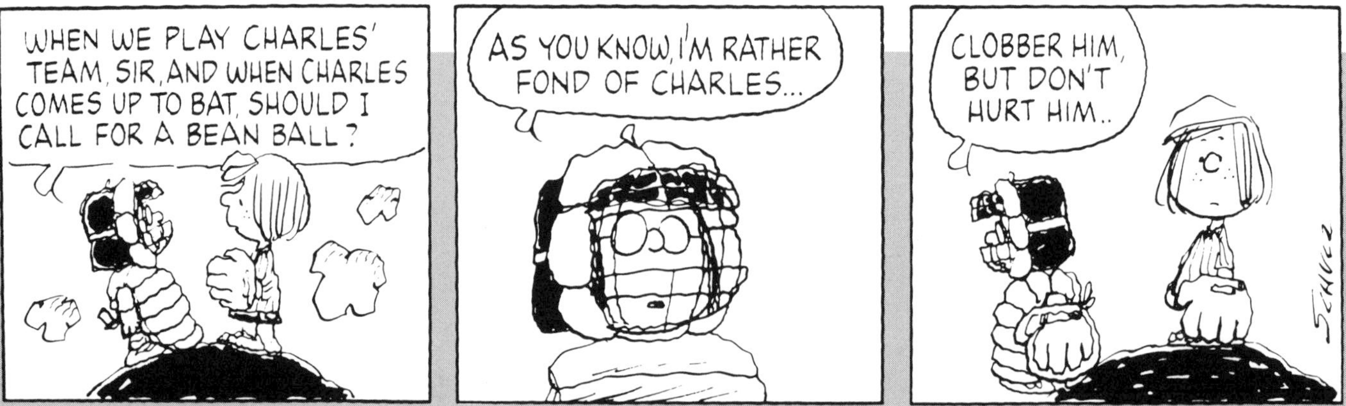
WHEN WE PLAY CHARLES' TEAM, SIR, AND WHEN CHARLES COMES UP TO BAT, SHOULD I CALL FOR A BEAN BALL ?
AS YOU KNOW, I'M RATHER FOND OF CHARLES...
CLOBBER HIM, BUT DON'T HURT HIM..
SCHULZ

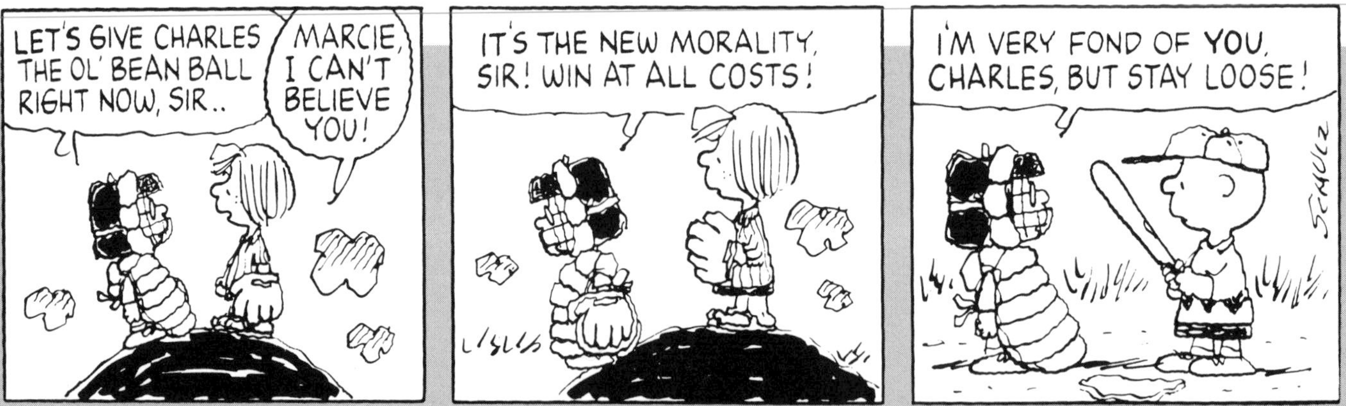
LET'S GIVE CHARLES THE OL' BEAN BALL RIGHT NOW, SIR..
MARCIE, I CAN'T BELIEVE YOU!
IT'S THE NEW MORALITY, SIR! WIN AT ALL COSTS!
I'M VERY FOND OF YOU, CHARLES, BUT STAY LOOSE!
SCHULZ

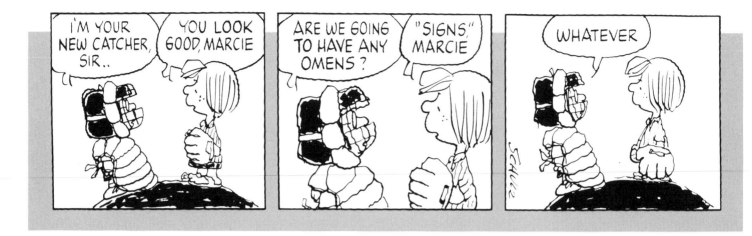

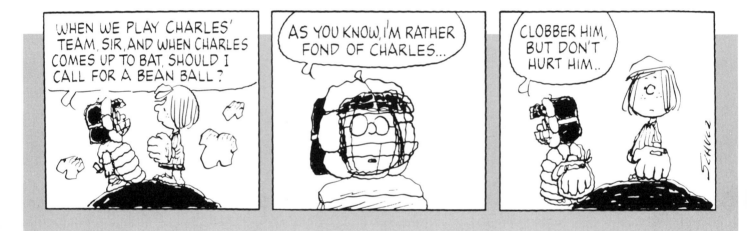

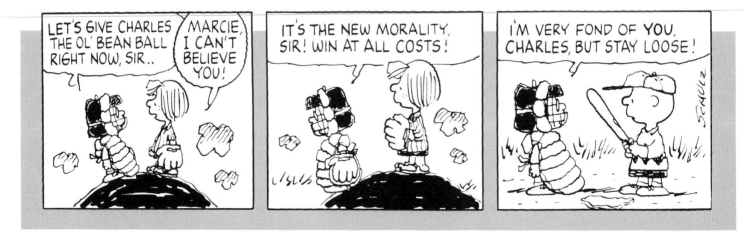

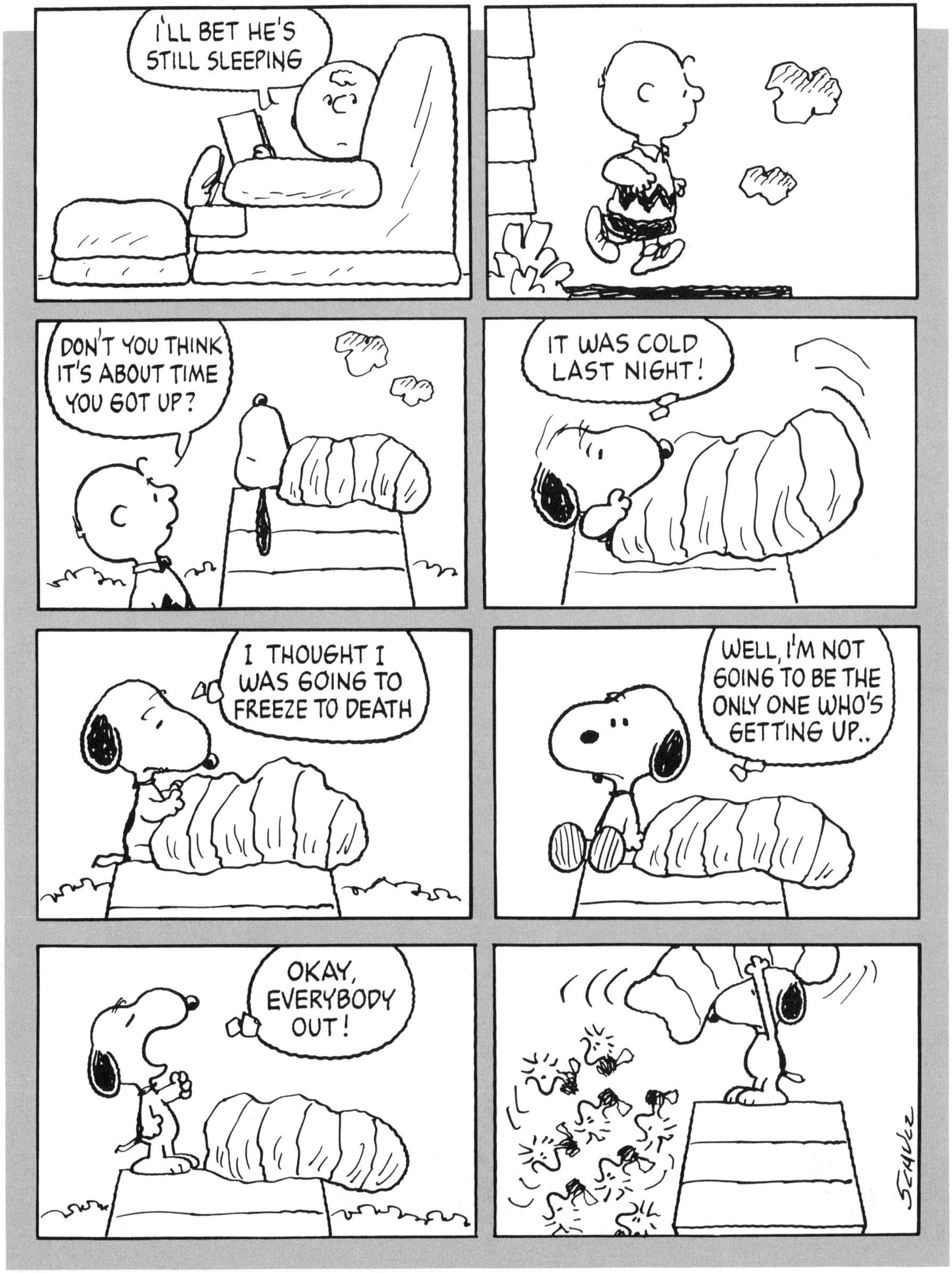
I'LL BET HE'S STILL SLEEPING
DON'T YOU THINK IT'S ABOUT TIME YOU GOT UP?
IT WAS COLD LAST NIGHT!
I THOUGHT I WAS GOING TO FREEZE TO DEATH
WELL, I'M NOT GOING TO BE THE ONLY ONE WHO'S GETTING UP..
OKAY, EVERYBODY OUT!
SCHULZ

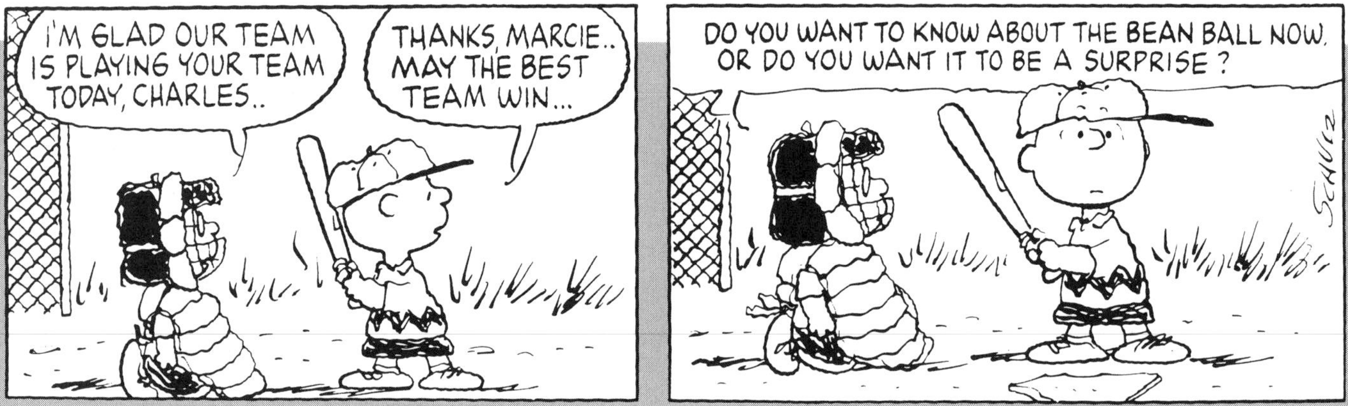
I'M GLAD OUR TEAM IS PLAYING YOUR TEAM TODAY, CHARLES..
THANKS, MARCIE.. MAY THE BEST TEAM WIN...
DO YOU WANT TO KNOW ABOUT THE BEAN BALL NOW, OR DO YOU WANT IT TO BE A SURPRISE ?
SCHULZ

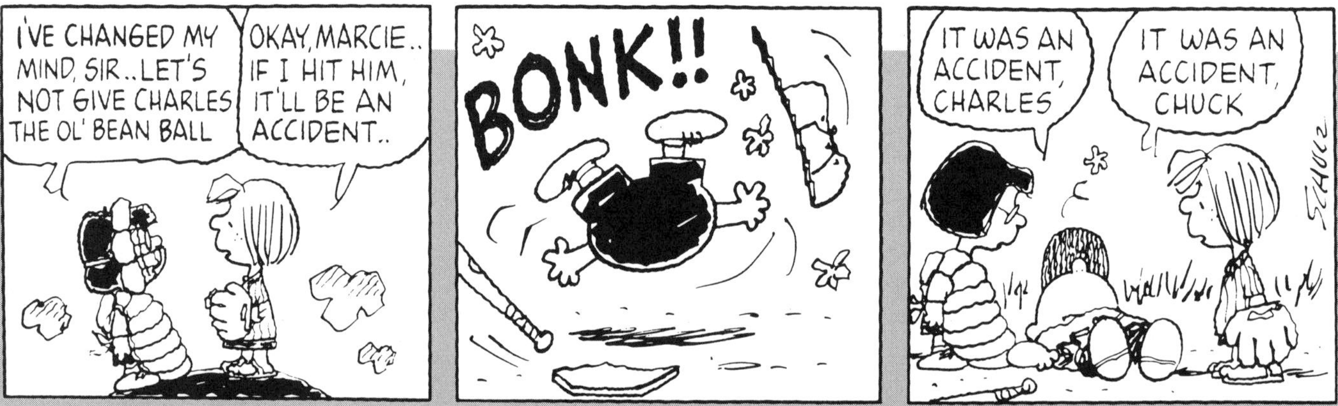
I'VE CHANGED MY MIND, SIR..LET'S NOT GIVE CHARLES THE OL' BEAN BALL
OKAY, MARCIE.. IF I HIT HIM, IT'LL BE AN ACCIDENT..
BONK!!
IT WAS AN ACCIDENT, CHARLES
IT WAS AN ACCIDENT, CHUCK
SCHULZ

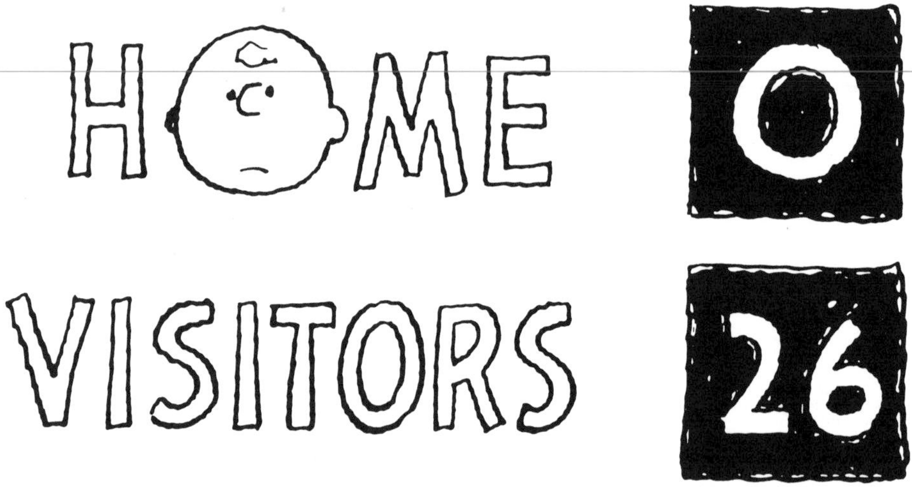
HOME 0
VISITORS 26

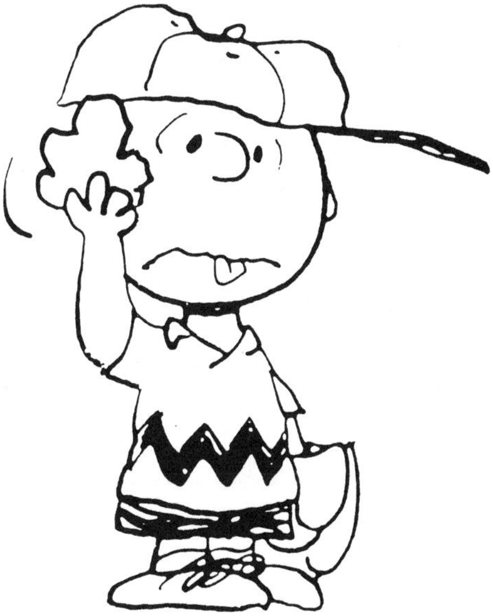

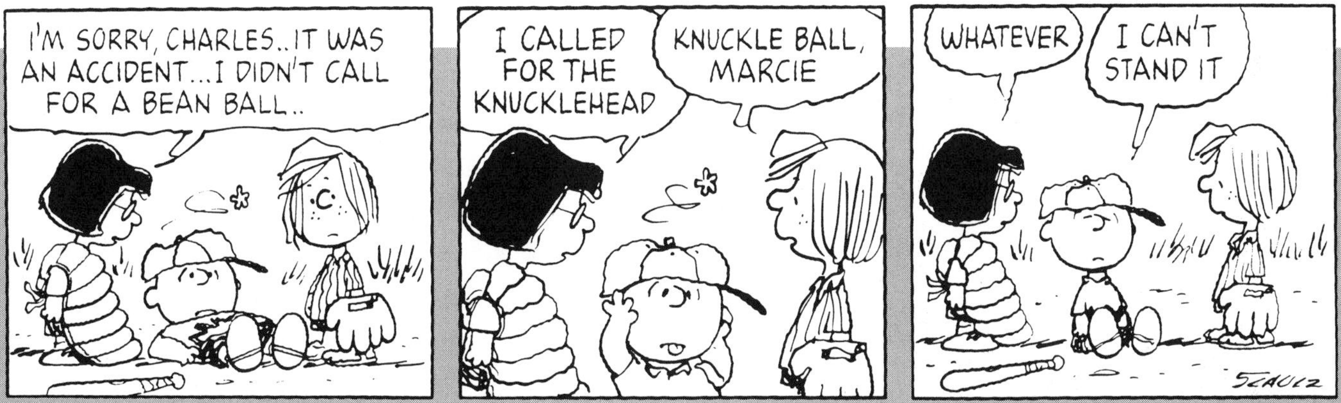
I'M SORRY, CHARLES..IT WAS AN ACCIDENT...I DIDN'T CALL FOR A BEAN BALL..
I CALLED FOR THE KNUCKLEHEAD
KNUCKLE BALL, MARCIE
WHATEVER
I CAN'T STAND IT

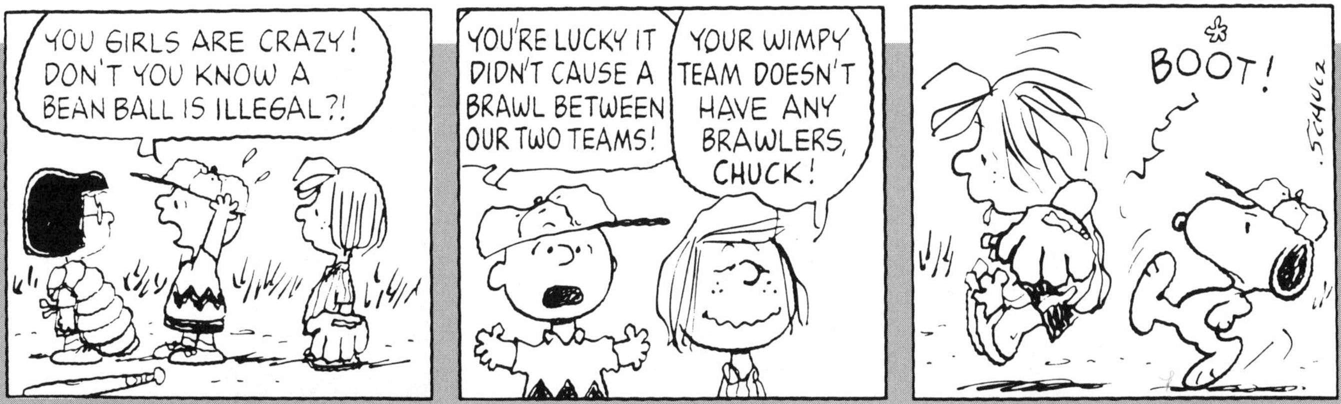
YOU GIRLS ARE CRAZY! DON'T YOU KNOW A BEAN BALL IS ILLEGAL?!
YOU'RE LUCKY IT DIDN'T CAUSE A BRAWL BETWEEN OUR TWO TEAMS!
YOUR WIMPY TEAM DOESN'T HAVE ANY BRAWLERS, CHUCK!
BOOT!

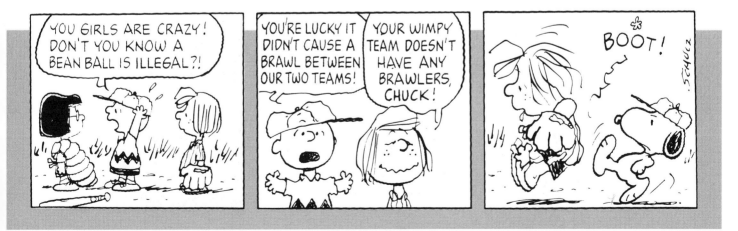

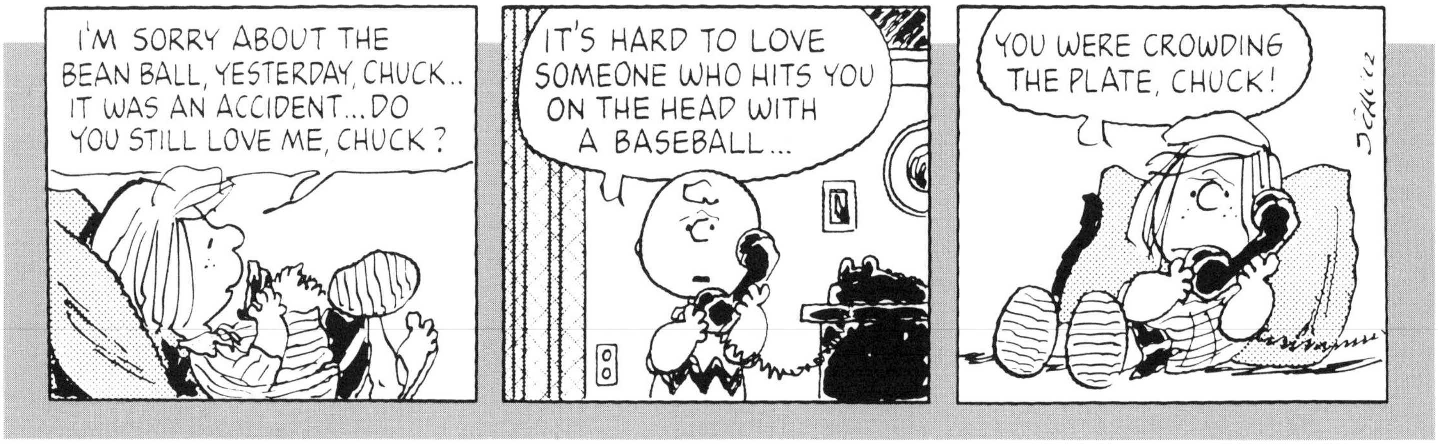
I'M SORRY ABOUT THE BEAN BALL, YESTERDAY, CHUCK.. IT WAS AN ACCIDENT...DO YOU STILL LOVE ME, CHUCK?
IT'S HARD TO LOVE SOMEONE WHO HITS YOU ON THE HEAD WITH A BASEBALL...
YOU WERE CROWDING THE PLATE, CHUCK!
SCHULZ

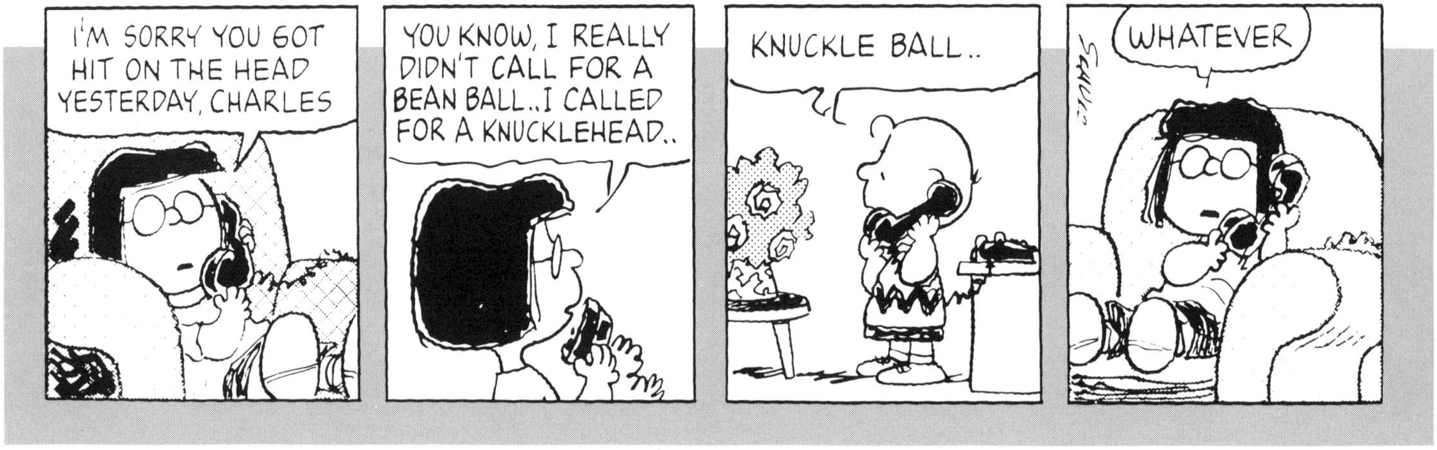
I'M SORRY YOU GOT HIT ON THE HEAD YESTERDAY, CHARLES
YOU KNOW, I REALLY DIDN'T CALL FOR A BEAN BALL..I CALLED FOR A KNUCKLEHEAD..
KNUCKLE BALL..
SCHULZ
WHATEVER

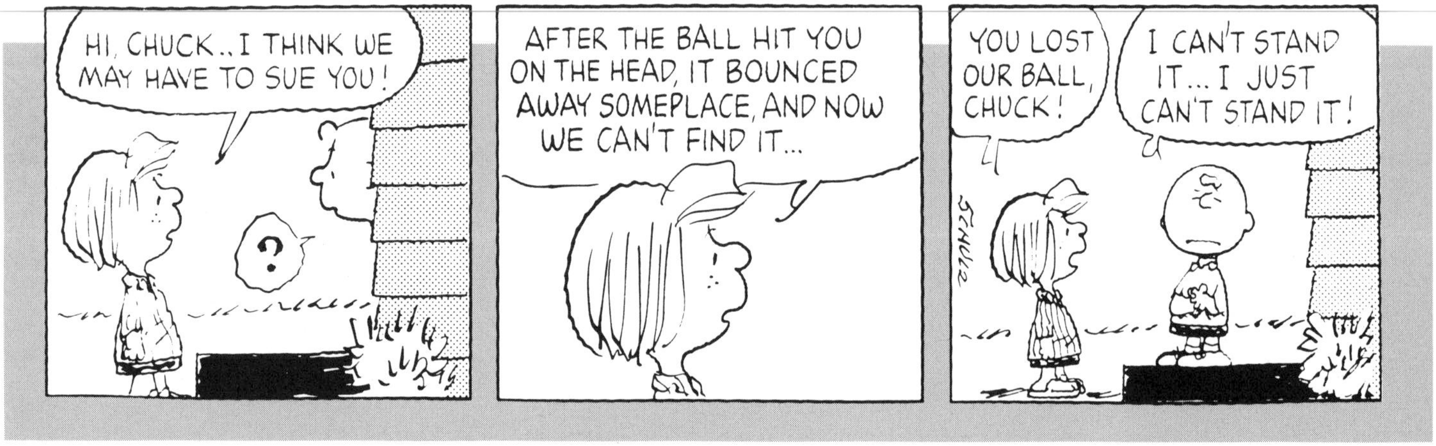
HI, CHUCK..I THINK WE MAY HAVE TO SUE YOU!
?
AFTER THE BALL HIT YOU ON THE HEAD, IT BOUNCED AWAY SOMEPLACE, AND NOW WE CAN'T FIND IT...
YOU LOST OUR BALL, CHUCK!
I CAN'T STAND IT... I JUST CAN'T STAND IT!
SCHULZ

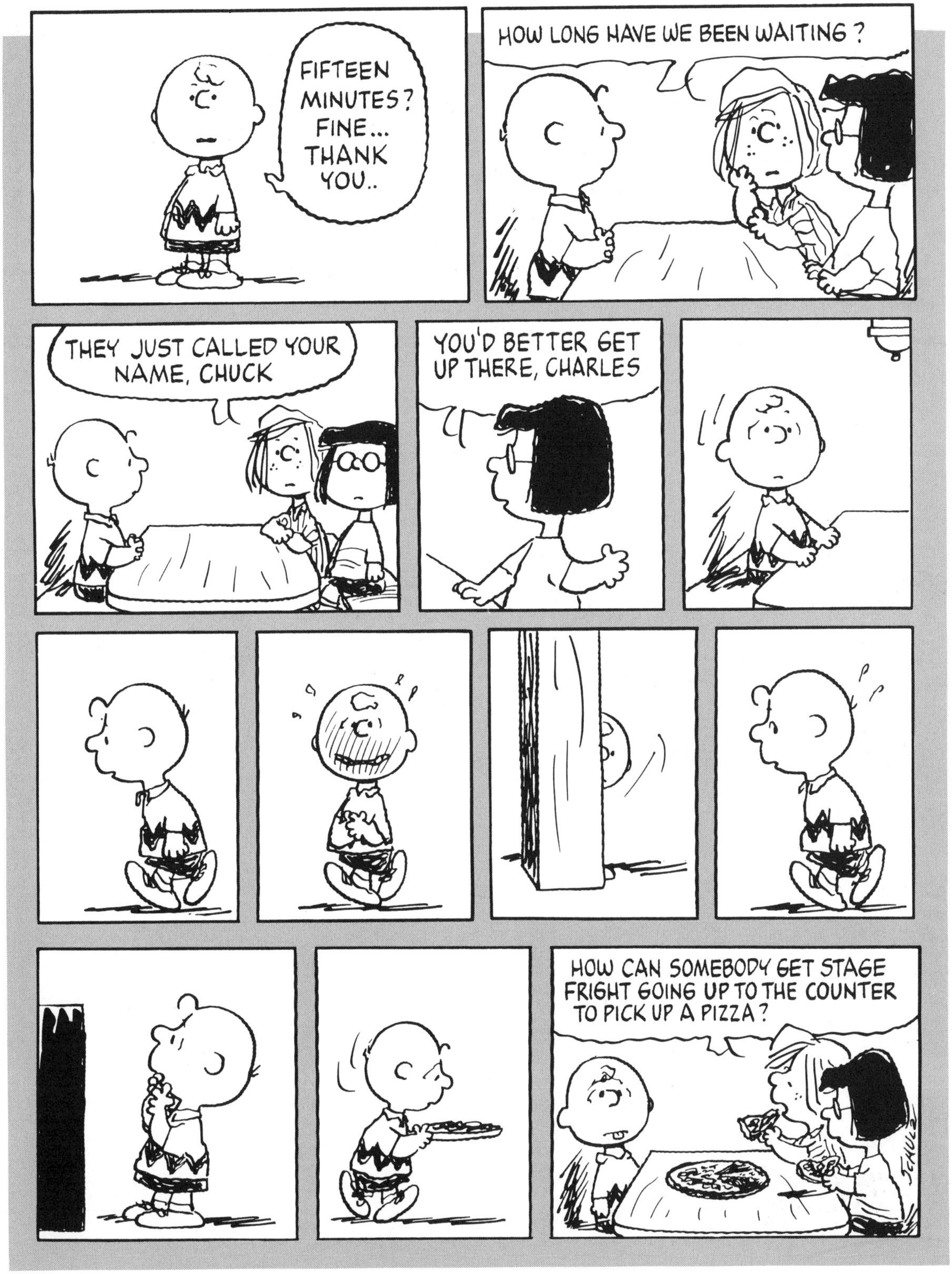
FIFTEEN MINUTES? FINE... THANK YOU..
HOW LONG HAVE WE BEEN WAITING ?
THEY JUST CALLED YOUR NAME, CHUCK
YOU'D BETTER GET UP THERE, CHARLES
HOW CAN SOMEBODY GET STAGE FRIGHT GOING UP TO THE COUNTER TO PICK UP A PIZZA ?
SCHULZ

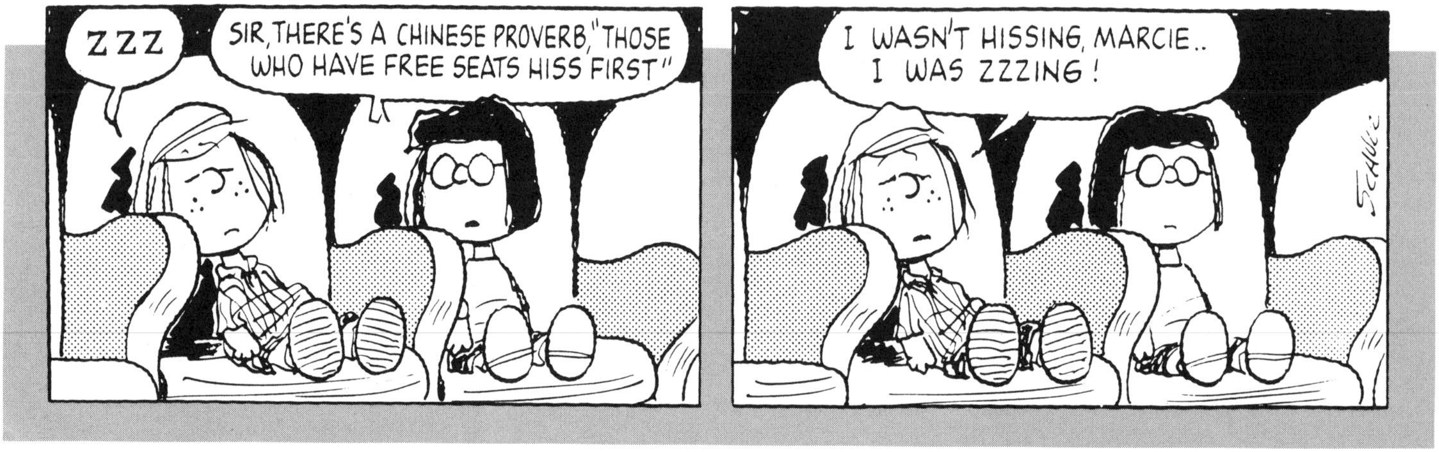
ZZZ
SIR, THERE'S A CHINESE PROVERB, "THOSE WHO HAVE FREE SEATS HISS FIRST"
I WASN'T HISSING, MARCIE.. I WAS ZZZING!

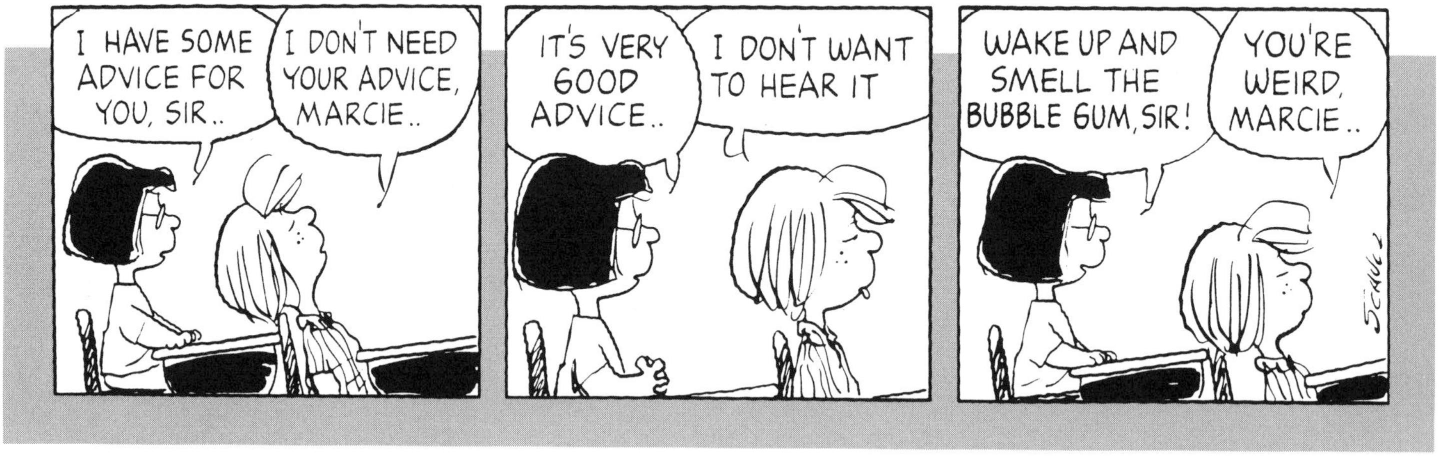
I HAVE SOME ADVICE FOR YOU, SIR..
I DON'T NEED YOUR ADVICE, MARCIE..
IT'S VERY GOOD ADVICE..
I DON'T WANT TO HEAR IT
WAKE UP AND SMELL THE BUBBLE GUM, SIR!
YOU'RE WEIRD, MARCIE..

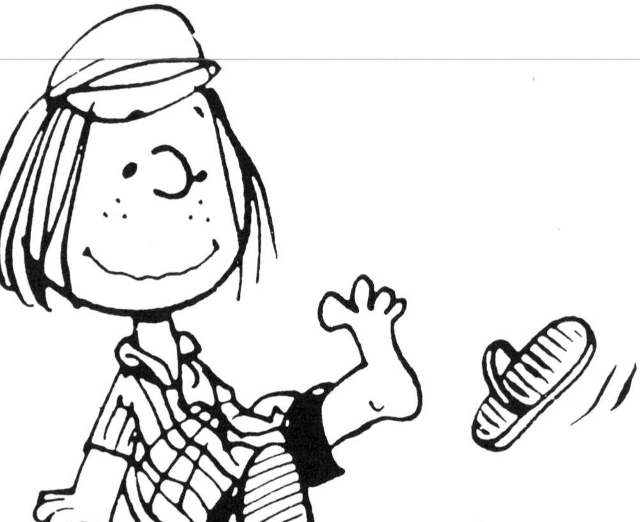

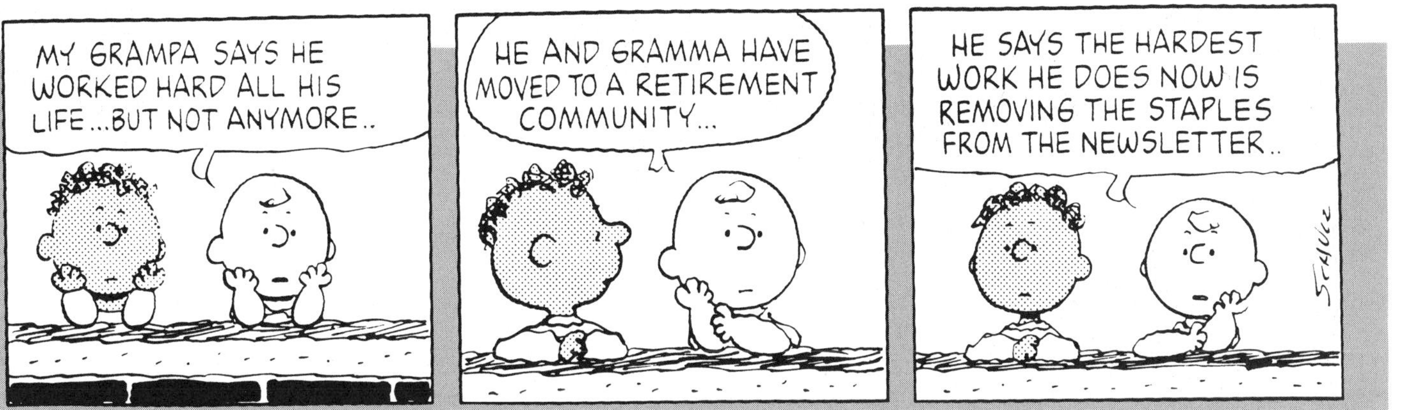
MY GRAMPA SAYS HE WORKED HARD ALL HIS LIFE...BUT NOT ANYMORE..
HE AND GRAMMA HAVE MOVED TO A RETIREMENT COMMUNITY...
HE SAYS THE HARDEST WORK HE DOES NOW IS REMOVING THE STAPLES FROM THE NEWSLETTER..
SCHULZ

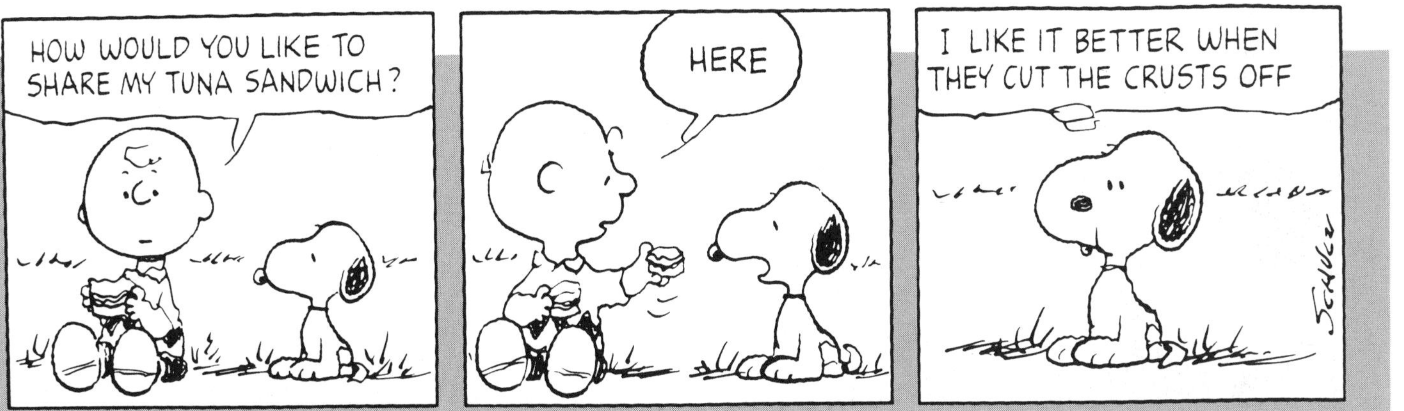
HOW WOULD YOU LIKE TO SHARE MY TUNA SANDWICH?
HERE
I LIKE IT BETTER WHEN THEY CUT THE CRUSTS OFF
SCHULZ

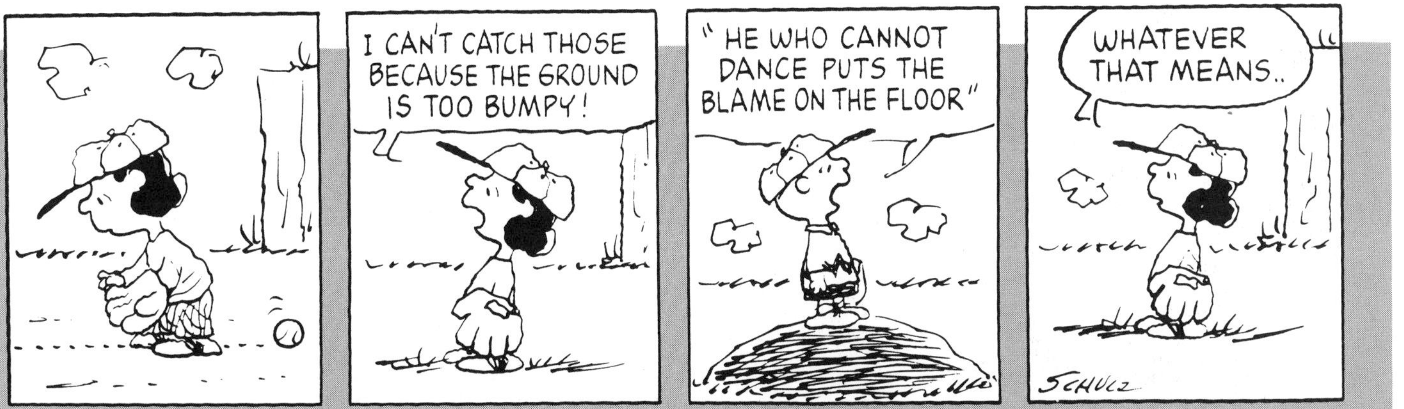
I CAN'T CATCH THOSE BECAUSE THE GROUND IS TOO BUMPY!
"HE WHO CANNOT DANCE PUTS THE BLAME ON THE FLOOR"
WHATEVER THAT MEANS..
SCHULZ

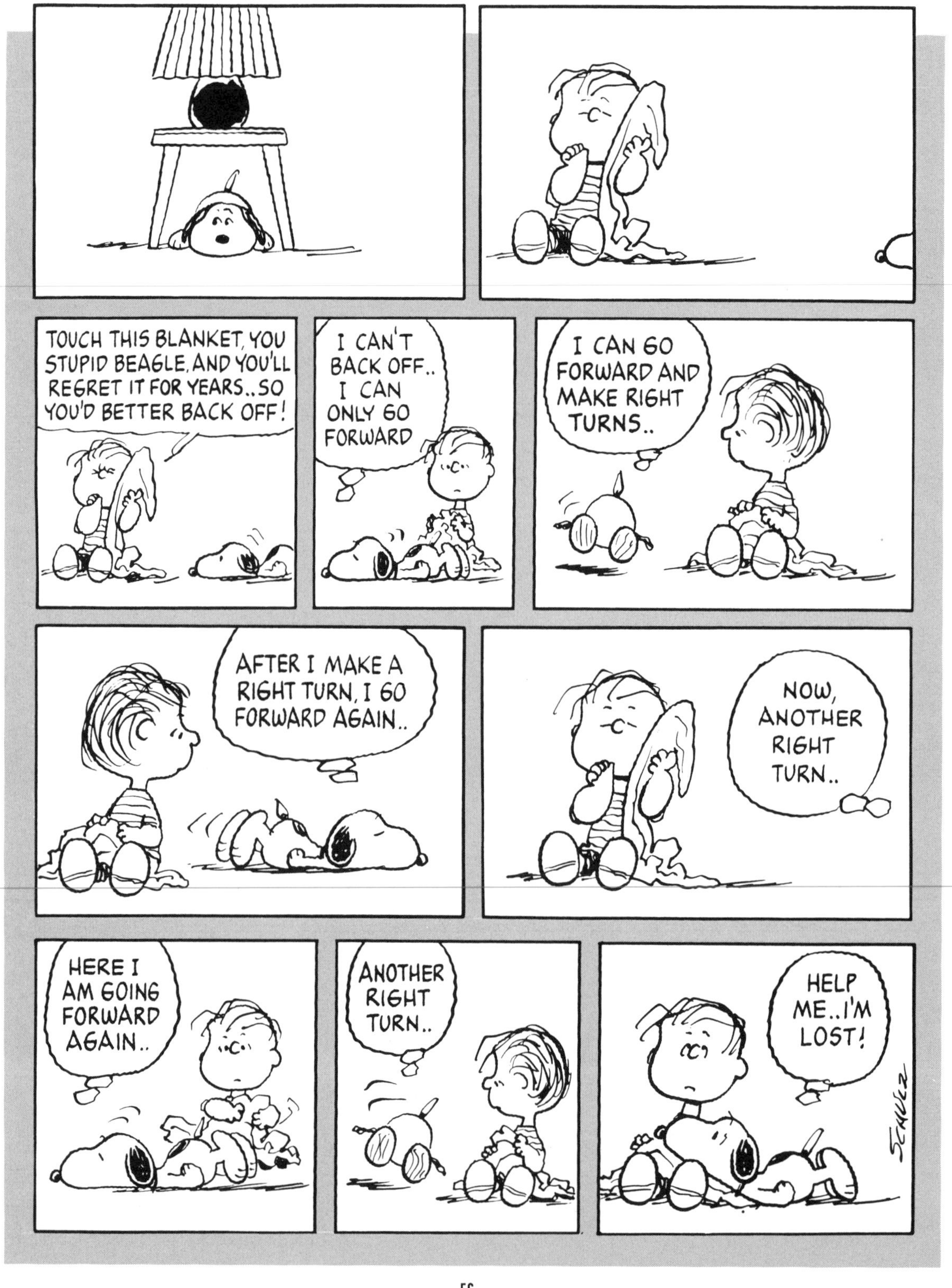
TOUCH THIS BLANKET, YOU STUPID BEAGLE, AND YOU'LL REGRET IT FOR YEARS..SO YOU'D BETTER BACK OFF!
I CAN'T BACK OFF.. I CAN ONLY GO FORWARD
I CAN GO FORWARD AND MAKE RIGHT TURNS..
AFTER I MAKE A RIGHT TURN, I GO FORWARD AGAIN..
NOW, ANOTHER RIGHT TURN..
HERE I AM GOING FORWARD AGAIN..
ANOTHER RIGHT TURN..
HELP ME..I'M LOST!
SCHULZ

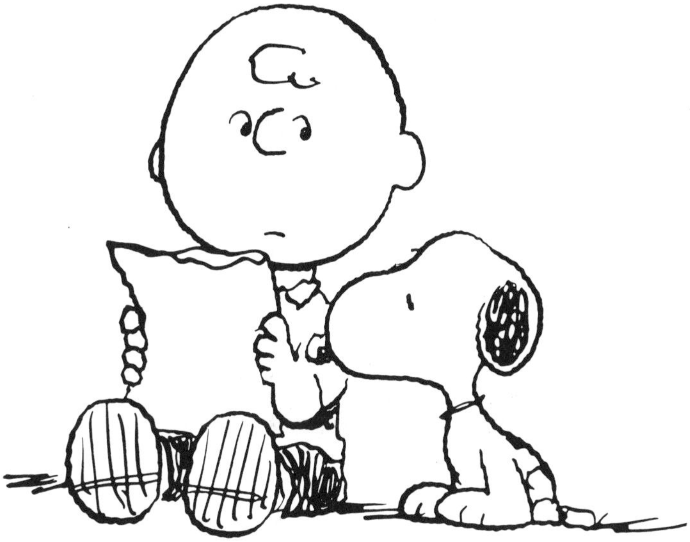

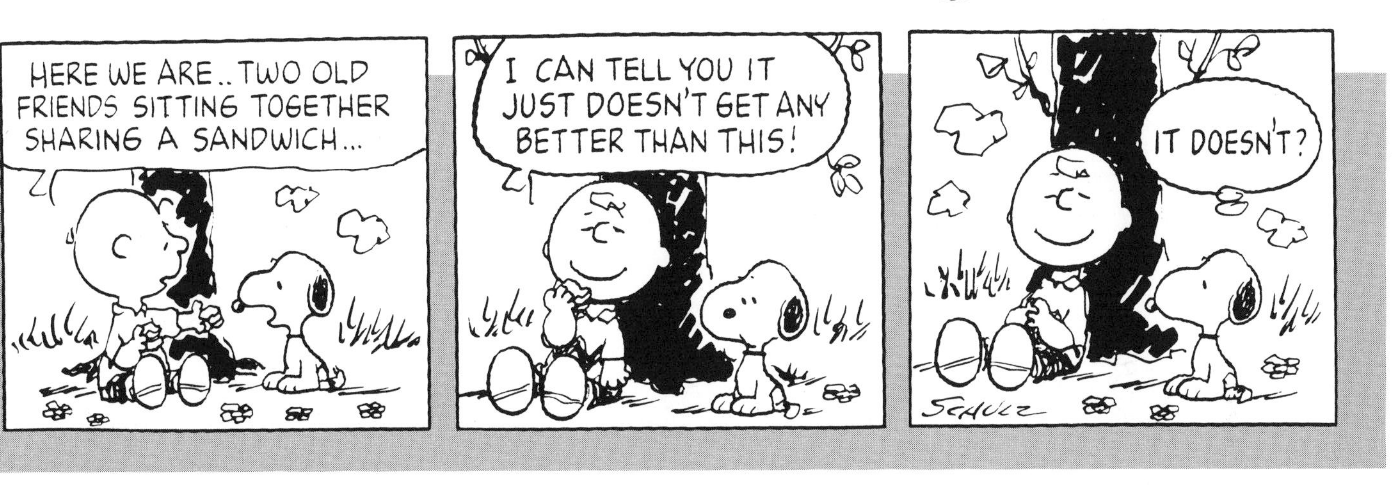
HERE WE ARE.. TWO OLD FRIENDS SITTING TOGETHER SHARING A SANDWICH...
I CAN TELL YOU IT JUST DOESN'T GET ANY BETTER THAN THIS!
IT DOESN'T?
SCHULZ

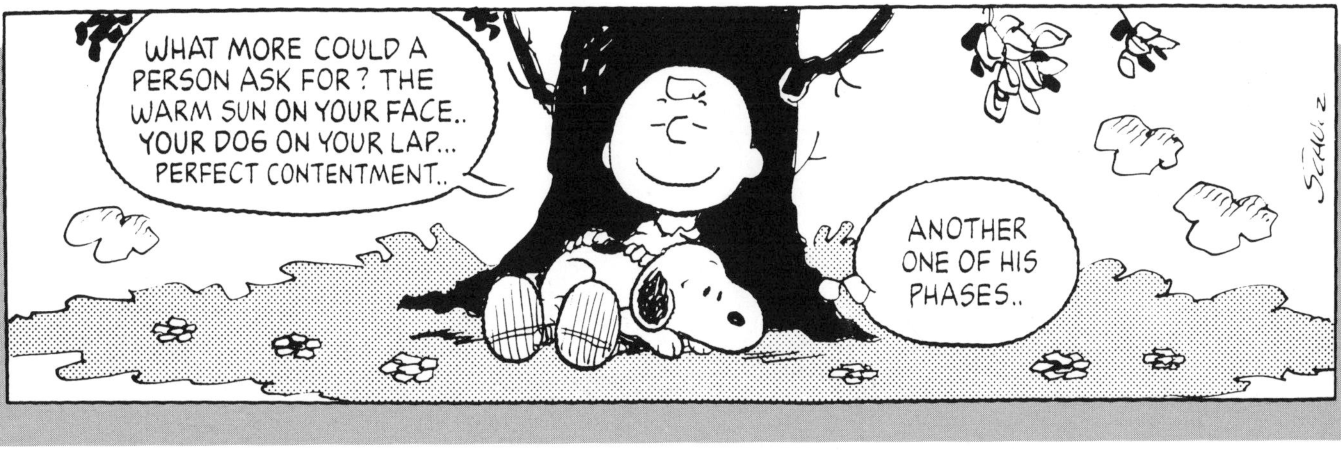
WHAT MORE COULD A PERSON ASK FOR? THE WARM SUN ON YOUR FACE.. YOUR DOG ON YOUR LAP... PERFECT CONTENTMENT..
ANOTHER ONE OF HIS PHASES..
SCHULZ

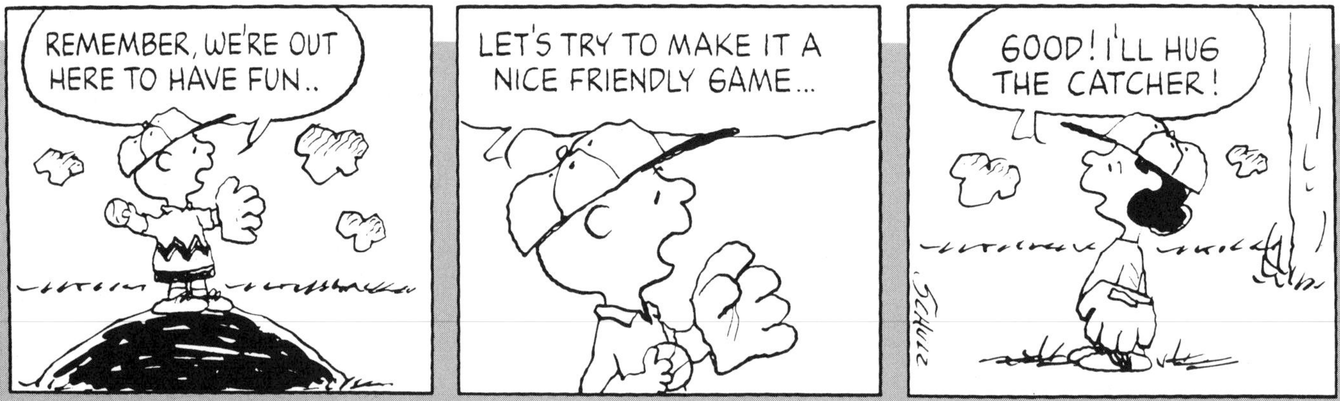
REMEMBER, WE'RE OUT HERE TO HAVE FUN..
LET'S TRY TO MAKE IT A NICE FRIENDLY GAME...
GOOD! I'LL HUG THE CATCHER!

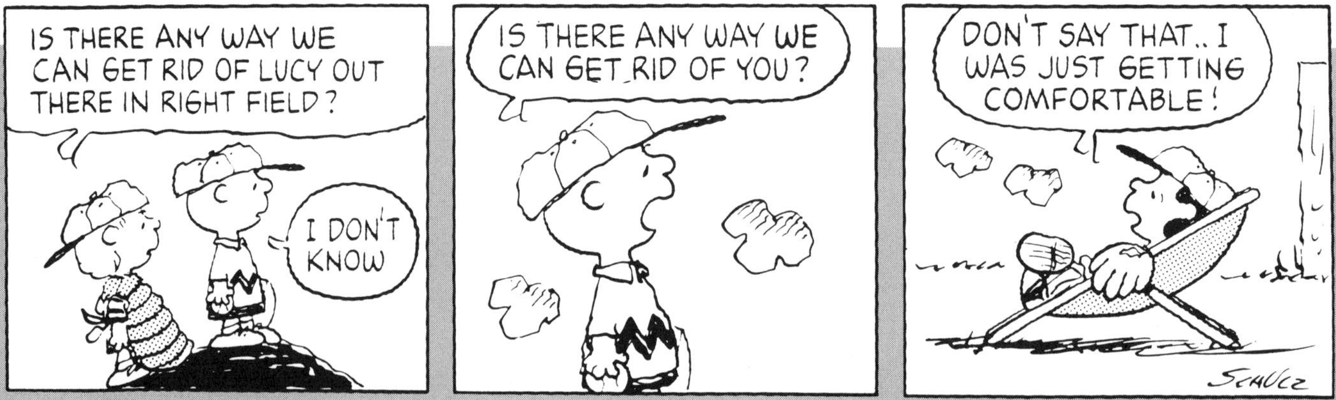
IS THERE ANY WAY WE CAN GET RID OF LUCY OUT THERE IN RIGHT FIELD?
I DON'T KNOW
IS THERE ANY WAY WE CAN GET RID OF YOU?
DON'T SAY THAT.. I WAS JUST GETTING COMFORTABLE!

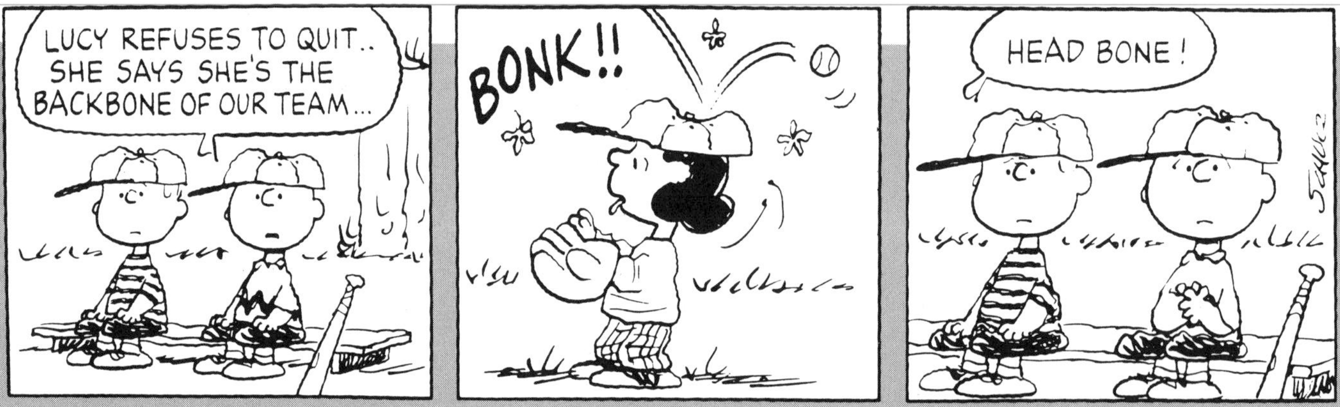
LUCY REFUSES TO QUIT.. SHE SAYS SHE'S THE BACKBONE OF OUR TEAM...
BONK!!
HEAD BONE!

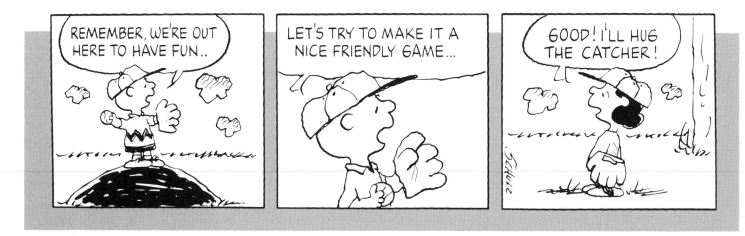

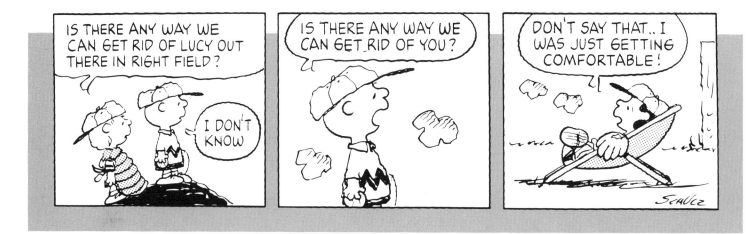

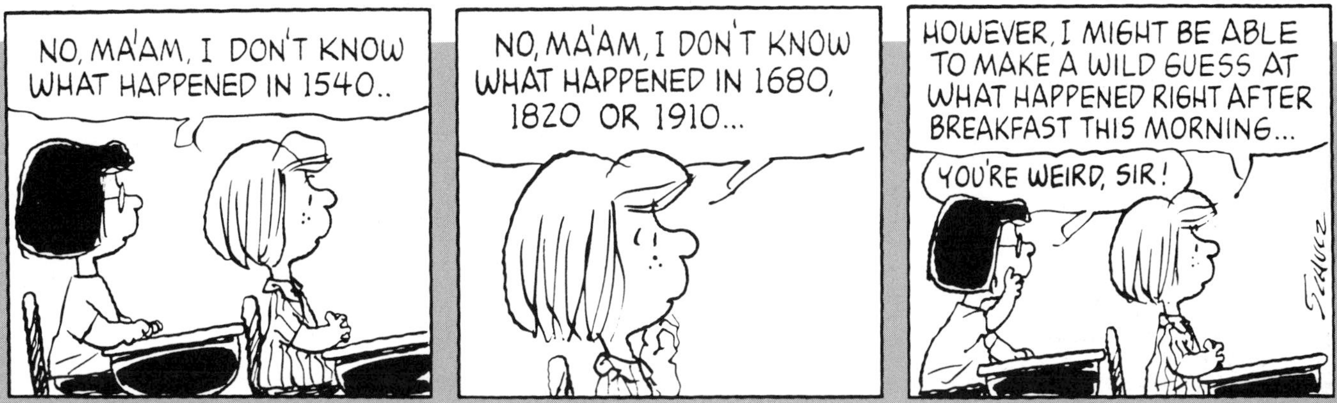
NO, MA'AM, I DON'T KNOW WHAT HAPPENED IN 1540..
NO, MA'AM, I DON'T KNOW WHAT HAPPENED IN 1680, 1820 OR 1910...
HOWEVER, I MIGHT BE ABLE TO MAKE A WILD GUESS AT WHAT HAPPENED RIGHT AFTER BREAKFAST THIS MORNING...
YOU'RE WEIRD, SIR!

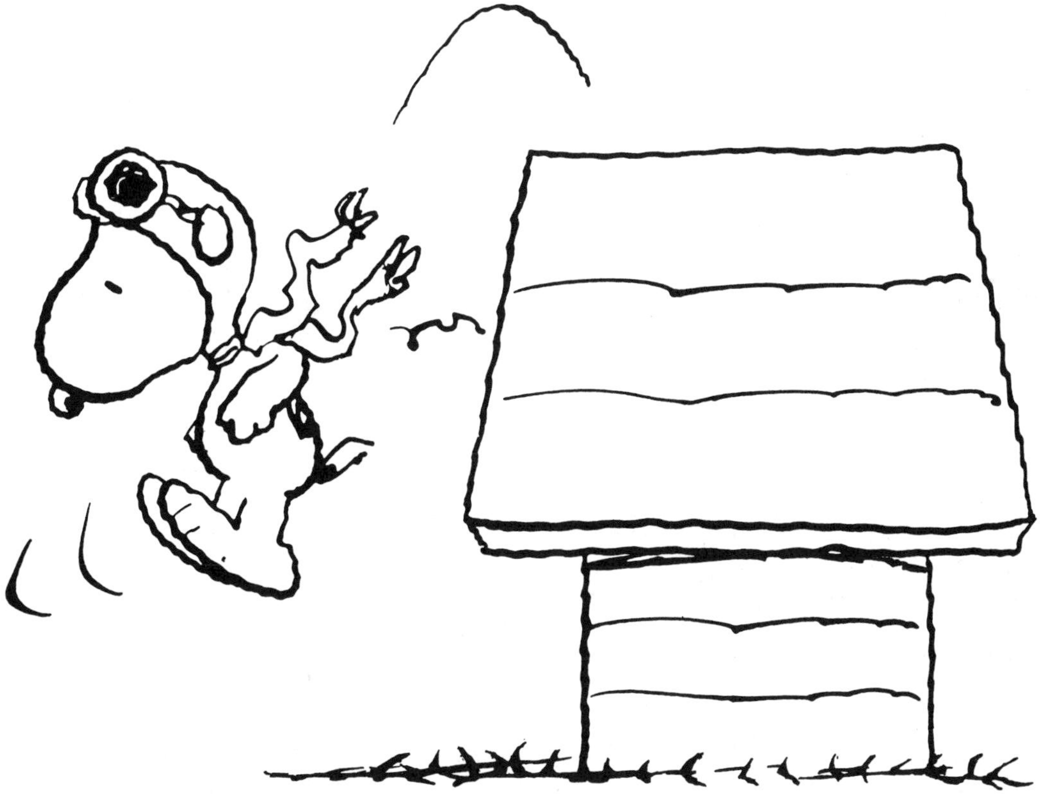

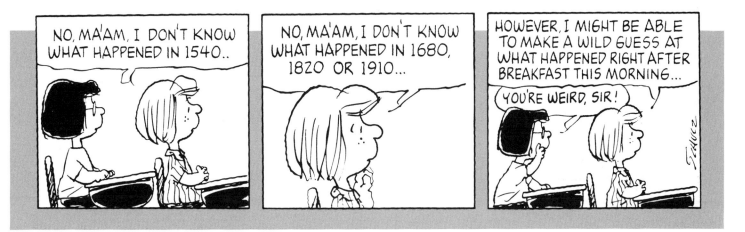

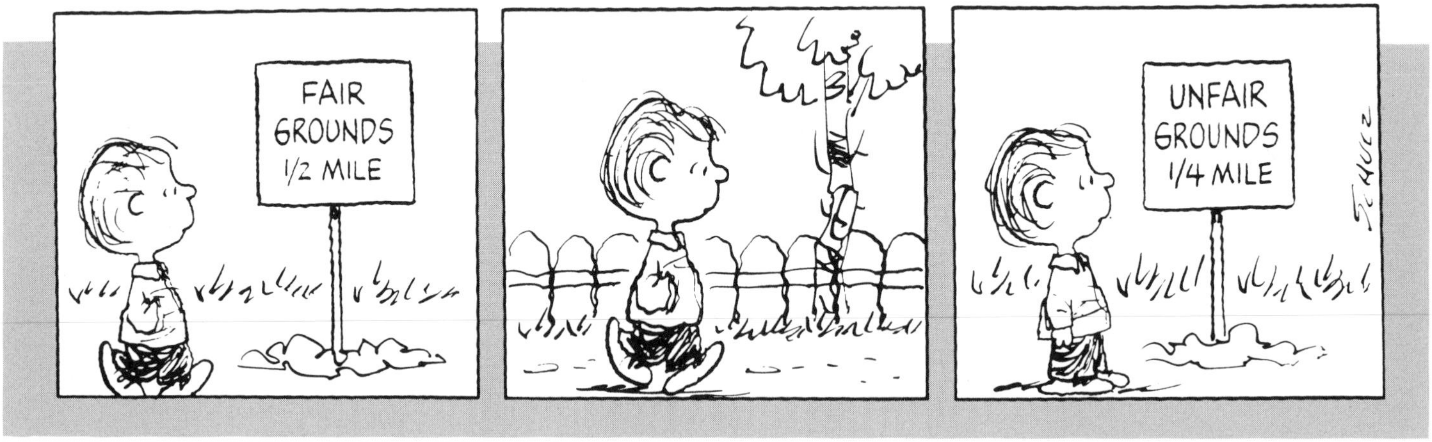
FAIR
GROUNDS
1/2 MILE
UNFAIR
GROUNDS
1/4 MILE
SCHULZ

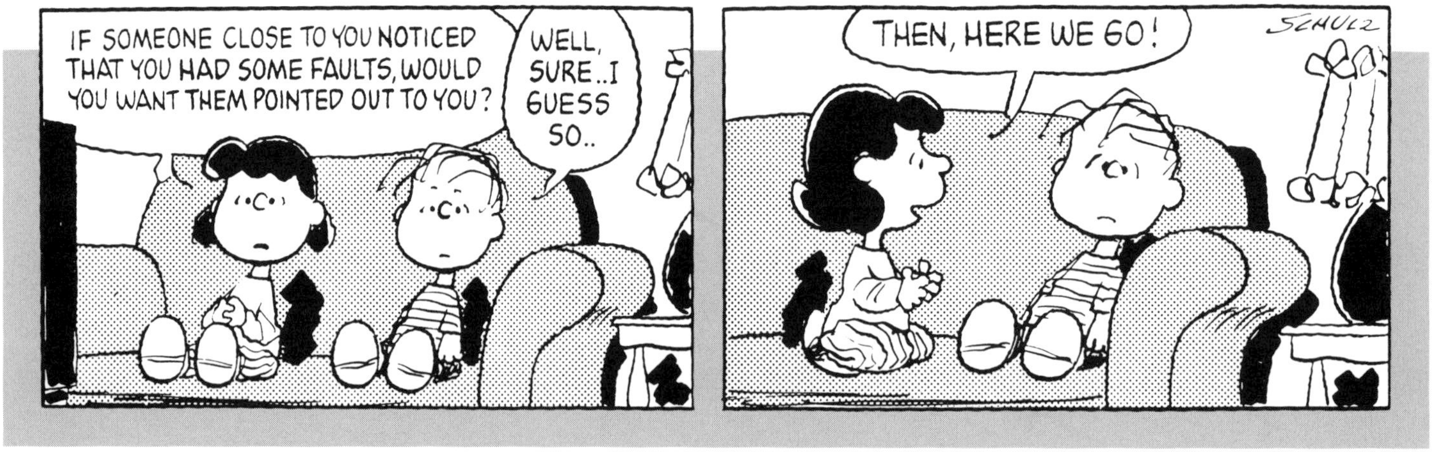
IF SOMEONE CLOSE TO YOU NOTICED THAT YOU HAD SOME FAULTS, WOULD YOU WANT THEM POINTED OUT TO YOU?
WELL, SURE..I GUESS SO..
THEN, HERE WE GO!
SCHULZ

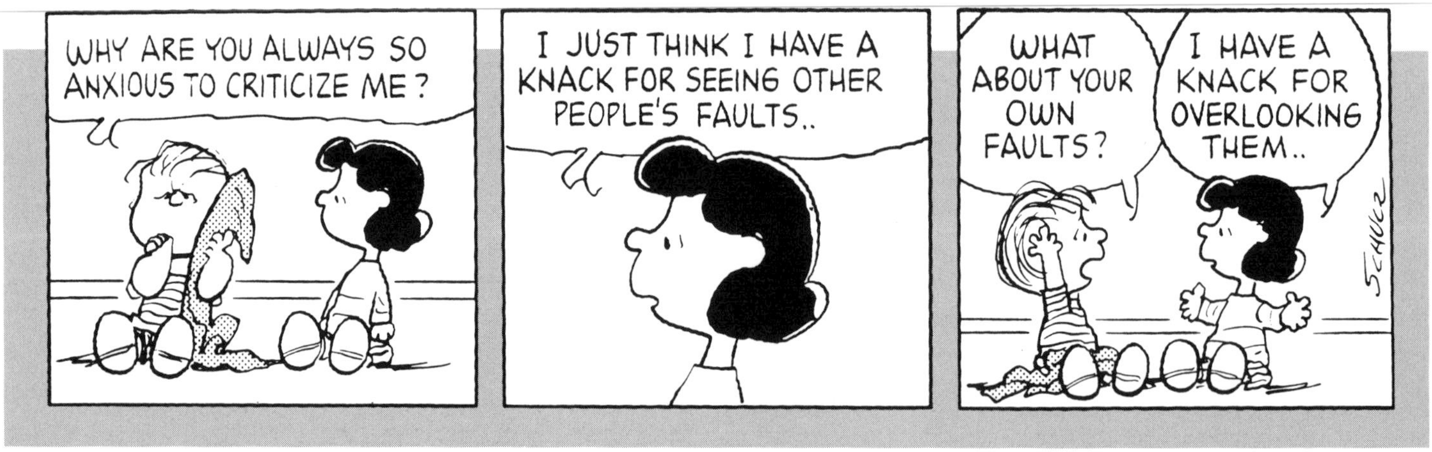
WHY ARE YOU ALWAYS SO ANXIOUS TO CRITICIZE ME?
I JUST THINK I HAVE A KNACK FOR SEEING OTHER PEOPLE'S FAULTS..
WHAT ABOUT YOUR OWN FAULTS?
I HAVE A KNACK FOR OVERLOOKING THEM..
SCHULZ

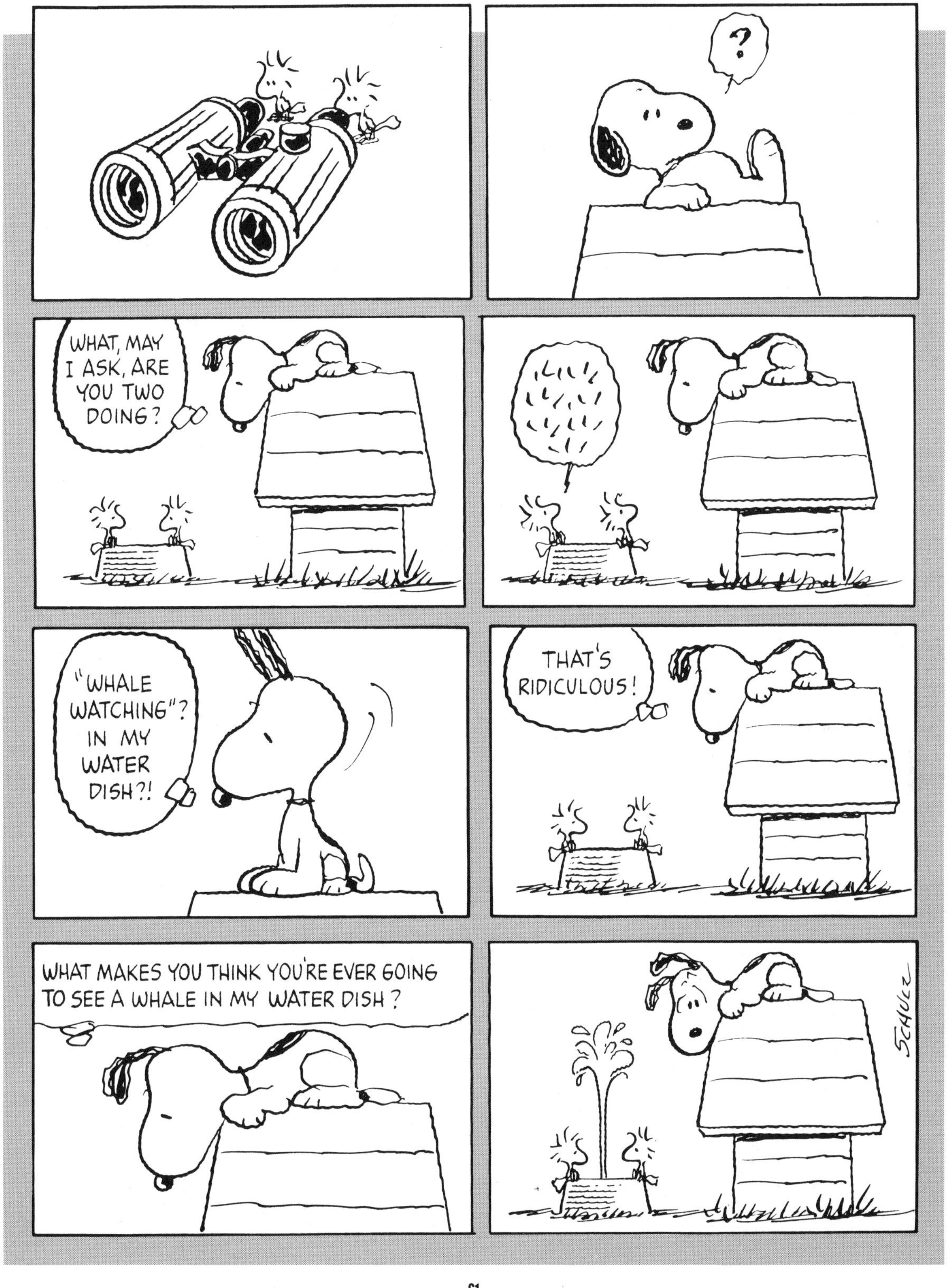
?
WHAT, MAY I ASK, ARE YOU TWO DOING?
"WHALE WATCHING"? IN MY WATER DISH?!
THAT'S RIDICULOUS!
WHAT MAKES YOU THINK YOU'RE EVER GOING TO SEE A WHALE IN MY WATER DISH?
SCHULZ

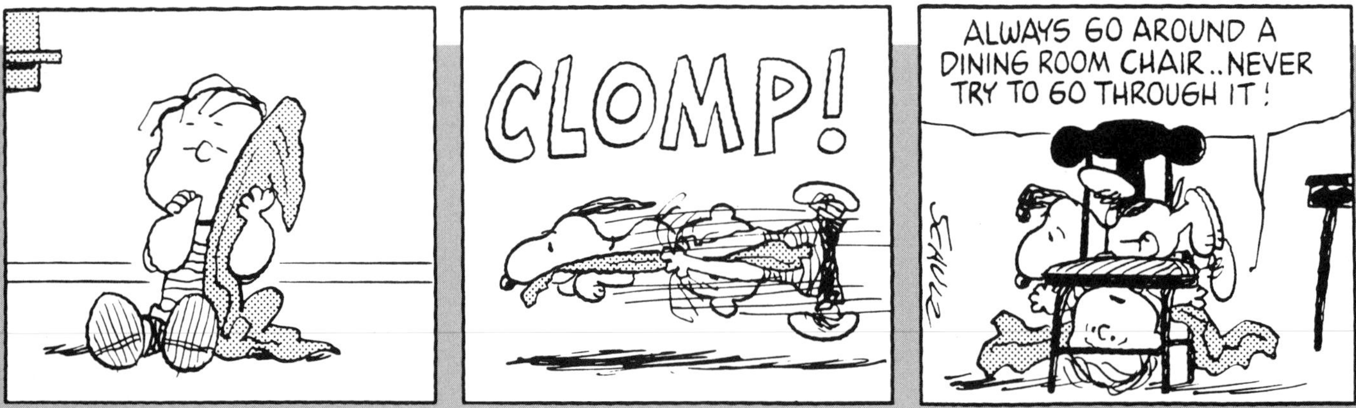
CLOMP!
ALWAYS GO AROUND A DINING ROOM CHAIR..NEVER TRY TO GO THROUGH IT!

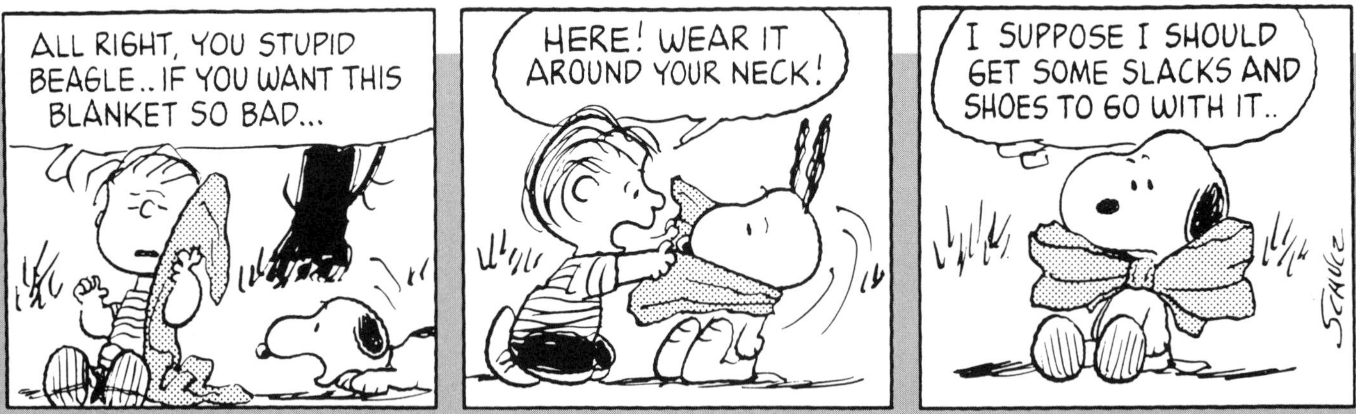
ALL RIGHT, YOU STUPID BEAGLE..IF YOU WANT THIS BLANKET SO BAD...
HERE! WEAR IT AROUND YOUR NECK!
I SUPPOSE I SHOULD GET SOME SLACKS AND SHOES TO GO WITH IT..

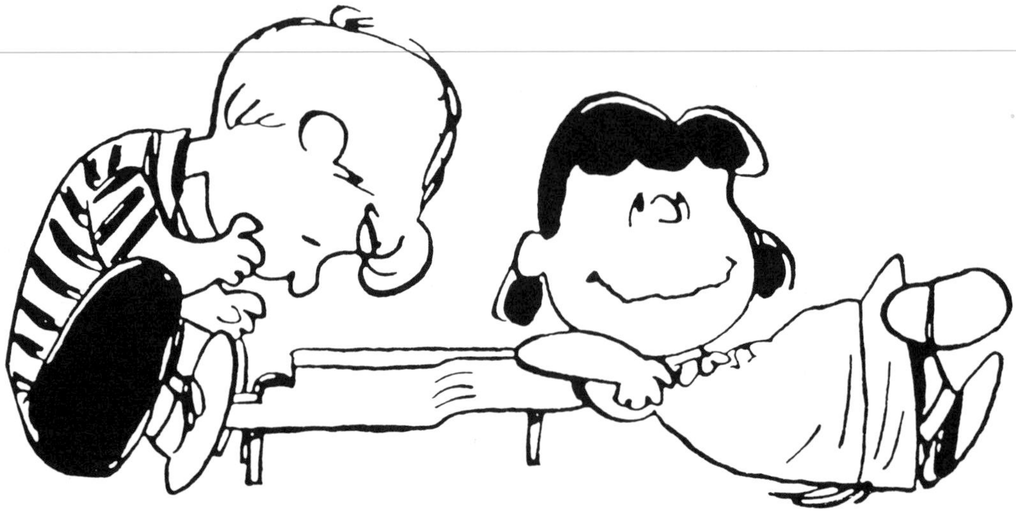

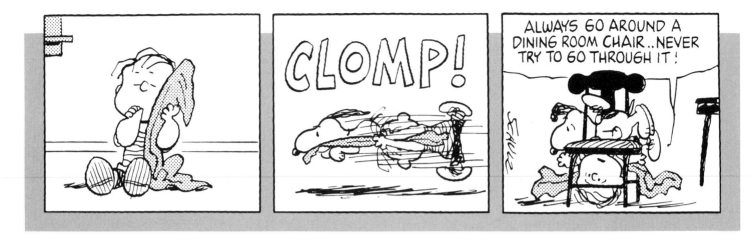

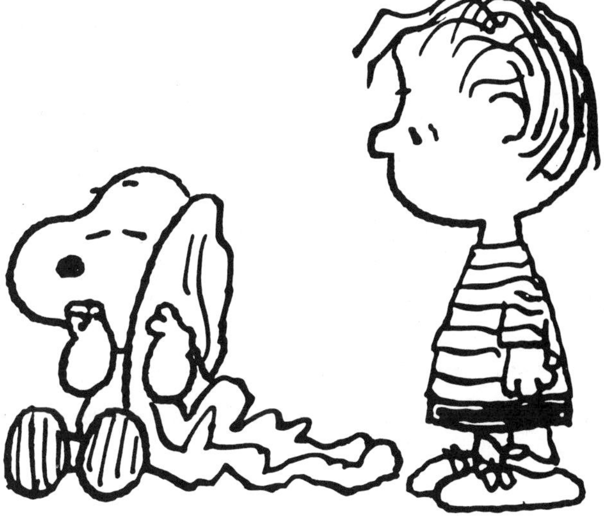

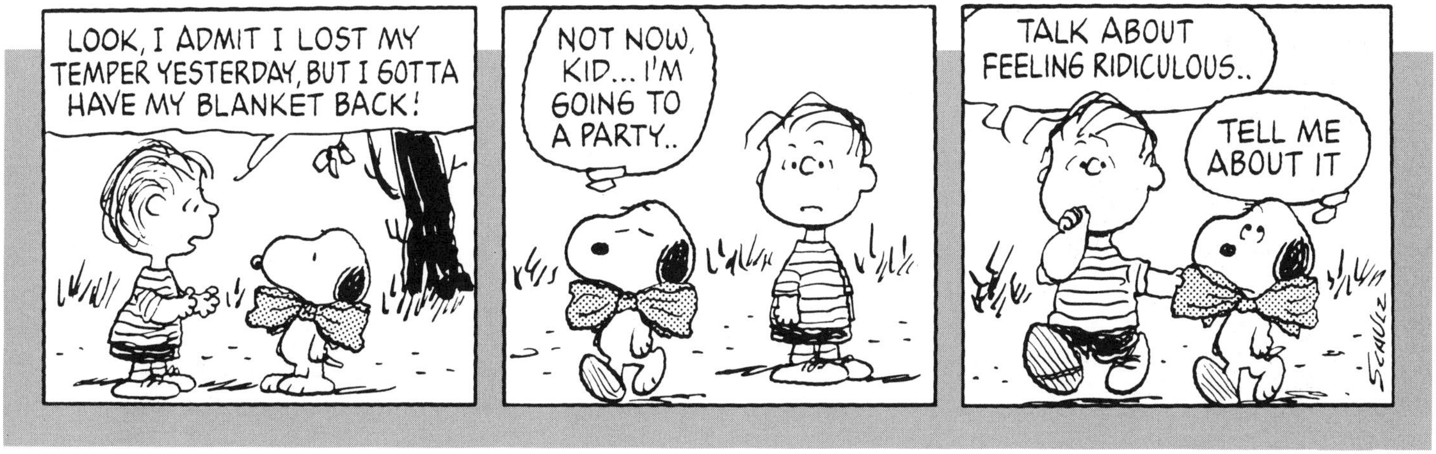
LOOK, I ADMIT I LOST MY TEMPER YESTERDAY, BUT I GOTTA HAVE MY BLANKET BACK!
NOT NOW, KID... I'M GOING TO A PARTY..
TALK ABOUT FEELING RIDICULOUS..
TELL ME ABOUT IT
SCHULZ

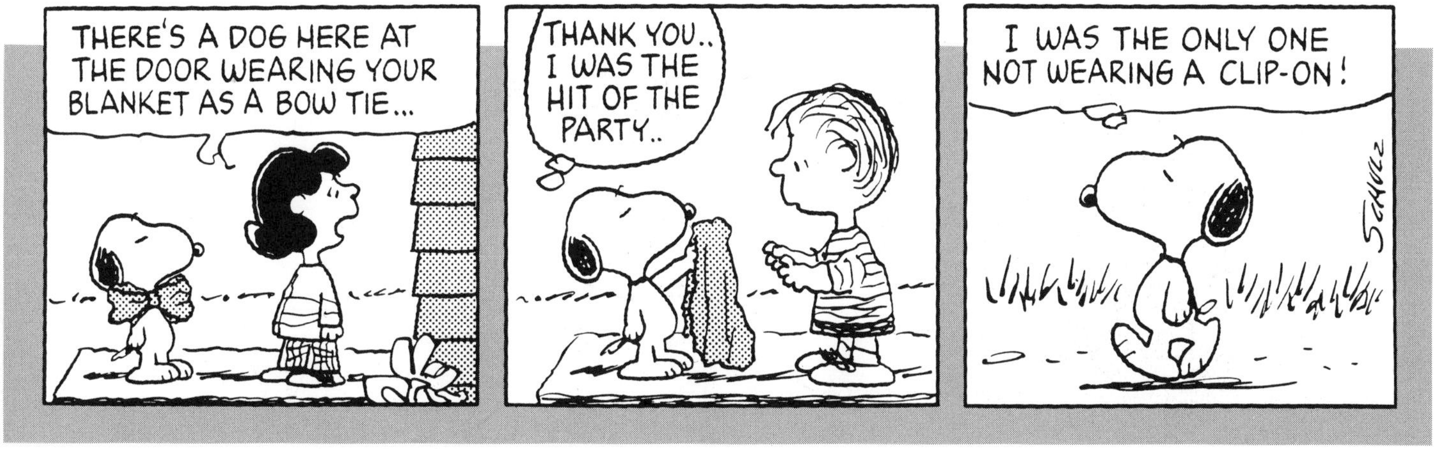
THERE'S A DOG HERE AT THE DOOR WEARING YOUR BLANKET AS A BOW TIE...
THANK YOU.. I WAS THE HIT OF THE PARTY..
I WAS THE ONLY ONE NOT WEARING A CLIP-ON!
SCHULZ

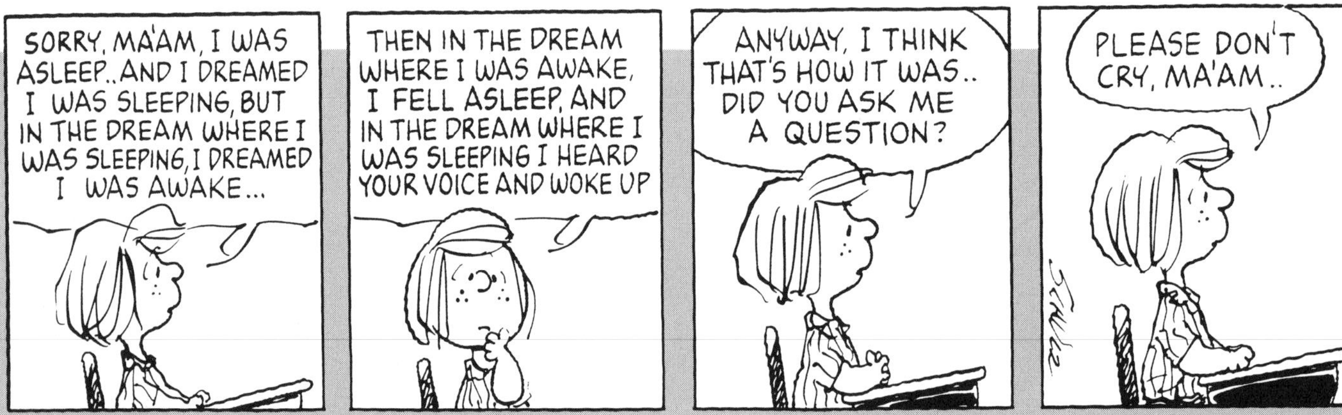
SORRY, MA'AM, I WAS ASLEEP.. AND I DREAMED I WAS SLEEPING, BUT IN THE DREAM WHERE I WAS SLEEPING, I DREAMED I WAS AWAKE...
THEN IN THE DREAM WHERE I WAS AWAKE, I FELL ASLEEP, AND IN THE DREAM WHERE I WAS SLEEPING I HEARD YOUR VOICE AND WOKE UP
ANYWAY, I THINK THAT'S HOW IT WAS.. DID YOU ASK ME A QUESTION?
PLEASE DON'T CRY, MA'AM..
SCHULZ

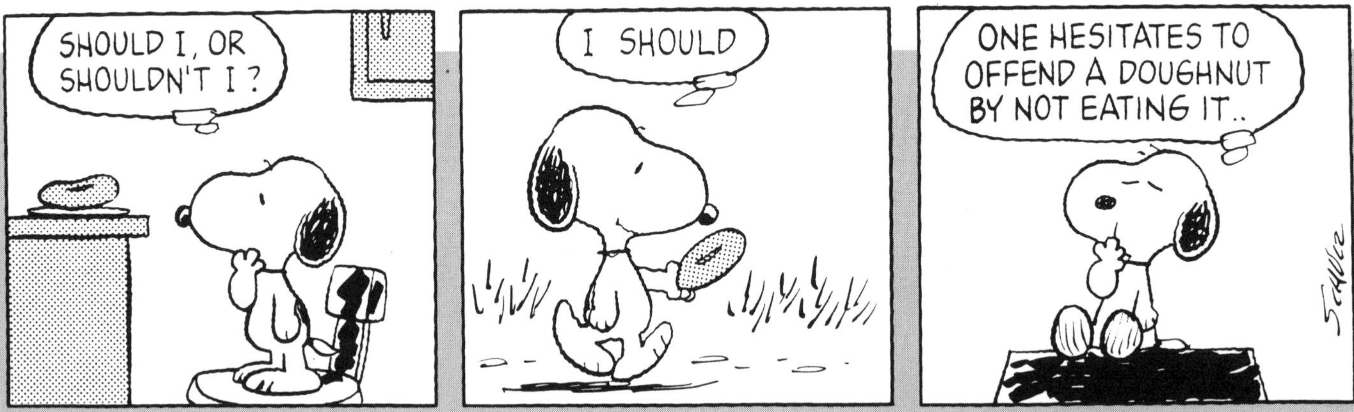
SHOULD I, OR SHOULDN'T I?
I SHOULD
ONE HESITATES TO OFFEND A DOUGHNUT BY NOT EATING IT..
SCHULZ

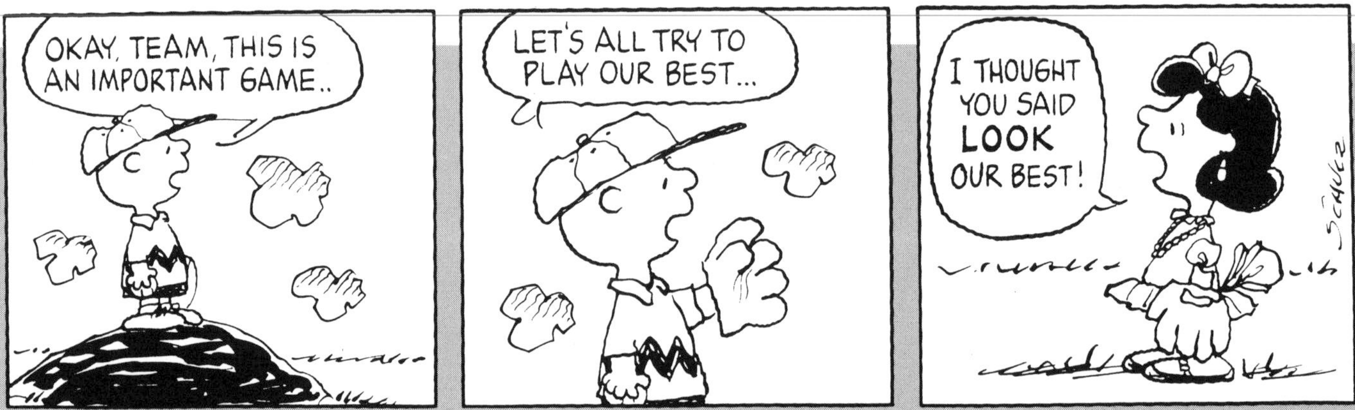
OKAY, TEAM, THIS IS AN IMPORTANT GAME..
LET'S ALL TRY TO PLAY OUR BEST...
I THOUGHT YOU SAID **LOOK** OUR BEST!
SCHULZ

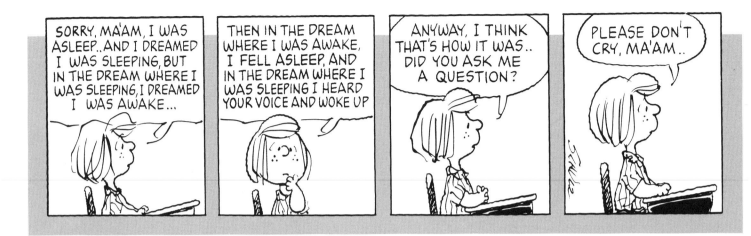

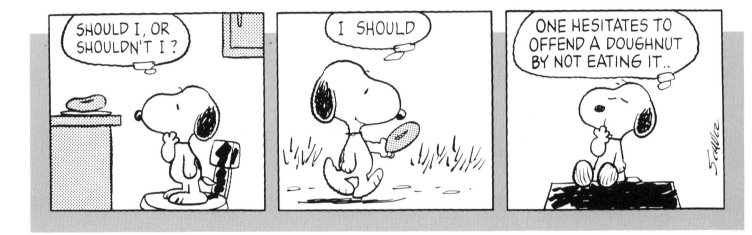

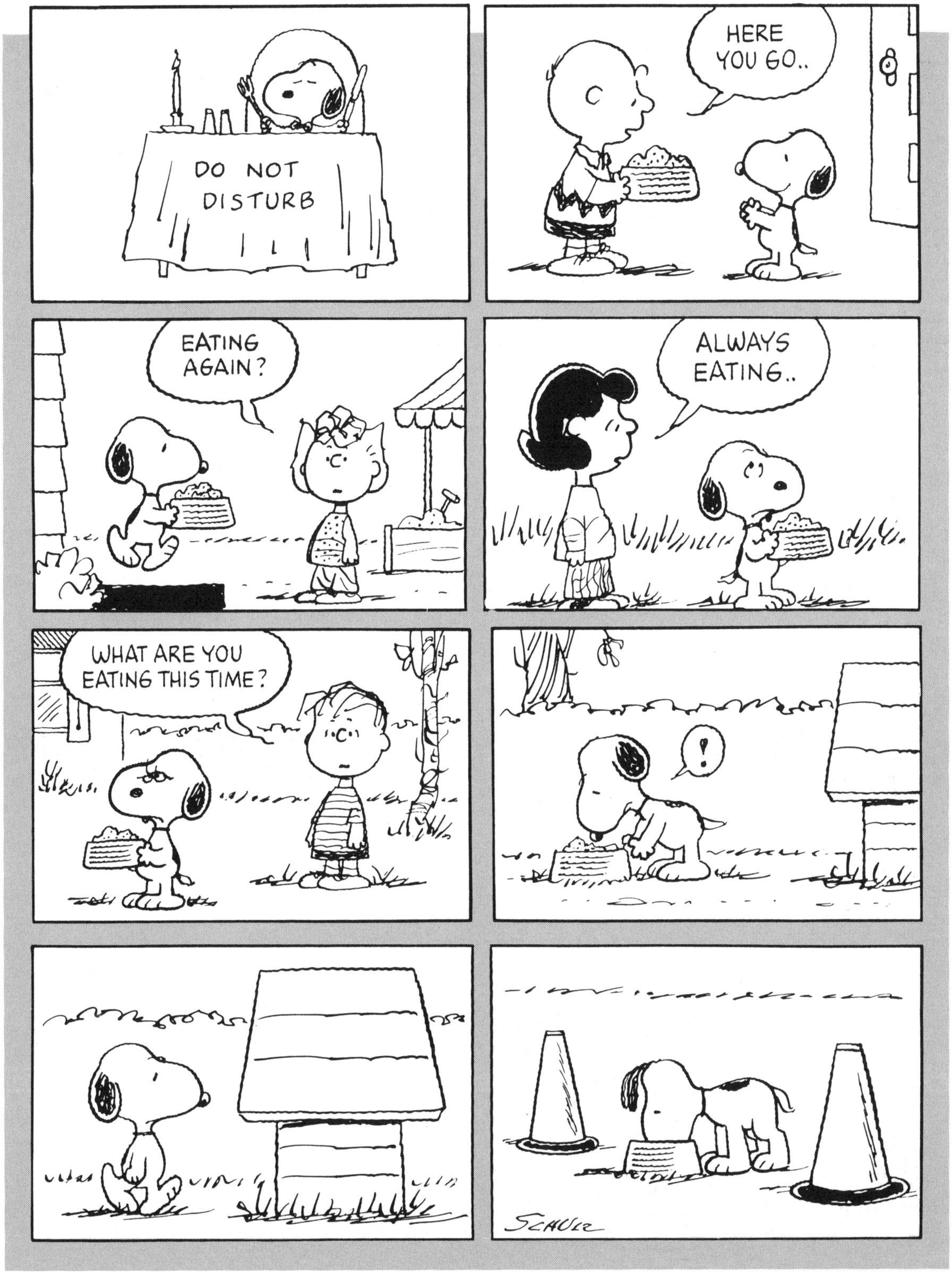
DO NOT DISTURB
HERE YOU GO..
EATING AGAIN?
ALWAYS EATING..
WHAT ARE YOU EATING THIS TIME?
!
SCHULZ

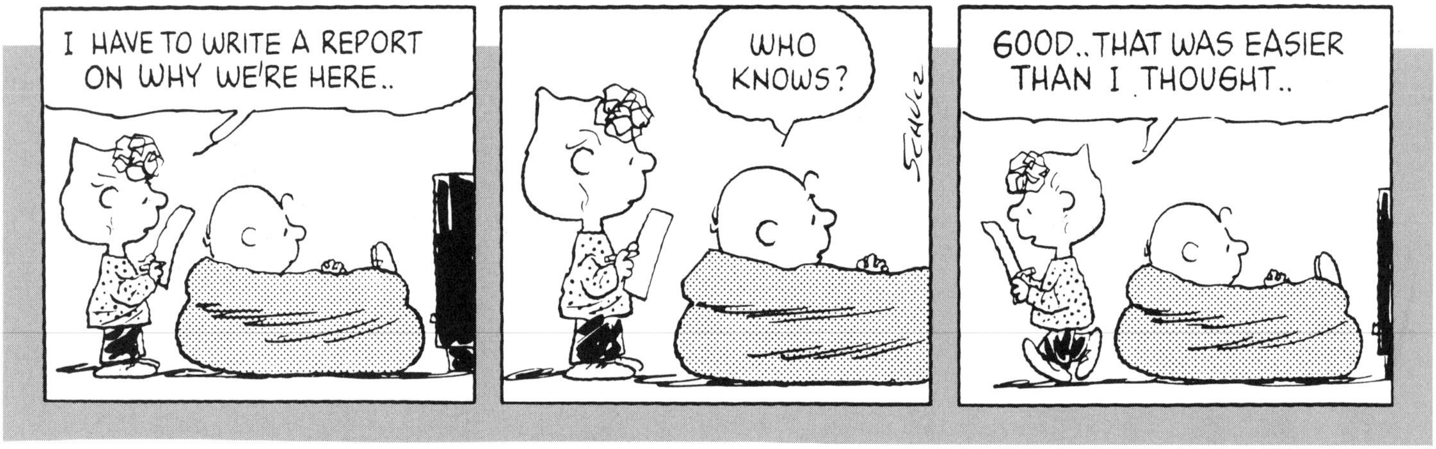
I HAVE TO WRITE A REPORT ON WHY WE'RE HERE..
WHO KNOWS?
SCHULZ
GOOD..THAT WAS EASIER THAN I THOUGHT..

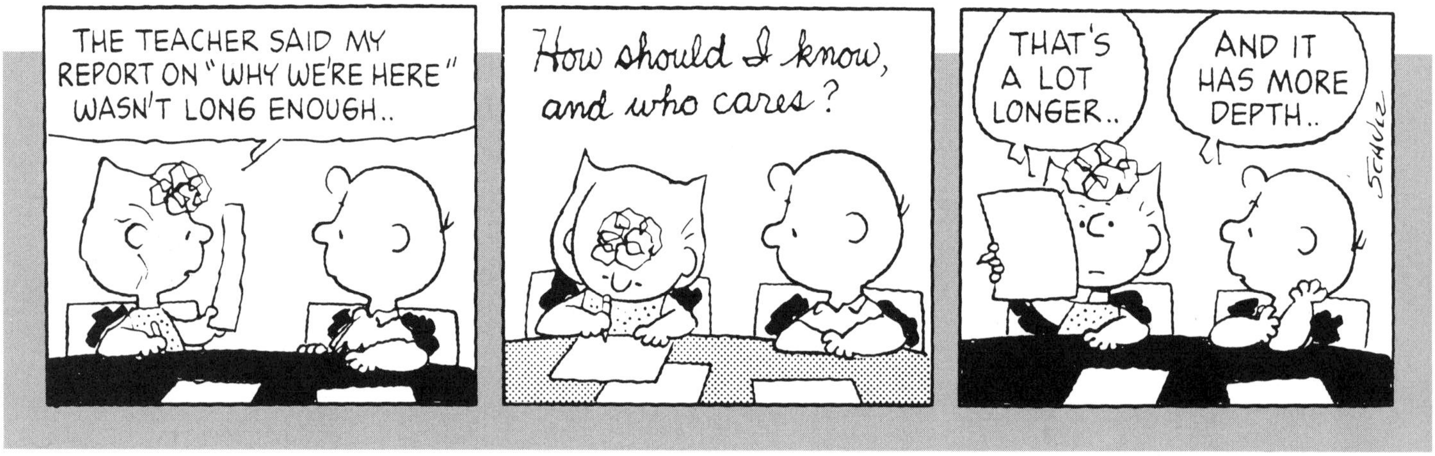
THE TEACHER SAID MY REPORT ON "WHY WE'RE HERE" WASN'T LONG ENOUGH..
How should I know, and who cares?
THAT'S A LOT LONGER..
AND IT HAS MORE DEPTH..
SCHULZ

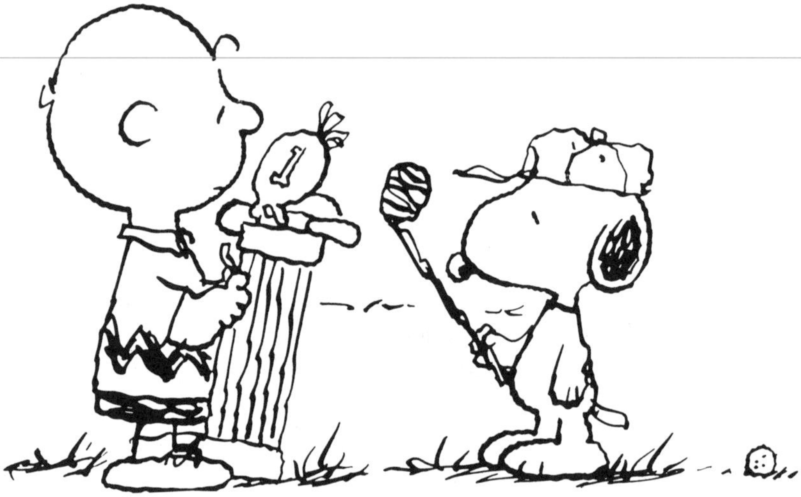

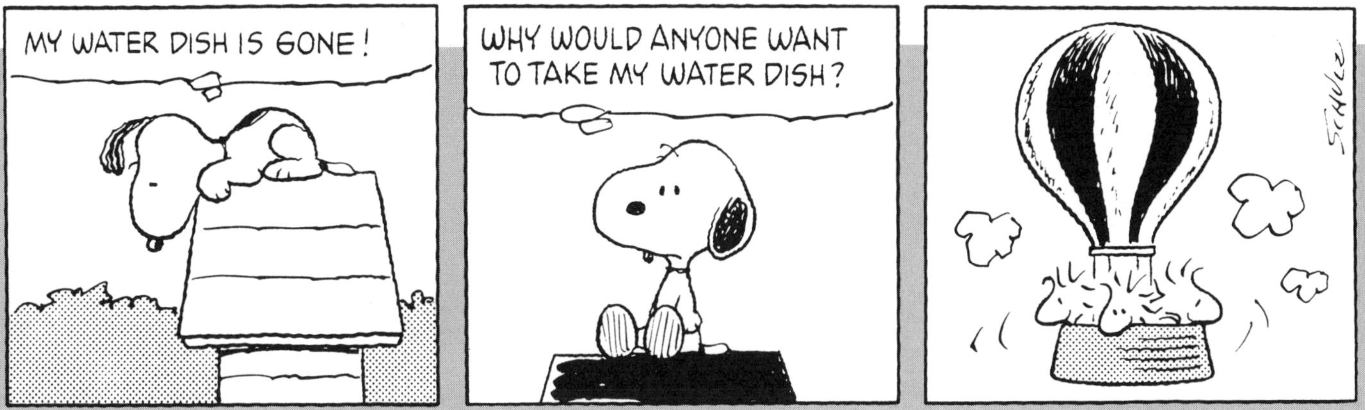
MY WATER DISH IS GONE!
WHY WOULD ANYONE WANT TO TAKE MY WATER DISH?

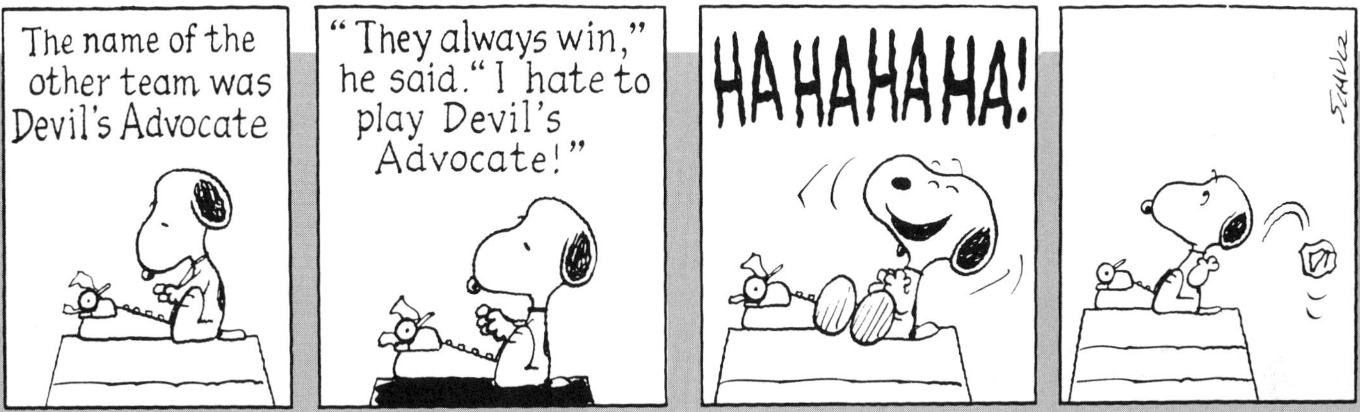
The name of the other team was Devil's Advocate
"They always win," he said. "I hate to play Devil's Advocate!"
HA HA HA HA HA!

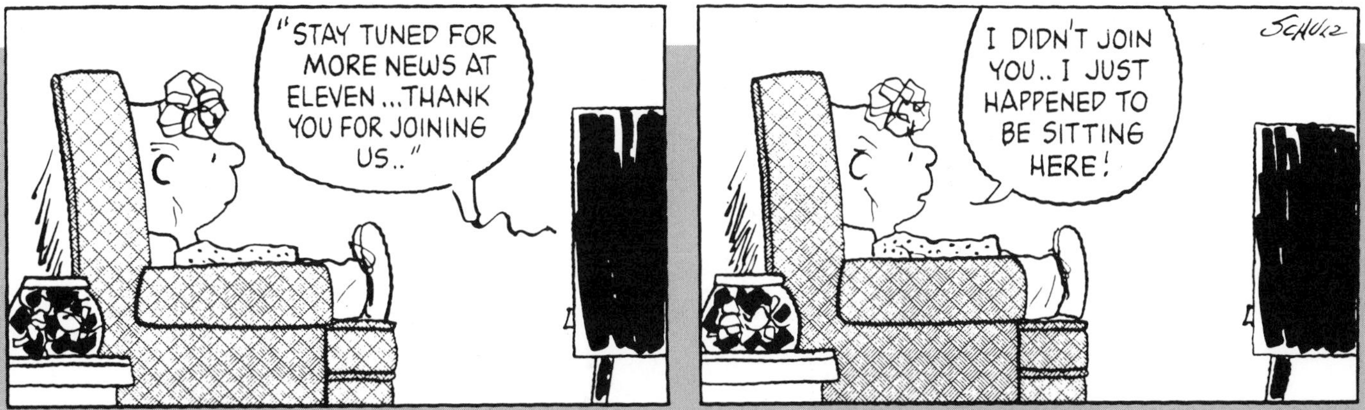
"STAY TUNED FOR MORE NEWS AT ELEVEN ... THANK YOU FOR JOINING US.."
I DIDN'T JOIN YOU.. I JUST HAPPENED TO BE SITTING HERE!

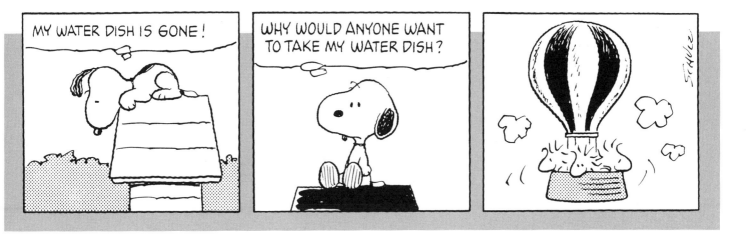

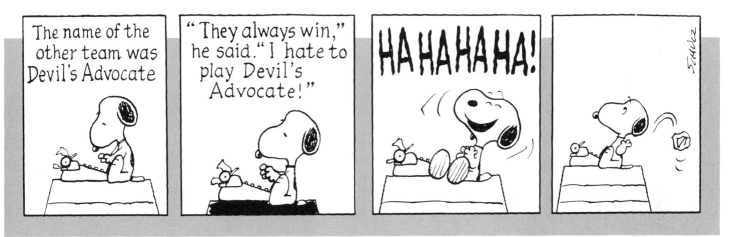

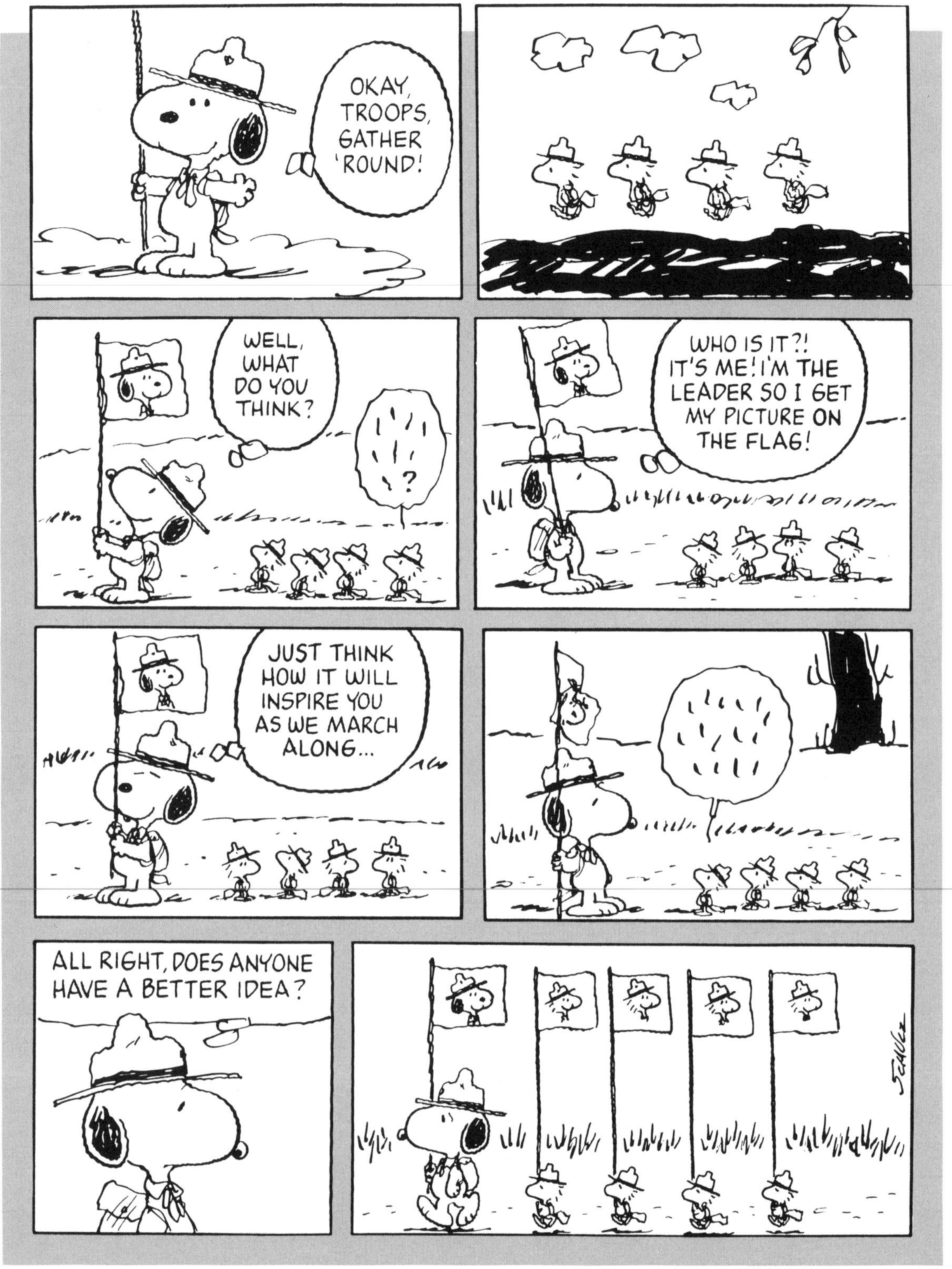
OKAY, TROOPS, GATHER 'ROUND!
WELL, WHAT DO YOU THINK?
?
WHO IS IT?! IT'S ME! I'M THE LEADER SO I GET MY PICTURE ON THE FLAG!
JUST THINK HOW IT WILL INSPIRE YOU AS WE MARCH ALONG...
ALL RIGHT, DOES ANYONE HAVE A BETTER IDEA?
SCHULZ

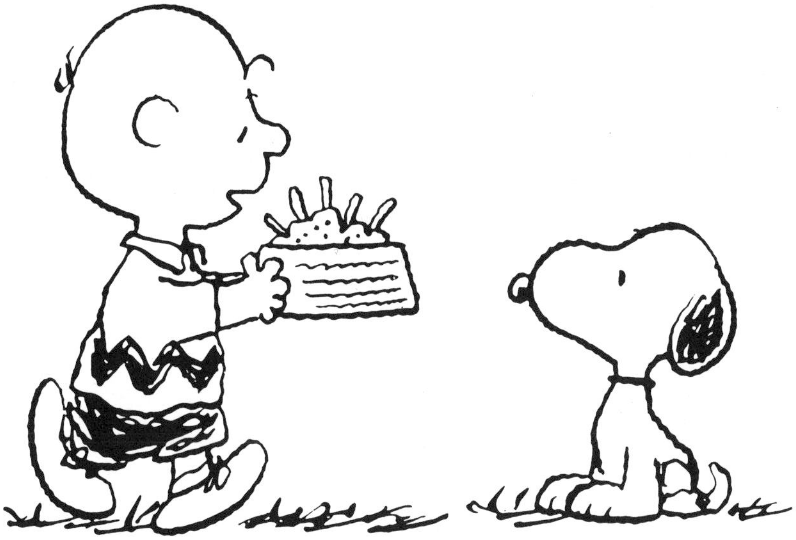

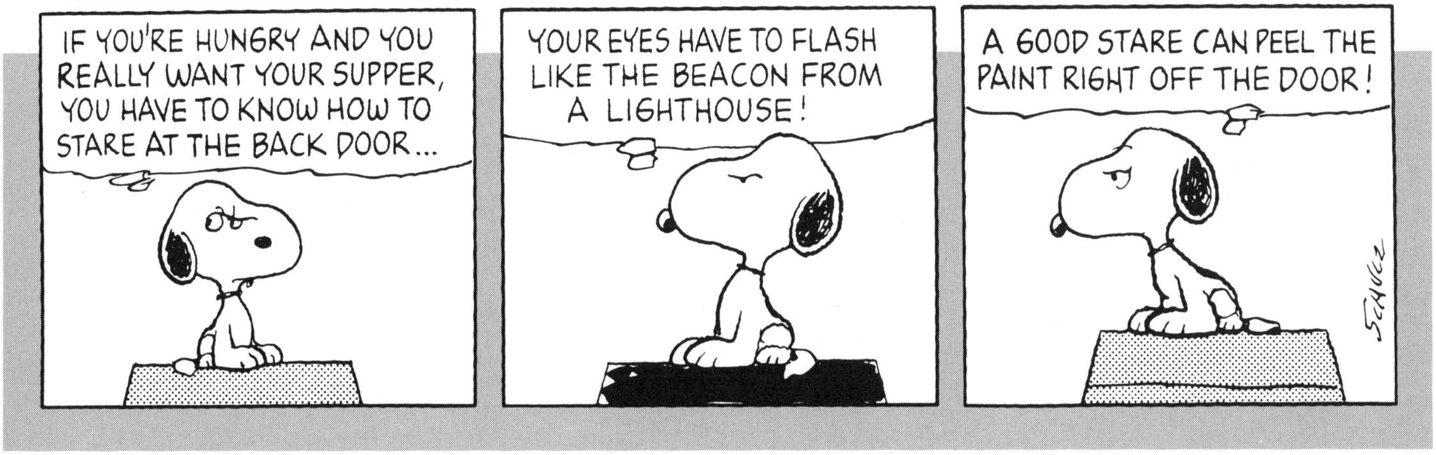
IF YOU'RE HUNGRY AND YOU REALLY WANT YOUR SUPPER, YOU HAVE TO KNOW HOW TO STARE AT THE BACK DOOR...
YOUR EYES HAVE TO FLASH LIKE THE BEACON FROM A LIGHTHOUSE!
A GOOD STARE CAN PEEL THE PAINT RIGHT OFF THE DOOR!
SCHULZ

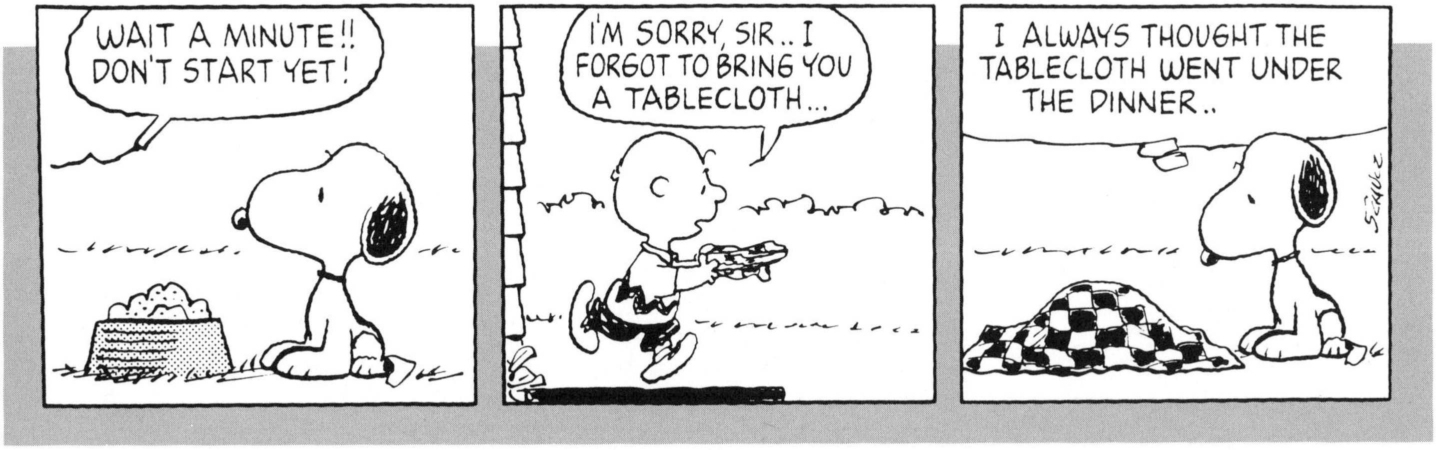
WAIT A MINUTE!! DON'T START YET!
I'M SORRY, SIR.. I FORGOT TO BRING YOU A TABLECLOTH...
I ALWAYS THOUGHT THE TABLECLOTH WENT UNDER THE DINNER..
SCHULZ

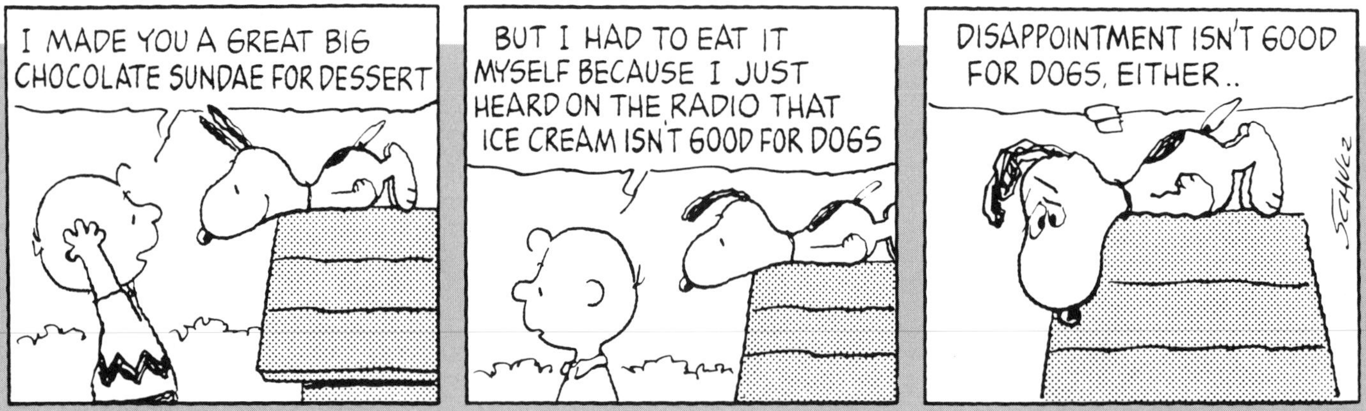
I MADE YOU A GREAT BIG CHOCOLATE SUNDAE FOR DESSERT
BUT I HAD TO EAT IT MYSELF BECAUSE I JUST HEARD ON THE RADIO THAT ICE CREAM ISN'T GOOD FOR DOGS
DISAPPOINTMENT ISN'T GOOD FOR DOGS, EITHER..
SCHULZ

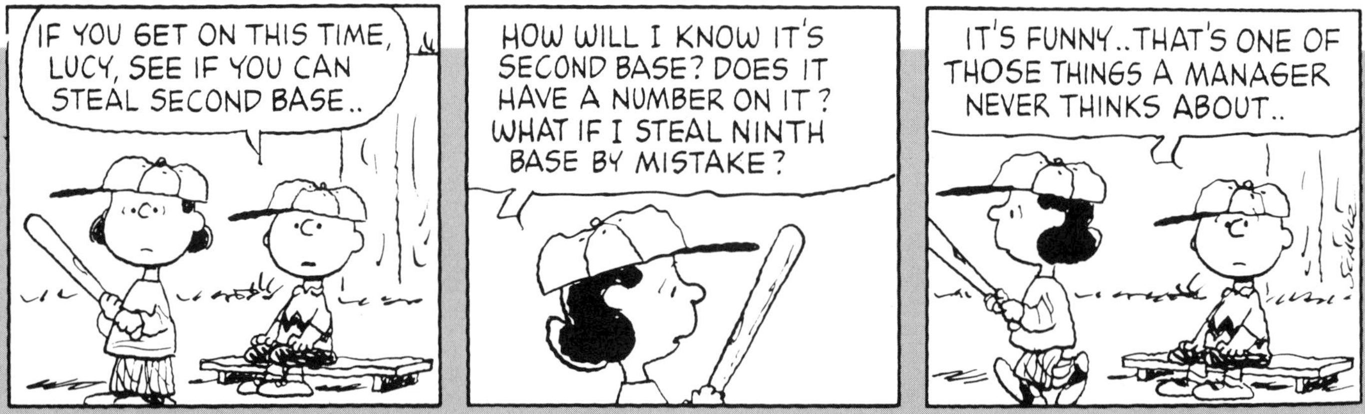
IF YOU GET ON THIS TIME, LUCY, SEE IF YOU CAN STEAL SECOND BASE..
HOW WILL I KNOW IT'S SECOND BASE? DOES IT HAVE A NUMBER ON IT? WHAT IF I STEAL NINTH BASE BY MISTAKE?
IT'S FUNNY..THAT'S ONE OF THOSE THINGS A MANAGER NEVER THINKS ABOUT..
SCHULZ

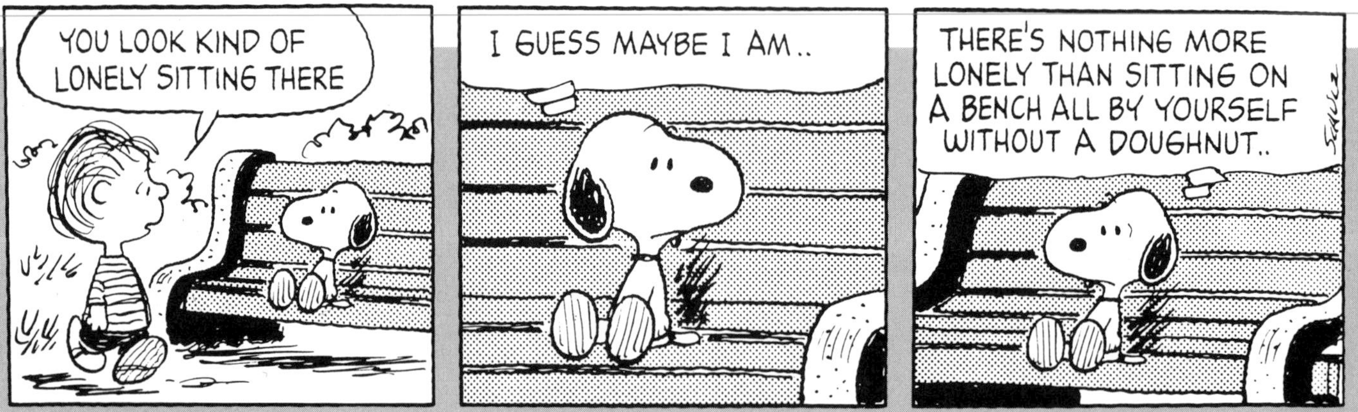
YOU LOOK KIND OF LONELY SITTING THERE
I GUESS MAYBE I AM..
THERE'S NOTHING MORE LONELY THAN SITTING ON A BENCH ALL BY YOURSELF WITHOUT A DOUGHNUT..
SCHULZ

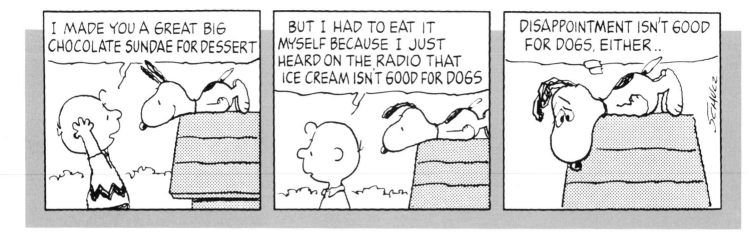

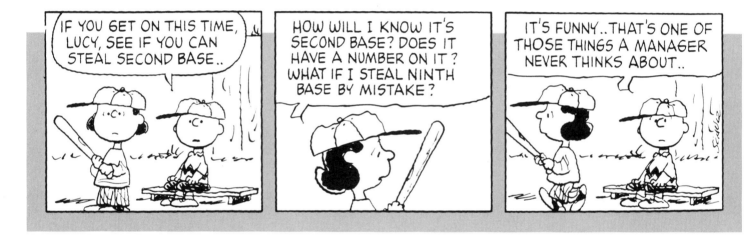

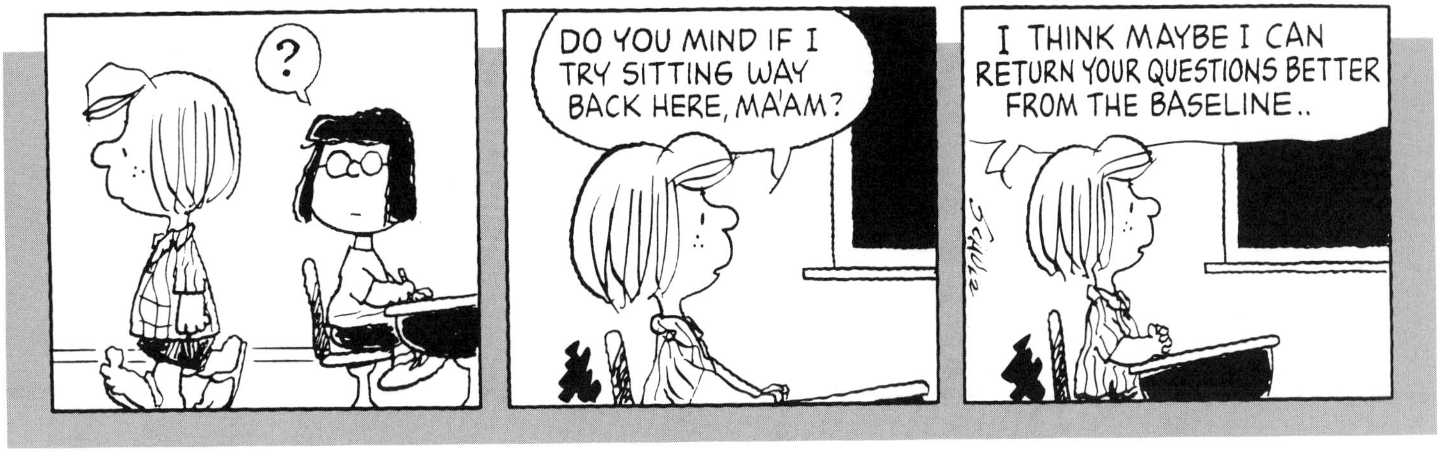
?
DO YOU MIND IF I TRY SITTING WAY BACK HERE, MA'AM?
I THINK MAYBE I CAN RETURN YOUR QUESTIONS BETTER FROM THE BASELINE..

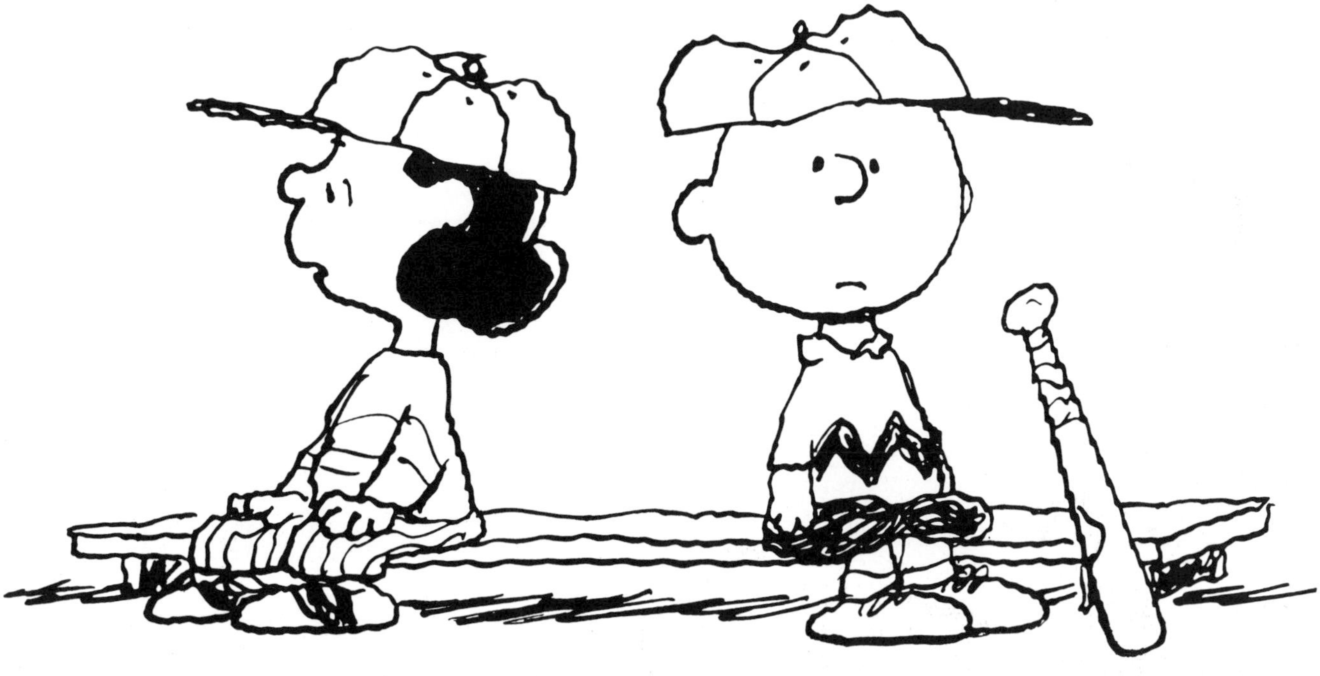

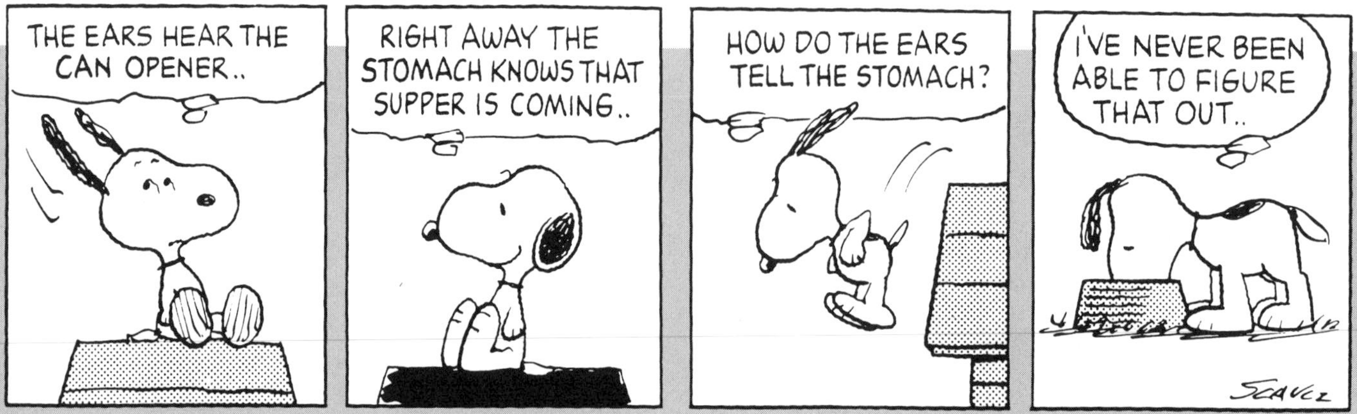
THE EARS HEAR THE CAN OPENER..
RIGHT AWAY THE STOMACH KNOWS THAT SUPPER IS COMING..
HOW DO THE EARS TELL THE STOMACH?
I'VE NEVER BEEN ABLE TO FIGURE THAT OUT..

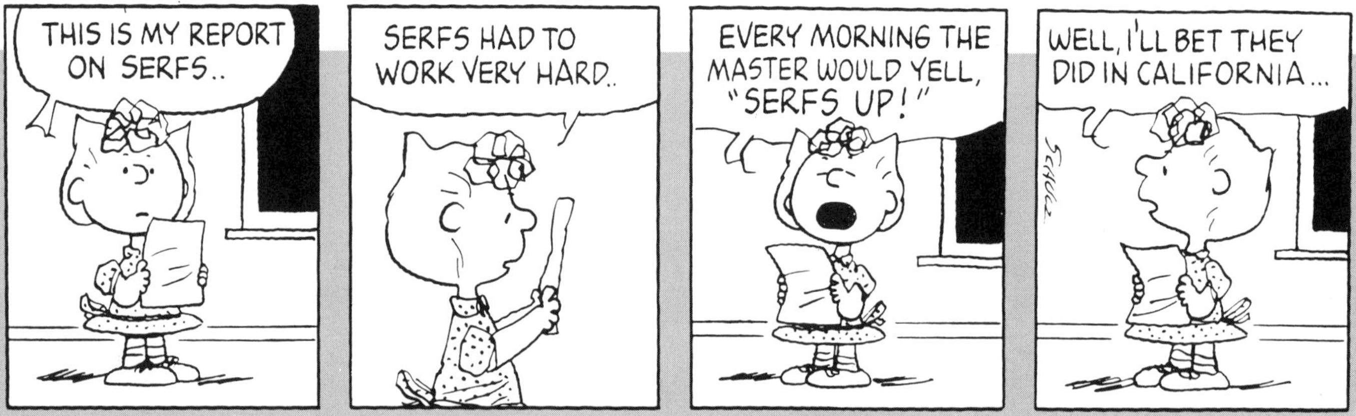
THIS IS MY REPORT ON SERFS..
SERFS HAD TO WORK VERY HARD..
EVERY MORNING THE MASTER WOULD YELL, "SERFS UP!"
WELL, I'LL BET THEY DID IN CALIFORNIA...

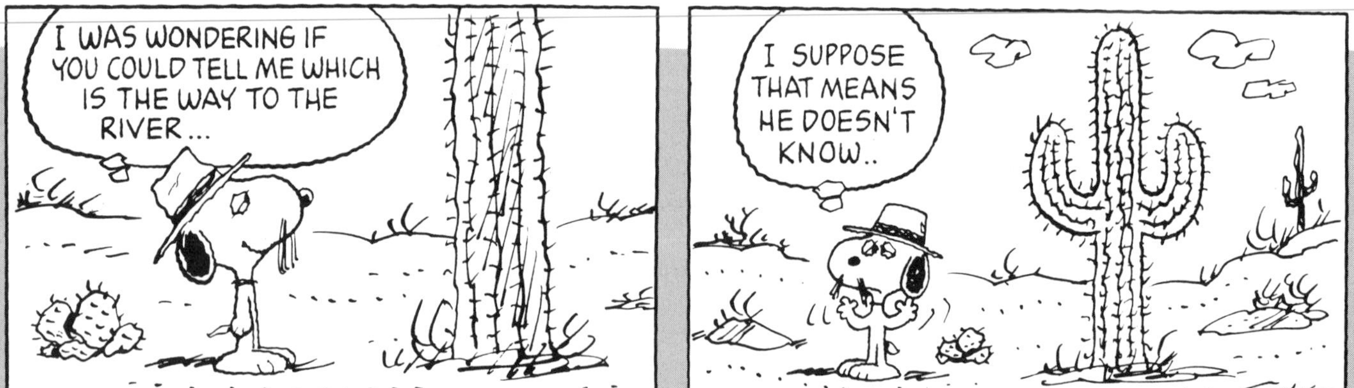
I WAS WONDERING IF YOU COULD TELL ME WHICH IS THE WAY TO THE RIVER...
I SUPPOSE THAT MEANS HE DOESN'T KNOW..

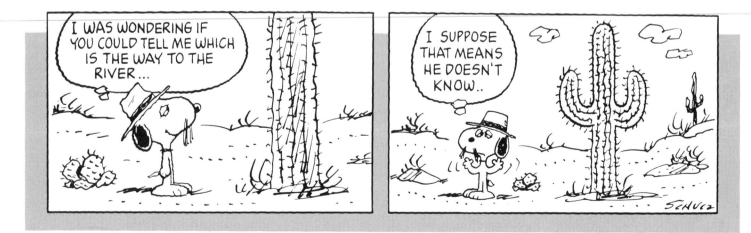

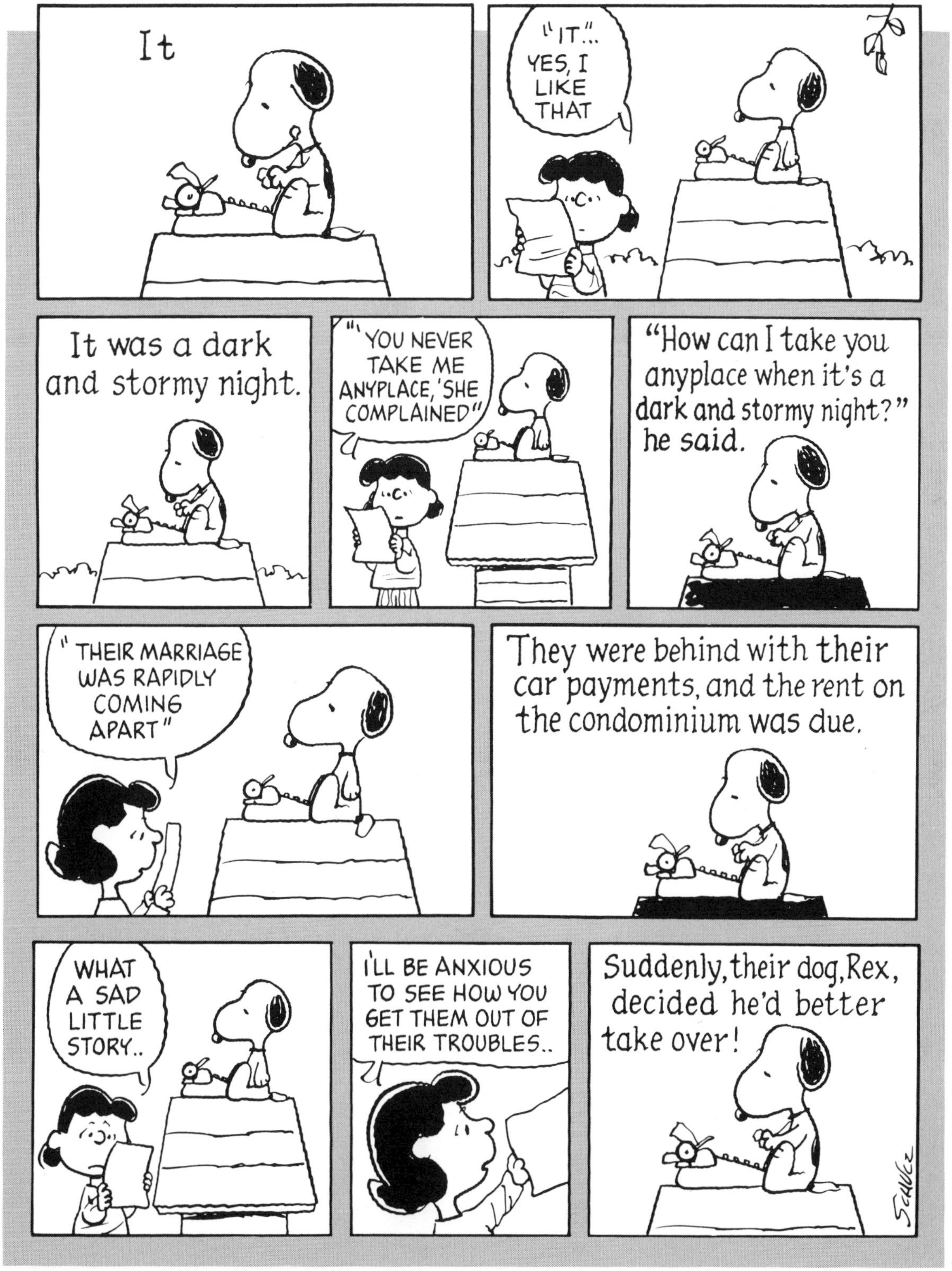
It
"IT"... YES, I LIKE THAT
It was a dark and stormy night.
"'YOU NEVER TAKE ME ANYPLACE,' SHE COMPLAINED"
"How can I take you anyplace when it's a dark and stormy night?" he said.
"THEIR MARRIAGE WAS RAPIDLY COMING APART"
They were behind with their car payments, and the rent on the condominium was due.
WHAT A SAD LITTLE STORY..
I'LL BE ANXIOUS TO SEE HOW YOU GET THEM OUT OF THEIR TROUBLES..
Suddenly, their dog, Rex, decided he'd better take over!
SCHULZ

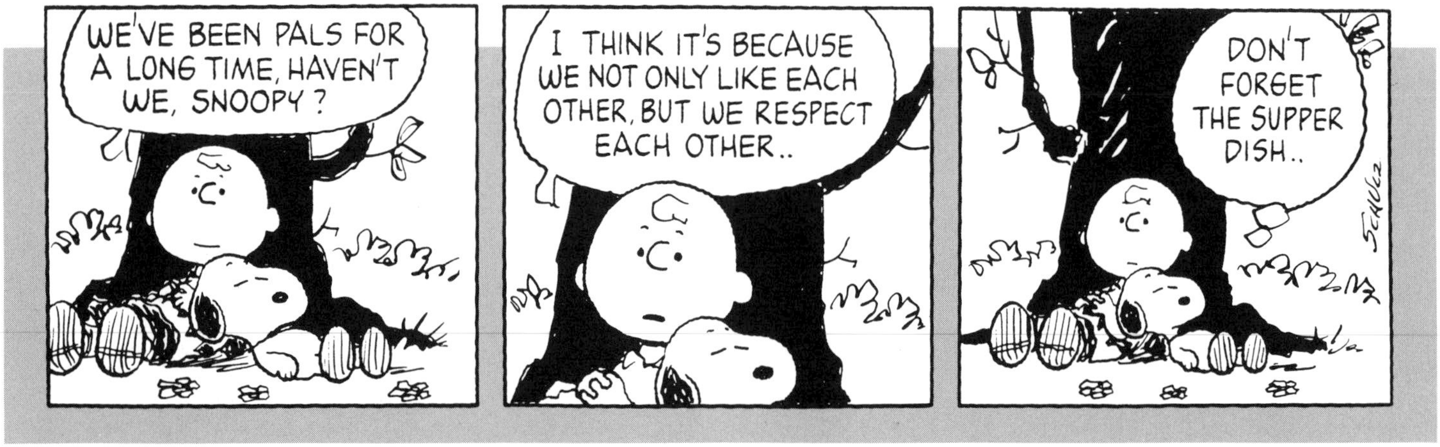
WE'VE BEEN PALS FOR A LONG TIME, HAVEN'T WE, SNOOPY ?
I THINK IT'S BECAUSE WE NOT ONLY LIKE EACH OTHER, BUT WE RESPECT EACH OTHER..
DON'T FORGET THE SUPPER DISH..
SCHULZ

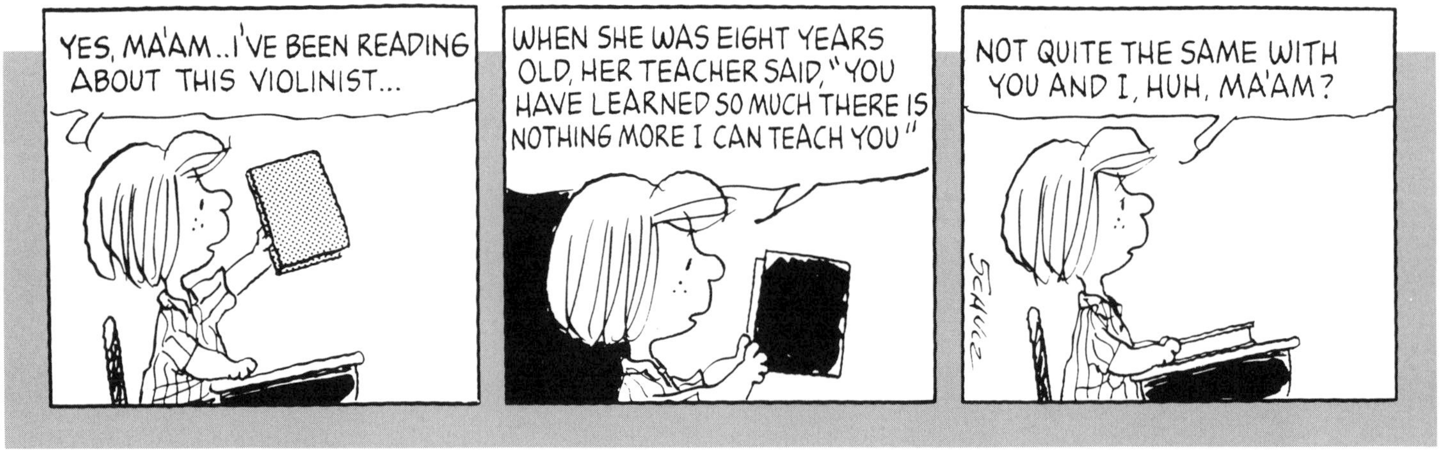
YES, MA'AM..I'VE BEEN READING ABOUT THIS VIOLINIST...
WHEN SHE WAS EIGHT YEARS OLD, HER TEACHER SAID, "YOU HAVE LEARNED SO MUCH THERE IS NOTHING MORE I CAN TEACH YOU"
NOT QUITE THE SAME WITH YOU AND I, HUH, MA'AM?
SCHULZ

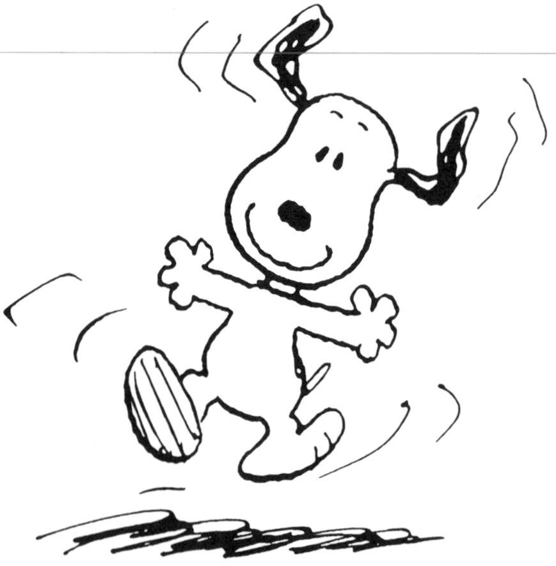

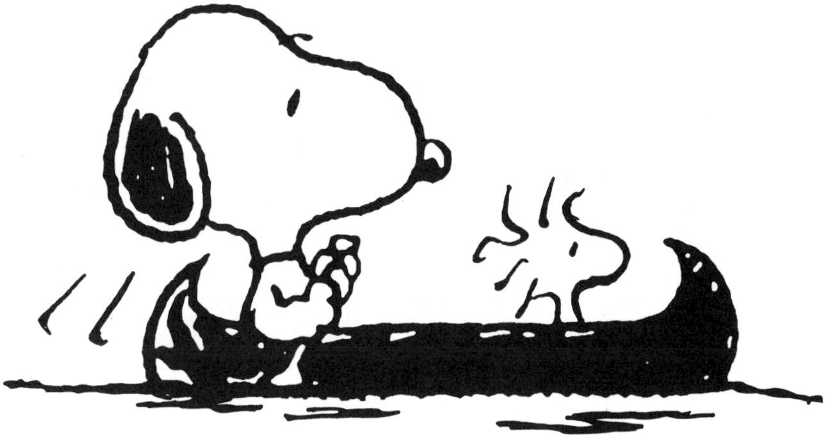

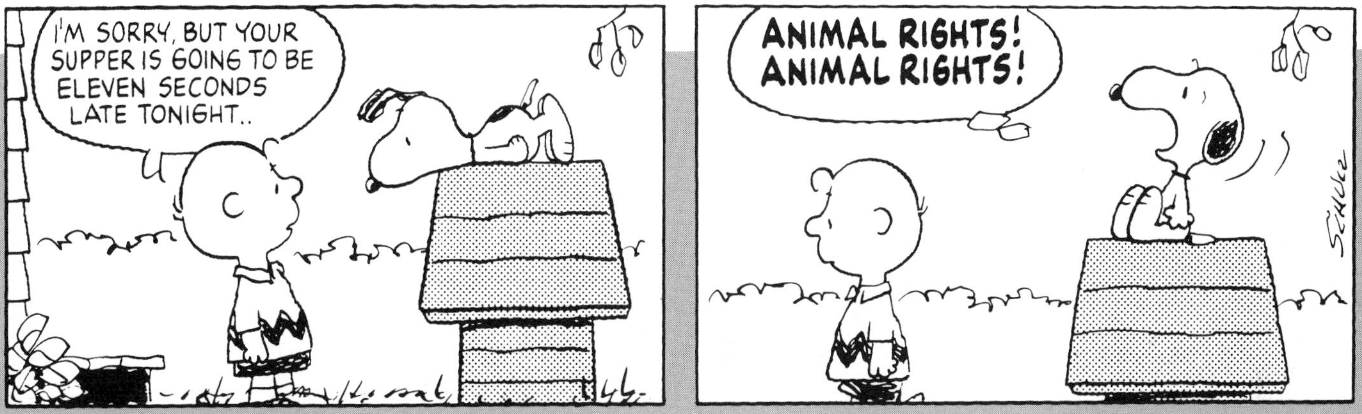
I'M SORRY, BUT YOUR SUPPER IS GOING TO BE ELEVEN SECONDS LATE TONIGHT..
ANIMAL RIGHTS! ANIMAL RIGHTS!
SCHULZ

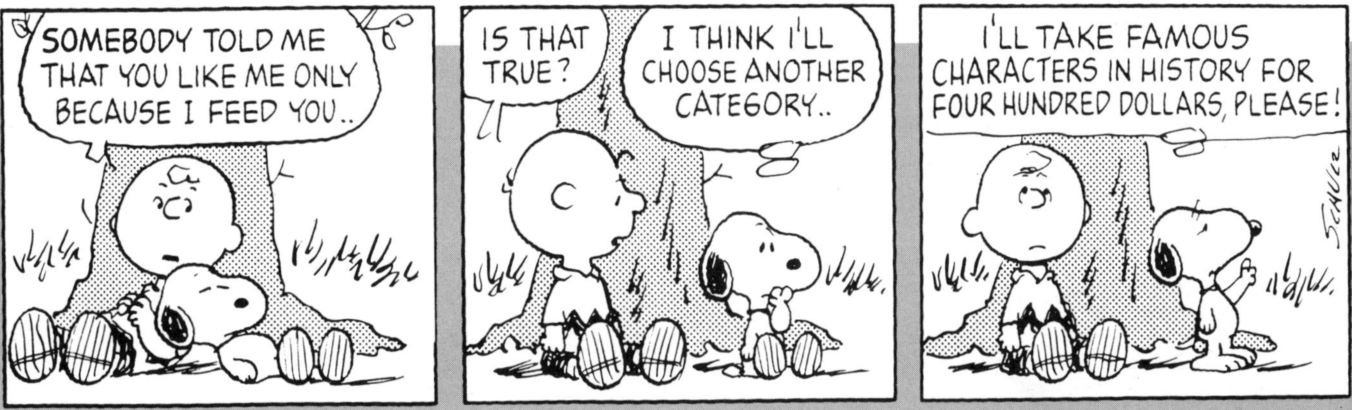
SOMEBODY TOLD ME THAT YOU LIKE ME ONLY BECAUSE I FEED YOU..
IS THAT TRUE?
I THINK I'LL CHOOSE ANOTHER CATEGORY..
I'LL TAKE FAMOUS CHARACTERS IN HISTORY FOR FOUR HUNDRED DOLLARS, PLEASE!
SCHULZ

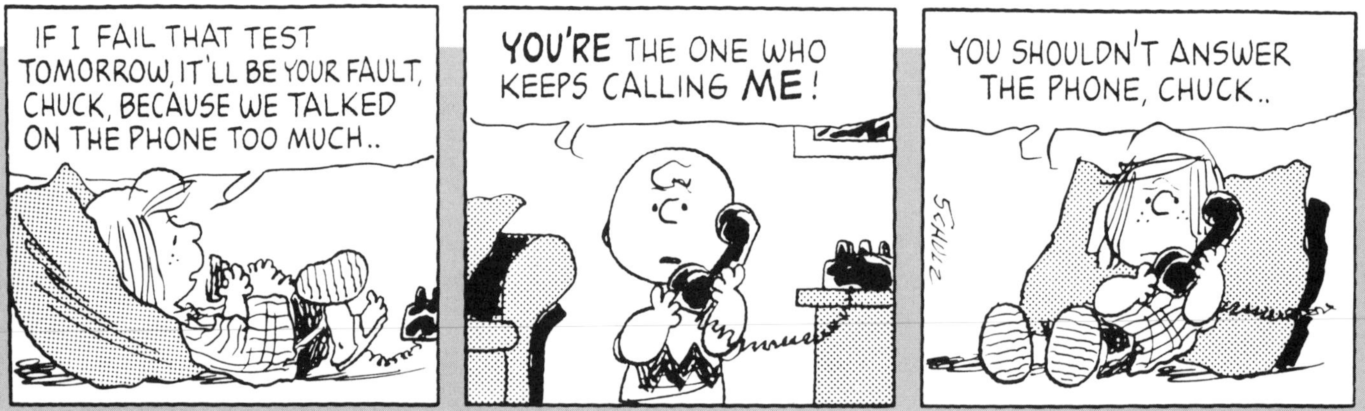
IF I FAIL THAT TEST TOMORROW, IT'LL BE YOUR FAULT, CHUCK, BECAUSE WE TALKED ON THE PHONE TOO MUCH..
YOU'RE THE ONE WHO KEEPS CALLING ME!
YOU SHOULDN'T ANSWER THE PHONE, CHUCK..

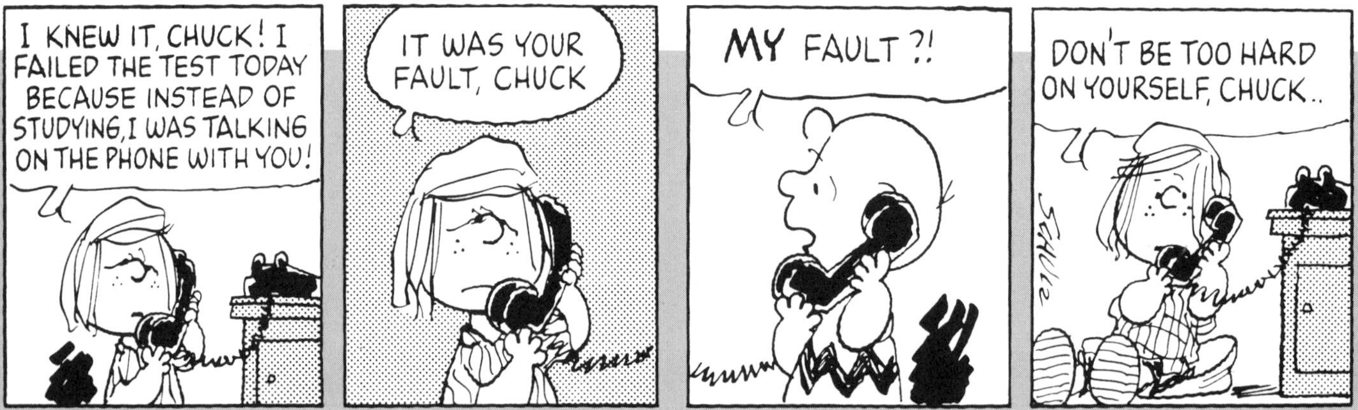
I KNEW IT, CHUCK! I FAILED THE TEST TODAY BECAUSE INSTEAD OF STUDYING, I WAS TALKING ON THE PHONE WITH YOU!
IT WAS YOUR FAULT, CHUCK
MY FAULT?!
DON'T BE TOO HARD ON YOURSELF, CHUCK..

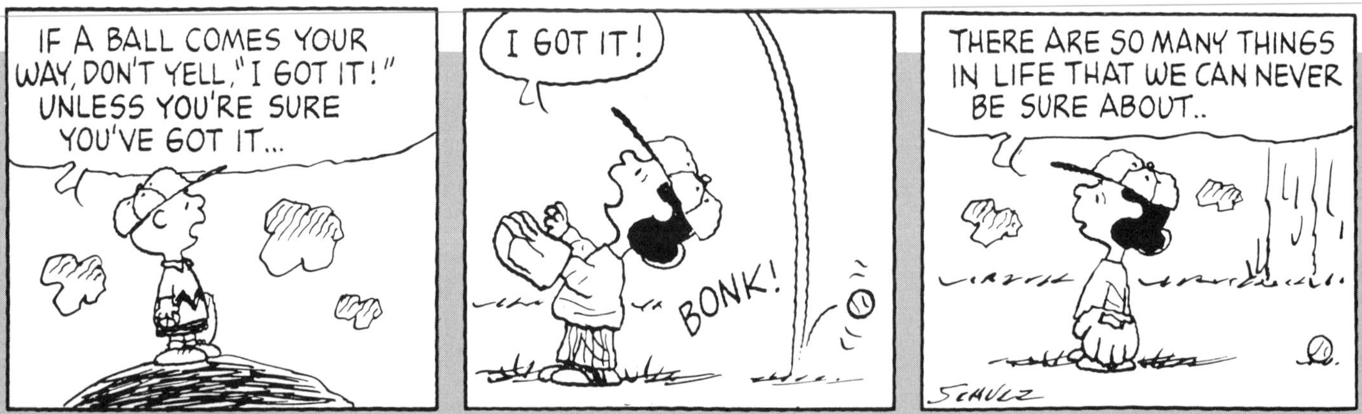
IF A BALL COMES YOUR WAY, DON'T YELL, "I GOT IT!" UNLESS YOU'RE SURE YOU'VE GOT IT...
I GOT IT!
BONK!
THERE ARE SO MANY THINGS IN LIFE THAT WE CAN NEVER BE SURE ABOUT..

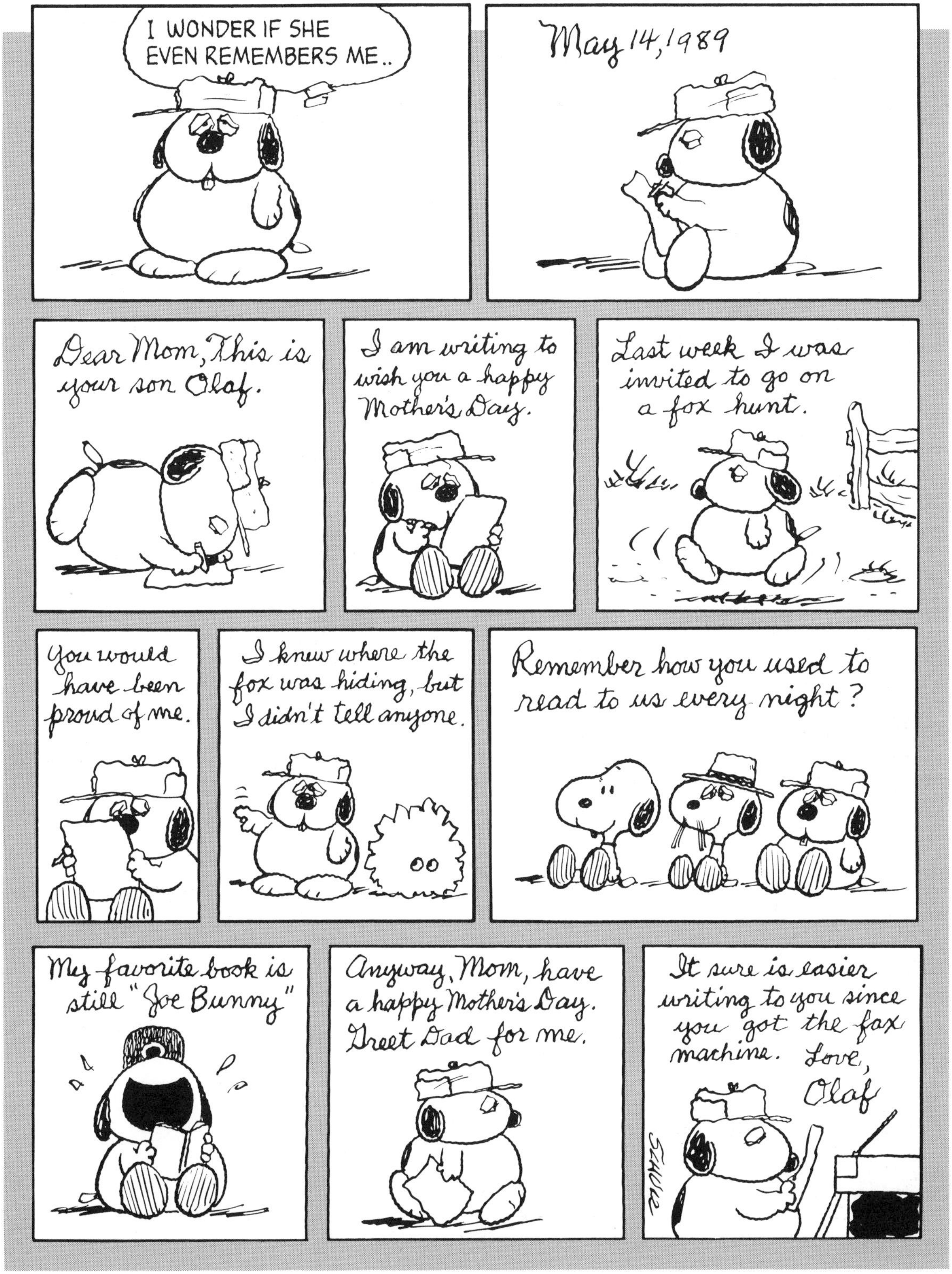
I WONDER IF SHE EVEN REMEMBERS ME..
May 14, 1989
Dear Mom, This is your son Olaf.
I am writing to wish you a happy Mother's Day.
Last week I was invited to go on a fox hunt.
You would have been proud of me.
I knew where the fox was hiding, but I didn't tell anyone.
Remember how you used to read to us every night?
My favorite book is still "Joe Bunny"
Anyway, Mom, have a happy Mother's Day. Greet Dad for me.
It sure is easier writing to you since you got the fax machine. Love, Olaf
SCHULZ

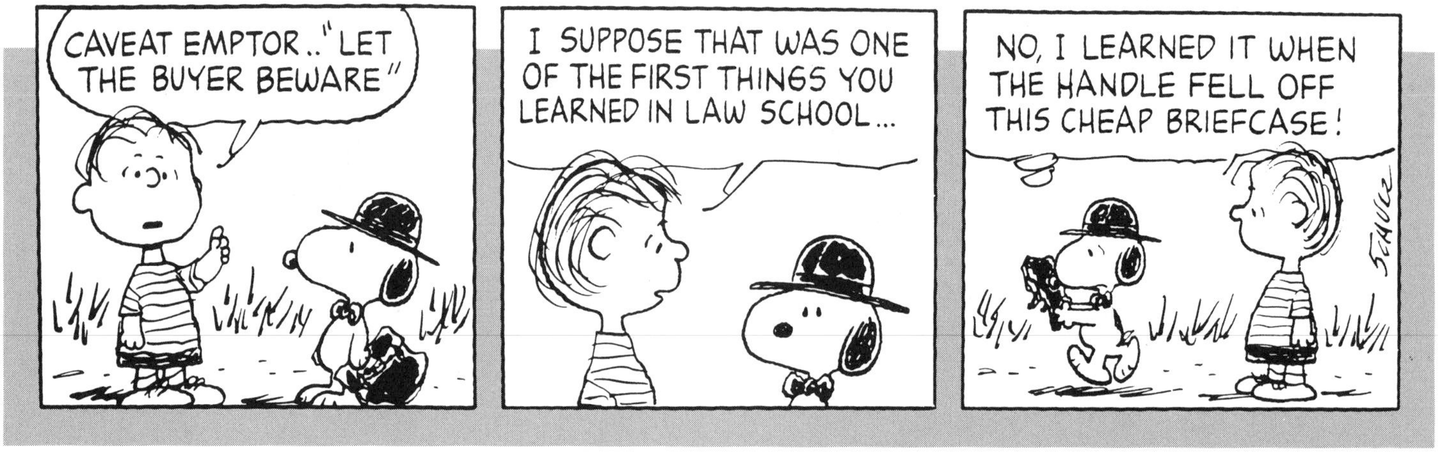
CAVEAT EMPTOR.."LET THE BUYER BEWARE"
I SUPPOSE THAT WAS ONE OF THE FIRST THINGS YOU LEARNED IN LAW SCHOOL...
NO, I LEARNED IT WHEN THE HANDLE FELL OFF THIS CHEAP BRIEFCASE!
SCHULZ

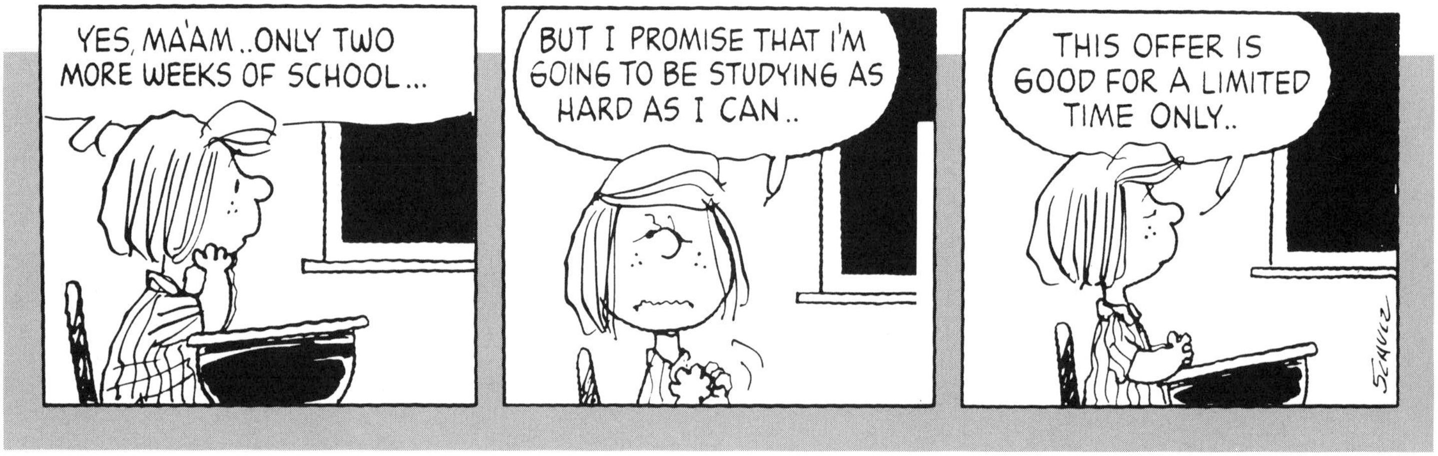
YES, MA'AM..ONLY TWO MORE WEEKS OF SCHOOL...
BUT I PROMISE THAT I'M GOING TO BE STUDYING AS HARD AS I CAN..
THIS OFFER IS GOOD FOR A LIMITED TIME ONLY..
SCHULZ

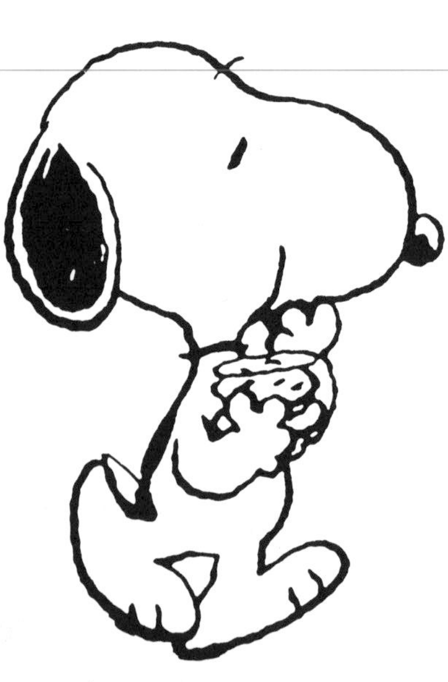

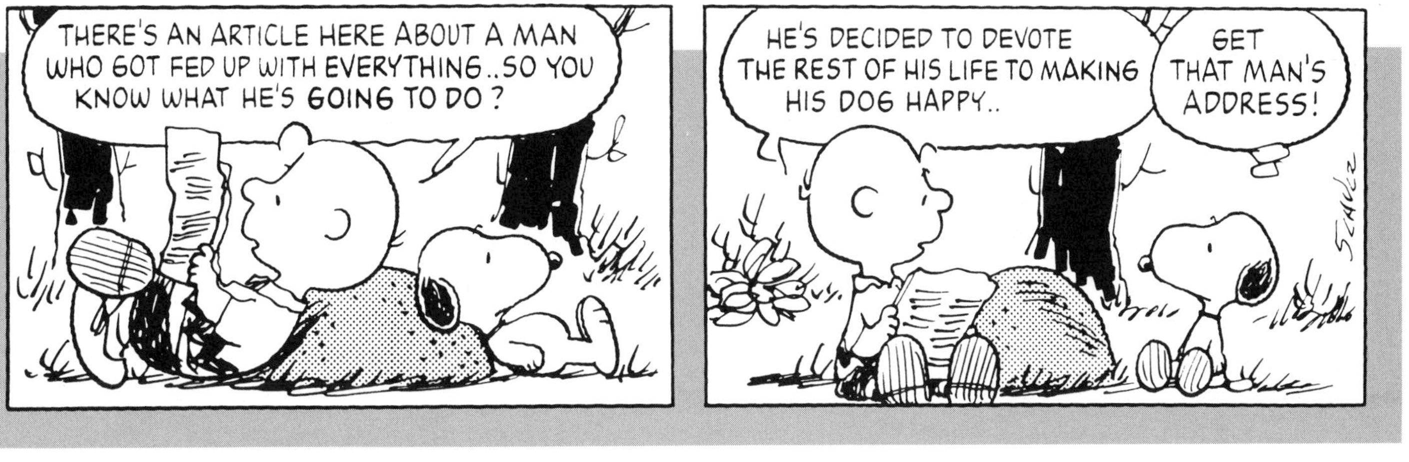
THERE'S AN ARTICLE HERE ABOUT A MAN WHO GOT FED UP WITH EVERYTHING..SO YOU KNOW WHAT HE'S GOING TO DO ?
HE'S DECIDED TO DEVOTE THE REST OF HIS LIFE TO MAKING HIS DOG HAPPY..
GET THAT MAN'S ADDRESS!

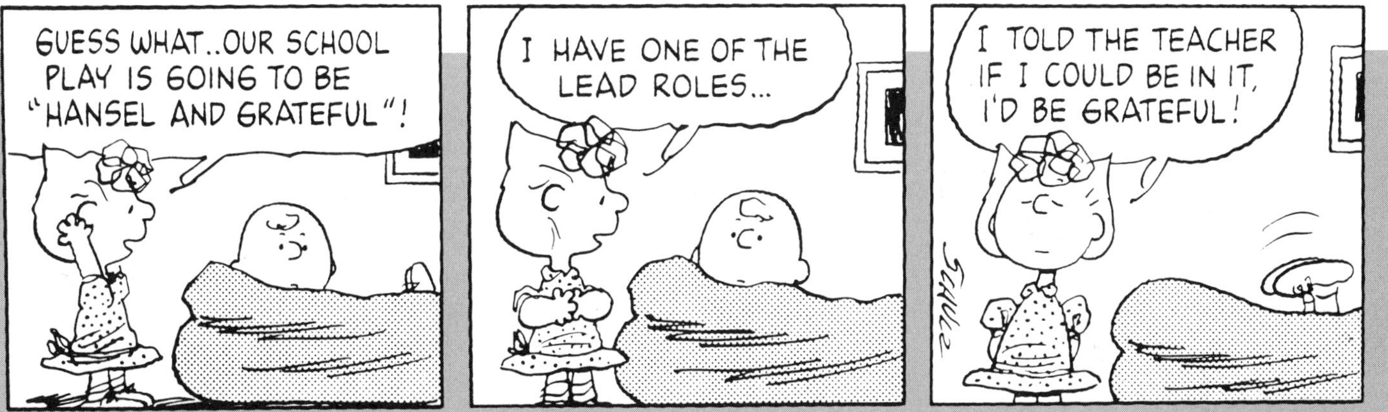
GUESS WHAT..OUR SCHOOL PLAY IS GOING TO BE "HANSEL AND GRATEFUL"!
I HAVE ONE OF THE LEAD ROLES...
I TOLD THE TEACHER IF I COULD BE IN IT, I'D BE GRATEFUL!

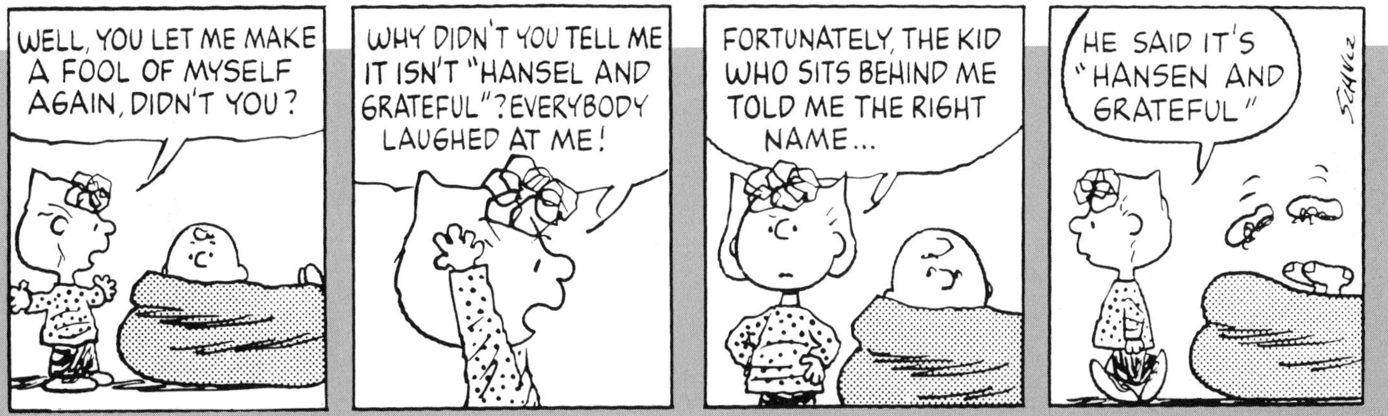
WELL, YOU LET ME MAKE A FOOL OF MYSELF AGAIN, DIDN'T YOU ?
WHY DIDN'T YOU TELL ME IT ISN'T "HANSEL AND GRATEFUL"? EVERYBODY LAUGHED AT ME!
FORTUNATELY, THE KID WHO SITS BEHIND ME TOLD ME THE RIGHT NAME...
HE SAID IT'S "HANSEN AND GRATEFUL"

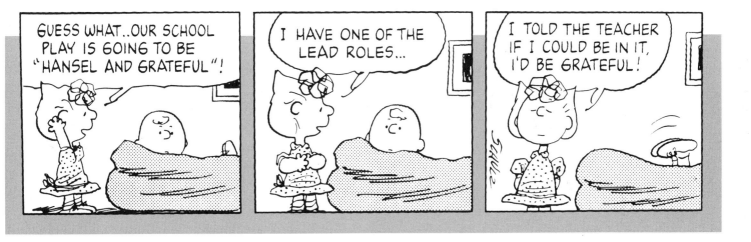

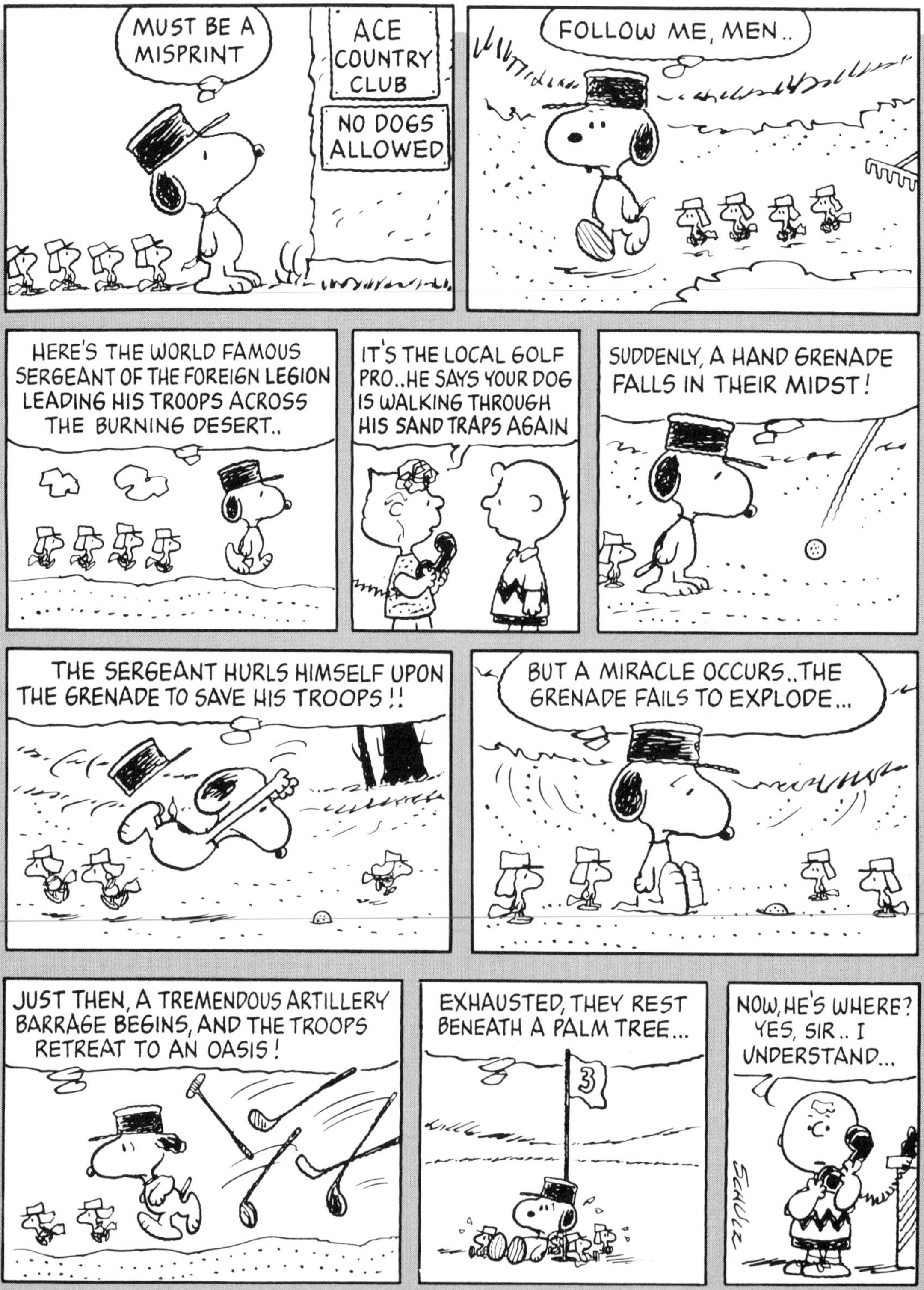
MUST BE A MISPRINT
ACE COUNTRY CLUB
NO DOGS ALLOWED
FOLLOW ME, MEN..
HERE'S THE WORLD FAMOUS SERGEANT OF THE FOREIGN LEGION LEADING HIS TROOPS ACROSS THE BURNING DESERT..
IT'S THE LOCAL GOLF PRO..HE SAYS YOUR DOG IS WALKING THROUGH HIS SAND TRAPS AGAIN
SUDDENLY, A HAND GRENADE FALLS IN THEIR MIDST!
THE SERGEANT HURLS HIMSELF UPON THE GRENADE TO SAVE HIS TROOPS!!
BUT A MIRACLE OCCURS..THE GRENADE FAILS TO EXPLODE...
JUST THEN, A TREMENDOUS ARTILLERY BARRAGE BEGINS, AND THE TROOPS RETREAT TO AN OASIS!
EXHAUSTED, THEY REST BENEATH A PALM TREE...
3
NOW, HE'S WHERE? YES, SIR.. I UNDERSTAND...
SCHULZ

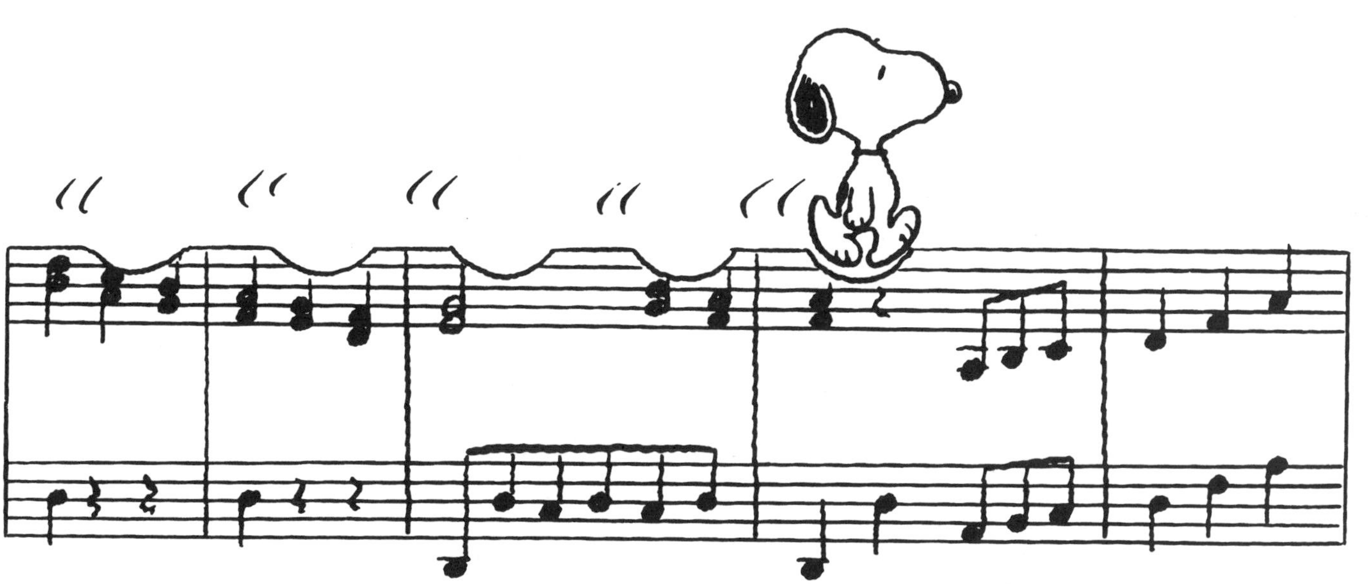

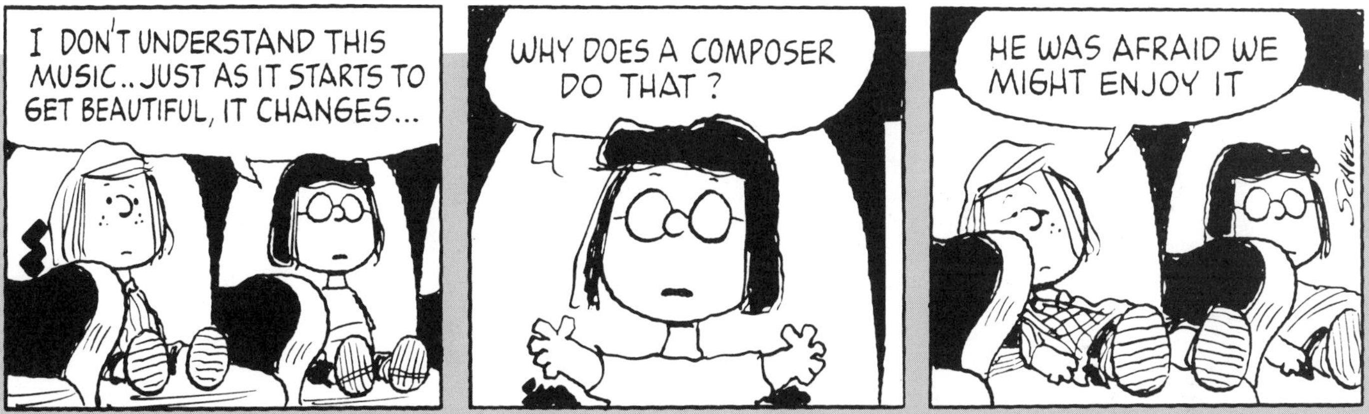
I DON'T UNDERSTAND THIS MUSIC.. JUST AS IT STARTS TO GET BEAUTIFUL, IT CHANGES...
WHY DOES A COMPOSER DO THAT ?
HE WAS AFRAID WE MIGHT ENJOY IT
SCHULZ

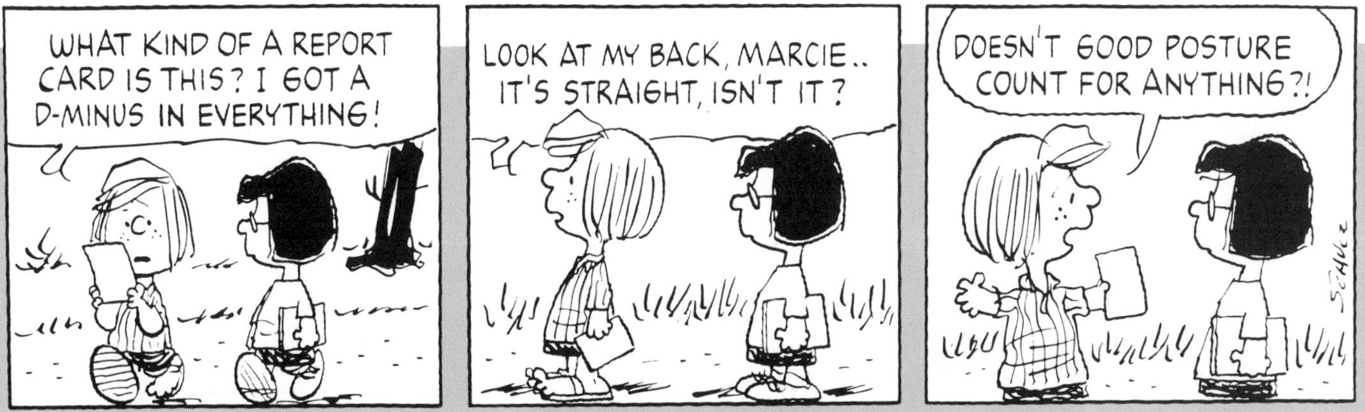
WHAT KIND OF A REPORT CARD IS THIS? I GOT A D-MINUS IN EVERYTHING!
LOOK AT MY BACK, MARCIE.. IT'S STRAIGHT, ISN'T IT?
DOESN'T GOOD POSTURE COUNT FOR ANYTHING?!
SCHULZ

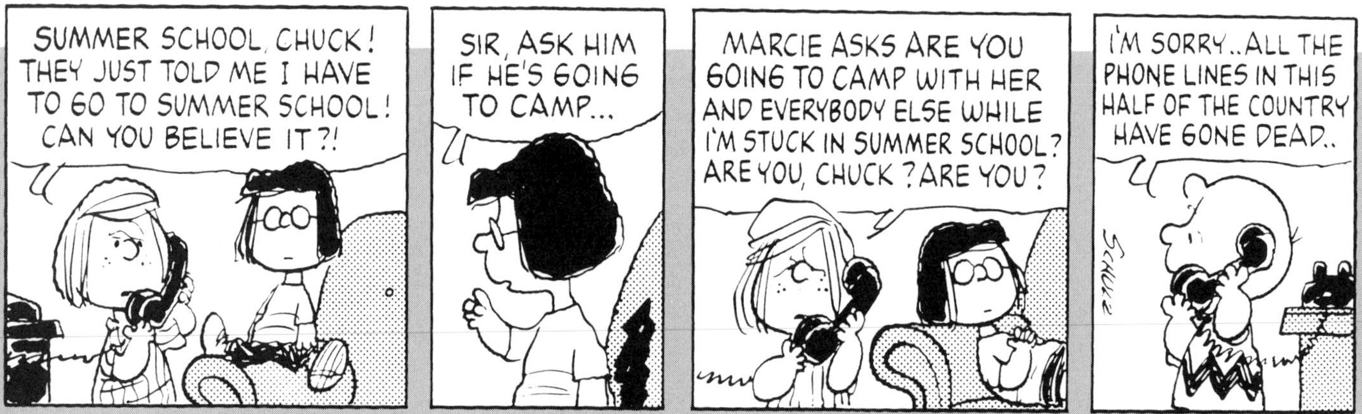
SUMMER SCHOOL, CHUCK! THEY JUST TOLD ME I HAVE TO GO TO SUMMER SCHOOL! CAN YOU BELIEVE IT?!
SIR, ASK HIM IF HE'S GOING TO CAMP...
MARCIE ASKS ARE YOU GOING TO CAMP WITH HER AND EVERYBODY ELSE WHILE I'M STUCK IN SUMMER SCHOOL? ARE YOU, CHUCK? ARE YOU?
I'M SORRY..ALL THE PHONE LINES IN THIS HALF OF THE COUNTRY HAVE GONE DEAD..

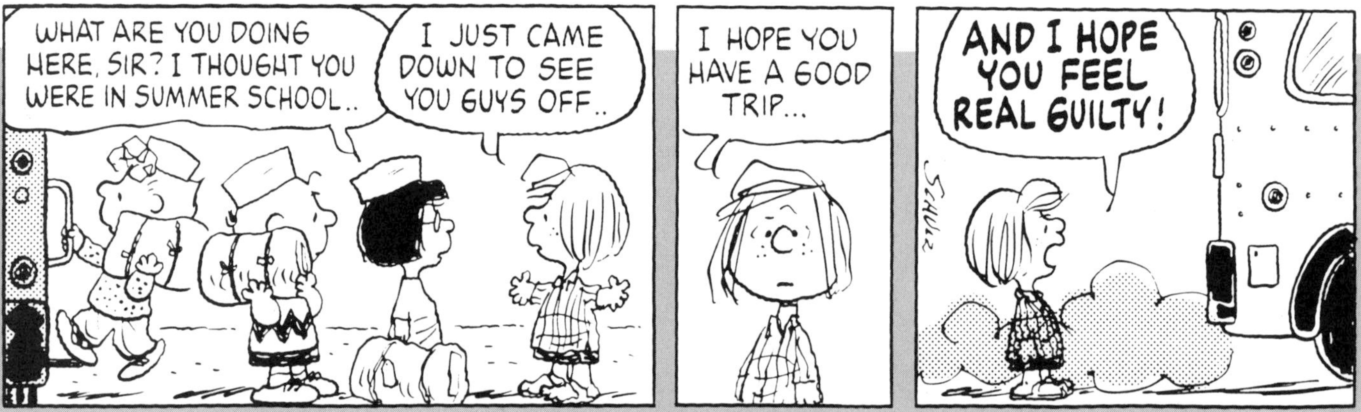
WHAT ARE YOU DOING HERE, SIR? I THOUGHT YOU WERE IN SUMMER SCHOOL..
I JUST CAME DOWN TO SEE YOU GUYS OFF..
I HOPE YOU HAVE A GOOD TRIP...
AND I HOPE YOU FEEL REAL GUILTY!

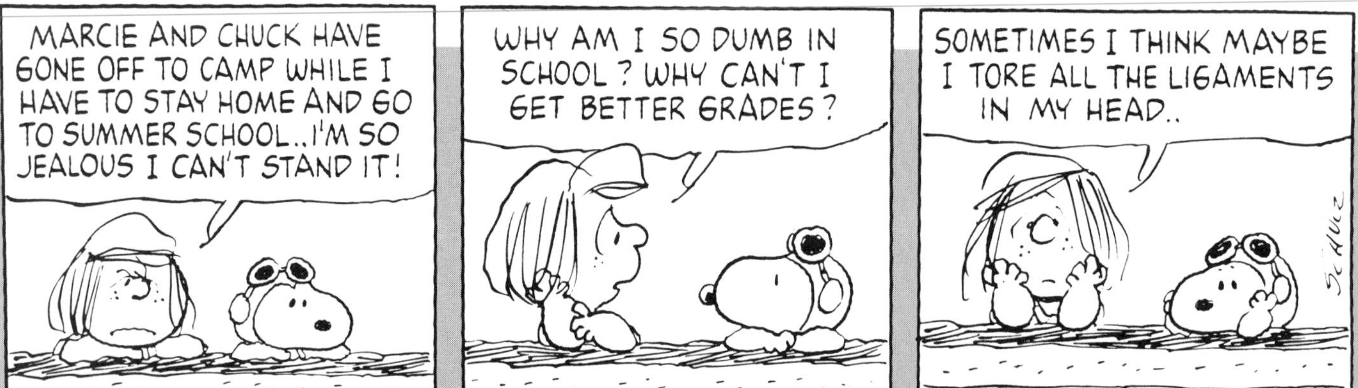
MARCIE AND CHUCK HAVE GONE OFF TO CAMP WHILE I HAVE TO STAY HOME AND GO TO SUMMER SCHOOL..I'M SO JEALOUS I CAN'T STAND IT!
WHY AM I SO DUMB IN SCHOOL? WHY CAN'T I GET BETTER GRADES?
SOMETIMES I THINK MAYBE I TORE ALL THE LIGAMENTS IN MY HEAD..

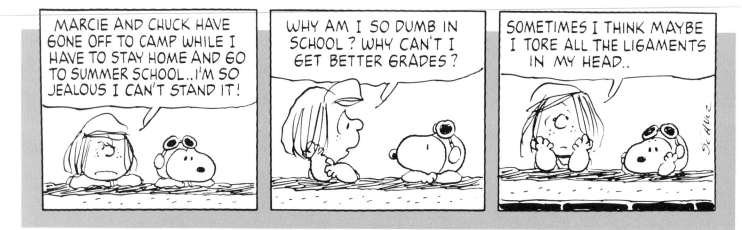

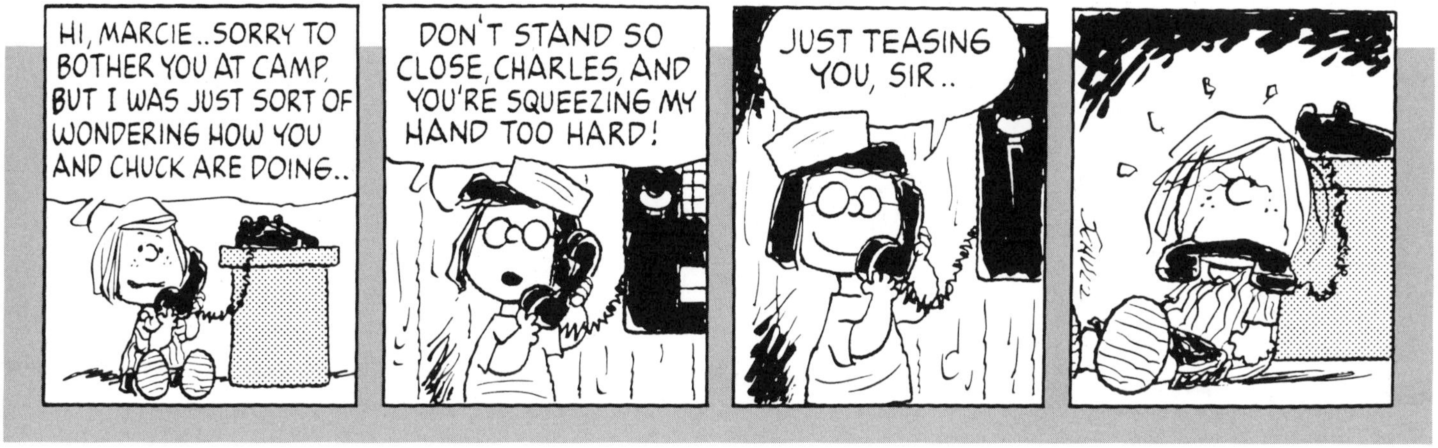
HI, MARCIE..SORRY TO BOTHER YOU AT CAMP, BUT I WAS JUST SORT OF WONDERING HOW YOU AND CHUCK ARE DOING..
DON'T STAND SO CLOSE, CHARLES, AND YOU'RE SQUEEZING MY HAND TOO HARD!
JUST TEASING YOU, SIR..

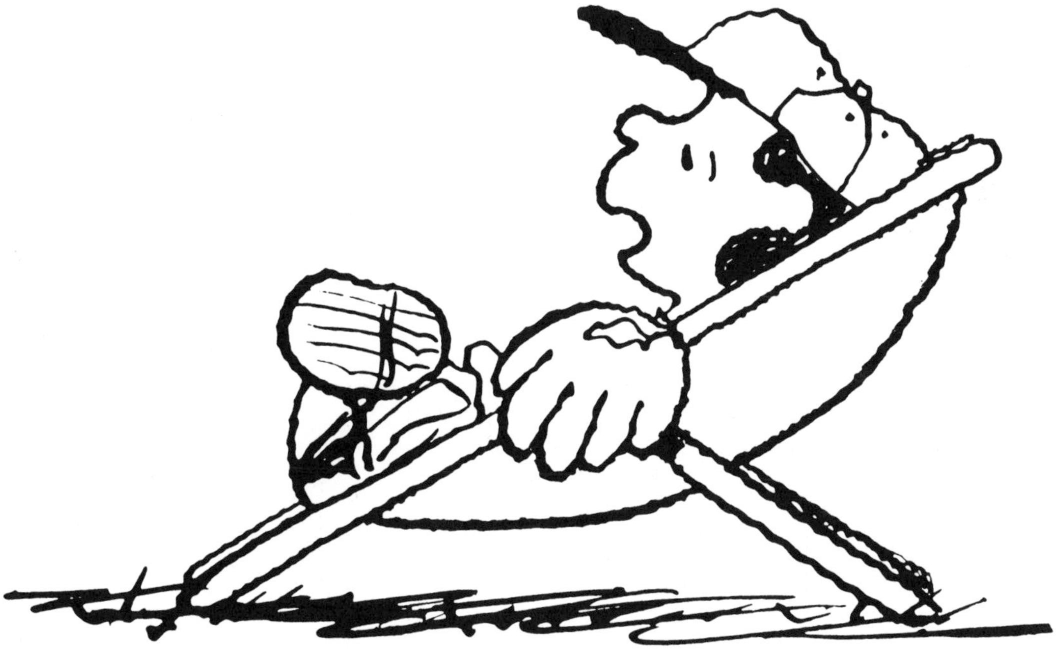

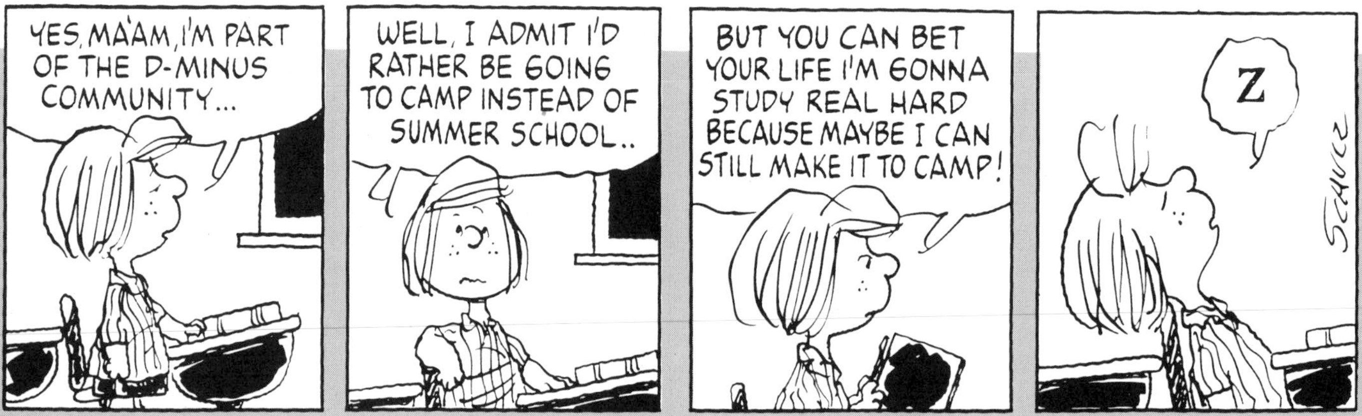
YES, MA'AM, I'M PART OF THE D-MINUS COMMUNITY...
WELL, I ADMIT I'D RATHER BE GOING TO CAMP INSTEAD OF SUMMER SCHOOL..
BUT YOU CAN BET YOUR LIFE I'M GONNA STUDY REAL HARD BECAUSE MAYBE I CAN STILL MAKE IT TO CAMP!
Z
SCHULZ

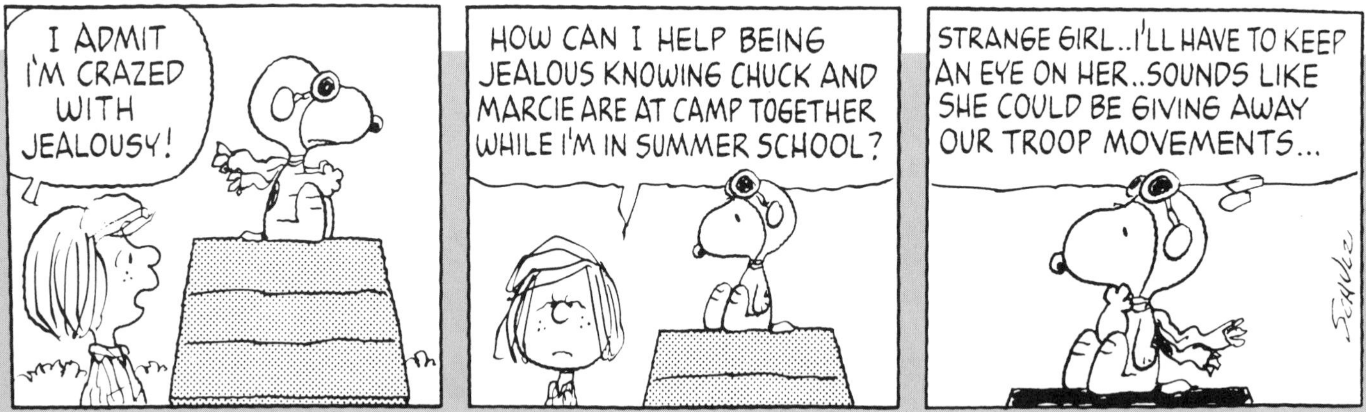
I ADMIT I'M CRAZED WITH JEALOUSY!
HOW CAN I HELP BEING JEALOUS KNOWING CHUCK AND MARCIE ARE AT CAMP TOGETHER WHILE I'M IN SUMMER SCHOOL?
STRANGE GIRL..I'LL HAVE TO KEEP AN EYE ON HER..SOUNDS LIKE SHE COULD BE GIVING AWAY OUR TROOP MOVEMENTS...
SCHULZ

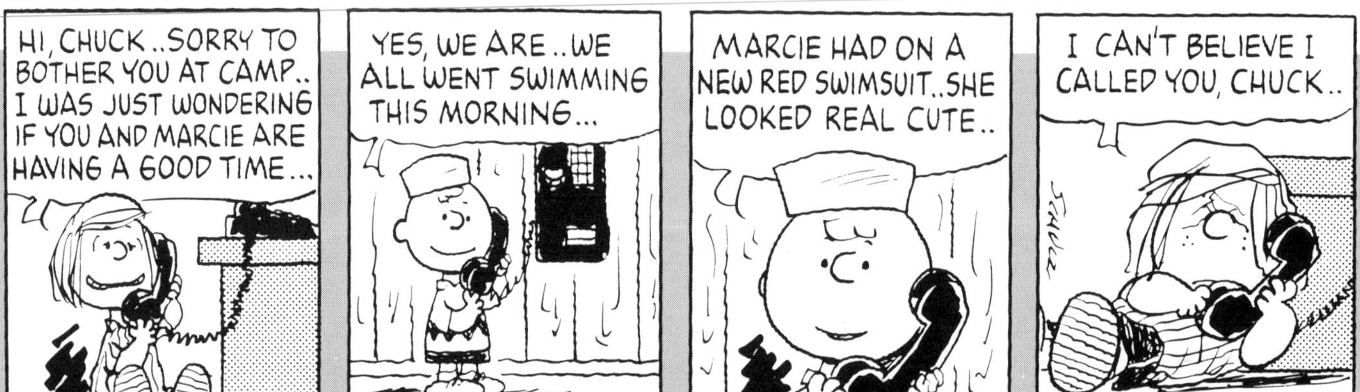
HI, CHUCK..SORRY TO BOTHER YOU AT CAMP.. I WAS JUST WONDERING IF YOU AND MARCIE ARE HAVING A GOOD TIME...
YES, WE ARE..WE ALL WENT SWIMMING THIS MORNING...
MARCIE HAD ON A NEW RED SWIMSUIT..SHE LOOKED REAL CUTE..
I CAN'T BELIEVE I CALLED YOU, CHUCK..
SCHULZ

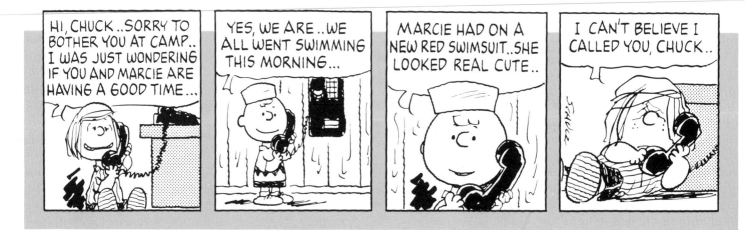

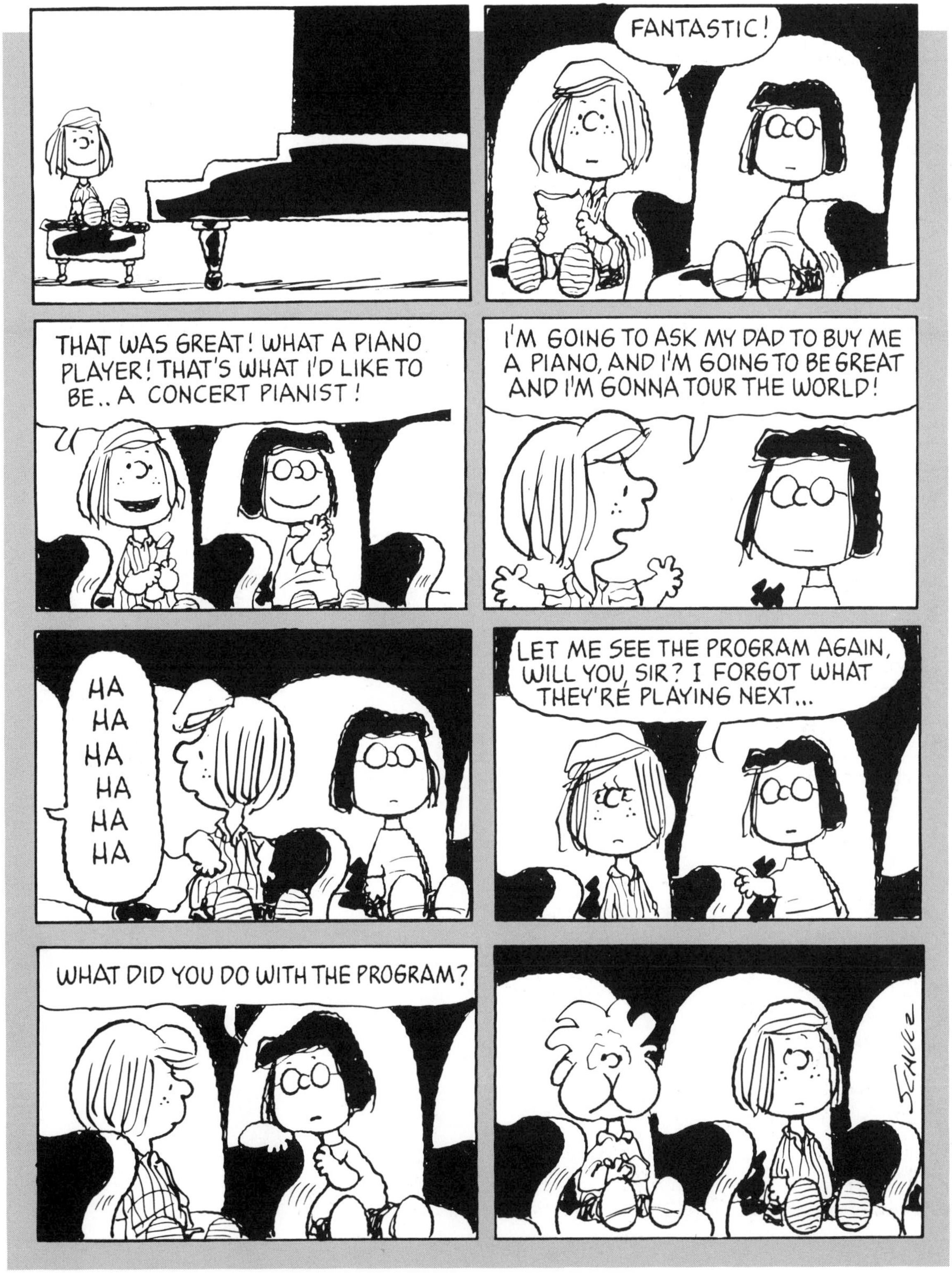
FANTASTIC!
THAT WAS GREAT! WHAT A PIANO PLAYER! THAT'S WHAT I'D LIKE TO BE.. A CONCERT PIANIST!
I'M GOING TO ASK MY DAD TO BUY ME A PIANO, AND I'M GOING TO BE GREAT AND I'M GONNA TOUR THE WORLD!
HA HA HA HA HA HA
LET ME SEE THE PROGRAM AGAIN, WILL YOU, SIR? I FORGOT WHAT THEY'RE PLAYING NEXT...
WHAT DID YOU DO WITH THE PROGRAM?
SCHULZ

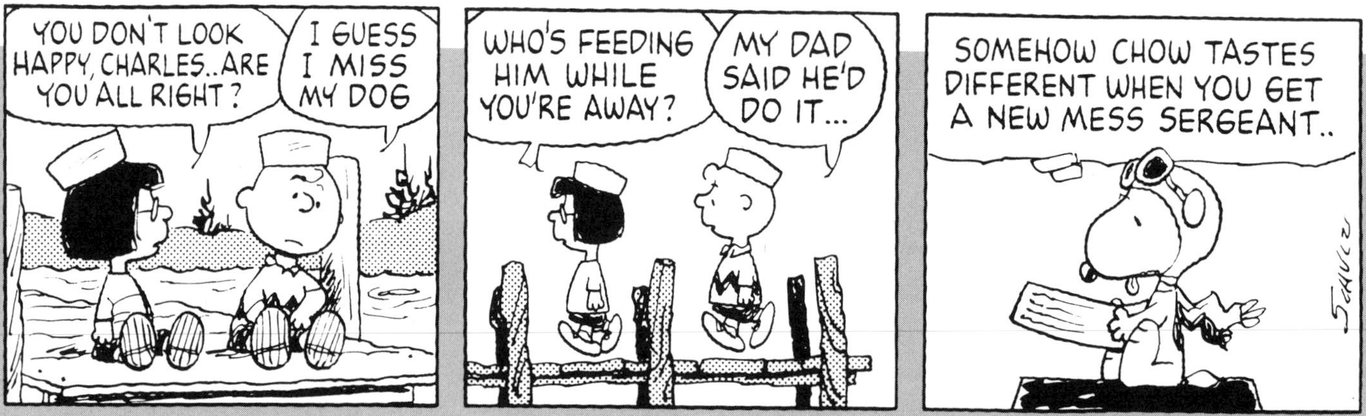
YOU DON'T LOOK HAPPY, CHARLES..ARE YOU ALL RIGHT?
I GUESS I MISS MY DOG
WHO'S FEEDING HIM WHILE YOU'RE AWAY?
MY DAD SAID HE'D DO IT...
SOMEHOW CHOW TASTES DIFFERENT WHEN YOU GET A NEW MESS SERGEANT..

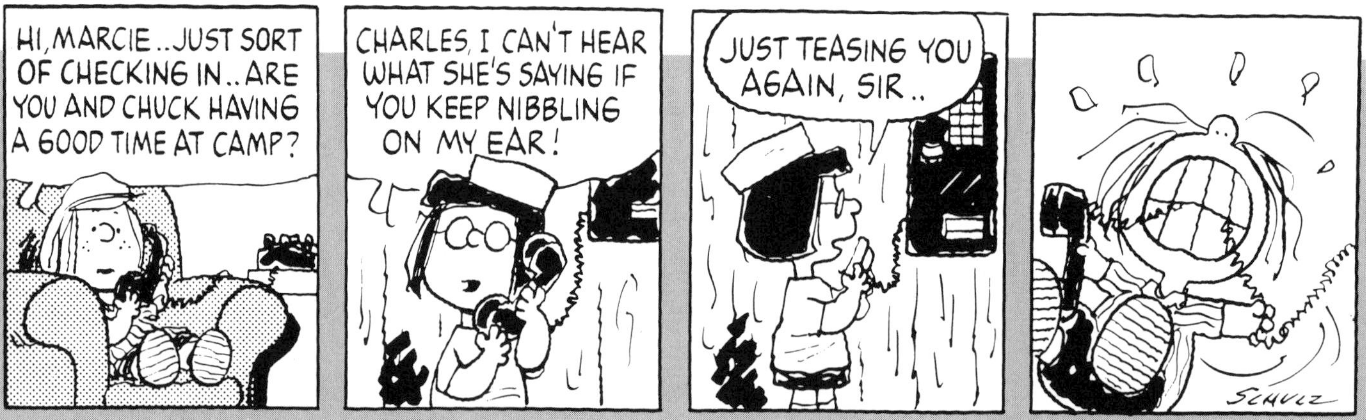
HI, MARCIE..JUST SORT OF CHECKING IN..ARE YOU AND CHUCK HAVING A GOOD TIME AT CAMP?
CHARLES, I CAN'T HEAR WHAT SHE'S SAYING IF YOU KEEP NIBBLING ON MY EAR!
JUST TEASING YOU AGAIN, SIR..

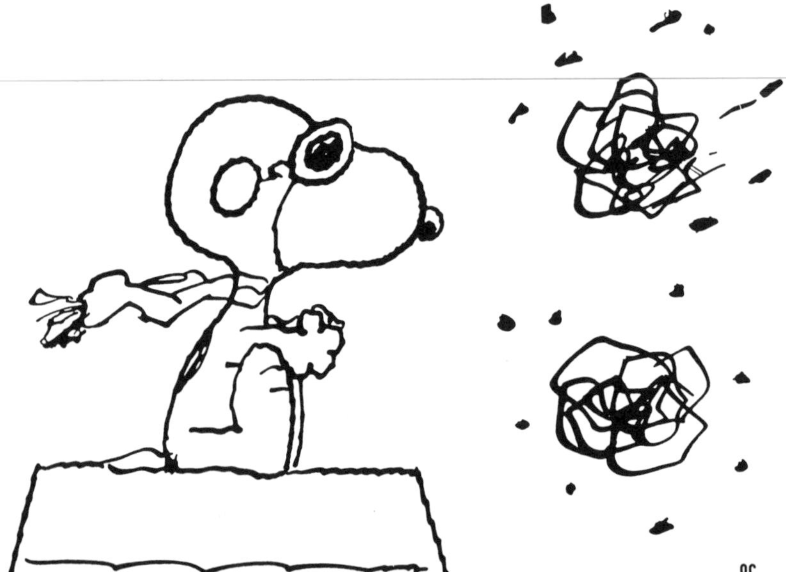

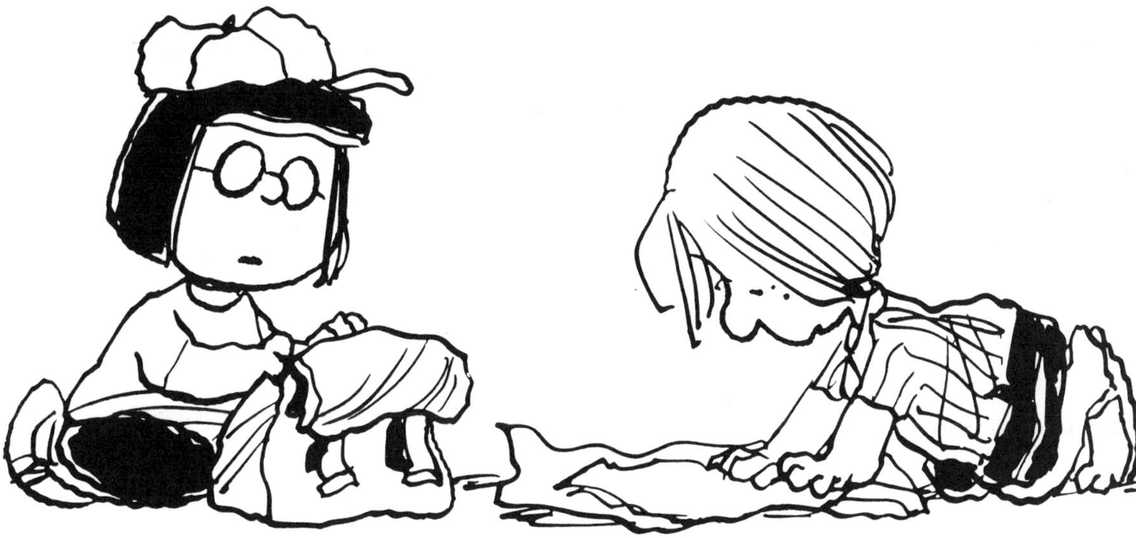

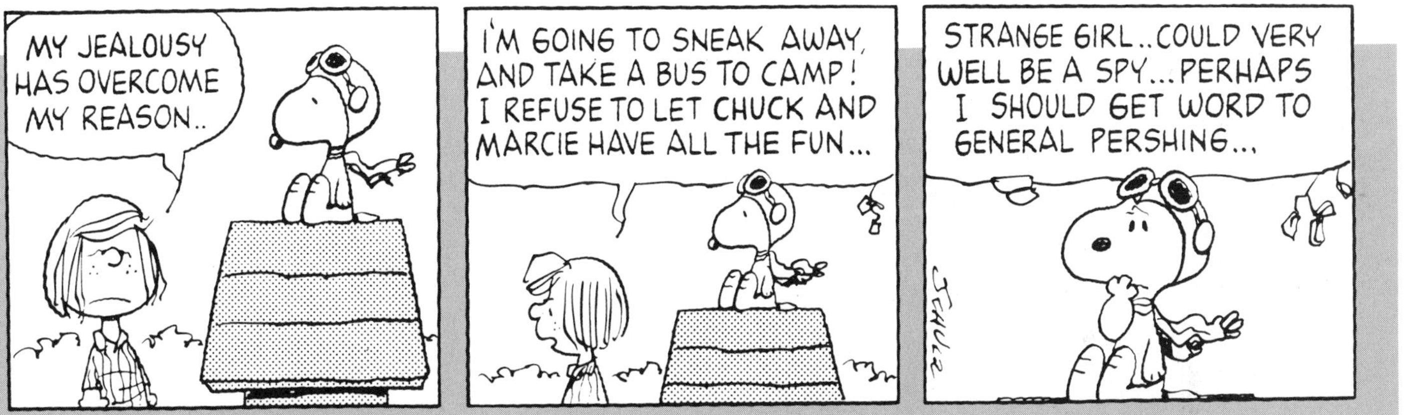
MY JEALOUSY HAS OVERCOME MY REASON..
I'M GOING TO SNEAK AWAY, AND TAKE A BUS TO CAMP! I REFUSE TO LET CHUCK AND MARCIE HAVE ALL THE FUN...
STRANGE GIRL..COULD VERY WELL BE A SPY...PERHAPS I SHOULD GET WORD TO GENERAL PERSHING...

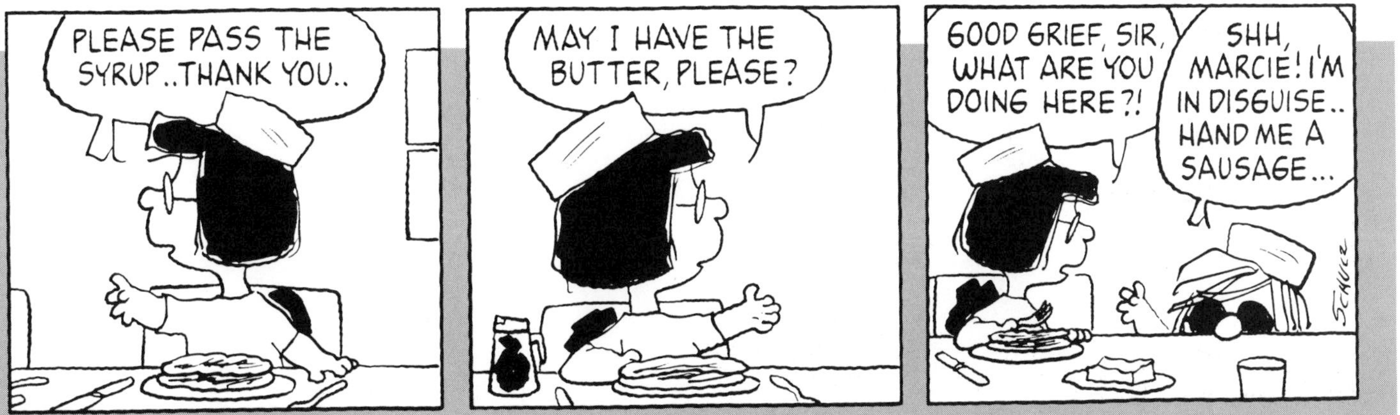
PLEASE PASS THE SYRUP..THANK YOU..
MAY I HAVE THE BUTTER, PLEASE?
GOOD GRIEF, SIR, WHAT ARE YOU DOING HERE?!
SHH, MARCIE! I'M IN DISGUISE.. HAND ME A SAUSAGE...

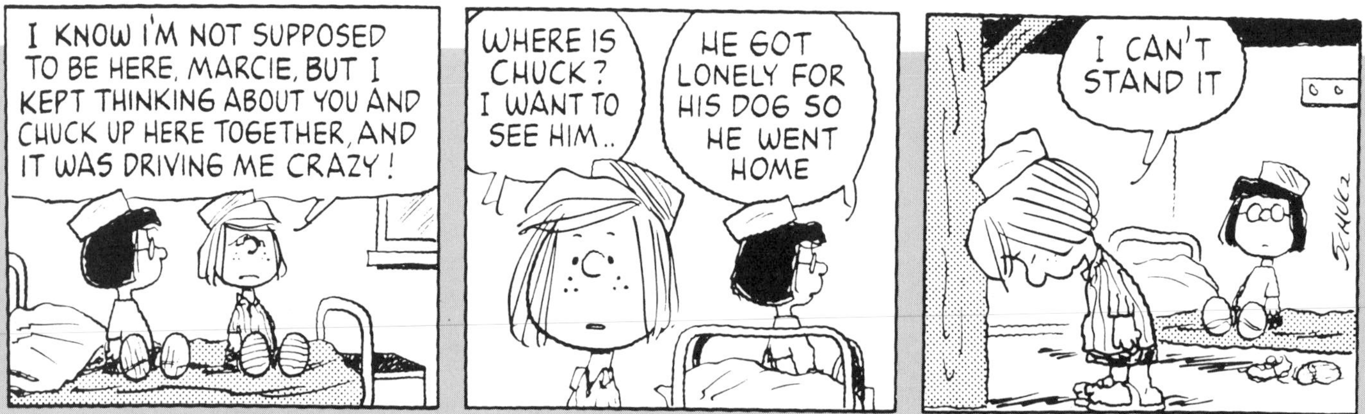
I KNOW I'M NOT SUPPOSED TO BE HERE, MARCIE, BUT I KEPT THINKING ABOUT YOU AND CHUCK UP HERE TOGETHER, AND IT WAS DRIVING ME CRAZY!
WHERE IS CHUCK? I WANT TO SEE HIM..
HE GOT LONELY FOR HIS DOG SO HE WENT HOME
I CAN'T STAND IT

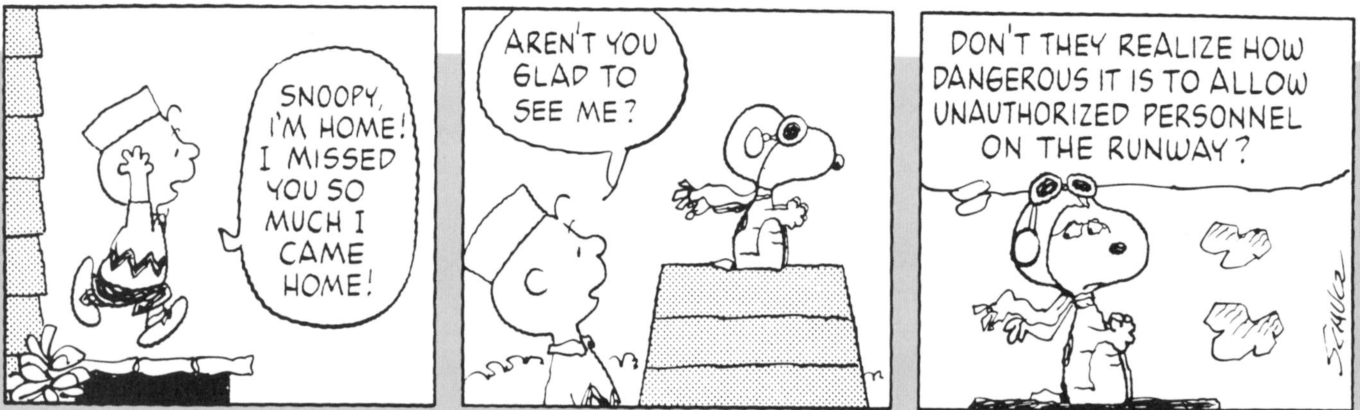
SNOOPY, I'M HOME! I MISSED YOU SO MUCH I CAME HOME!
AREN'T YOU GLAD TO SEE ME?
DON'T THEY REALIZE HOW DANGEROUS IT IS TO ALLOW UNAUTHORIZED PERSONNEL ON THE RUNWAY?

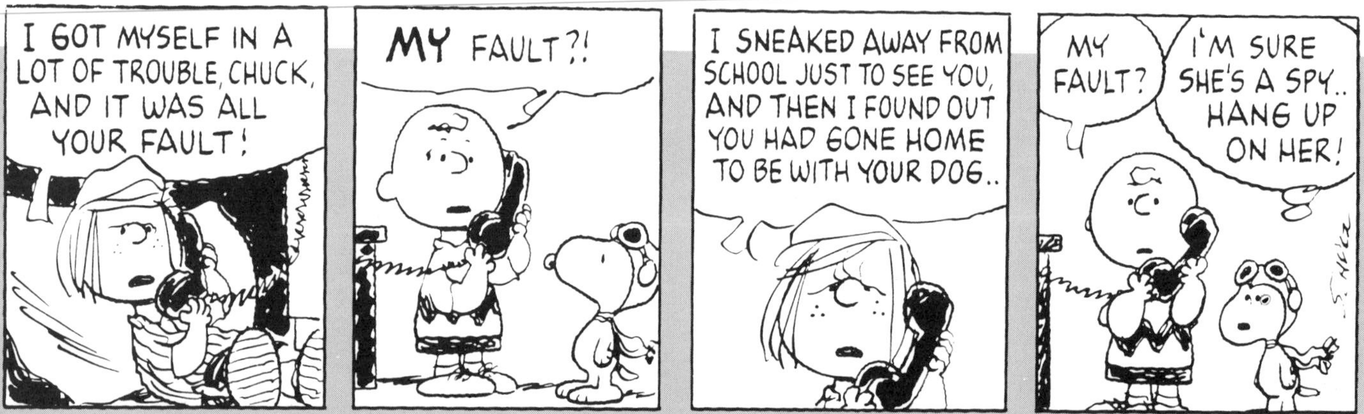
I GOT MYSELF IN A LOT OF TROUBLE, CHUCK, AND IT WAS ALL YOUR FAULT!
MY FAULT?!
I SNEAKED AWAY FROM SCHOOL JUST TO SEE YOU, AND THEN I FOUND OUT YOU HAD GONE HOME TO BE WITH YOUR DOG..
MY FAULT?
I'M SURE SHE'S A SPY.. HANG UP ON HER!

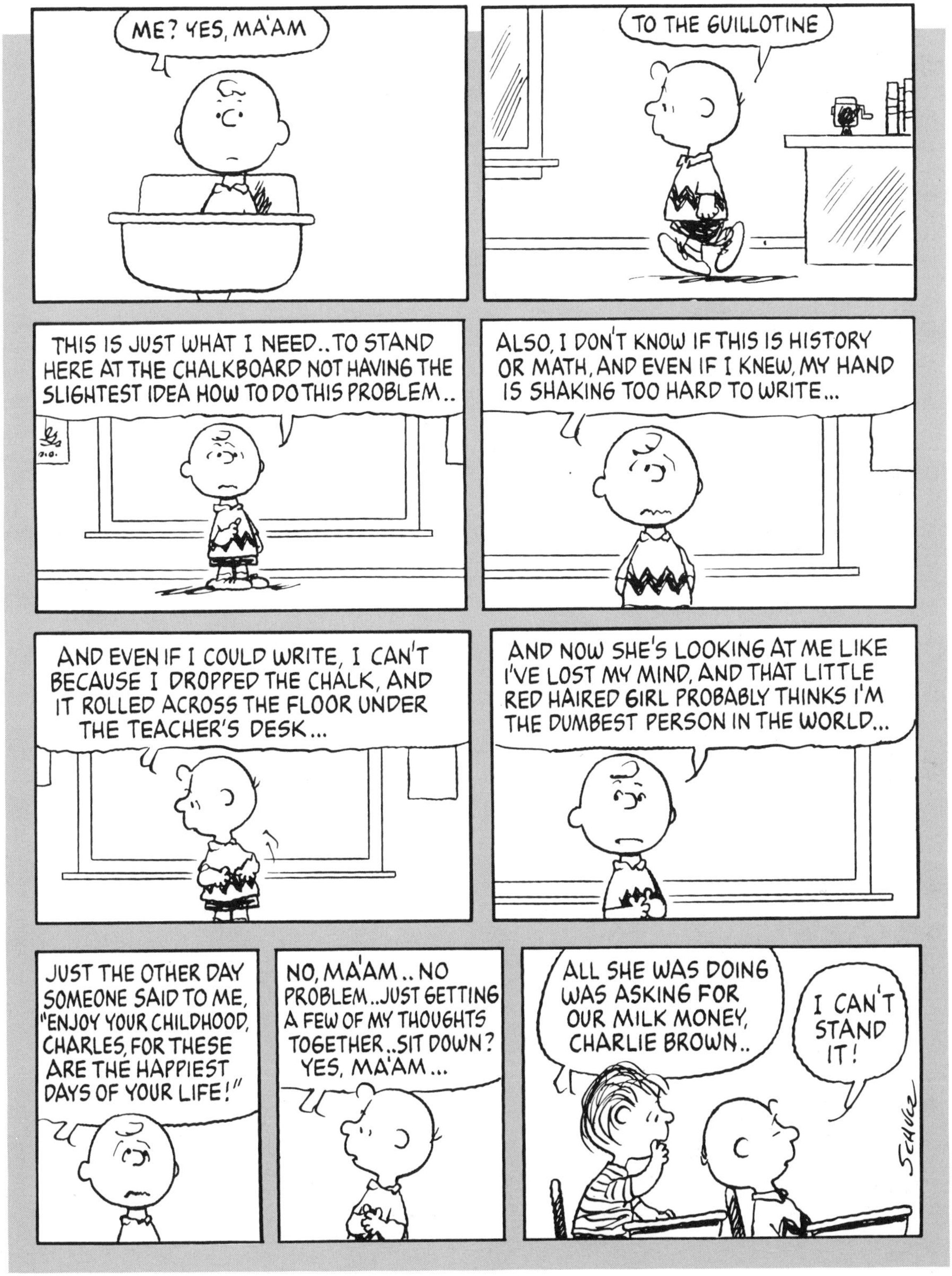
ME? YES, MA'AM
TO THE GUILLOTINE
THIS IS JUST WHAT I NEED..TO STAND HERE AT THE CHALKBOARD NOT HAVING THE SLIGHTEST IDEA HOW TO DO THIS PROBLEM..
ALSO, I DON'T KNOW IF THIS IS HISTORY OR MATH, AND EVEN IF I KNEW, MY HAND IS SHAKING TOO HARD TO WRITE...
AND EVEN IF I COULD WRITE, I CAN'T BECAUSE I DROPPED THE CHALK, AND IT ROLLED ACROSS THE FLOOR UNDER THE TEACHER'S DESK...
AND NOW SHE'S LOOKING AT ME LIKE I'VE LOST MY MIND, AND THAT LITTLE RED HAIRED GIRL PROBABLY THINKS I'M THE DUMBEST PERSON IN THE WORLD...
JUST THE OTHER DAY SOMEONE SAID TO ME, "ENJOY YOUR CHILDHOOD, CHARLES, FOR THESE ARE THE HAPPIEST DAYS OF YOUR LIFE!"
NO, MA'AM.. NO PROBLEM..JUST GETTING A FEW OF MY THOUGHTS TOGETHER..SIT DOWN? YES, MA'AM...
ALL SHE WAS DOING WAS ASKING FOR OUR MILK MONEY, CHARLIE BROWN..
I CAN'T STAND IT!
SCHULZ

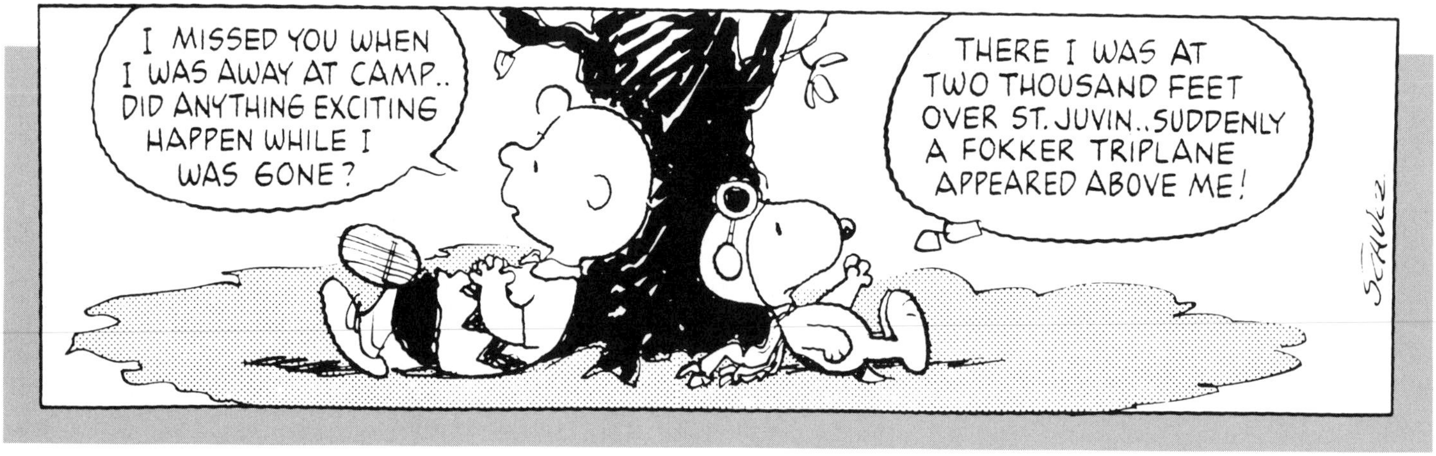
I MISSED YOU WHEN I WAS AWAY AT CAMP.. DID ANYTHING EXCITING HAPPEN WHILE I WAS GONE?
THERE I WAS AT TWO THOUSAND FEET OVER ST. JUVIN..SUDDENLY A FOKKER TRIPLANE APPEARED ABOVE ME!
SCHULZ

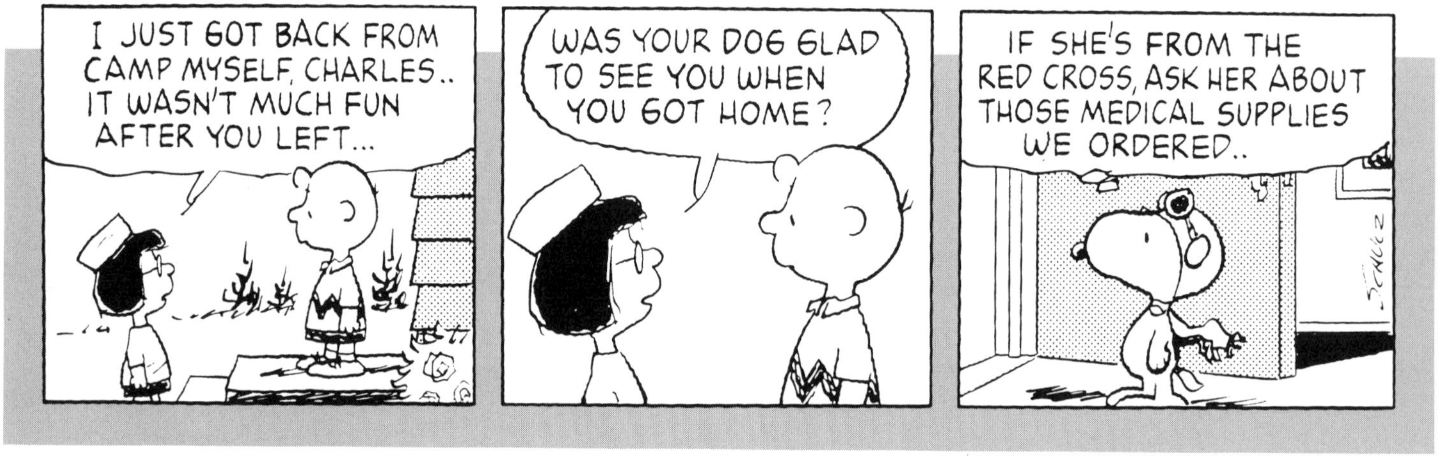
I JUST GOT BACK FROM CAMP MYSELF, CHARLES.. IT WASN'T MUCH FUN AFTER YOU LEFT...
WAS YOUR DOG GLAD TO SEE YOU WHEN YOU GOT HOME?
IF SHE'S FROM THE RED CROSS, ASK HER ABOUT THOSE MEDICAL SUPPLIES WE ORDERED..
SCHULZ

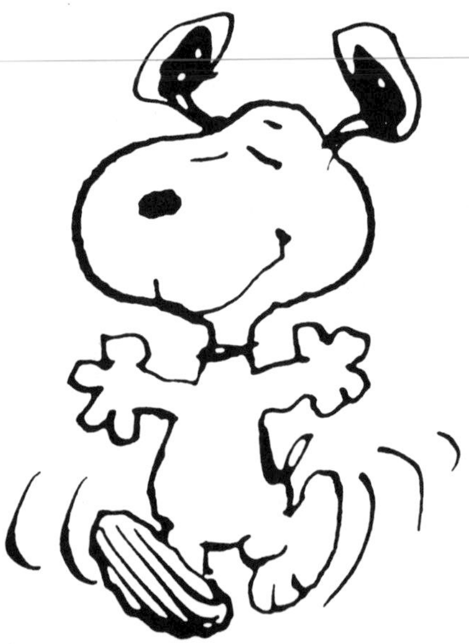

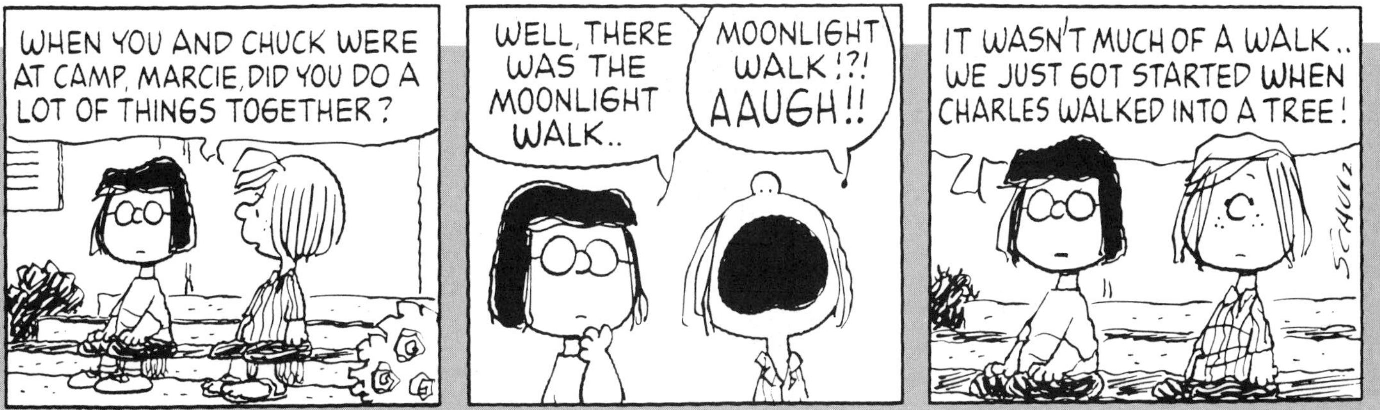
WHEN YOU AND CHUCK WERE AT CAMP, MARCIE, DID YOU DO A LOT OF THINGS TOGETHER?
WELL, THERE WAS THE MOONLIGHT WALK..
MOONLIGHT WALK!?! AAUGH!!
IT WASN'T MUCH OF A WALK.. WE JUST GOT STARTED WHEN CHARLES WALKED INTO A TREE!

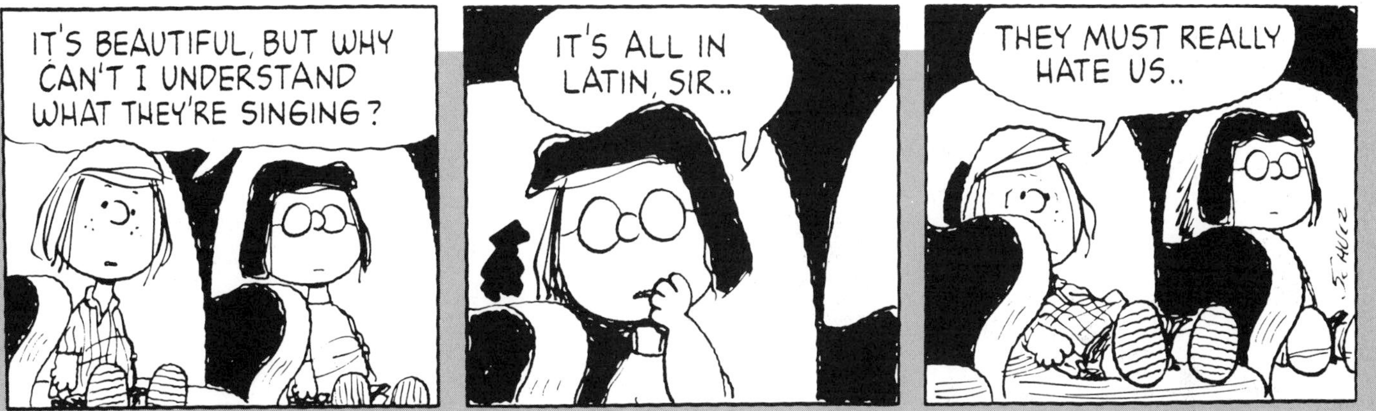
IT'S BEAUTIFUL, BUT WHY CAN'T I UNDERSTAND WHAT THEY'RE SINGING?
IT'S ALL IN LATIN, SIR..
THEY MUST REALLY HATE US..

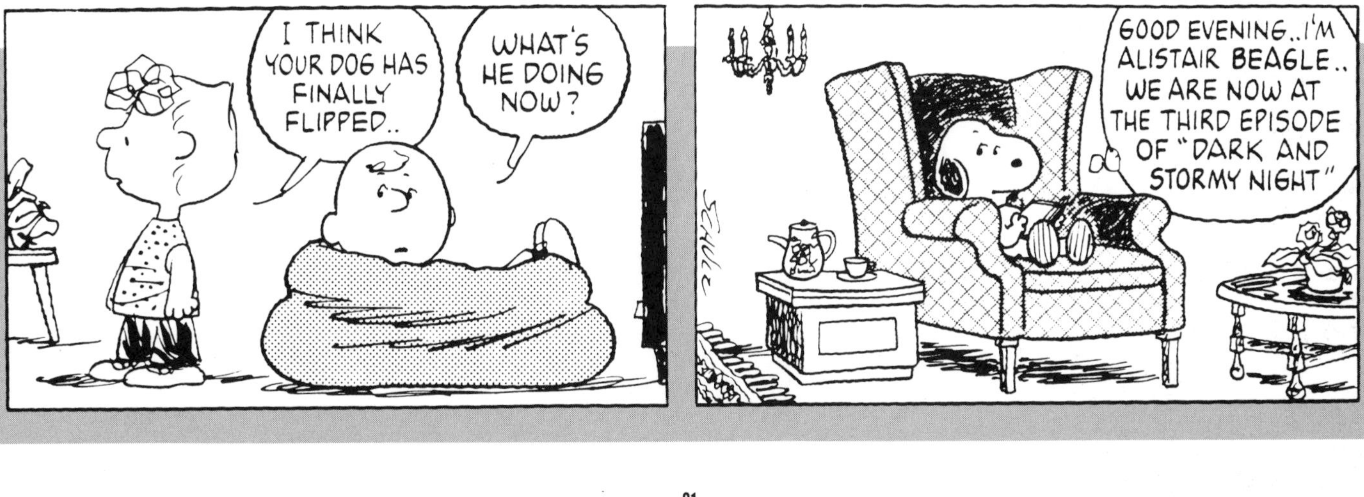
I THINK YOUR DOG HAS FINALLY FLIPPED..
WHAT'S HE DOING NOW?
GOOD EVENING..I'M ALISTAIR BEAGLE.. WE ARE NOW AT THE THIRD EPISODE OF "DARK AND STORMY NIGHT"

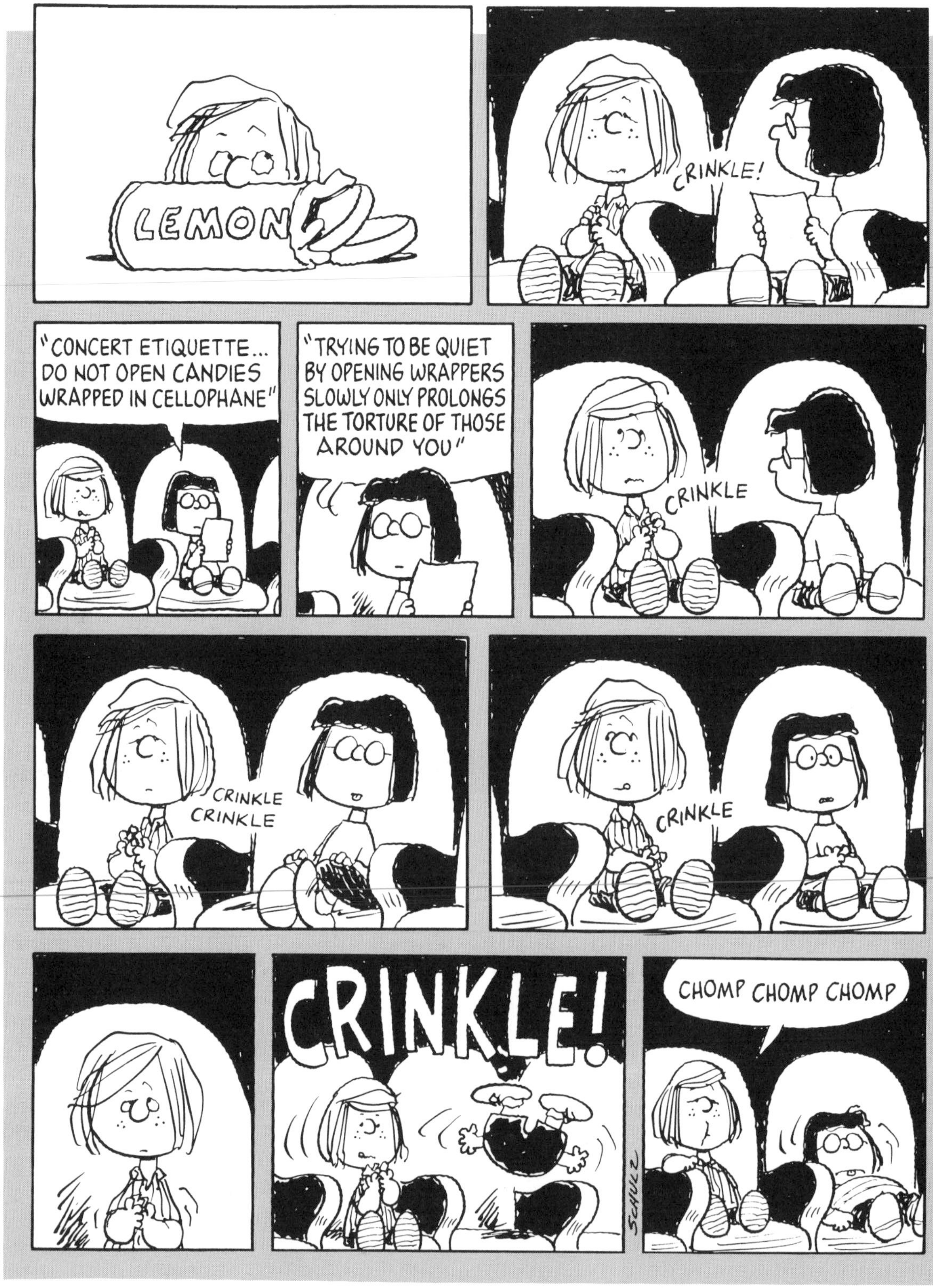
LEMON
CRINKLE!
"CONCERT ETIQUETTE... DO NOT OPEN CANDIES WRAPPED IN CELLOPHANE"
"TRYING TO BE QUIET BY OPENING WRAPPERS SLOWLY ONLY PROLONGS THE TORTURE OF THOSE AROUND YOU"
CRINKLE
CRINKLE CRINKLE
CRINKLE
CRINKLE!
SCHULZ
CHOMP CHOMP CHOMP

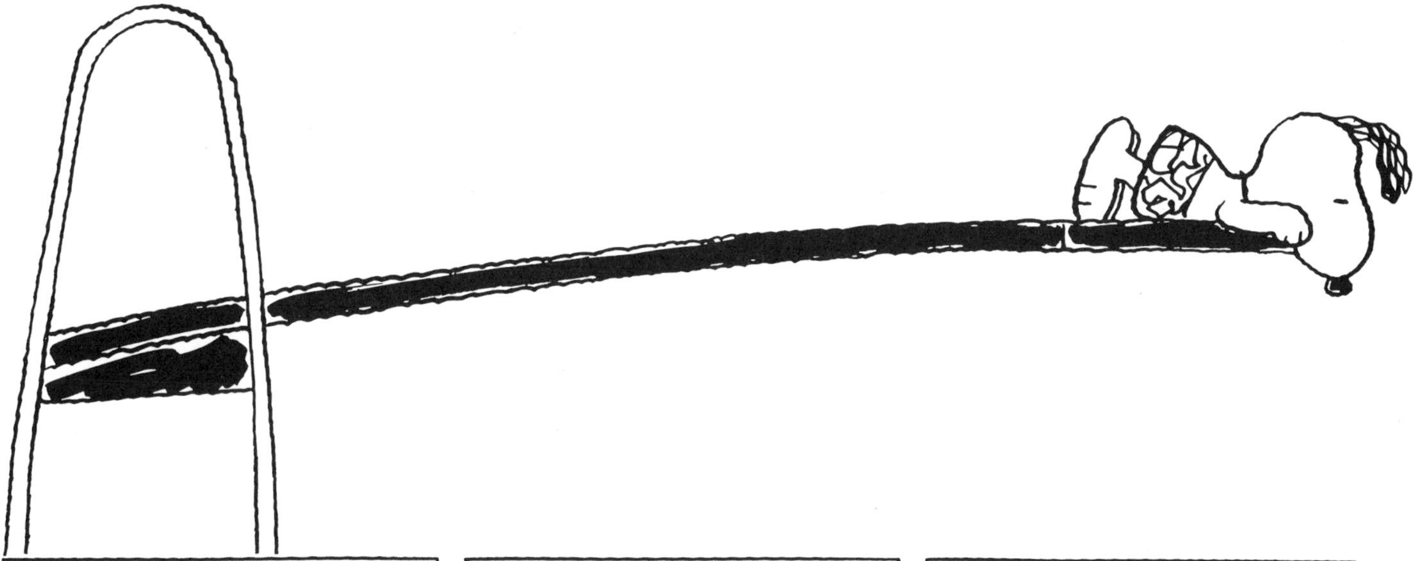

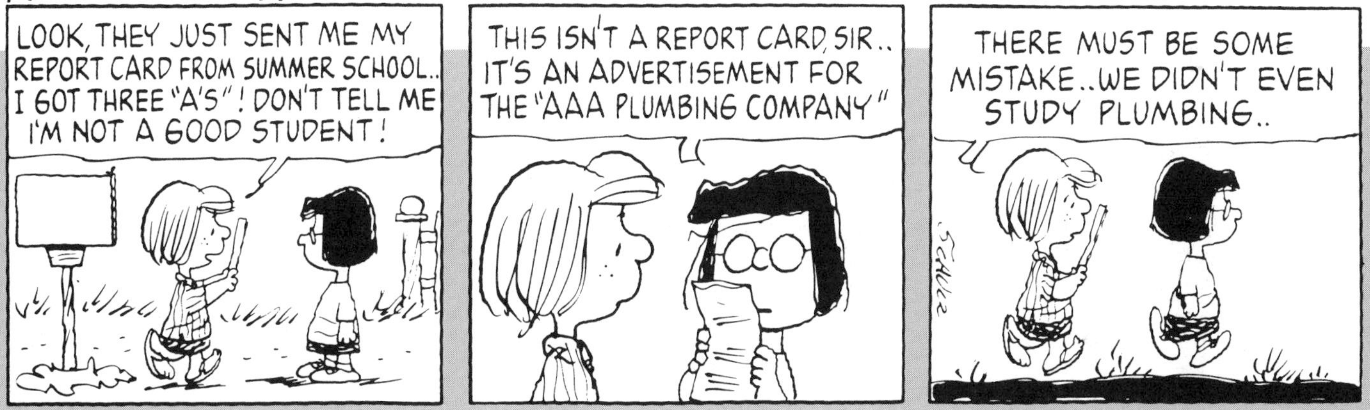
LOOK, THEY JUST SENT ME MY REPORT CARD FROM SUMMER SCHOOL.. I GOT THREE "A'S"! DON'T TELL ME I'M NOT A GOOD STUDENT!
THIS ISN'T A REPORT CARD, SIR.. IT'S AN ADVERTISEMENT FOR THE "AAA PLUMBING COMPANY"
THERE MUST BE SOME MISTAKE..WE DIDN'T EVEN STUDY PLUMBING..

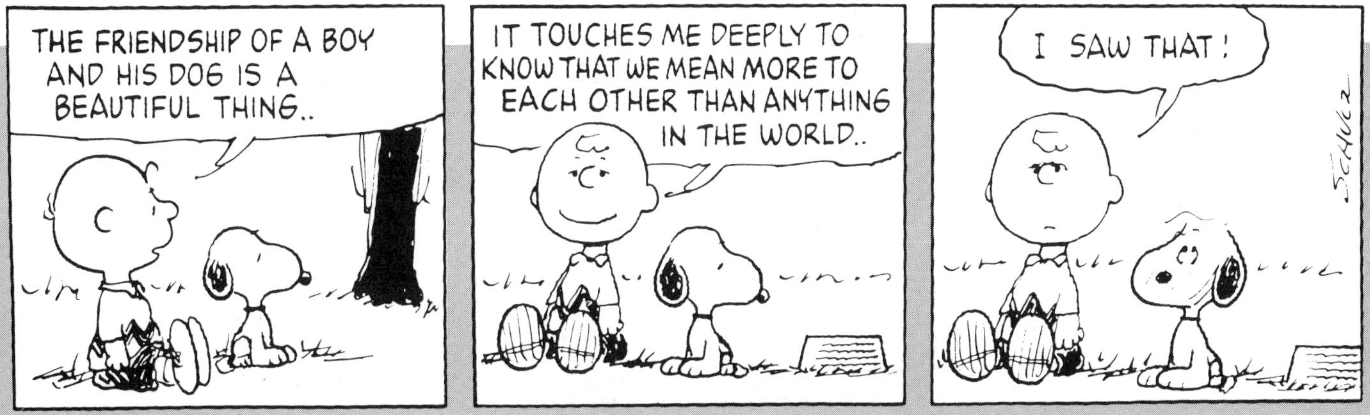
THE FRIENDSHIP OF A BOY AND HIS DOG IS A BEAUTIFUL THING..
IT TOUCHES ME DEEPLY TO KNOW THAT WE MEAN MORE TO EACH OTHER THAN ANYTHING IN THE WORLD..
I SAW THAT!

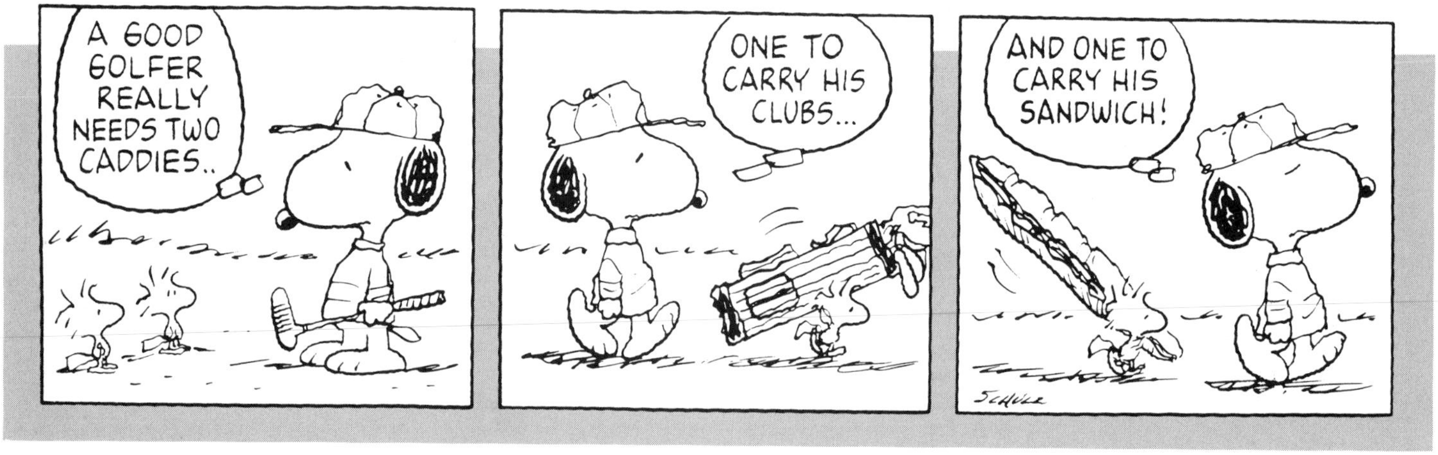
A GOOD GOLFER REALLY NEEDS TWO CADDIES..
ONE TO CARRY HIS CLUBS...
AND ONE TO CARRY HIS SANDWICH!
SCHULZ

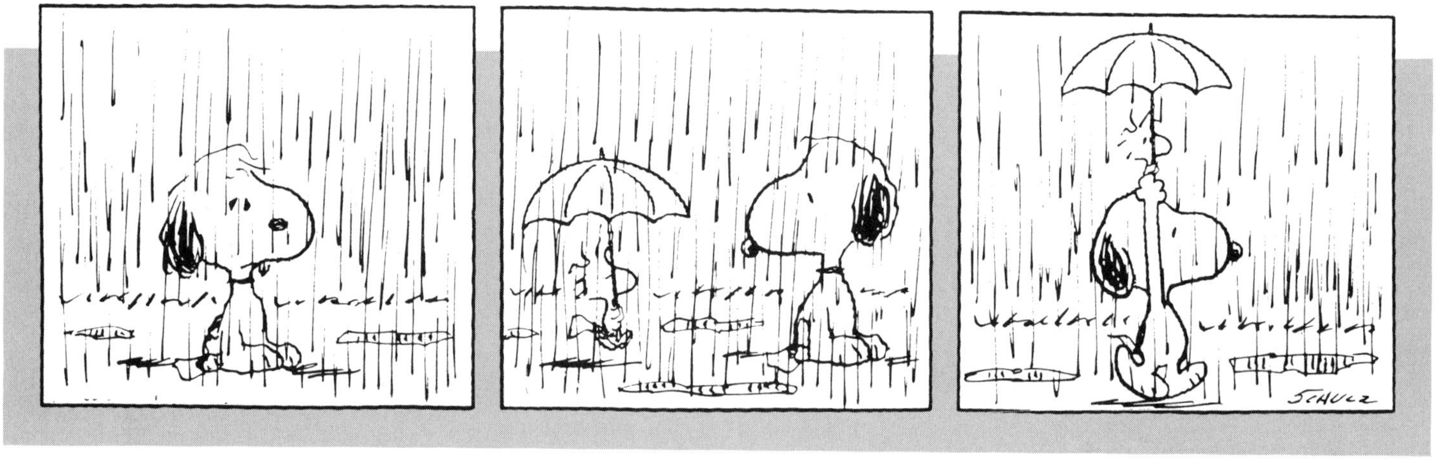
SCHULZ

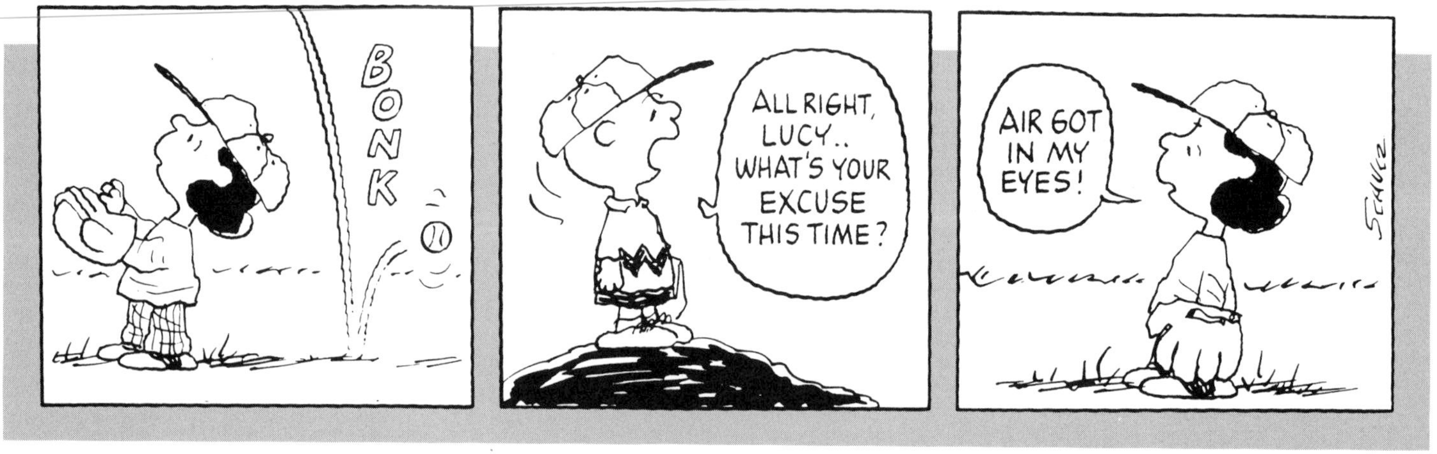
BONK
ALL RIGHT, LUCY.. WHAT'S YOUR EXCUSE THIS TIME?
AIR GOT IN MY EYES!
SCHULZ

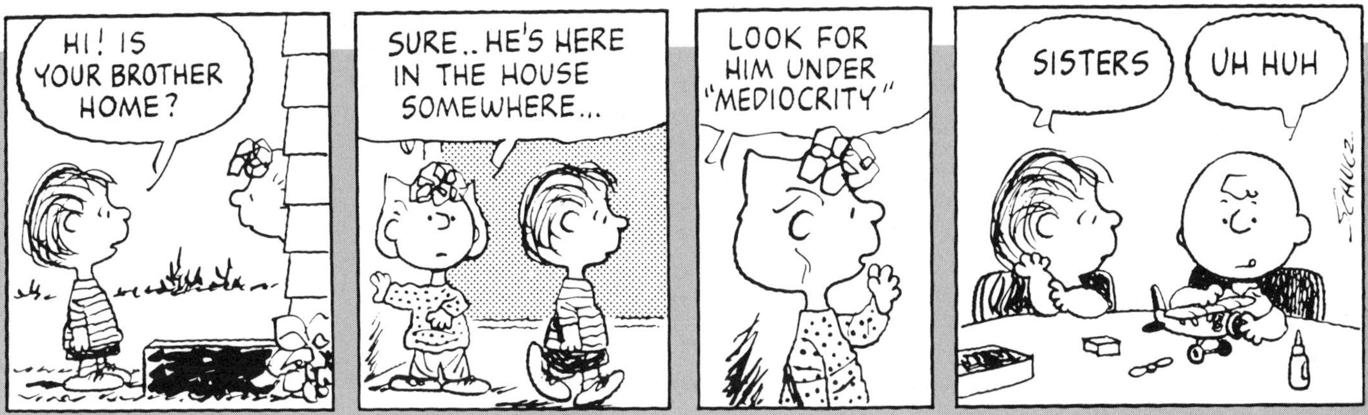
HI! IS YOUR BROTHER HOME?
SURE.. HE'S HERE IN THE HOUSE SOMEWHERE...
LOOK FOR HIM UNDER "MEDIOCRITY"
SISTERS
UH HUH
SCHULZ

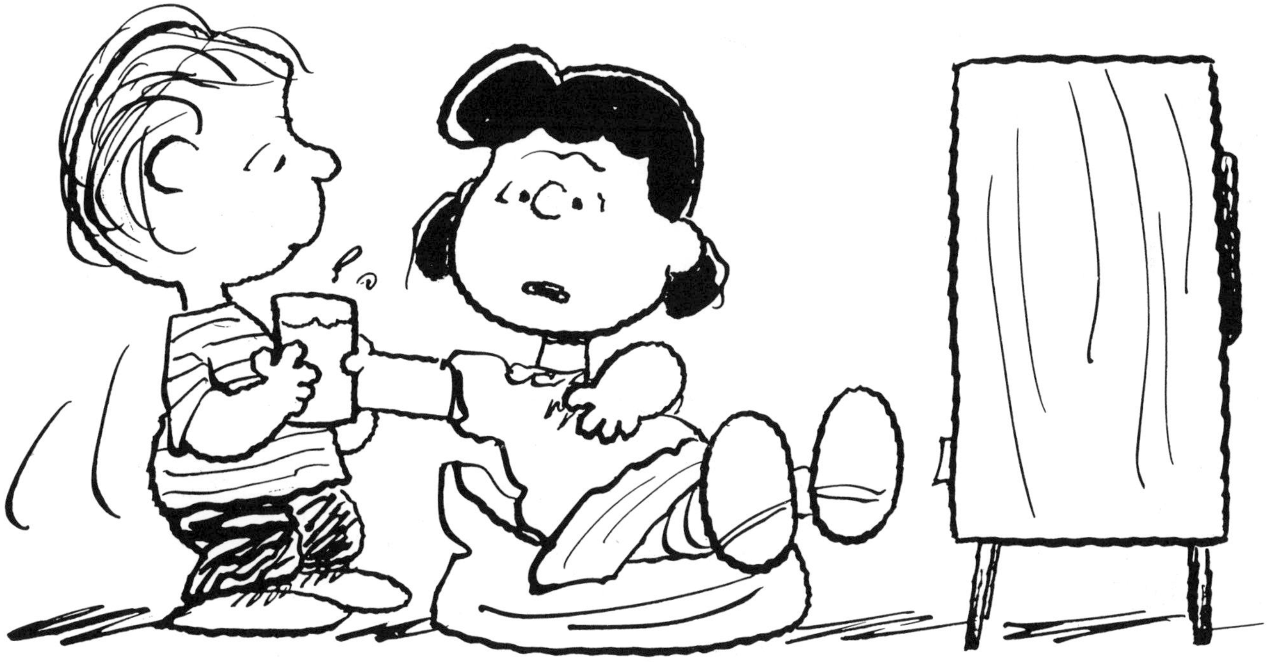

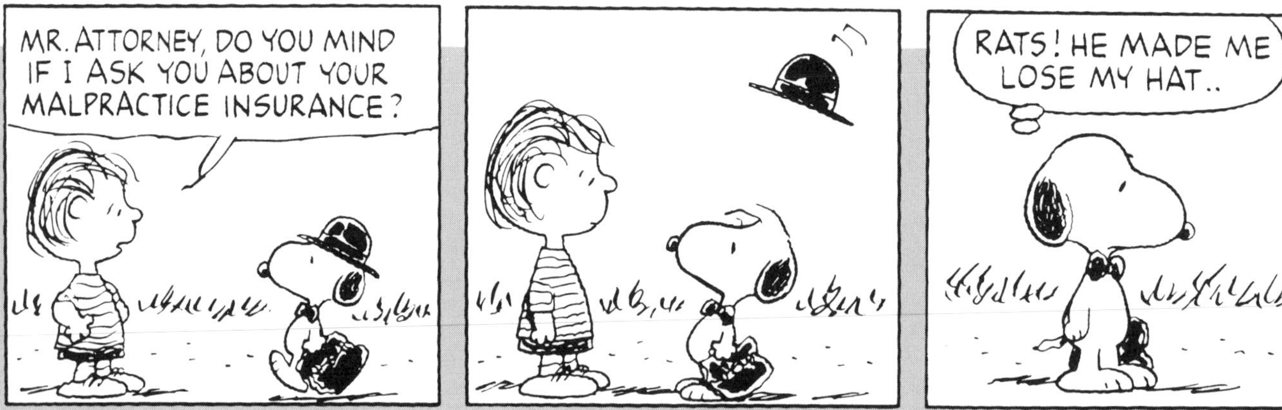
MR. ATTORNEY, DO YOU MIND IF I ASK YOU ABOUT YOUR MALPRACTICE INSURANCE?
RATS! HE MADE ME LOSE MY HAT..
SCHULZ

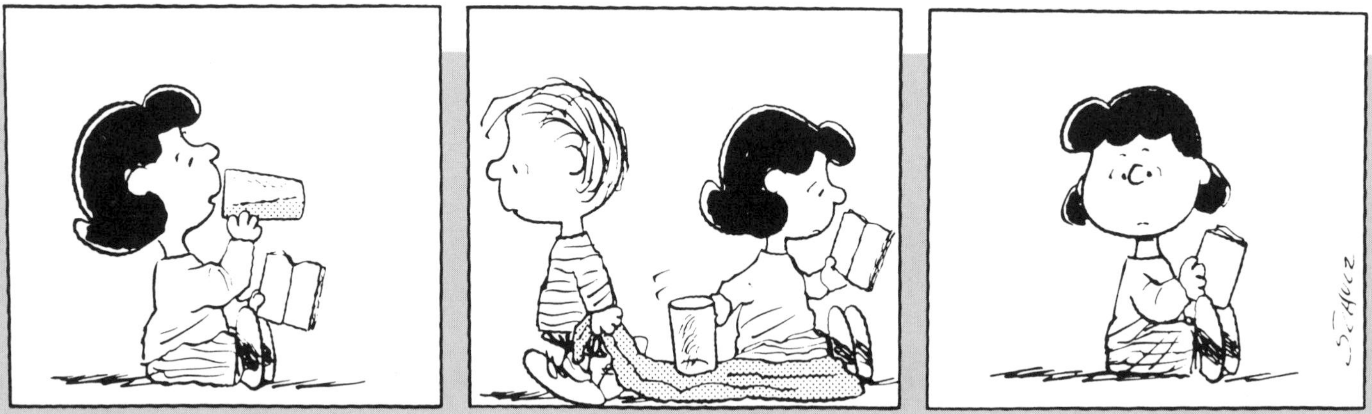
SCHULZ

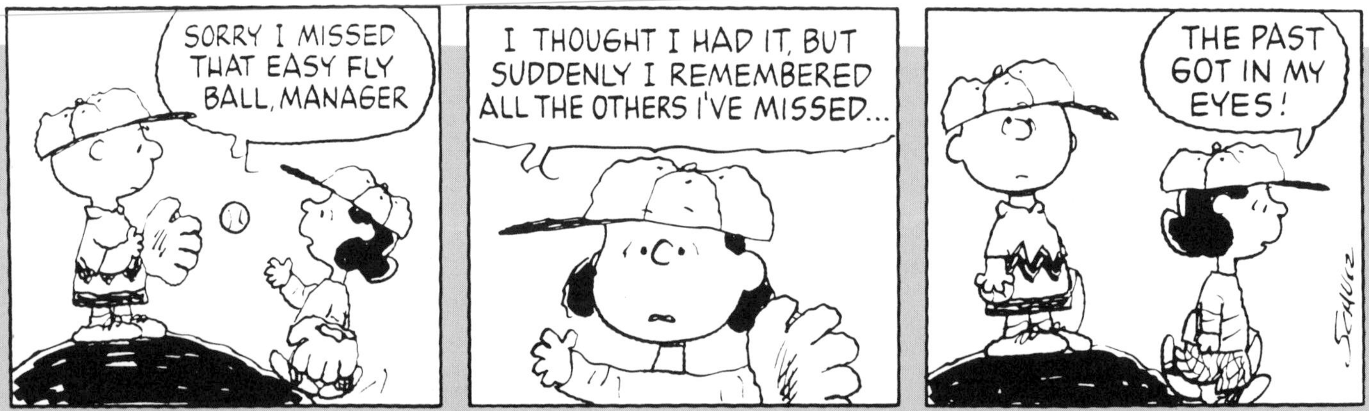
SORRY I MISSED THAT EASY FLY BALL, MANAGER
I THOUGHT I HAD IT, BUT SUDDENLY I REMEMBERED ALL THE OTHERS I'VE MISSED...
THE PAST GOT IN MY EYES!
SCHULZ

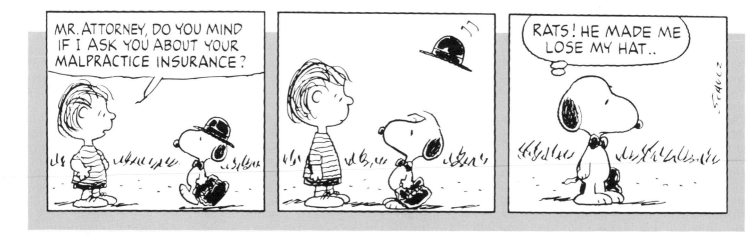

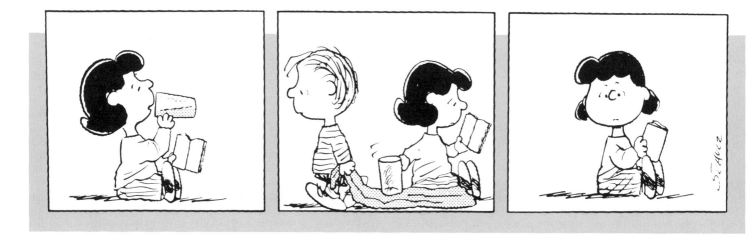

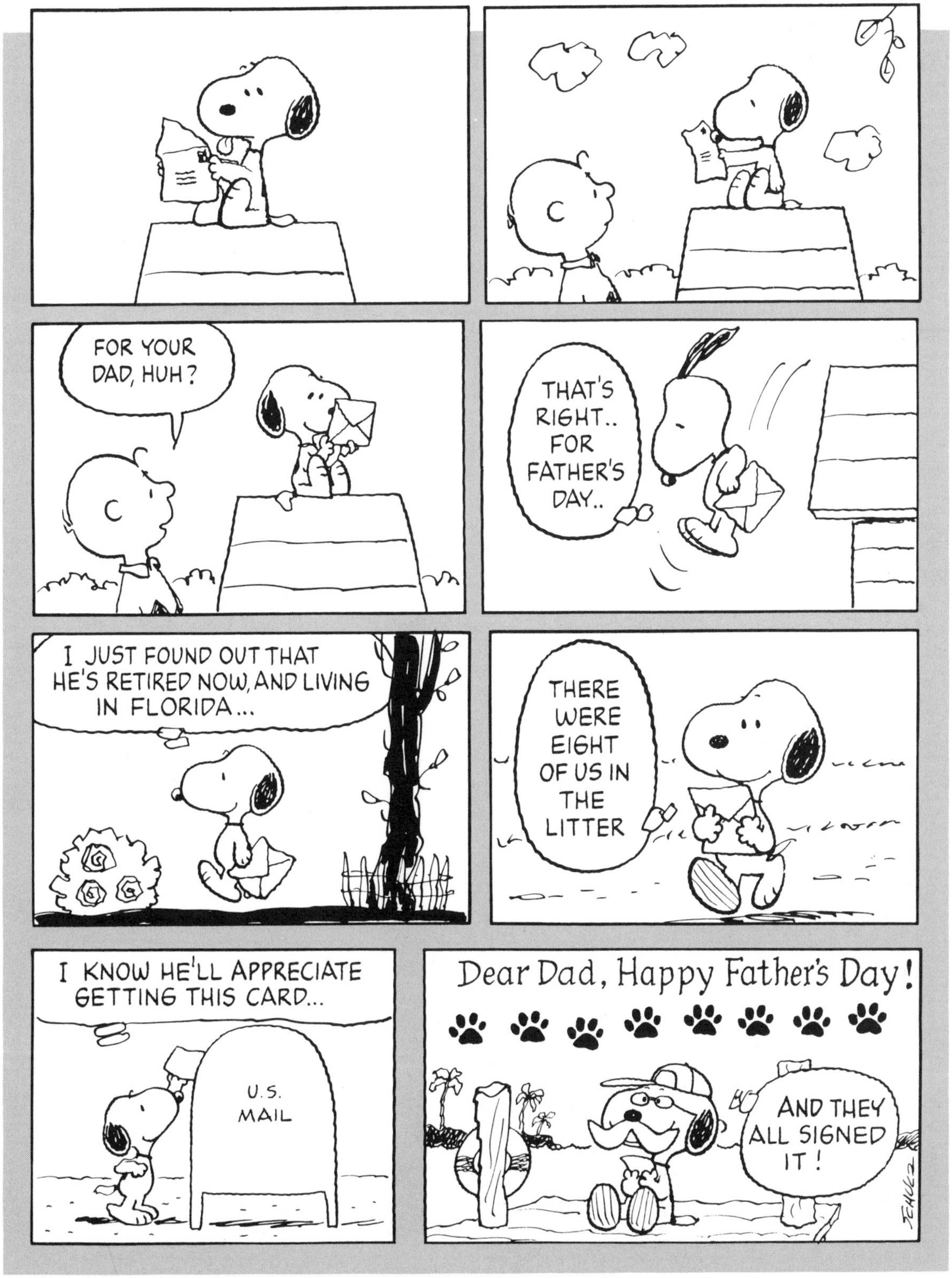
FOR YOUR DAD, HUH?
THAT'S RIGHT.. FOR FATHER'S DAY..
I JUST FOUND OUT THAT HE'S RETIRED NOW, AND LIVING IN FLORIDA...
THERE WERE EIGHT OF US IN THE LITTER
I KNOW HE'LL APPRECIATE GETTING THIS CARD...
U.S. MAIL
Dear Dad, Happy Father's Day!
AND THEY ALL SIGNED IT!
SCHULZ

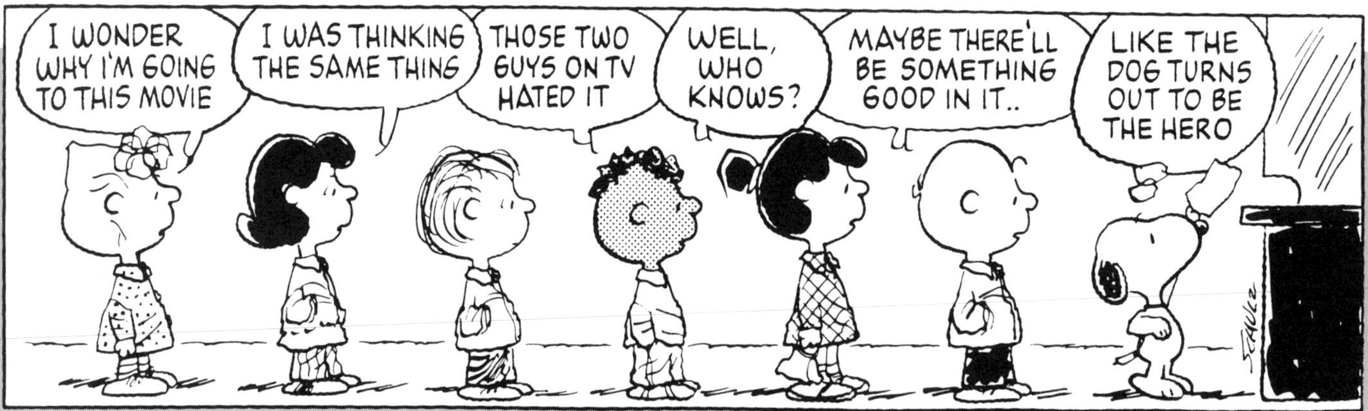
I WONDER WHY I'M GOING TO THIS MOVIE
I WAS THINKING THE SAME THING
THOSE TWO GUYS ON TV HATED IT
WELL, WHO KNOWS?
MAYBE THERE'LL BE SOMETHING GOOD IN IT..
LIKE THE DOG TURNS OUT TO BE THE HERO
SCHULZ

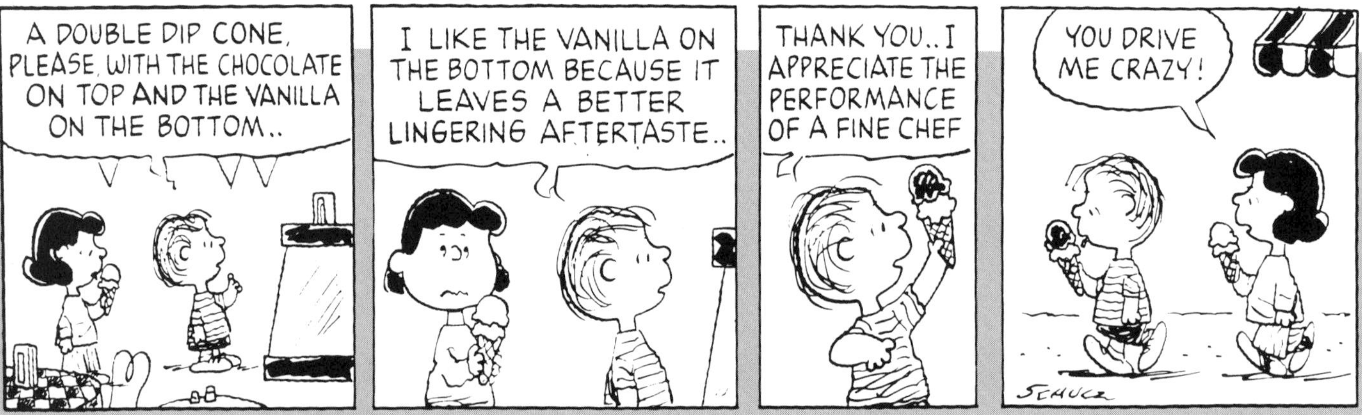
A DOUBLE DIP CONE, PLEASE, WITH THE CHOCOLATE ON TOP AND THE VANILLA ON THE BOTTOM..
I LIKE THE VANILLA ON THE BOTTOM BECAUSE IT LEAVES A BETTER LINGERING AFTERTASTE..
THANK YOU..I APPRECIATE THE PERFORMANCE OF A FINE CHEF
YOU DRIVE ME CRAZY!
SCHULZ

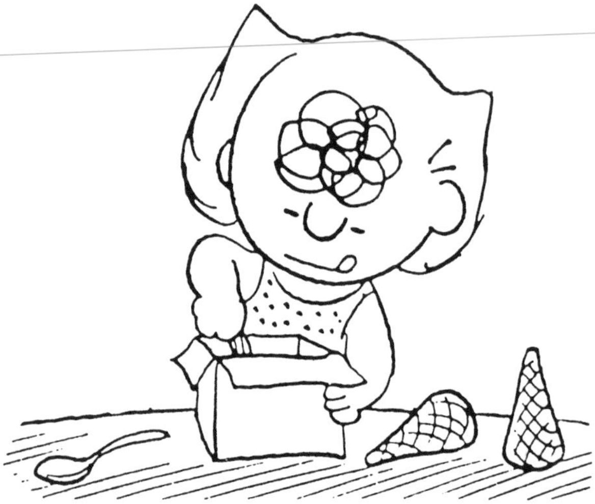

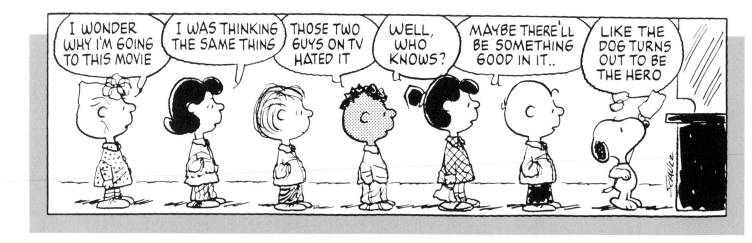

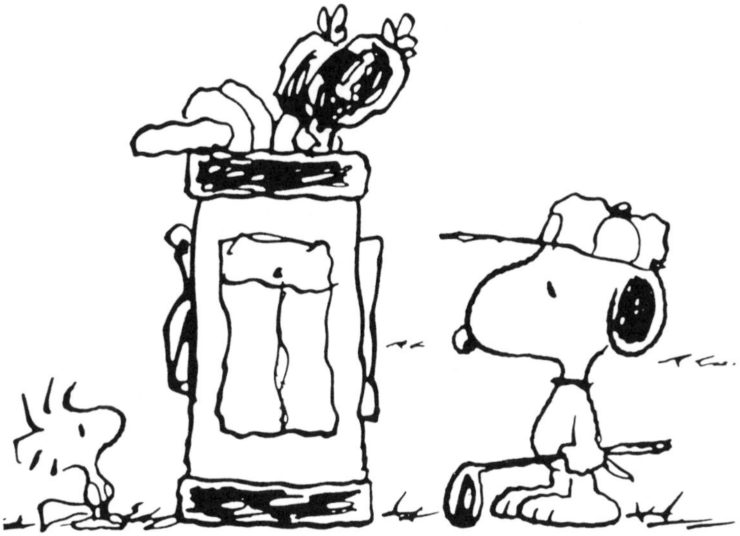

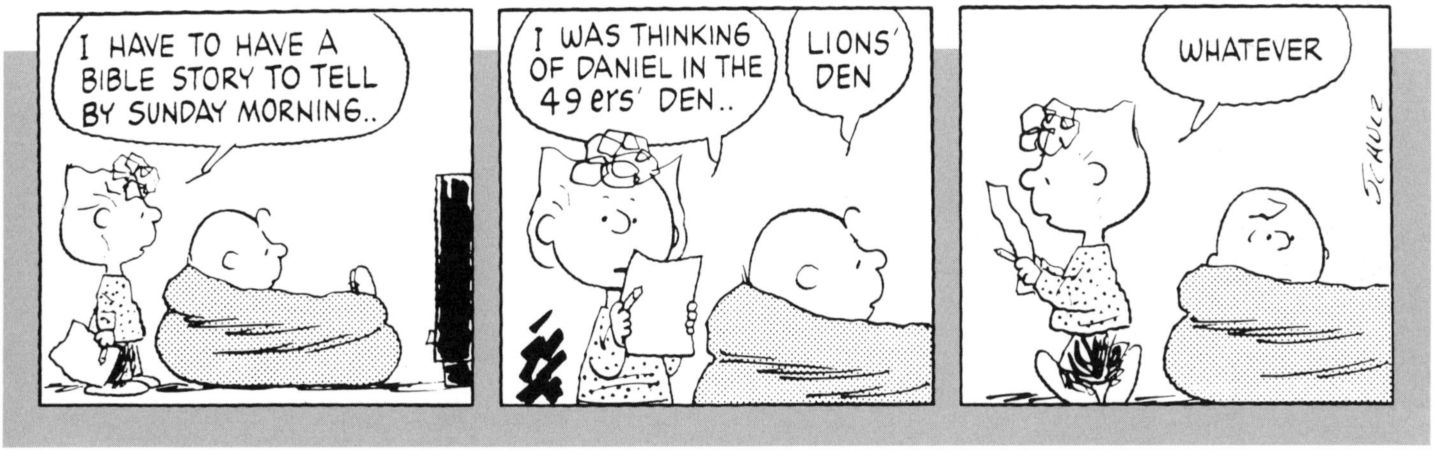
I HAVE TO HAVE A BIBLE STORY TO TELL BY SUNDAY MORNING..
I WAS THINKING OF DANIEL IN THE 49ers' DEN..
LIONS' DEN
WHATEVER

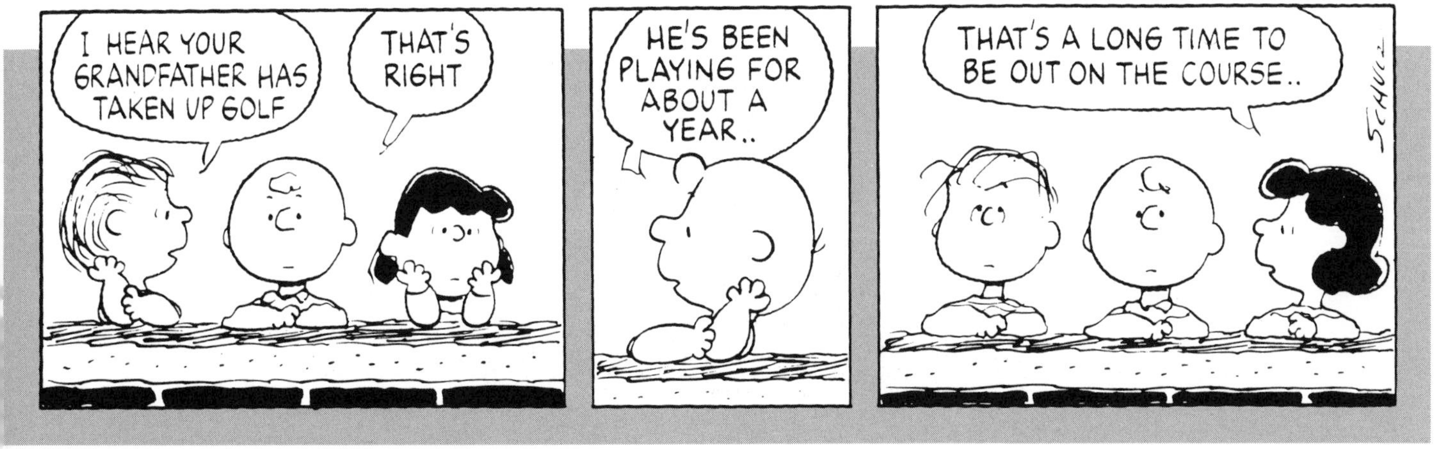
I HEAR YOUR GRANDFATHER HAS TAKEN UP GOLF
THAT'S RIGHT
HE'S BEEN PLAYING FOR ABOUT A YEAR..
THAT'S A LONG TIME TO BE OUT ON THE COURSE..

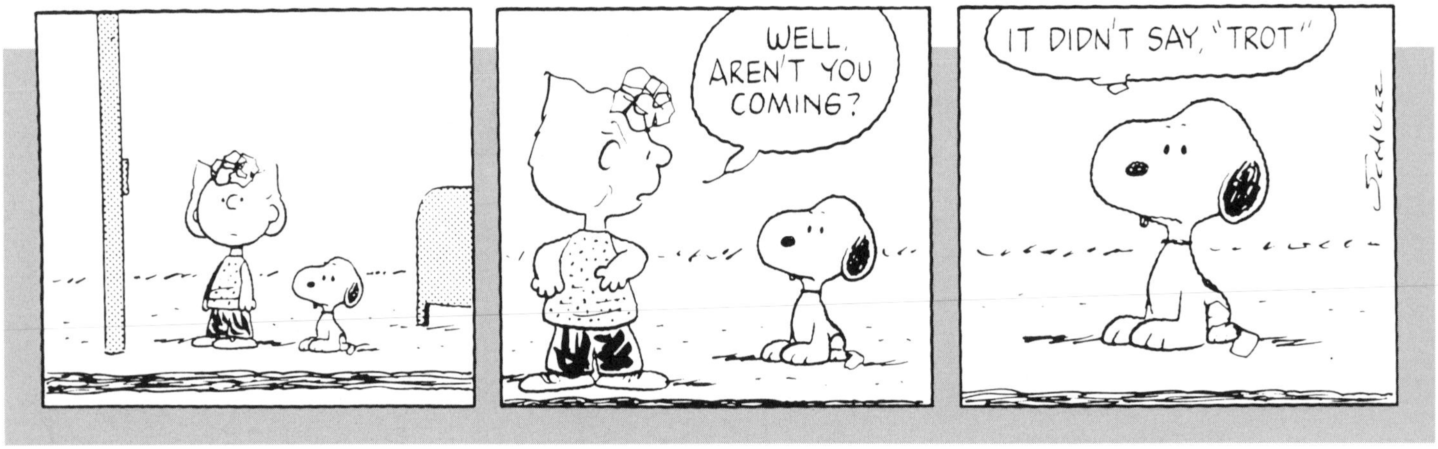
WELL, AREN'T YOU COMING?
IT DIDN'T SAY, "TROT"

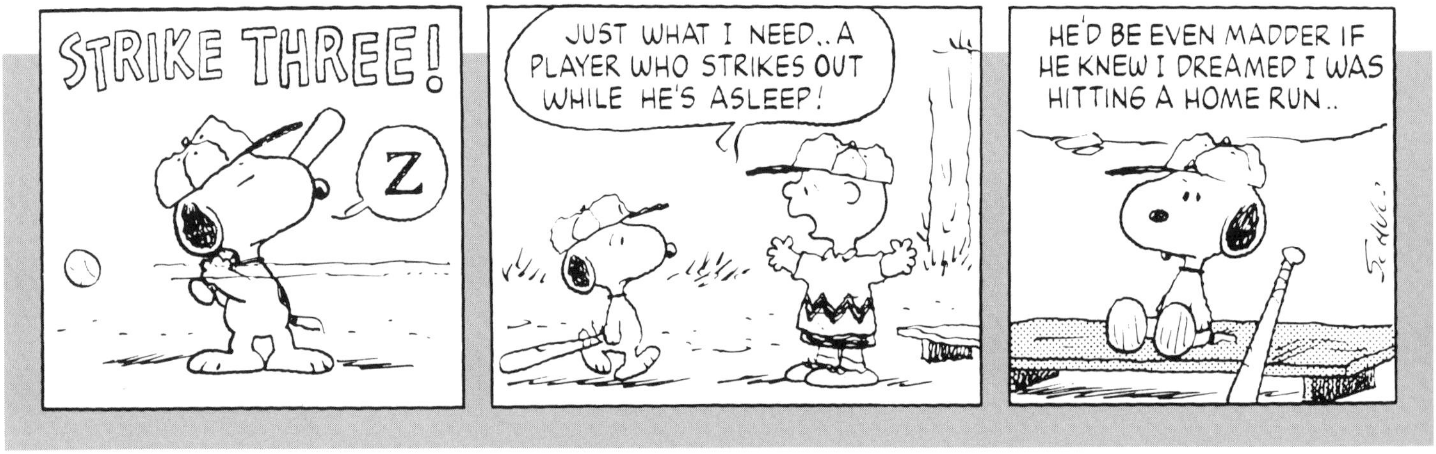
STRIKE THREE!
Z
JUST WHAT I NEED.. A PLAYER WHO STRIKES OUT WHILE HE'S ASLEEP!
HE'D BE EVEN MADDER IF HE KNEW I DREAMED I WAS HITTING A HOME RUN..

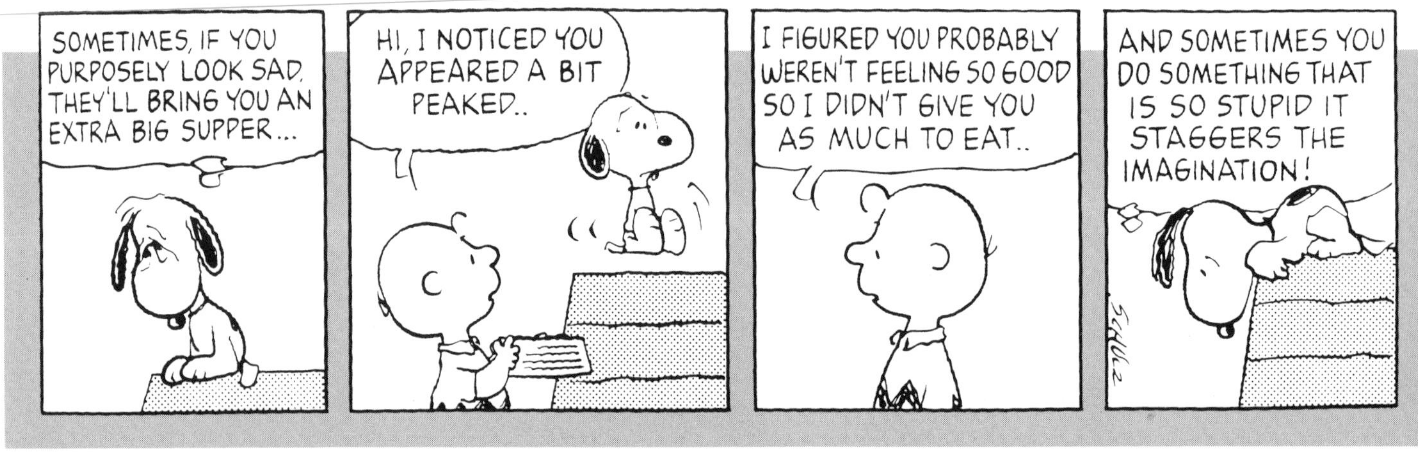
SOMETIMES, IF YOU PURPOSELY LOOK SAD, THEY'LL BRING YOU AN EXTRA BIG SUPPER...
HI, I NOTICED YOU APPEARED A BIT PEAKED..
I FIGURED YOU PROBABLY WEREN'T FEELING SO GOOD SO I DIDN'T GIVE YOU AS MUCH TO EAT..
AND SOMETIMES YOU DO SOMETHING THAT IS SO STUPID IT STAGGERS THE IMAGINATION!

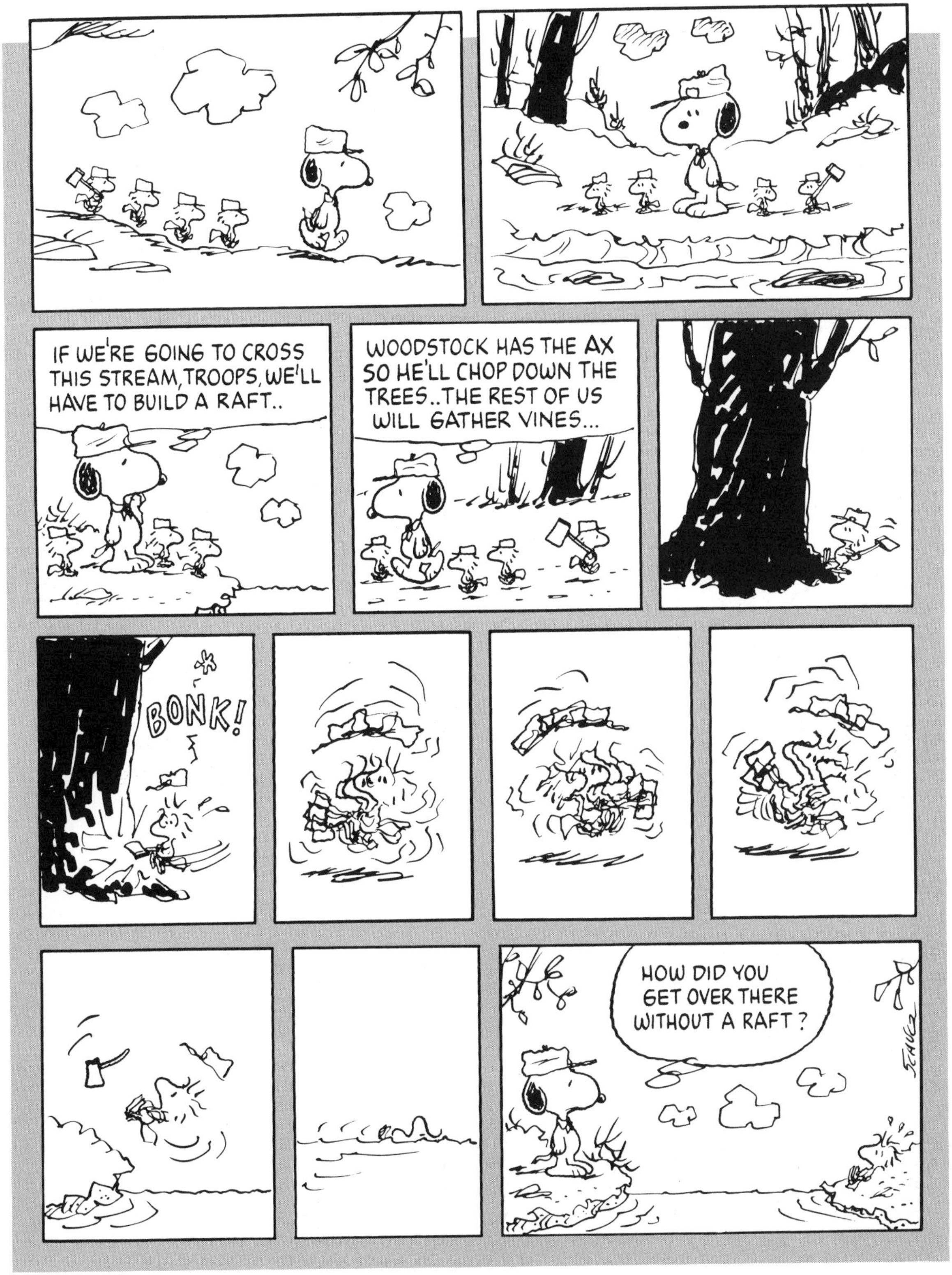
IF WE'RE GOING TO CROSS THIS STREAM, TROOPS, WE'LL HAVE TO BUILD A RAFT..
WOODSTOCK HAS THE AX SO HE'LL CHOP DOWN THE TREES..THE REST OF US WILL GATHER VINES...
BONK!
HOW DID YOU GET OVER THERE WITHOUT A RAFT?
SCHULZ

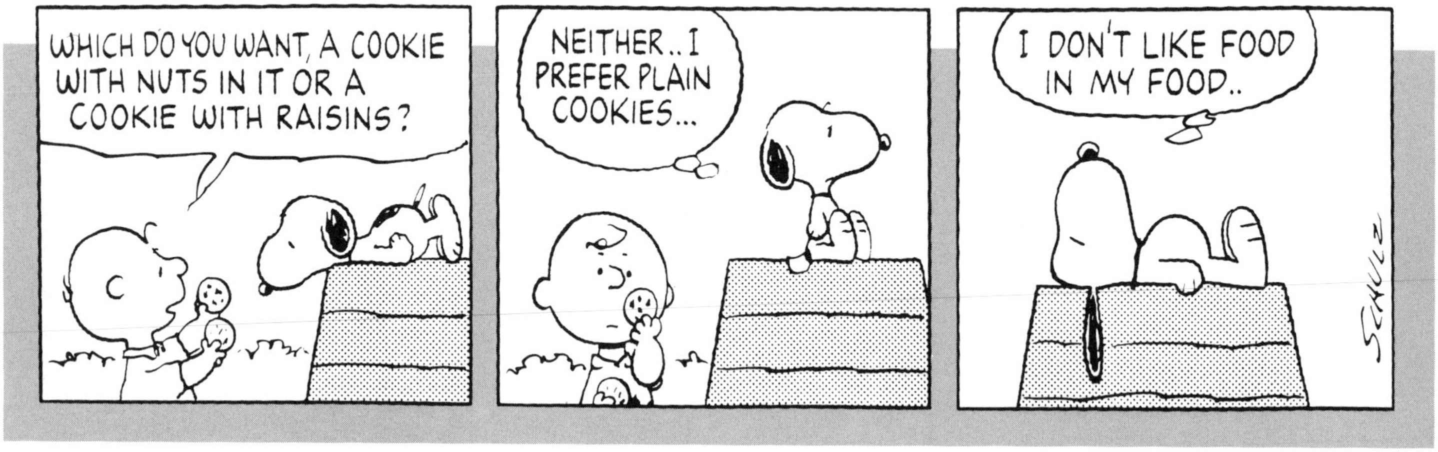
WHICH DO YOU WANT, A COOKIE WITH NUTS IN IT OR A COOKIE WITH RAISINS?
NEITHER.. I PREFER PLAIN COOKIES...
I DON'T LIKE FOOD IN MY FOOD..
SCHULZ

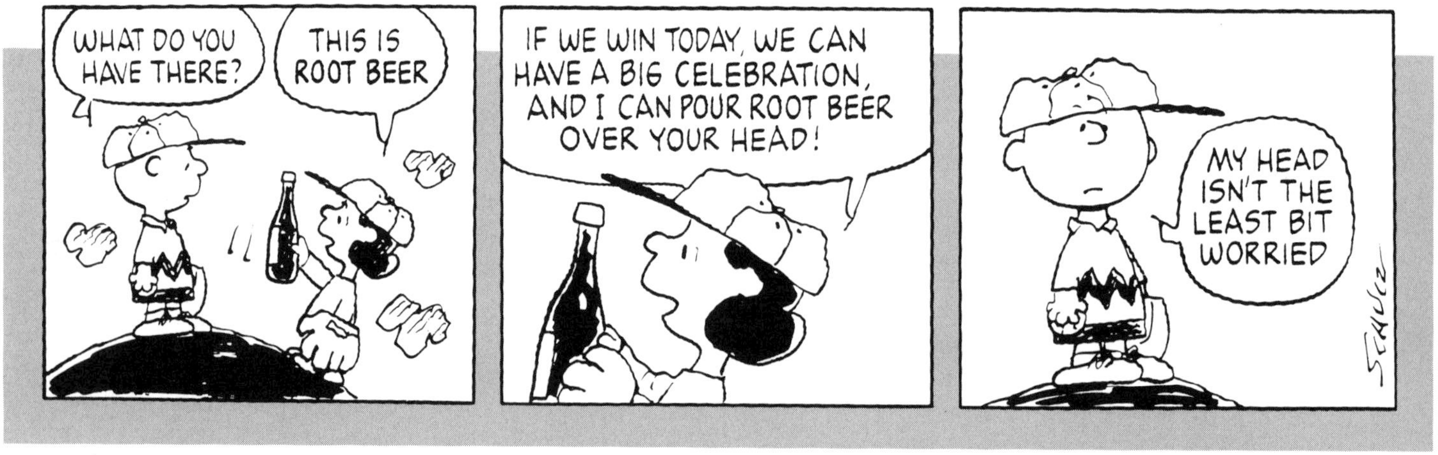
WHAT DO YOU HAVE THERE?
THIS IS ROOT BEER
IF WE WIN TODAY, WE CAN HAVE A BIG CELEBRATION, AND I CAN POUR ROOT BEER OVER YOUR HEAD!
MY HEAD ISN'T THE LEAST BIT WORRIED
SCHULZ

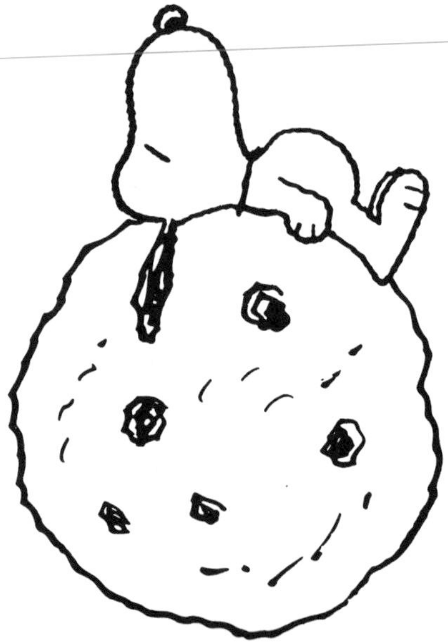

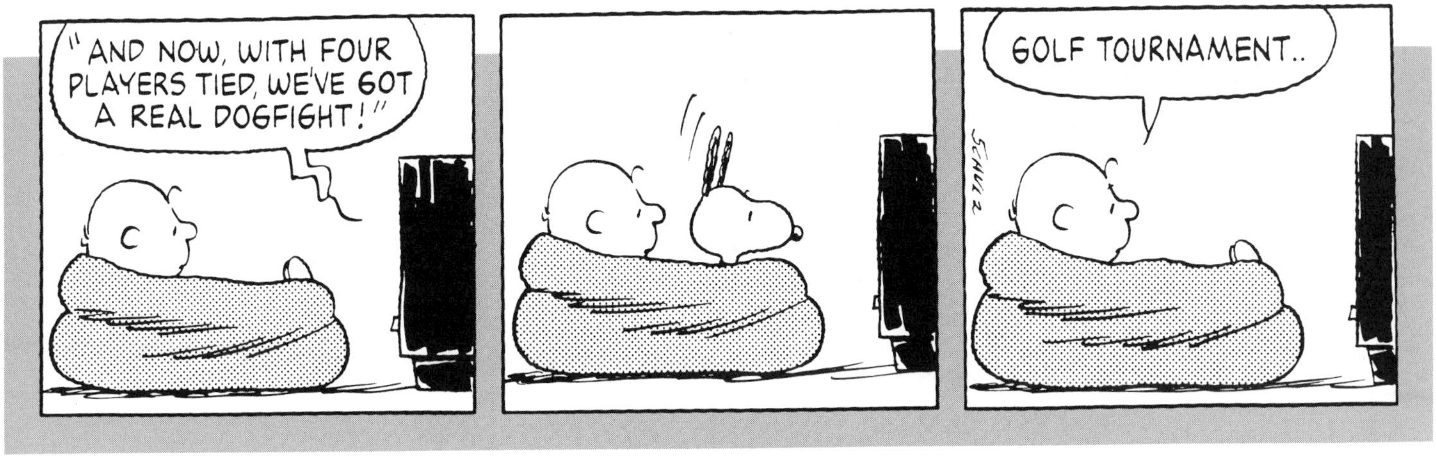
"AND NOW, WITH FOUR PLAYERS TIED, WE'VE GOT A REAL DOGFIGHT!"
GOLF TOURNAMENT..

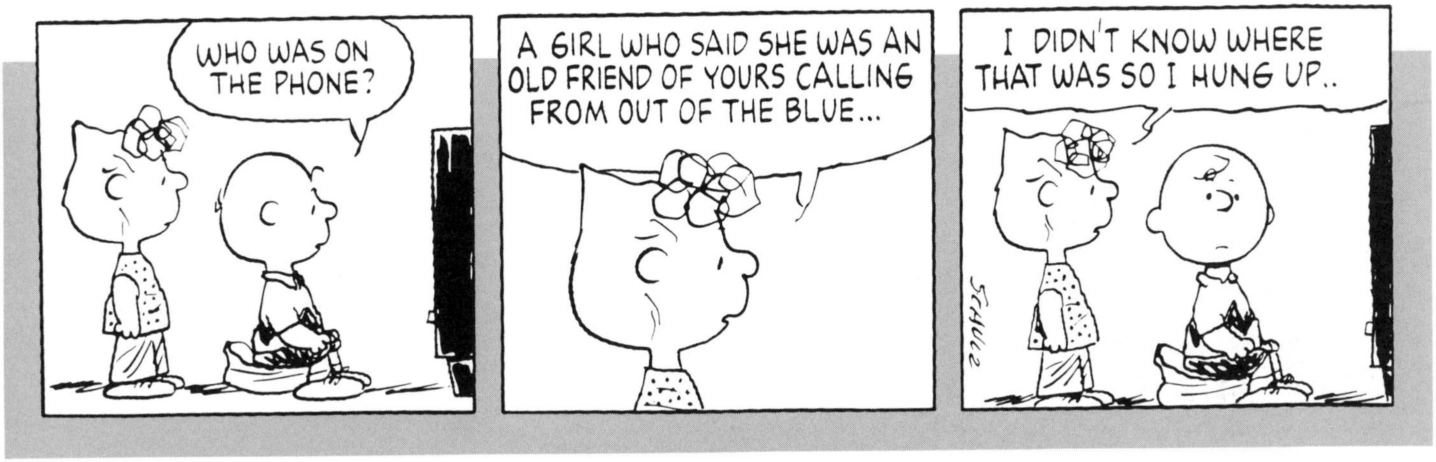
WHO WAS ON THE PHONE?
A GIRL WHO SAID SHE WAS AN OLD FRIEND OF YOURS CALLING FROM OUT OF THE BLUE...
I DIDN'T KNOW WHERE THAT WAS SO I HUNG UP..

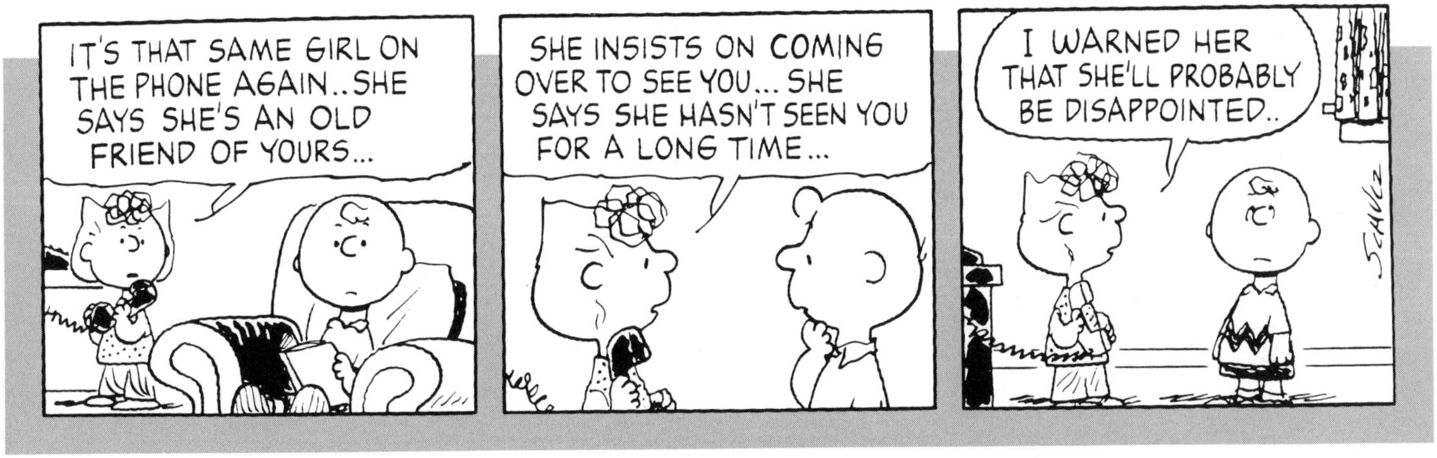
IT'S THAT SAME GIRL ON THE PHONE AGAIN..SHE SAYS SHE'S AN OLD FRIEND OF YOURS...
SHE INSISTS ON COMING OVER TO SEE YOU... SHE SAYS SHE HASN'T SEEN YOU FOR A LONG TIME...
I WARNED HER THAT SHE'LL PROBABLY BE DISAPPOINTED..

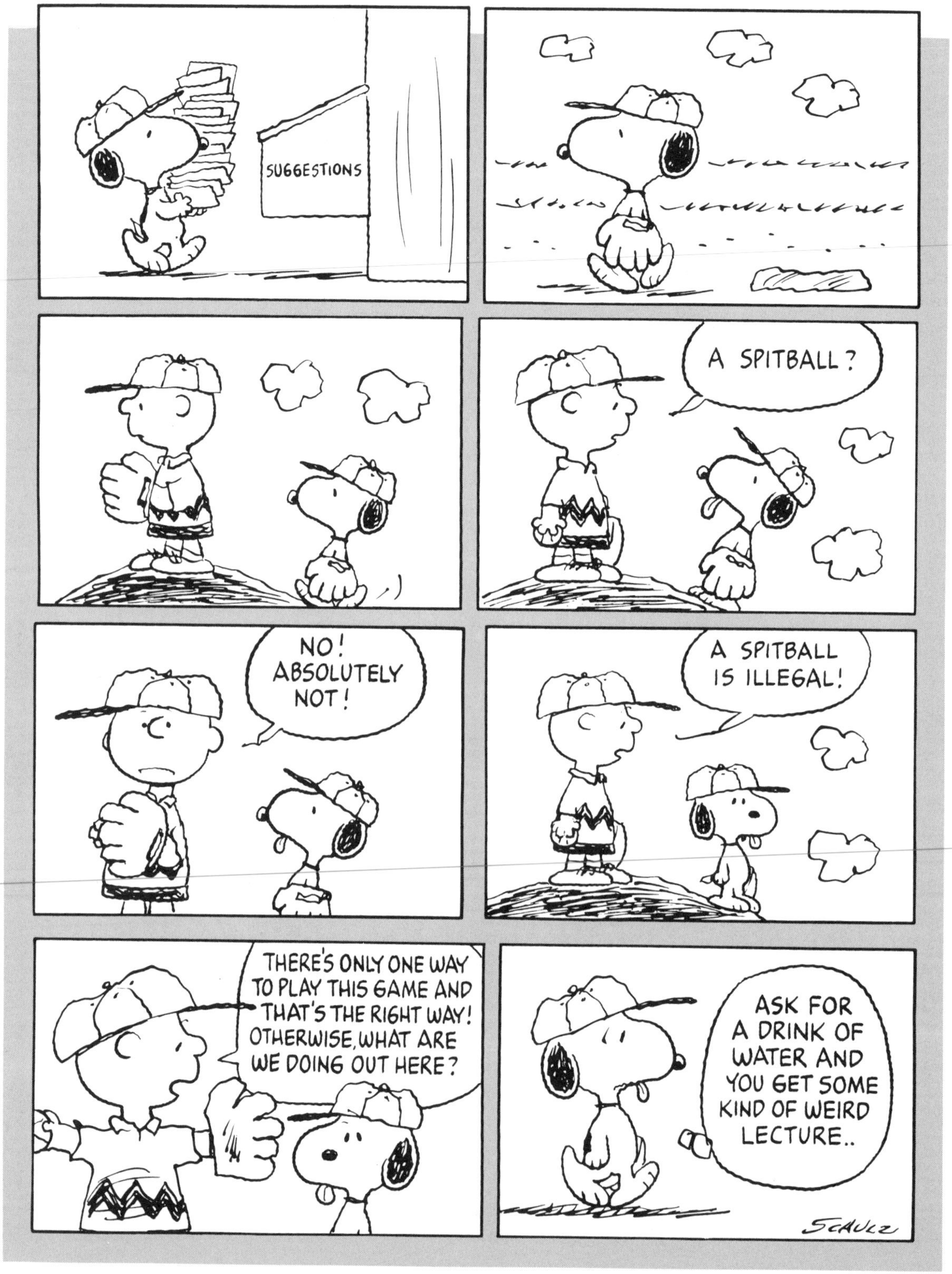
SUGGESTIONS
A SPITBALL?
NO! ABSOLUTELY NOT!
A SPITBALL IS ILLEGAL!
THERE'S ONLY ONE WAY TO PLAY THIS GAME AND THAT'S THE RIGHT WAY! OTHERWISE, WHAT ARE WE DOING OUT HERE?
ASK FOR A DRINK OF WATER AND YOU GET SOME KIND OF WEIRD LECTURE..
SCHULZ

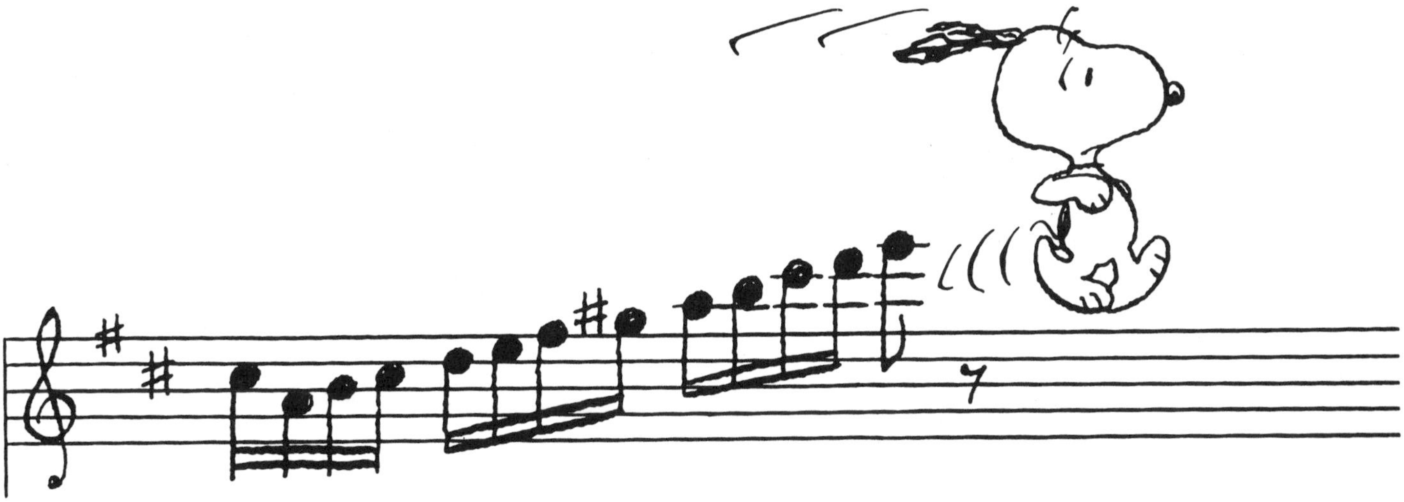

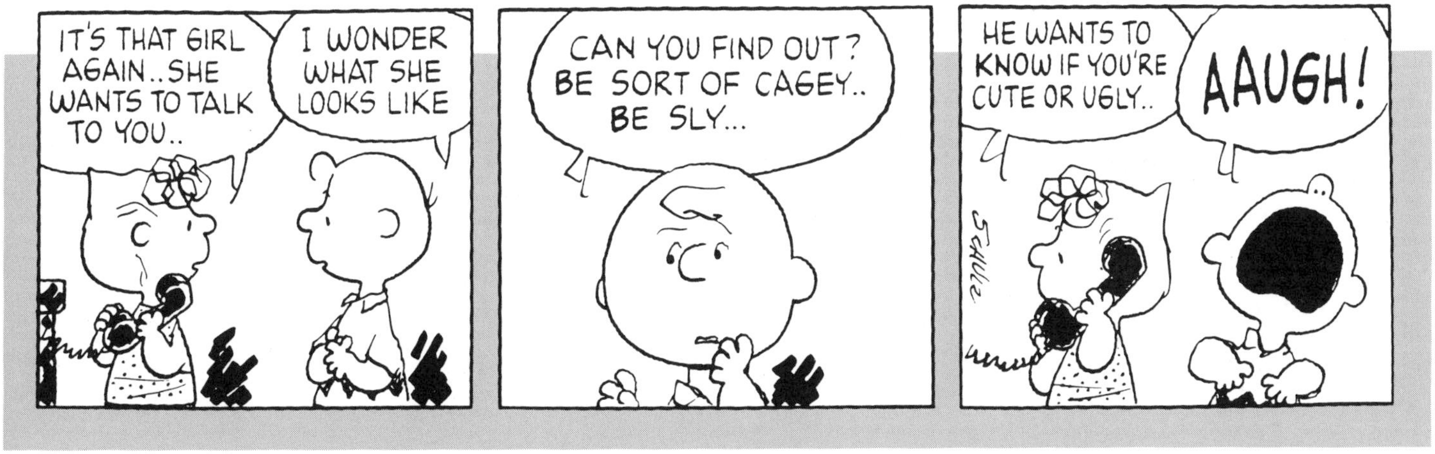
IT'S THAT GIRL AGAIN..SHE WANTS TO TALK TO YOU..
I WONDER WHAT SHE LOOKS LIKE
CAN YOU FIND OUT? BE SORT OF CAGEY.. BE SLY...
HE WANTS TO KNOW IF YOU'RE CUTE OR UGLY..
AAUGH!

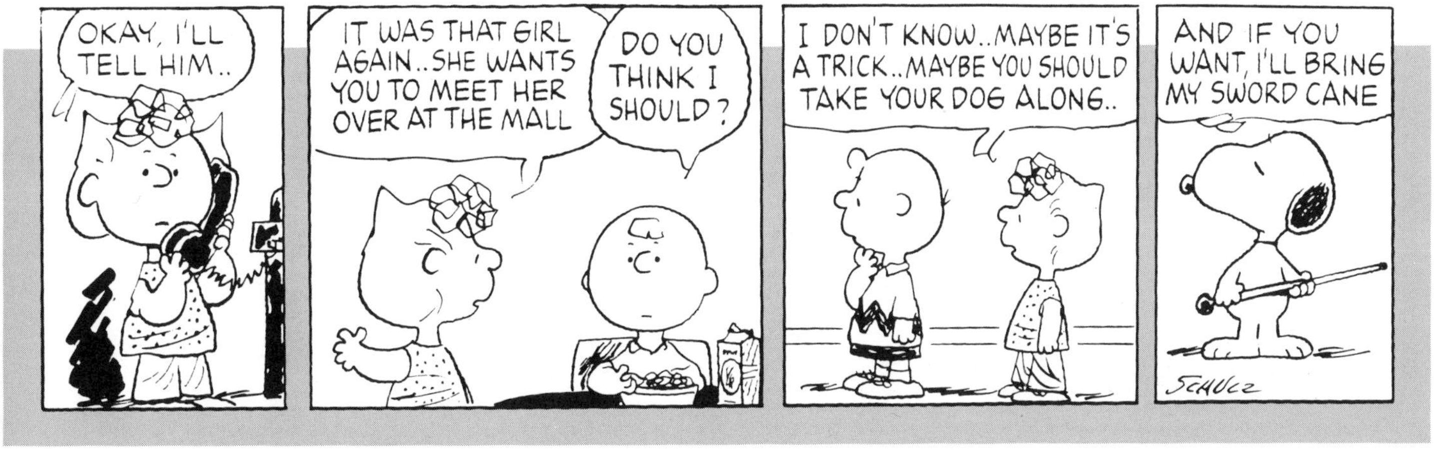
OKAY, I'LL TELL HIM..
IT WAS THAT GIRL AGAIN..SHE WANTS YOU TO MEET HER OVER AT THE MALL
DO YOU THINK I SHOULD?
I DON'T KNOW..MAYBE IT'S A TRICK..MAYBE YOU SHOULD TAKE YOUR DOG ALONG..
AND IF YOU WANT, I'LL BRING MY SWORD CANE

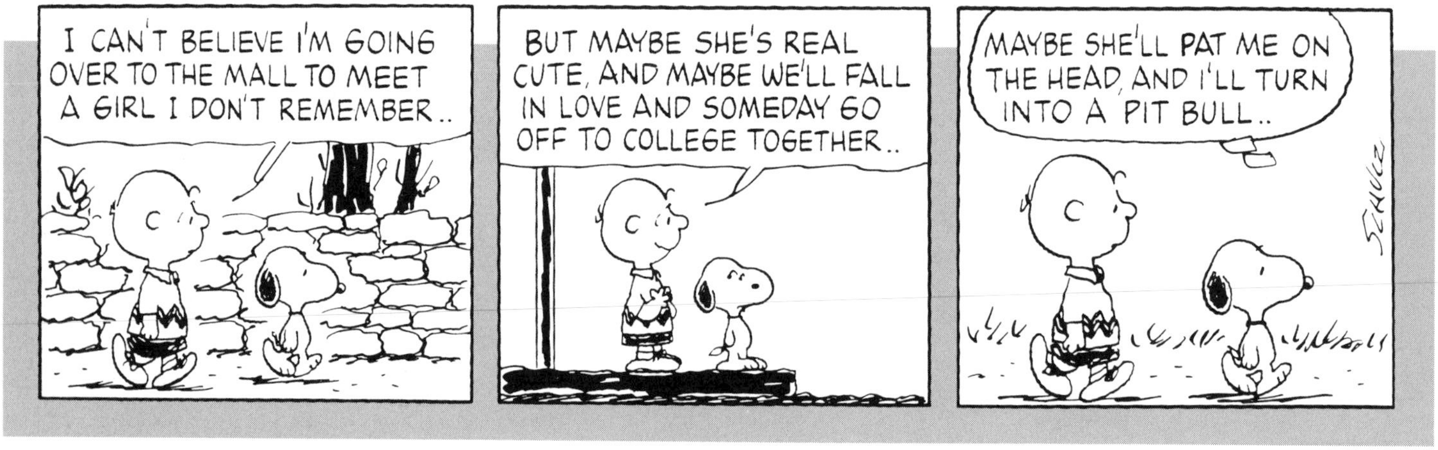
I CAN'T BELIEVE I'M GOING OVER TO THE MALL TO MEET A GIRL I DON'T REMEMBER..
BUT MAYBE SHE'S REAL CUTE, AND MAYBE WE'LL FALL IN LOVE AND SOMEDAY GO OFF TO COLLEGE TOGETHER..
MAYBE SHE'LL PAT ME ON THE HEAD, AND I'LL TURN INTO A PIT BULL..
SCHULZ

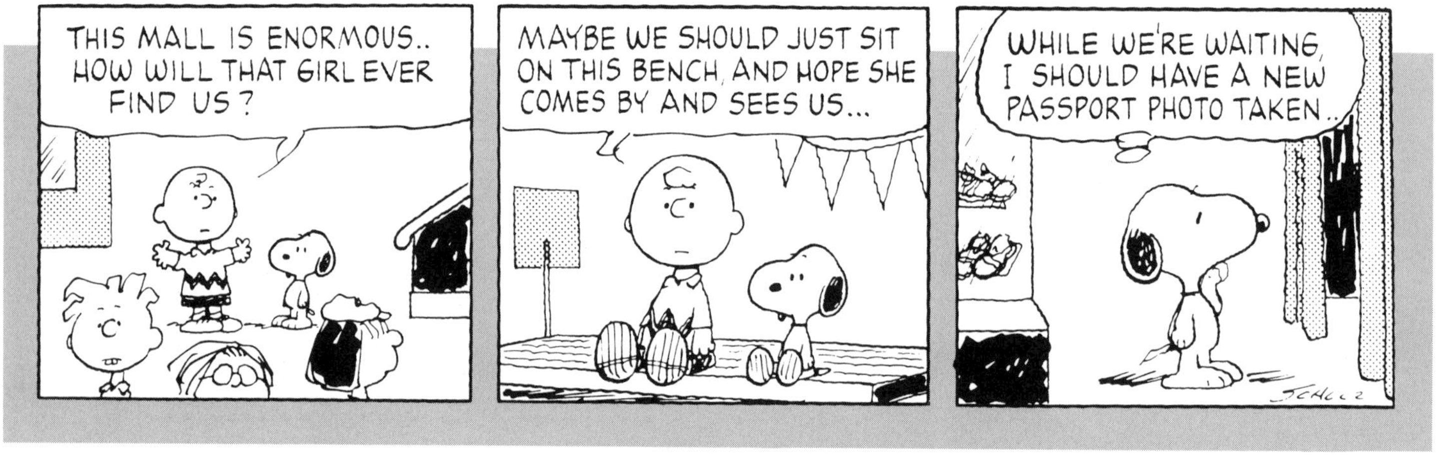
THIS MALL IS ENORMOUS.. HOW WILL THAT GIRL EVER FIND US?
MAYBE WE SHOULD JUST SIT ON THIS BENCH, AND HOPE SHE COMES BY AND SEES US...
WHILE WE'RE WAITING, I SHOULD HAVE A NEW PASSPORT PHOTO TAKEN..
SCHULZ

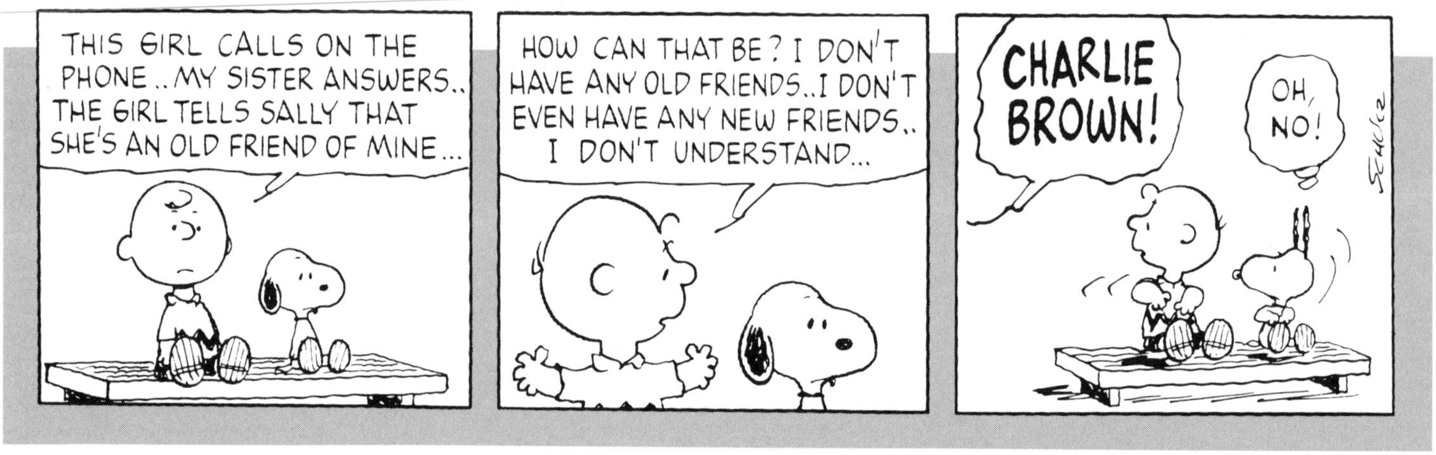
THIS GIRL CALLS ON THE PHONE..MY SISTER ANSWERS.. THE GIRL TELLS SALLY THAT SHE'S AN OLD FRIEND OF MINE...
HOW CAN THAT BE? I DON'T HAVE ANY OLD FRIENDS..I DON'T EVEN HAVE ANY NEW FRIENDS.. I DON'T UNDERSTAND...
CHARLIE BROWN!
OH, NO!
SCHULZ

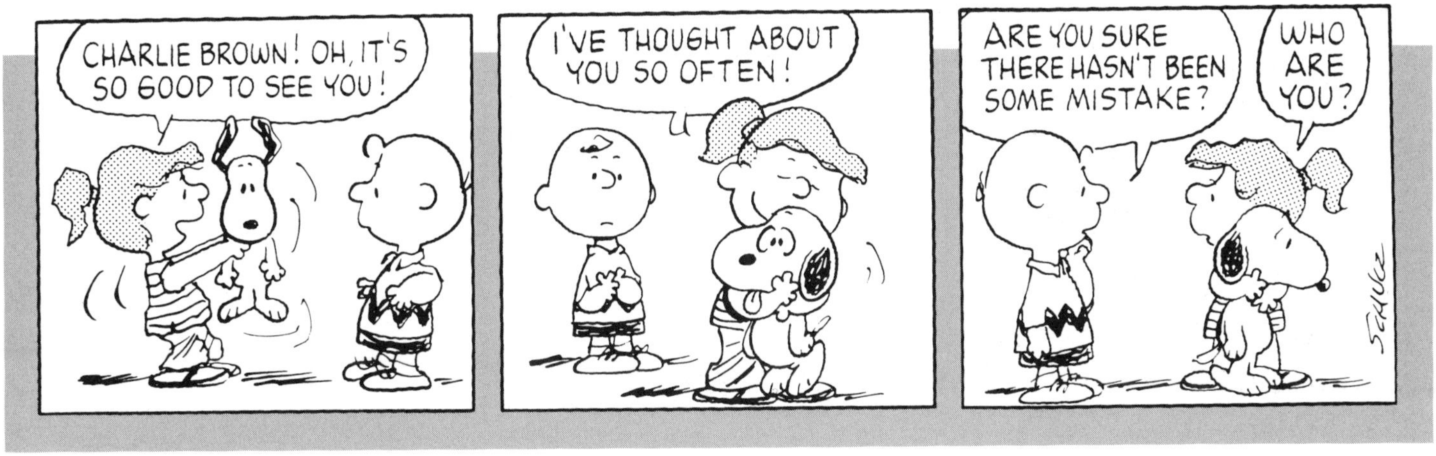
CHARLIE BROWN! OH, IT'S SO GOOD TO SEE YOU!
I'VE THOUGHT ABOUT YOU SO OFTEN!
ARE YOU SURE THERE HASN'T BEEN SOME MISTAKE?
WHO ARE YOU?

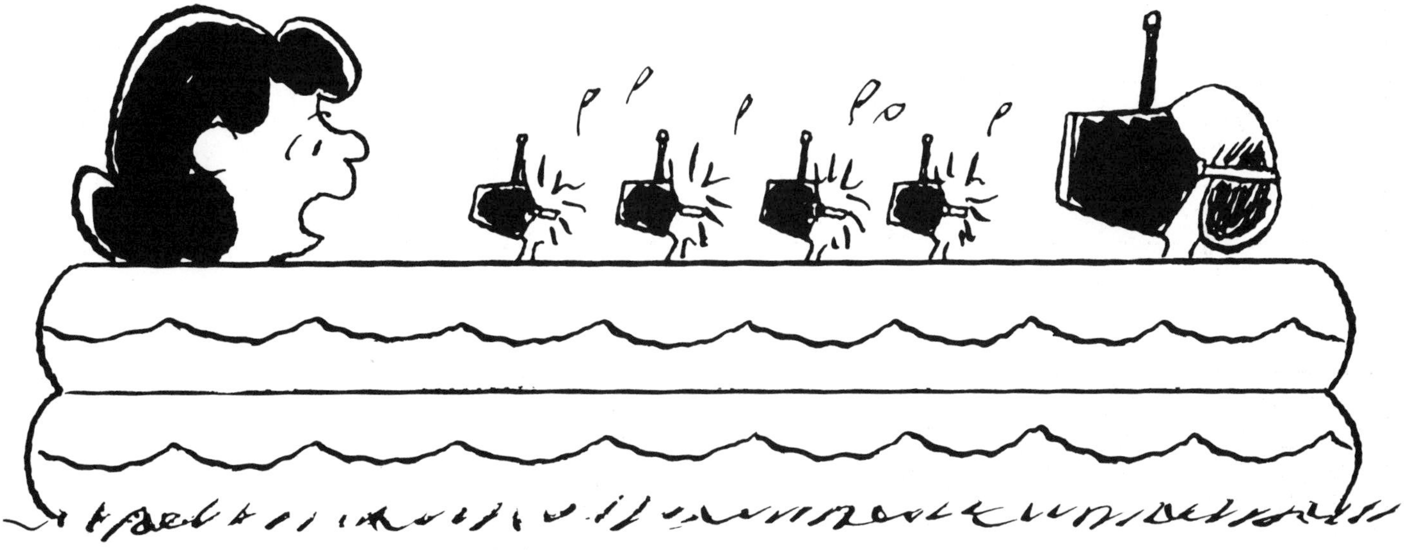

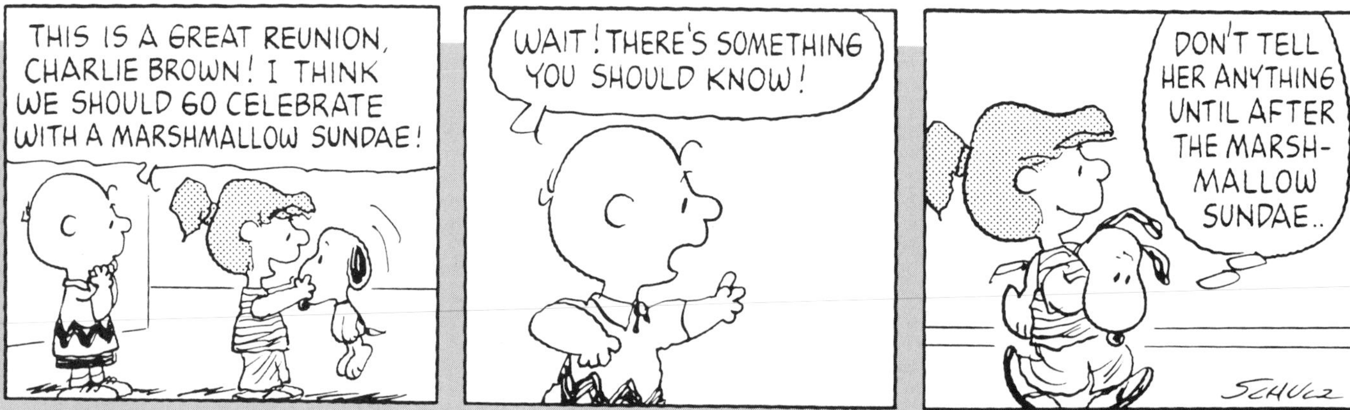
THIS IS A GREAT REUNION, CHARLIE BROWN! I THINK WE SHOULD GO CELEBRATE WITH A MARSHMALLOW SUNDAE!
WAIT! THERE'S SOMETHING YOU SHOULD KNOW!
DON'T TELL HER ANYTHING UNTIL AFTER THE MARSH-MALLOW SUNDAE..
SCHULZ

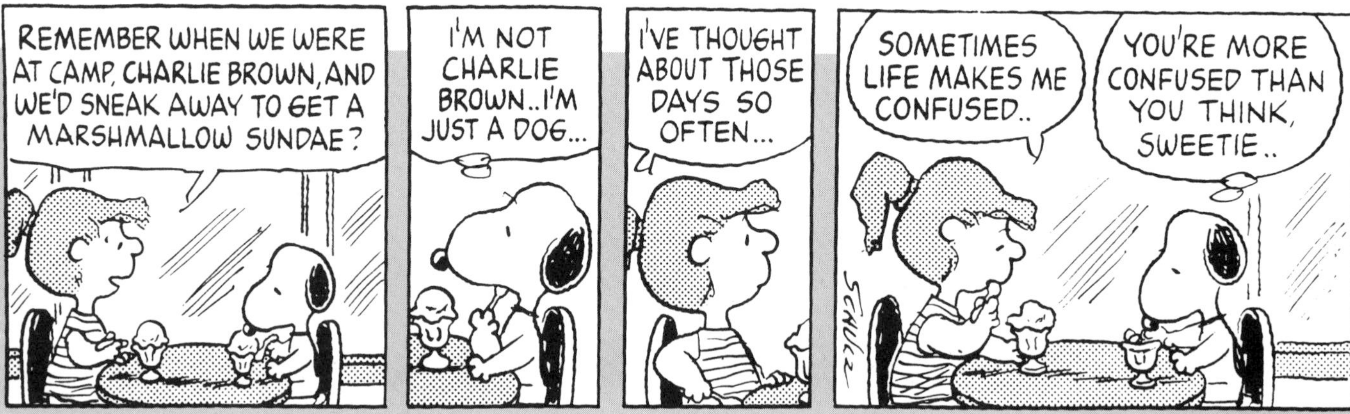
REMEMBER WHEN WE WERE AT CAMP, CHARLIE BROWN, AND WE'D SNEAK AWAY TO GET A MARSHMALLOW SUNDAE?
I'M NOT CHARLIE BROWN..I'M JUST A DOG...
I'VE THOUGHT ABOUT THOSE DAYS SO OFTEN...
SCHULZ
SOMETIMES LIFE MAKES ME CONFUSED..
YOU'RE MORE CONFUSED THAN YOU THINK, SWEETIE..

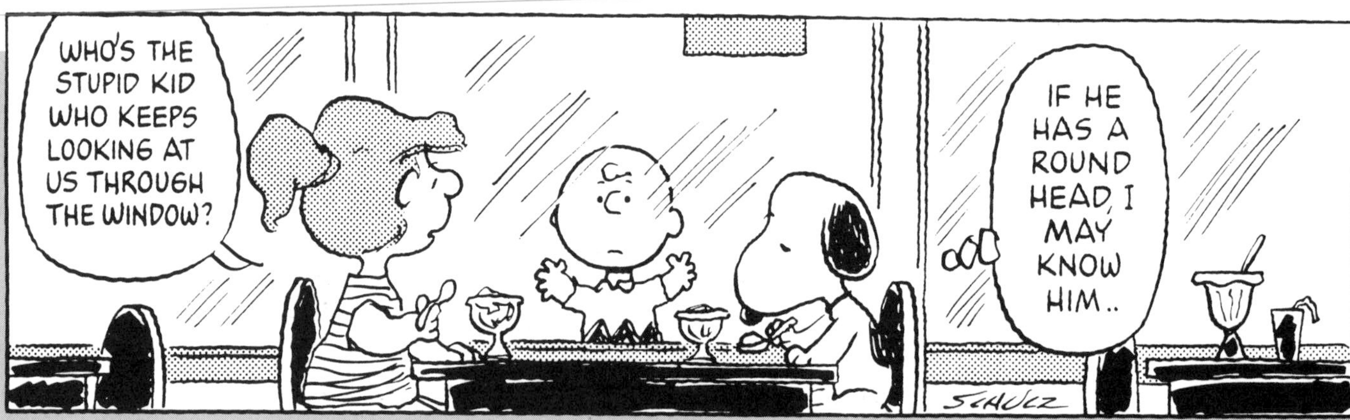
WHO'S THE STUPID KID WHO KEEPS LOOKING AT US THROUGH THE WINDOW?
IF HE HAS A ROUND HEAD, I MAY KNOW HIM..
SCHULZ

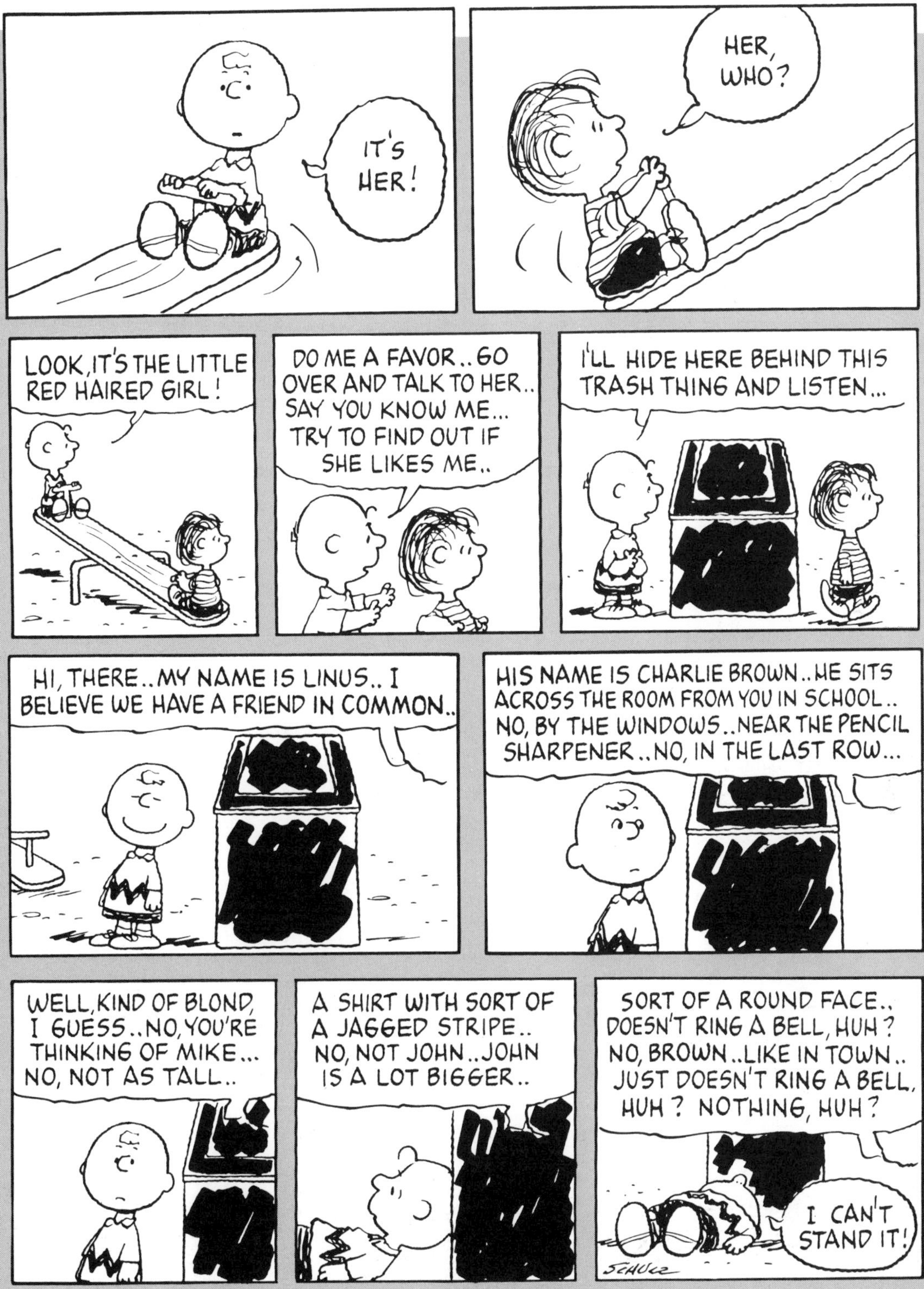
IT'S HER!
HER, WHO?
LOOK, IT'S THE LITTLE RED HAIRED GIRL!
DO ME A FAVOR.. GO OVER AND TALK TO HER.. SAY YOU KNOW ME... TRY TO FIND OUT IF SHE LIKES ME..
I'LL HIDE HERE BEHIND THIS TRASH THING AND LISTEN...
HI, THERE.. MY NAME IS LINUS.. I BELIEVE WE HAVE A FRIEND IN COMMON..
HIS NAME IS CHARLIE BROWN.. HE SITS ACROSS THE ROOM FROM YOU IN SCHOOL.. NO, BY THE WINDOWS.. NEAR THE PENCIL SHARPENER.. NO, IN THE LAST ROW...
WELL, KIND OF BLOND, I GUESS.. NO, YOU'RE THINKING OF MIKE... NO, NOT AS TALL..
A SHIRT WITH SORT OF A JAGGED STRIPE.. NO, NOT JOHN.. JOHN IS A LOT BIGGER..
SORT OF A ROUND FACE.. DOESN'T RING A BELL, HUH? NO, BROWN.. LIKE IN TOWN.. JUST DOESN'T RING A BELL, HUH? NOTHING, HUH?
I CAN'T STAND IT!
SCHULZ

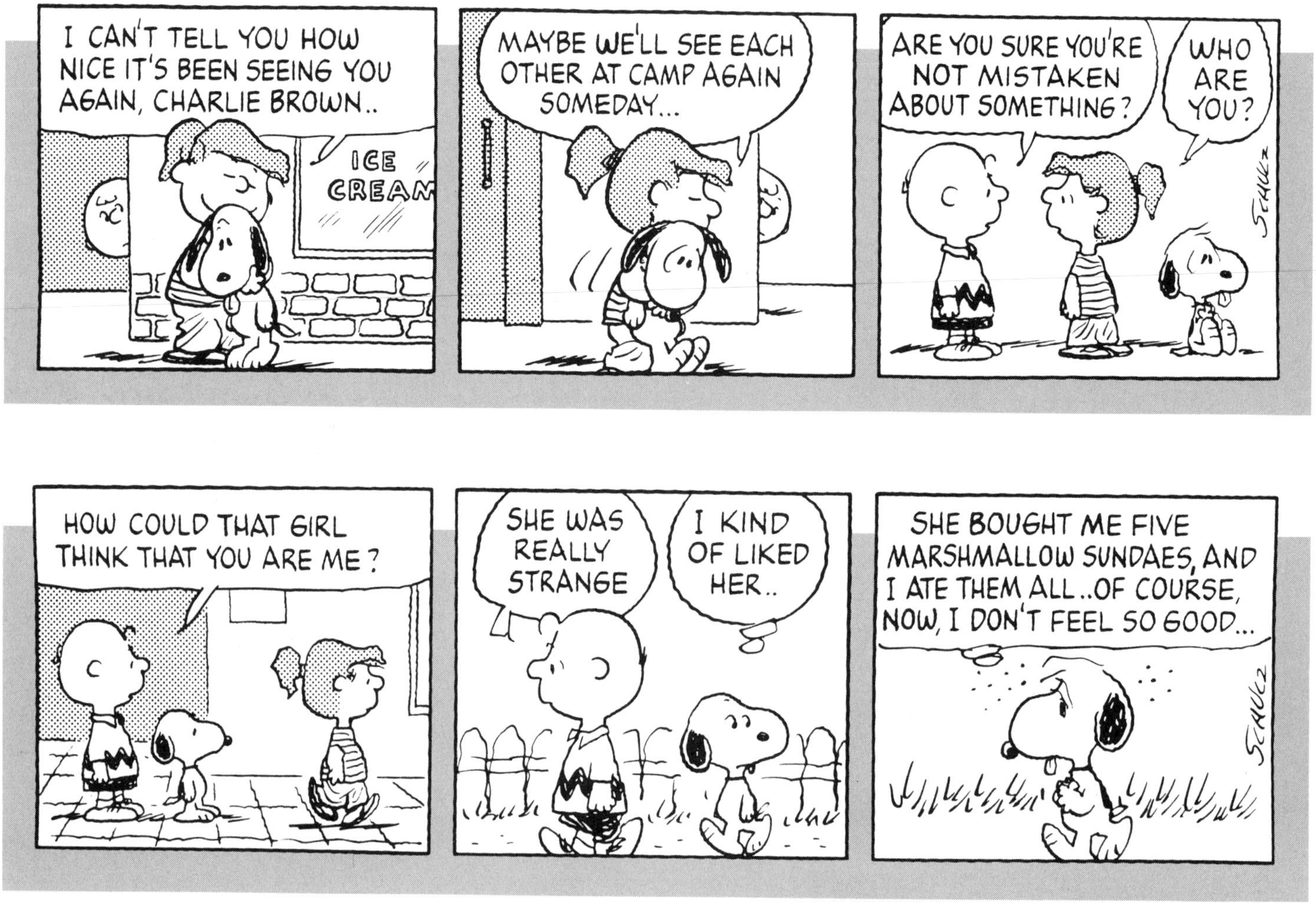
I CAN'T TELL YOU HOW NICE IT'S BEEN SEEING YOU AGAIN, CHARLIE BROWN..
ICE CREAM
MAYBE WE'LL SEE EACH OTHER AT CAMP AGAIN SOMEDAY...
ARE YOU SURE YOU'RE NOT MISTAKEN ABOUT SOMETHING?
WHO ARE YOU?
SCHULZ
HOW COULD THAT GIRL THINK THAT YOU ARE ME?
SHE WAS REALLY STRANGE
I KIND OF LIKED HER..
SHE BOUGHT ME FIVE MARSHMALLOW SUNDAES, AND I ATE THEM ALL..OF COURSE, NOW, I DON'T FEEL SO GOOD...
SCHULZ

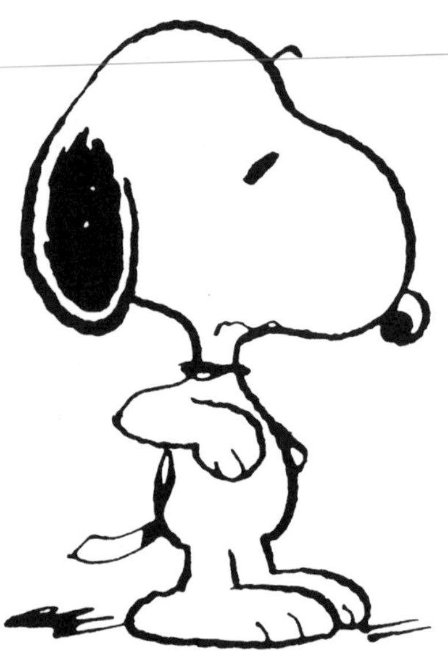

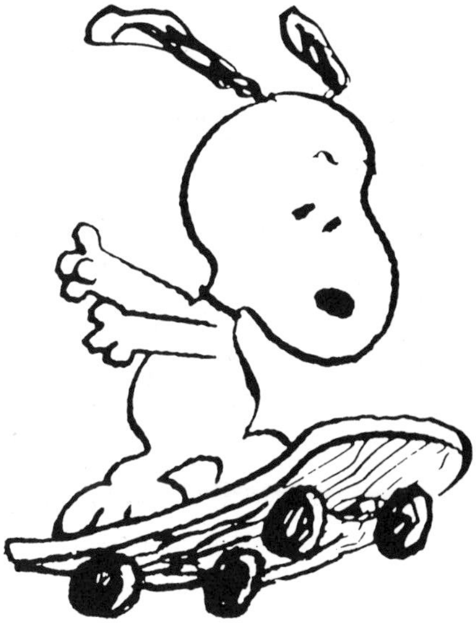

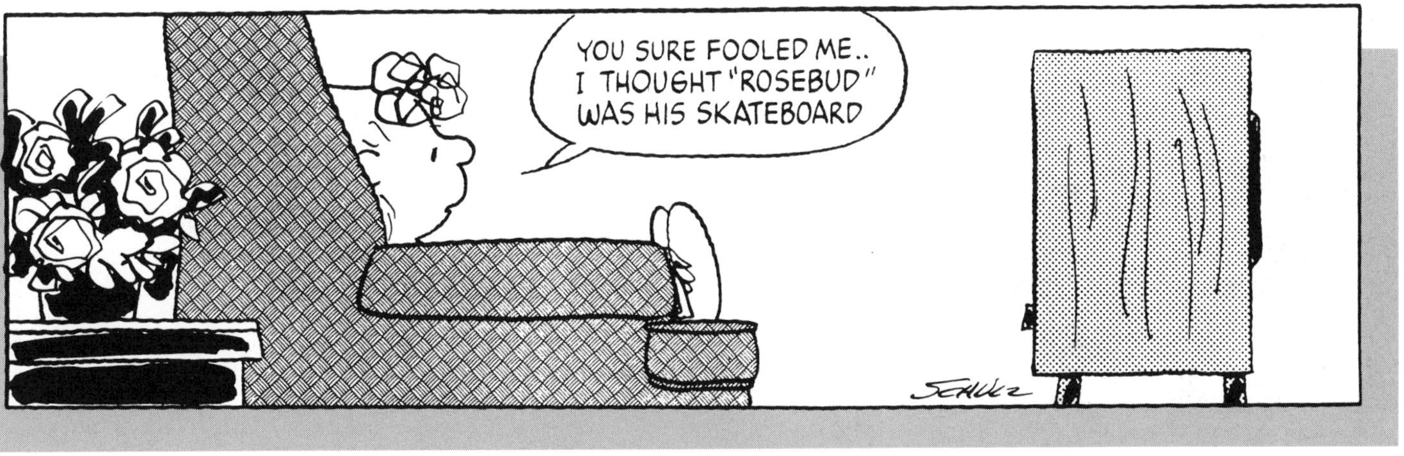
YOU SURE FOOLED ME..
I THOUGHT "ROSEBUD"
WAS HIS SKATEBOARD
SCHULZ

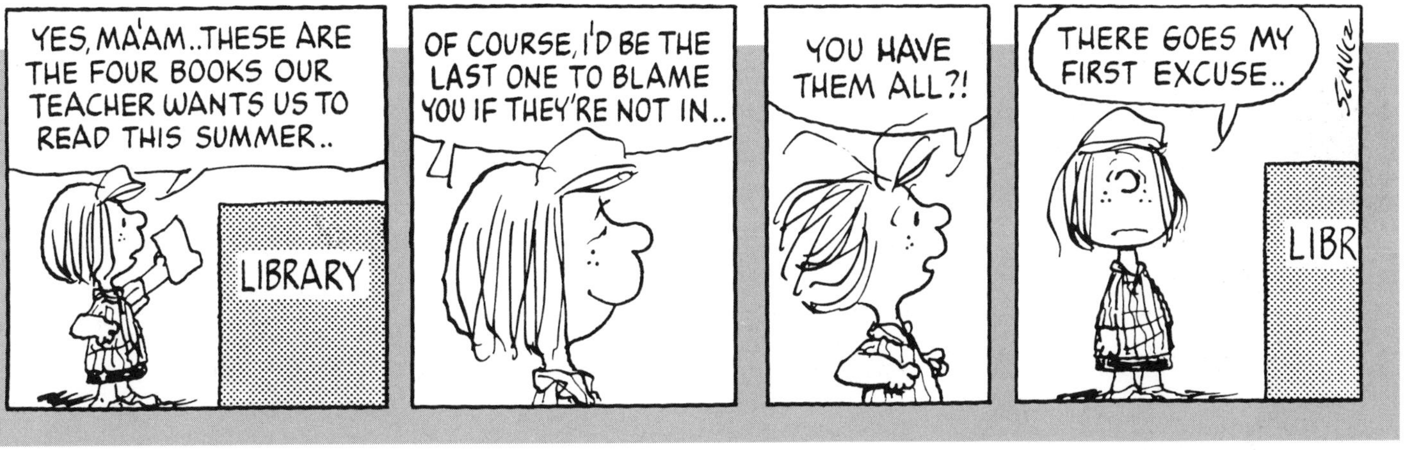
YES, MA'AM..THESE ARE THE FOUR BOOKS OUR TEACHER WANTS US TO READ THIS SUMMER..
LIBRARY
OF COURSE, I'D BE THE LAST ONE TO BLAME YOU IF THEY'RE NOT IN..
YOU HAVE THEM ALL?!
THERE GOES MY FIRST EXCUSE..
SCHULZ
LIBR

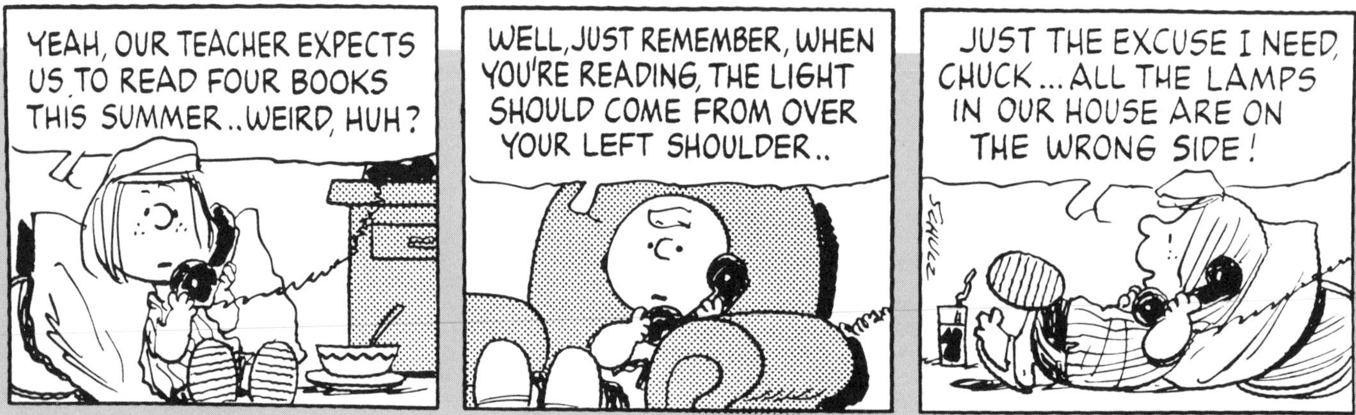
YEAH, OUR TEACHER EXPECTS US TO READ FOUR BOOKS THIS SUMMER.. WEIRD, HUH?
WELL, JUST REMEMBER, WHEN YOU'RE READING, THE LIGHT SHOULD COME FROM OVER YOUR LEFT SHOULDER..
JUST THE EXCUSE I NEED, CHUCK... ALL THE LAMPS IN OUR HOUSE ARE ON THE WRONG SIDE!
SCHULZ

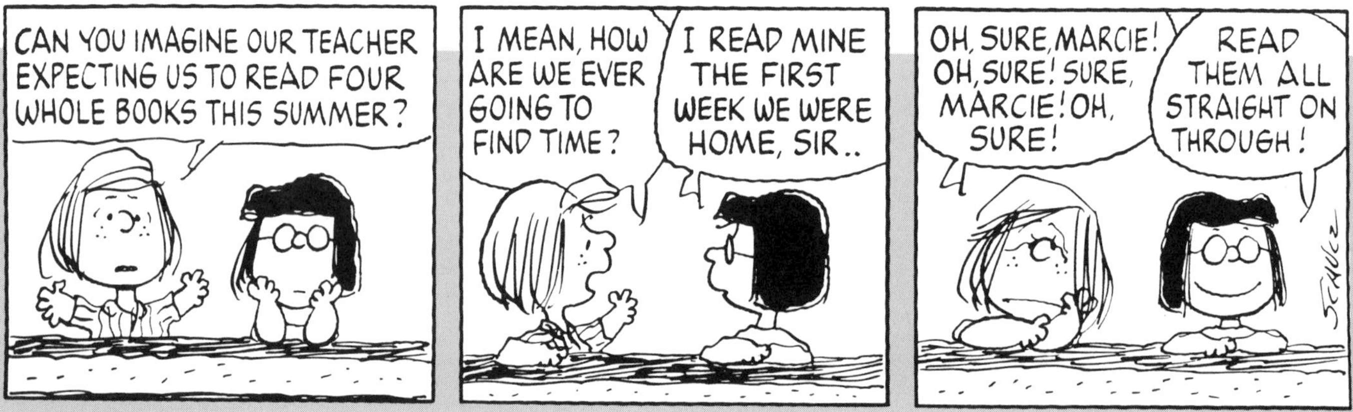
CAN YOU IMAGINE OUR TEACHER EXPECTING US TO READ FOUR WHOLE BOOKS THIS SUMMER?
I MEAN, HOW ARE WE EVER GOING TO FIND TIME?
I READ MINE THE FIRST WEEK WE WERE HOME, SIR..
OH, SURE, MARCIE! OH, SURE! SURE, MARCIE! OH, SURE!
READ THEM ALL STRAIGHT ON THROUGH!
SCHULZ

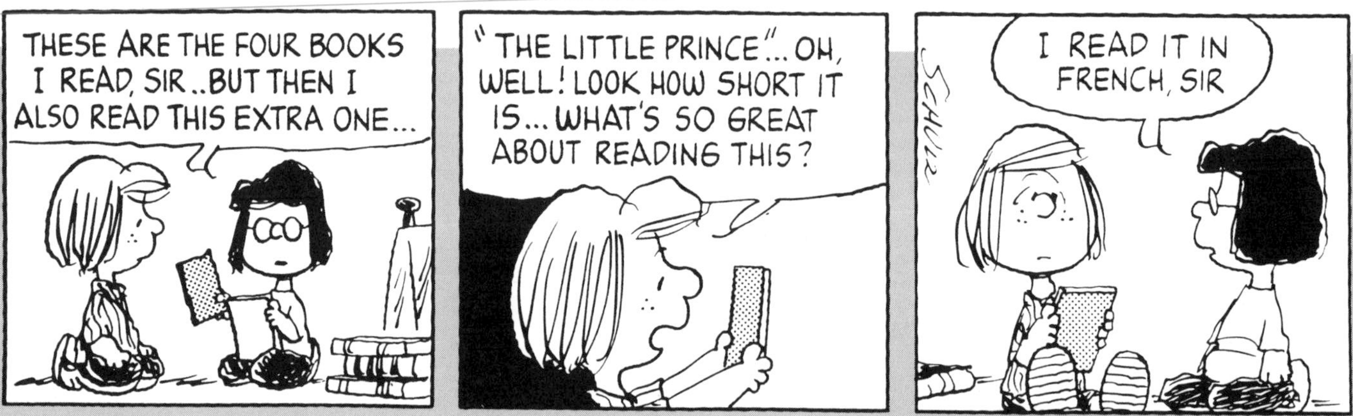
THESE ARE THE FOUR BOOKS I READ, SIR.. BUT THEN I ALSO READ THIS EXTRA ONE...
"THE LITTLE PRINCE"... OH, WELL! LOOK HOW SHORT IT IS... WHAT'S SO GREAT ABOUT READING THIS?
SCHULZ
I READ IT IN FRENCH, SIR

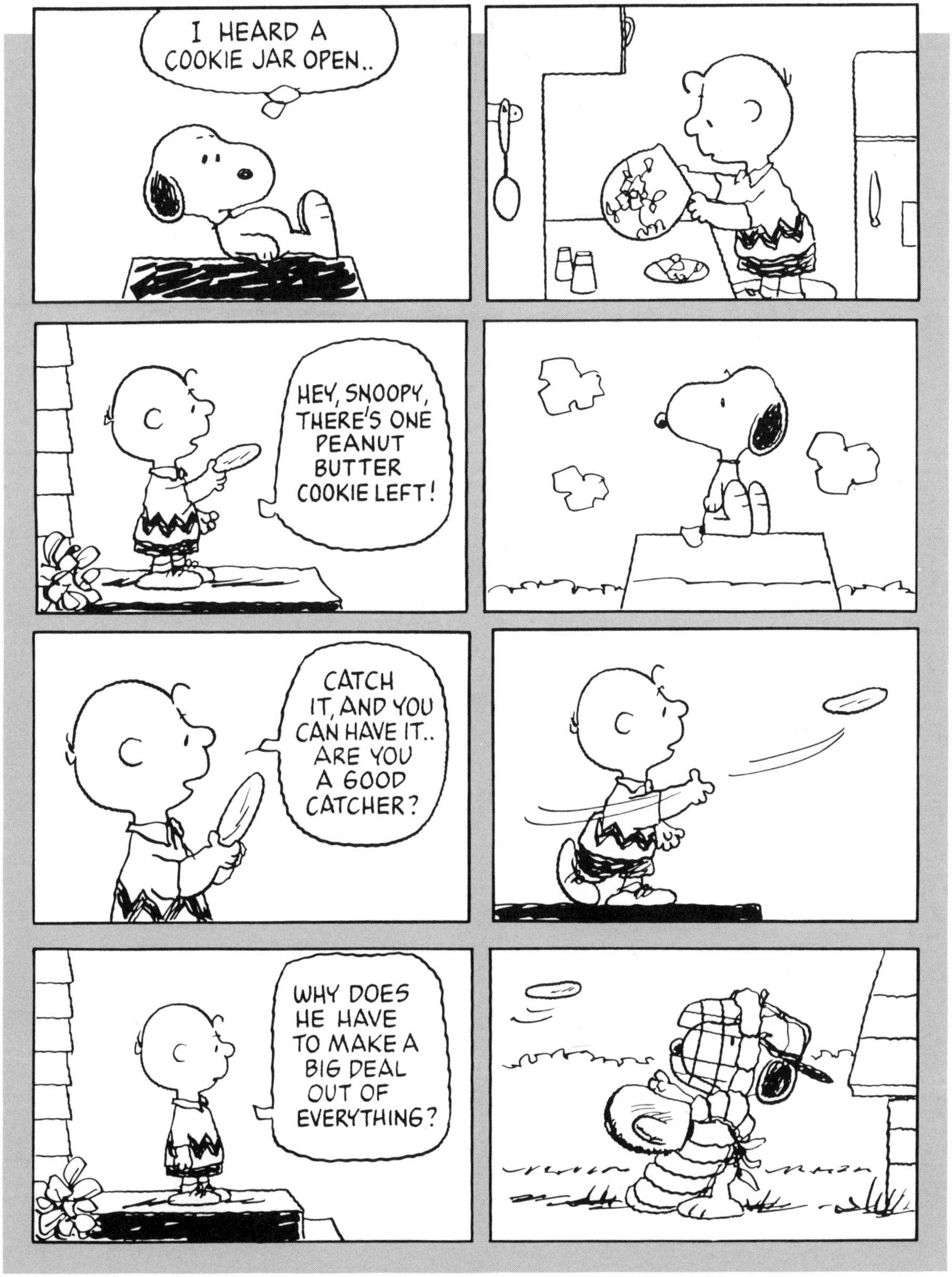
I HEARD A COOKIE JAR OPEN..
HEY, SNOOPY, THERE'S ONE PEANUT BUTTER COOKIE LEFT!
CATCH IT, AND YOU CAN HAVE IT.. ARE YOU A GOOD CATCHER?
WHY DOES HE HAVE TO MAKE A BIG DEAL OUT OF EVERYTHING?

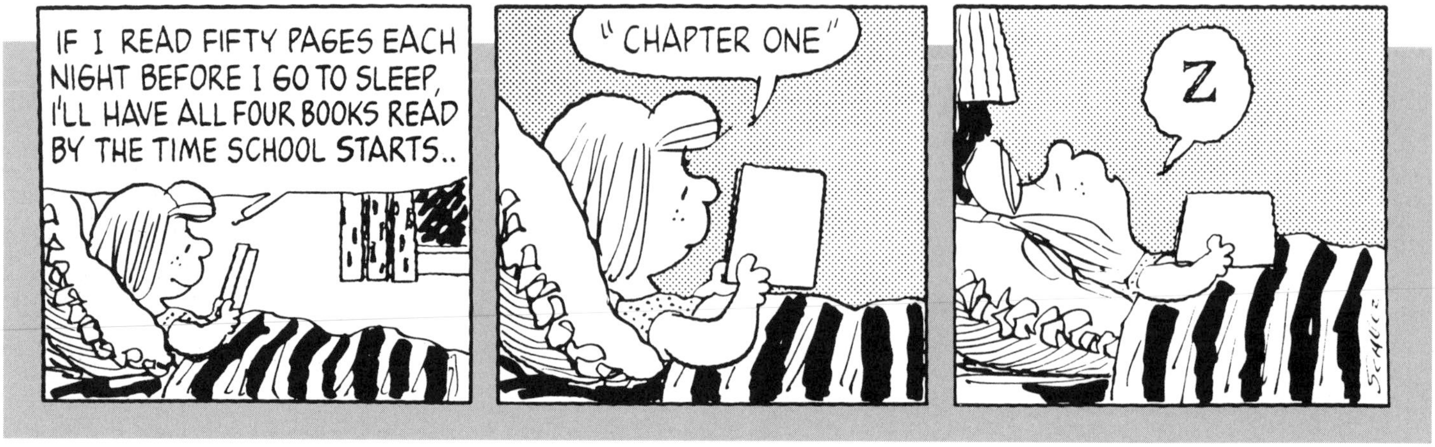
IF I READ FIFTY PAGES EACH NIGHT BEFORE I GO TO SLEEP, I'LL HAVE ALL FOUR BOOKS READ BY THE TIME SCHOOL STARTS..
"CHAPTER ONE"
Z

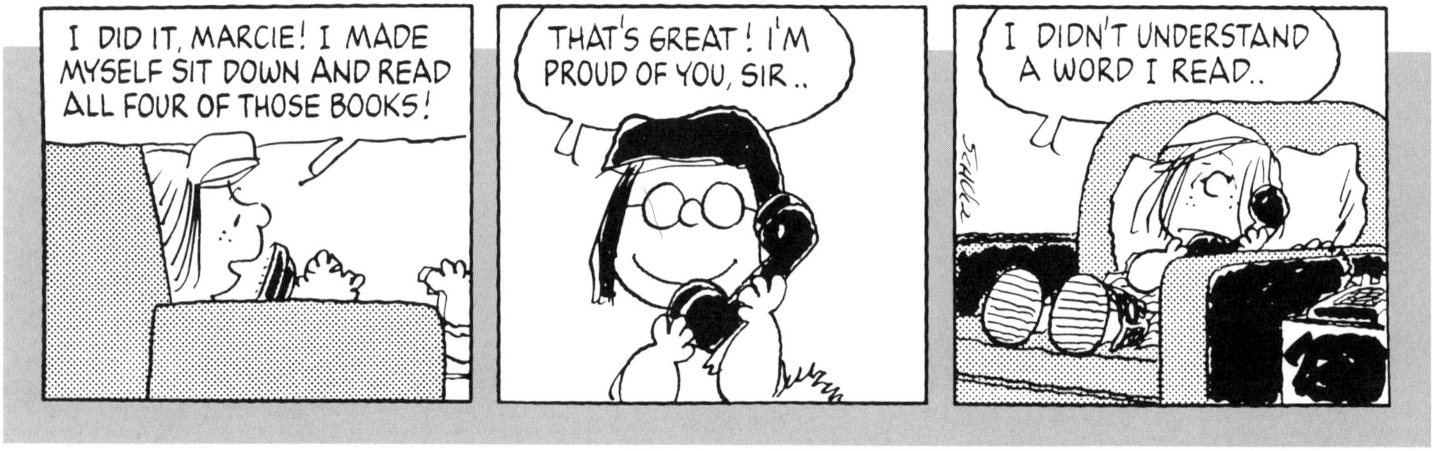
I DID IT, MARCIE! I MADE MYSELF SIT DOWN AND READ ALL FOUR OF THOSE BOOKS!
THAT'S GREAT! I'M PROUD OF YOU, SIR..
I DIDN'T UNDERSTAND A WORD I READ..

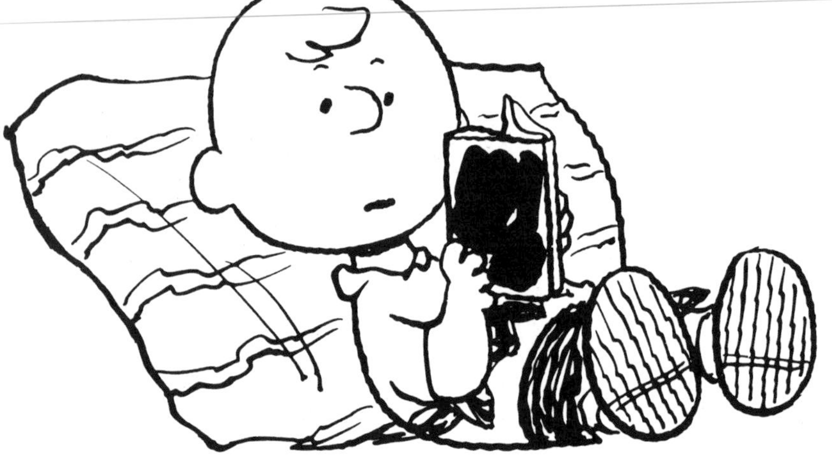

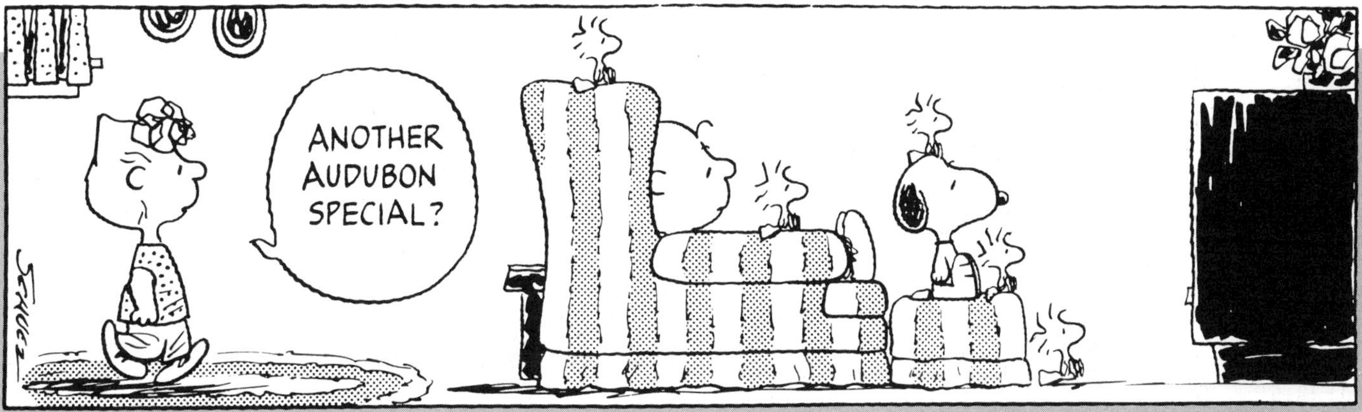
ANOTHER AUDUBON SPECIAL?

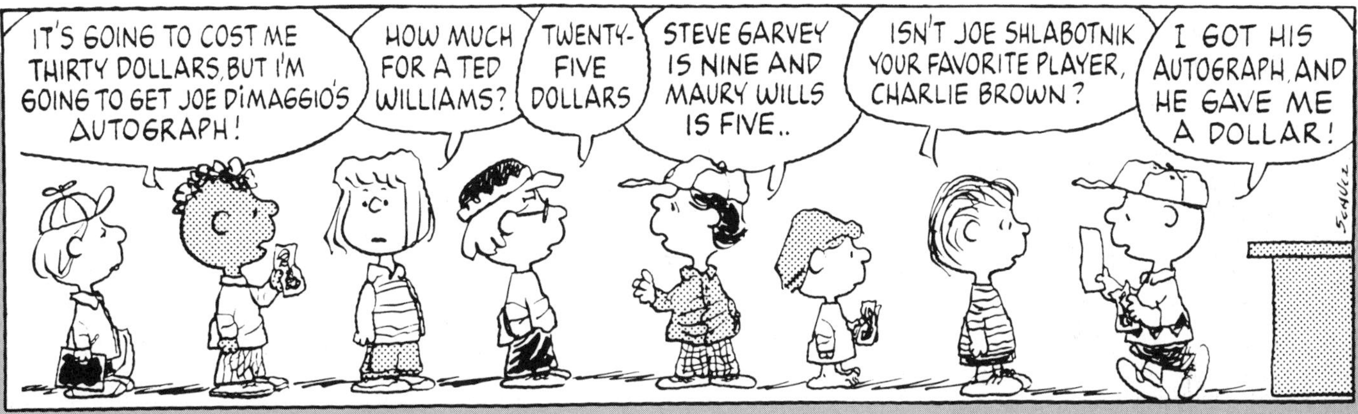
IT'S GOING TO COST ME THIRTY DOLLARS, BUT I'M GOING TO GET JOE DiMAGGIO'S AUTOGRAPH!
HOW MUCH FOR A TED WILLIAMS?
TWENTY-FIVE DOLLARS
STEVE GARVEY IS NINE AND MAURY WILLS IS FIVE..
ISN'T JOE SHLABOTNIK YOUR FAVORITE PLAYER, CHARLIE BROWN?
I GOT HIS AUTOGRAPH, AND HE GAVE ME A DOLLAR!

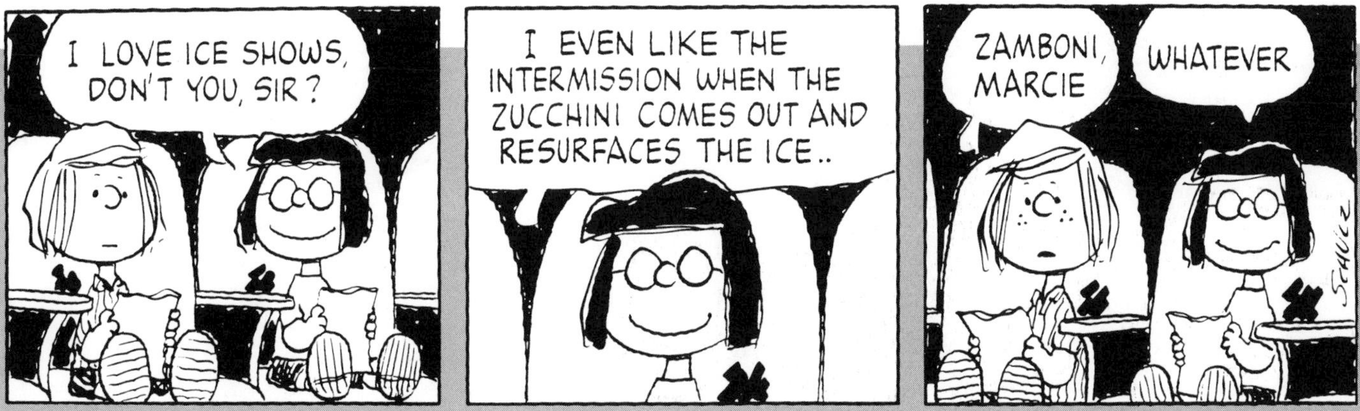
I LOVE ICE SHOWS, DON'T YOU, SIR?
I EVEN LIKE THE INTERMISSION WHEN THE ZUCCHINI COMES OUT AND RESURFACES THE ICE..
ZAMBONI, MARCIE
WHATEVER

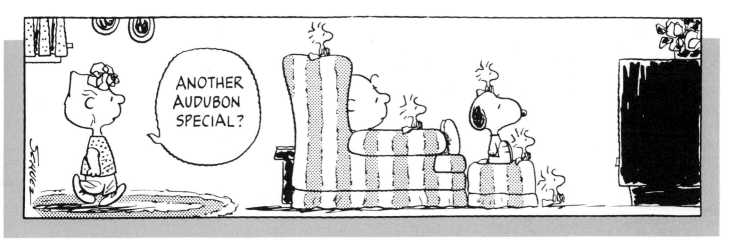

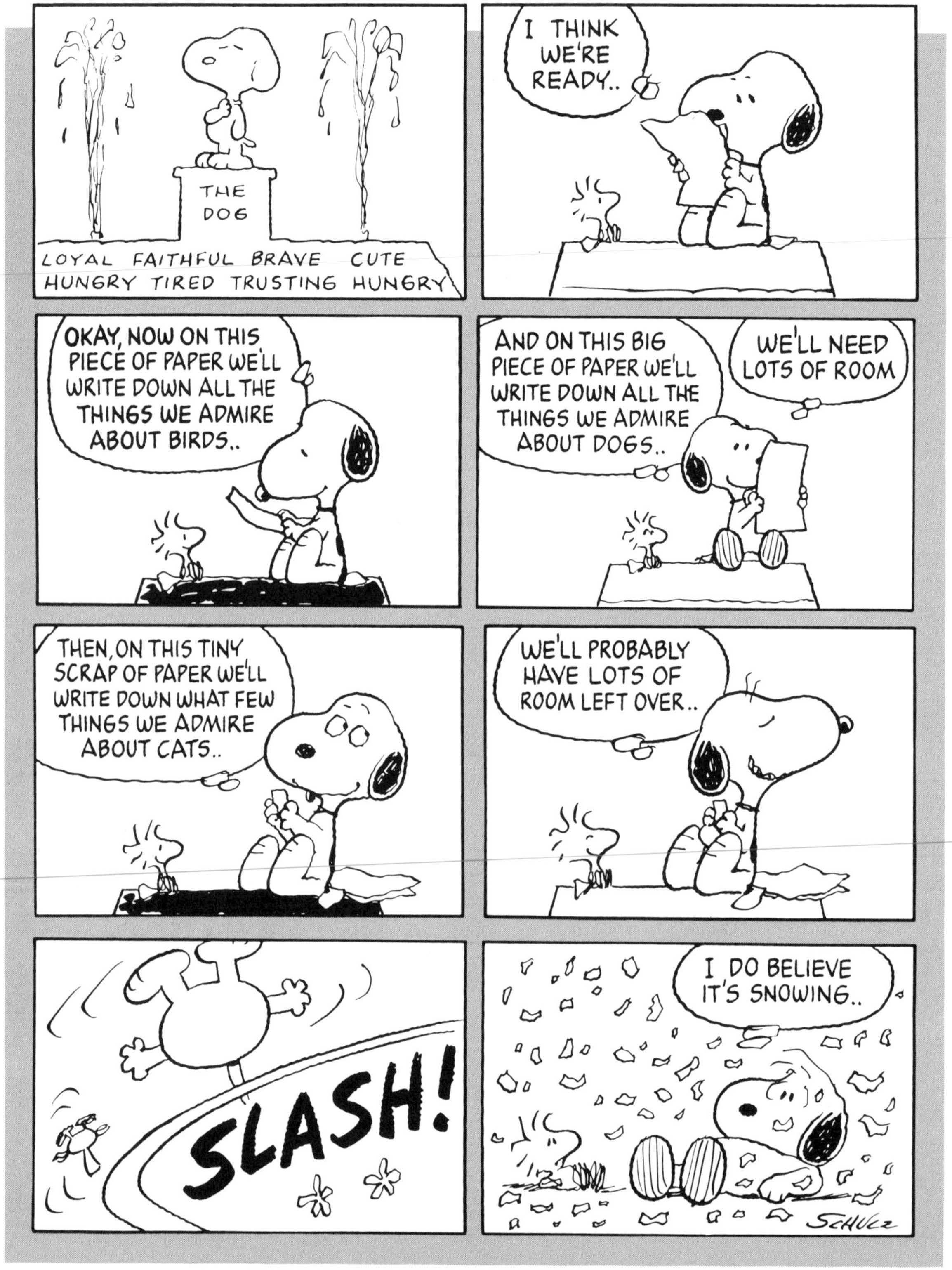
THE DOG
LOYAL FAITHFUL BRAVE CUTE
HUNGRY TIRED TRUSTING HUNGRY
I THINK WE'RE READY..
OKAY, NOW ON THIS PIECE OF PAPER WE'LL WRITE DOWN ALL THE THINGS WE ADMIRE ABOUT BIRDS..
AND ON THIS BIG PIECE OF PAPER WE'LL WRITE DOWN ALL THE THINGS WE ADMIRE ABOUT DOGS..
WE'LL NEED LOTS OF ROOM
THEN, ON THIS TINY SCRAP OF PAPER WE'LL WRITE DOWN WHAT FEW THINGS WE ADMIRE ABOUT CATS..
WE'LL PROBABLY HAVE LOTS OF ROOM LEFT OVER..
SLASH!
I DO BELIEVE IT'S SNOWING..
SCHULZ

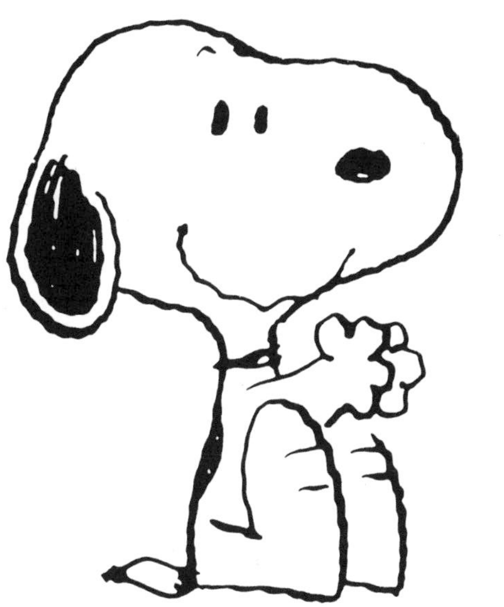

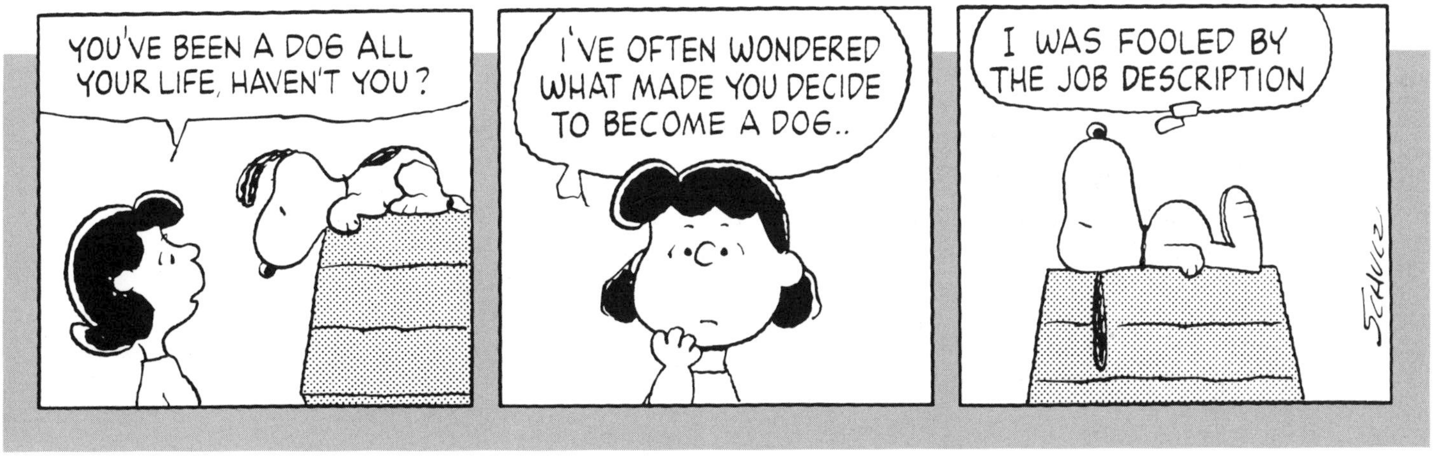
YOU'VE BEEN A DOG ALL YOUR LIFE, HAVEN'T YOU?
I'VE OFTEN WONDERED WHAT MADE YOU DECIDE TO BECOME A DOG..
I WAS FOOLED BY THE JOB DESCRIPTION
SCHULZ

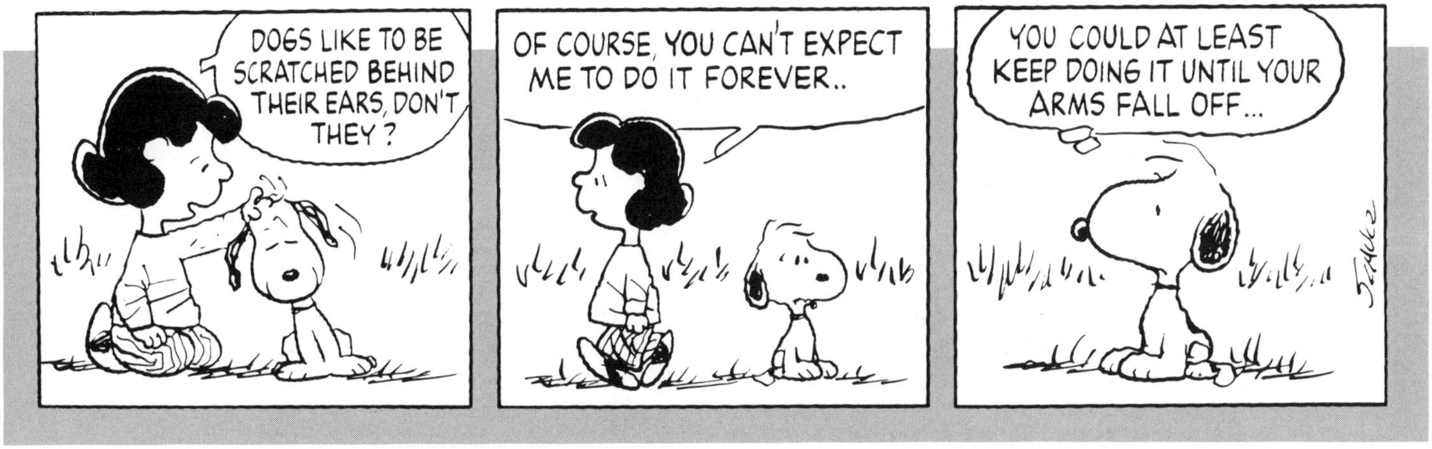
DOGS LIKE TO BE SCRATCHED BEHIND THEIR EARS, DON'T THEY?
OF COURSE, YOU CAN'T EXPECT ME TO DO IT FOREVER..
YOU COULD AT LEAST KEEP DOING IT UNTIL YOUR ARMS FALL OFF...
SCHULZ

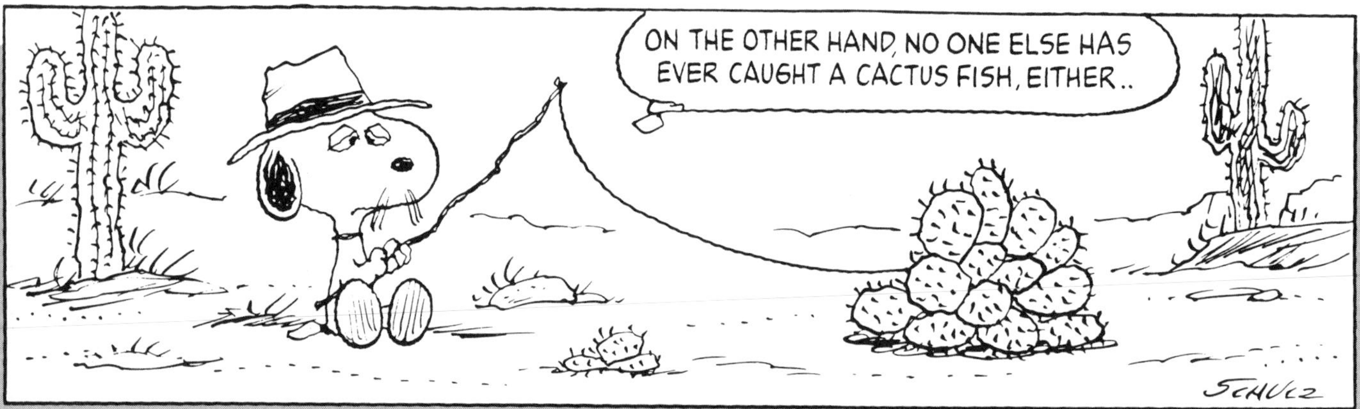
ON THE OTHER HAND, NO ONE ELSE HAS EVER CAUGHT A CACTUS FISH, EITHER..
SCHULZ

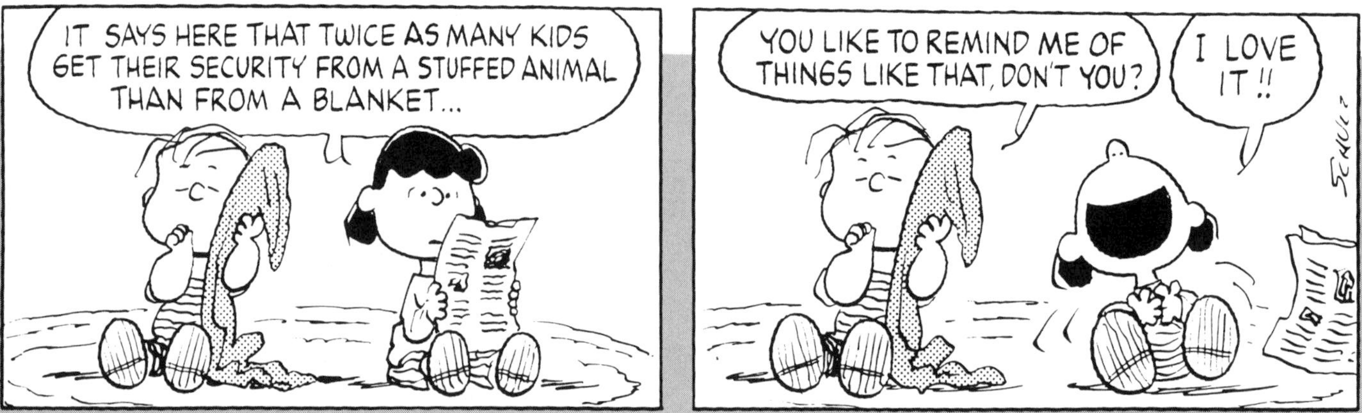
IT SAYS HERE THAT TWICE AS MANY KIDS GET THEIR SECURITY FROM A STUFFED ANIMAL THAN FROM A BLANKET...
YOU LIKE TO REMIND ME OF THINGS LIKE THAT, DON'T YOU?
I LOVE IT !!
SCHULZ

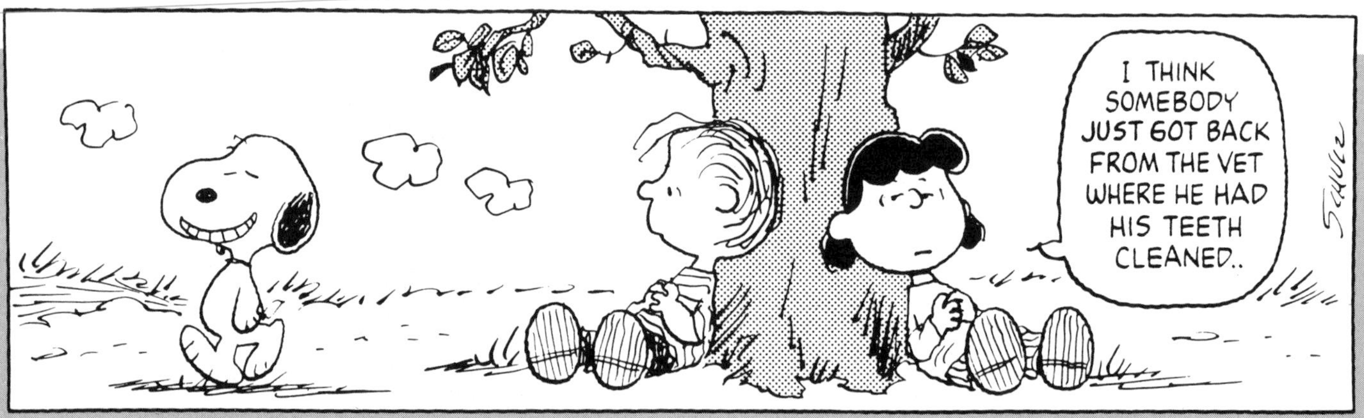
I THINK SOMEBODY JUST GOT BACK FROM THE VET WHERE HE HAD HIS TEETH CLEANED..
SCHULZ

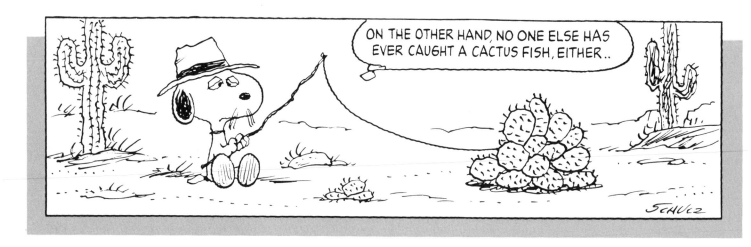

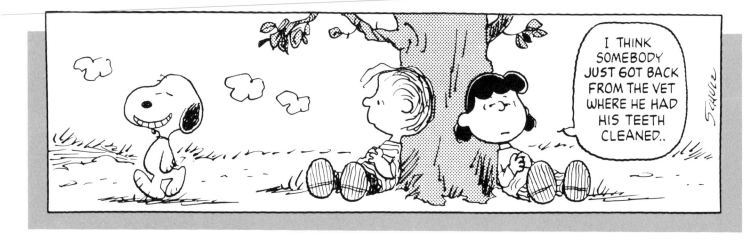

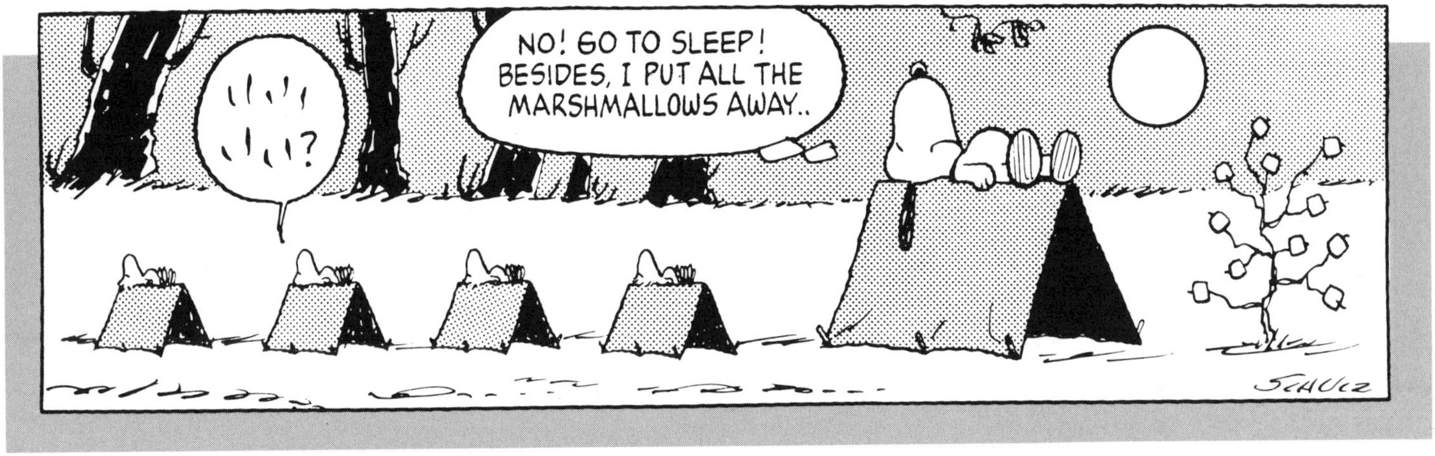
NO! GO TO SLEEP! BESIDES, I PUT ALL THE MARSHMALLOWS AWAY..
SCHULZ

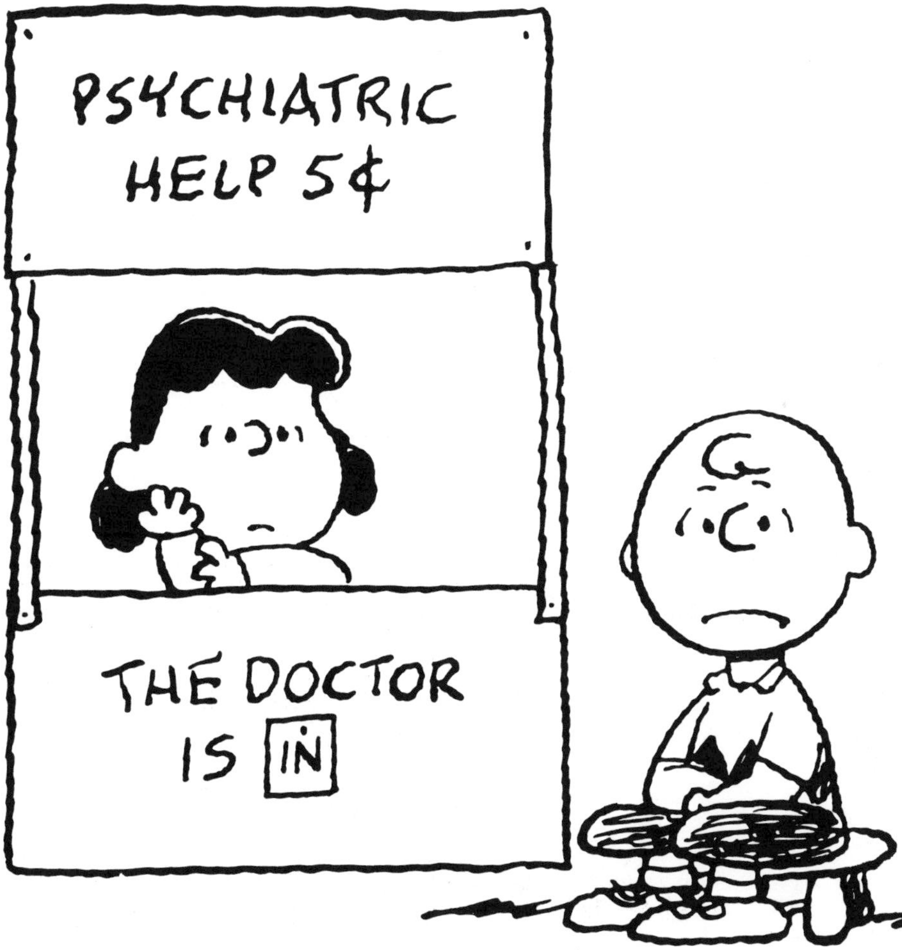
PSYCHIATRIC HELP 5¢
THE DOCTOR IS IN

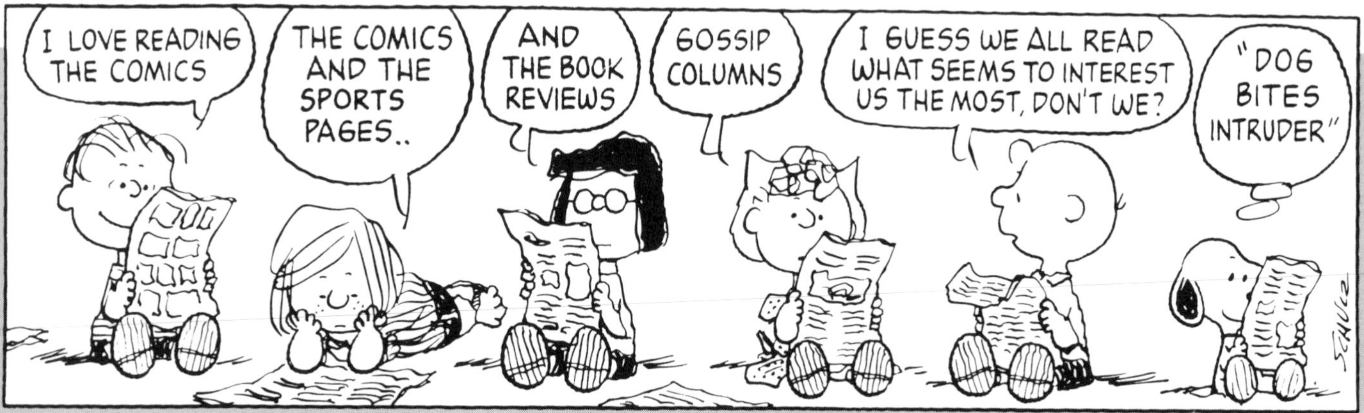
I LOVE READING THE COMICS
THE COMICS AND THE SPORTS PAGES..
AND THE BOOK REVIEWS
GOSSIP COLUMNS
I GUESS WE ALL READ WHAT SEEMS TO INTEREST US THE MOST, DON'T WE?
"DOG BITES INTRUDER"
SCHULZ

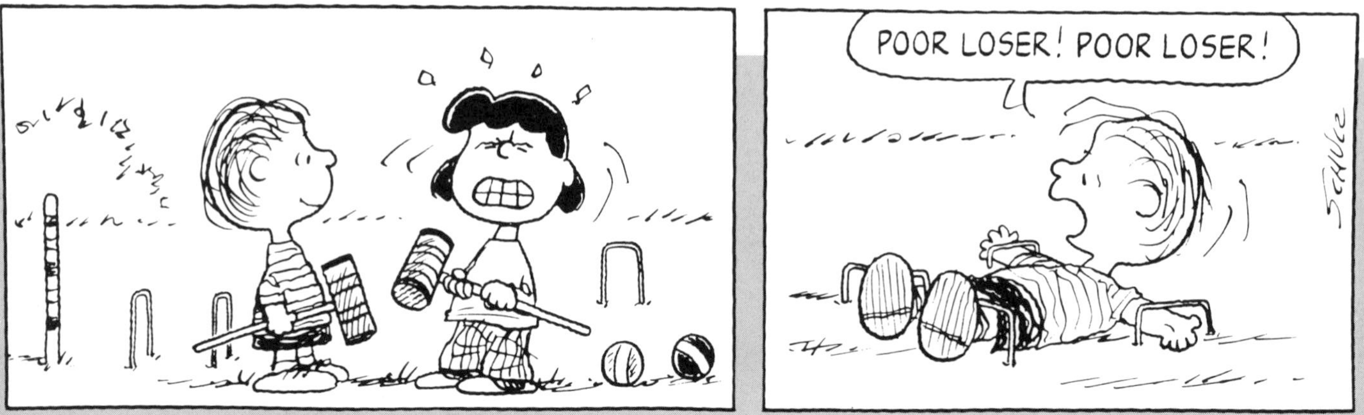
POOR LOSER! POOR LOSER!
SCHULZ

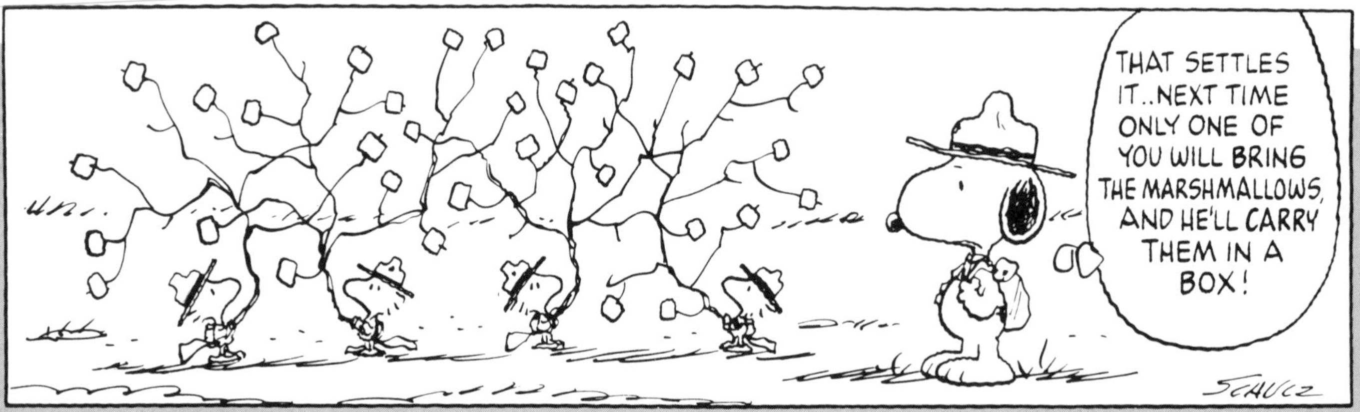
THAT SETTLES IT..NEXT TIME ONLY ONE OF YOU WILL BRING THE MARSHMALLOWS, AND HE'LL CARRY THEM IN A BOX!
SCHULZ

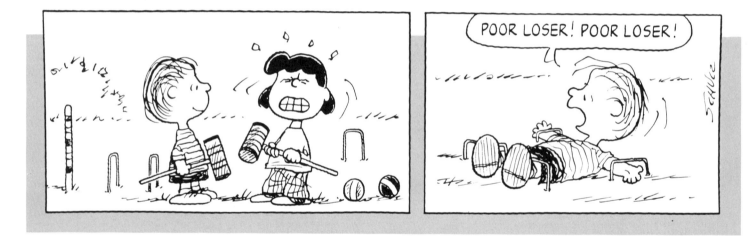

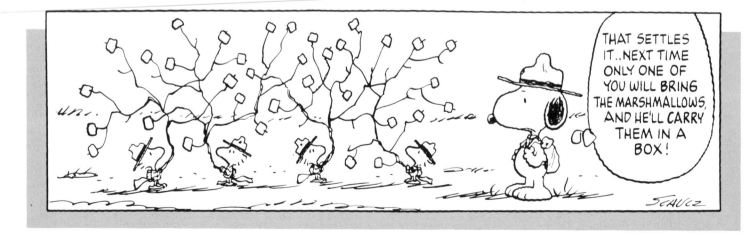

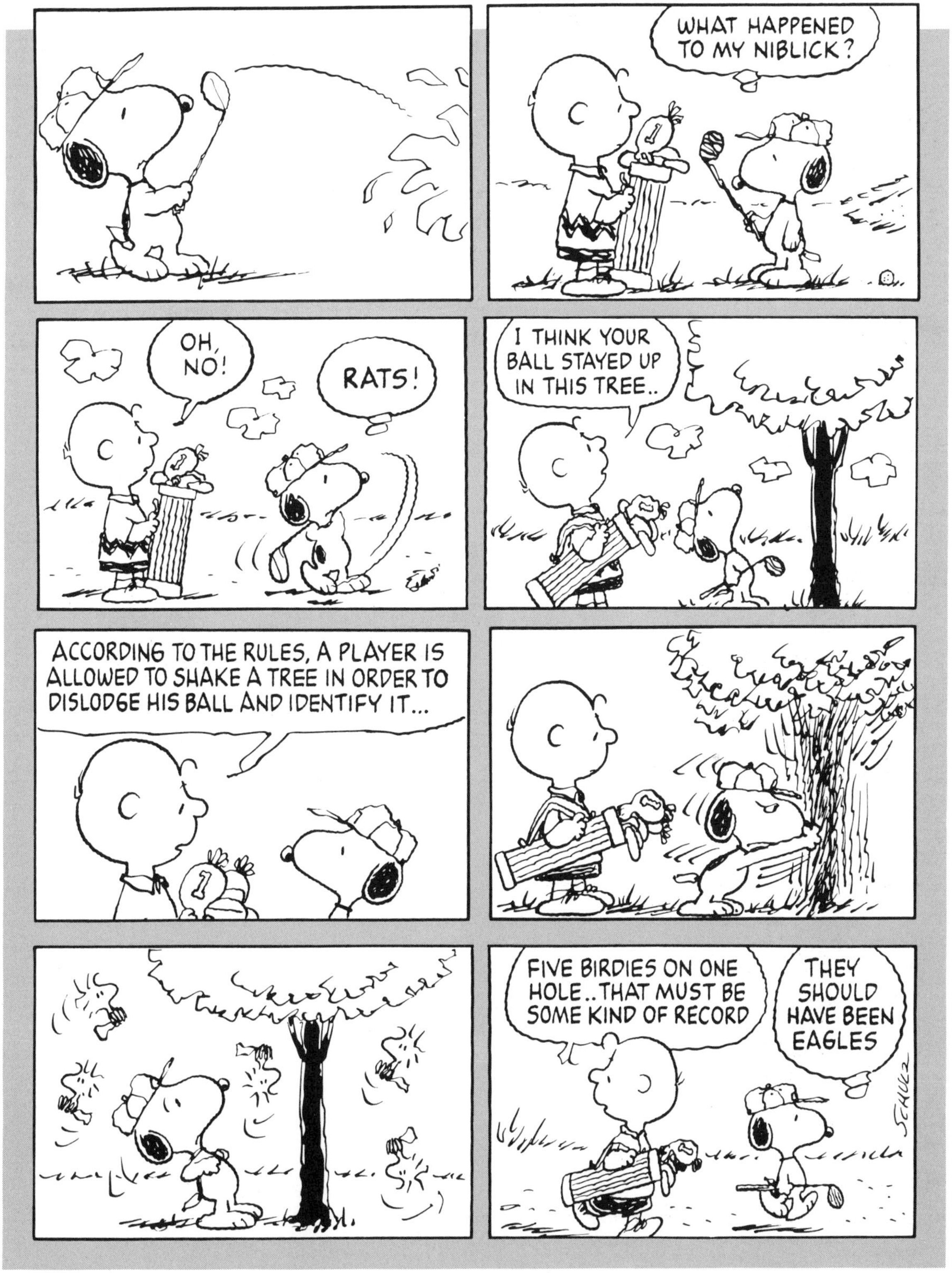
WHAT HAPPENED TO MY NIBLICK?
OH, NO!
RATS!
I THINK YOUR BALL STAYED UP IN THIS TREE..
ACCORDING TO THE RULES, A PLAYER IS ALLOWED TO SHAKE A TREE IN ORDER TO DISLODGE HIS BALL AND IDENTIFY IT...
FIVE BIRDIES ON ONE HOLE..THAT MUST BE SOME KIND OF RECORD
THEY SHOULD HAVE BEEN EAGLES
SCHULZ

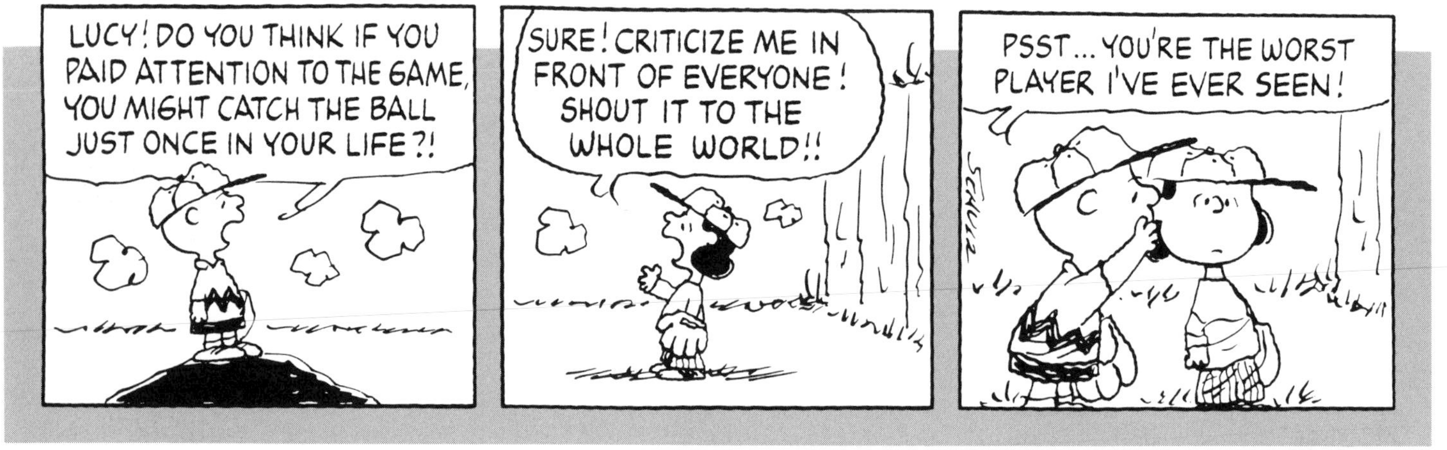
LUCY! DO YOU THINK IF YOU PAID ATTENTION TO THE GAME, YOU MIGHT CATCH THE BALL JUST ONCE IN YOUR LIFE?!
SURE! CRITICIZE ME IN FRONT OF EVERYONE! SHOUT IT TO THE WHOLE WORLD!!
PSST... YOU'RE THE WORST PLAYER I'VE EVER SEEN!

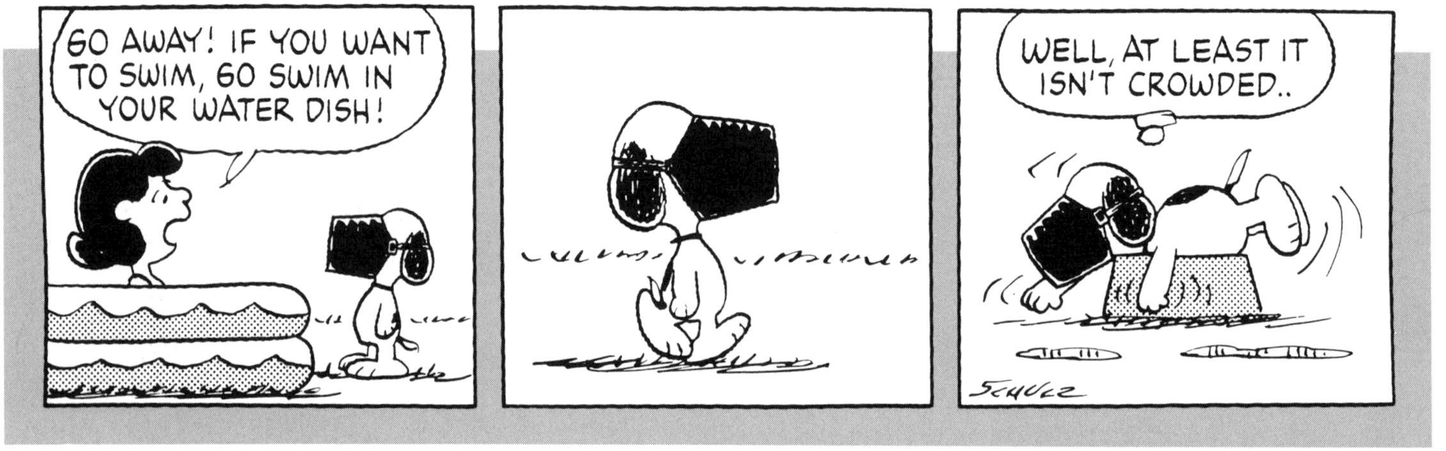
GO AWAY! IF YOU WANT TO SWIM, GO SWIM IN YOUR WATER DISH!
WELL, AT LEAST IT ISN'T CROWDED..

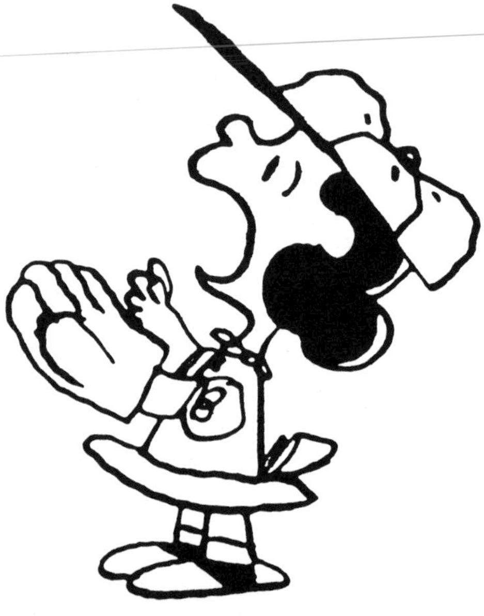

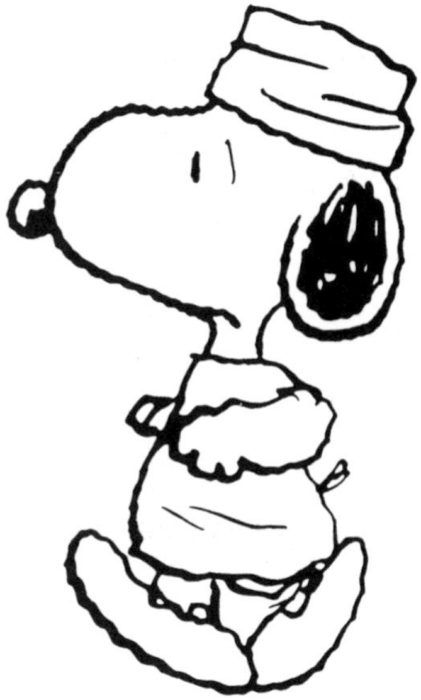

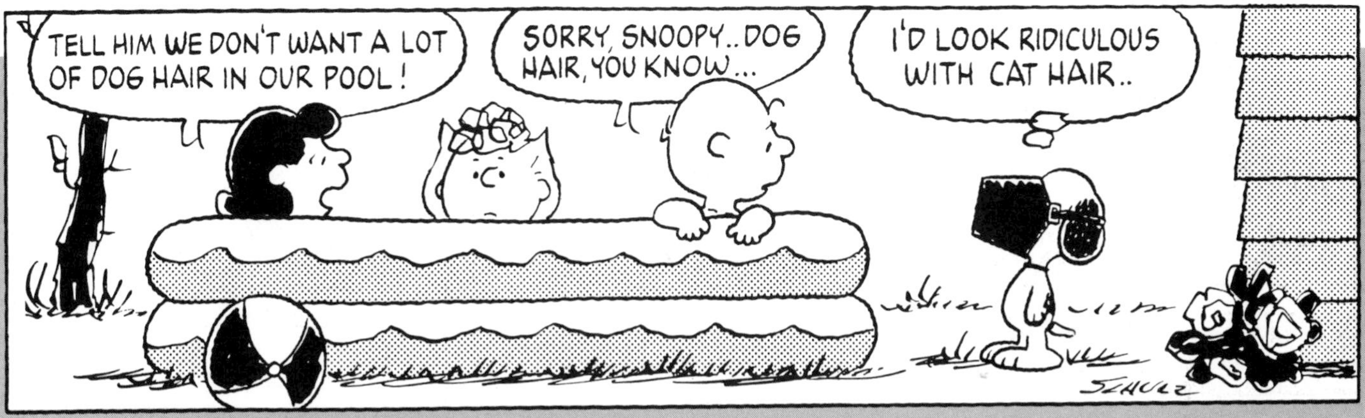
TELL HIM WE DON'T WANT A LOT OF DOG HAIR IN OUR POOL!
SORRY, SNOOPY..DOG HAIR, YOU KNOW...
I'D LOOK RIDICULOUS WITH CAT HAIR..
SCHULZ

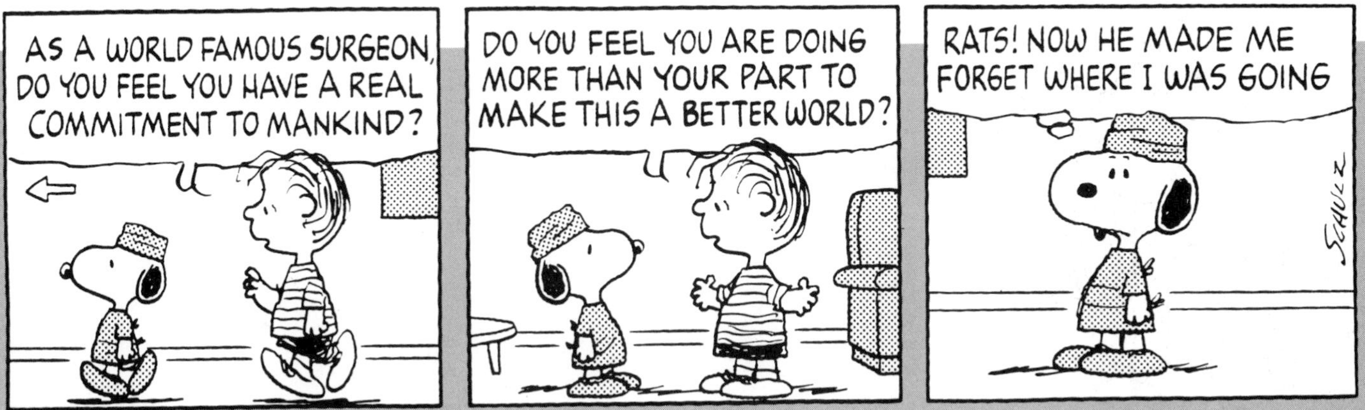
AS A WORLD FAMOUS SURGEON, DO YOU FEEL YOU HAVE A REAL COMMITMENT TO MANKIND?
DO YOU FEEL YOU ARE DOING MORE THAN YOUR PART TO MAKE THIS A BETTER WORLD?
RATS! NOW HE MADE ME FORGET WHERE I WAS GOING
SCHULZ

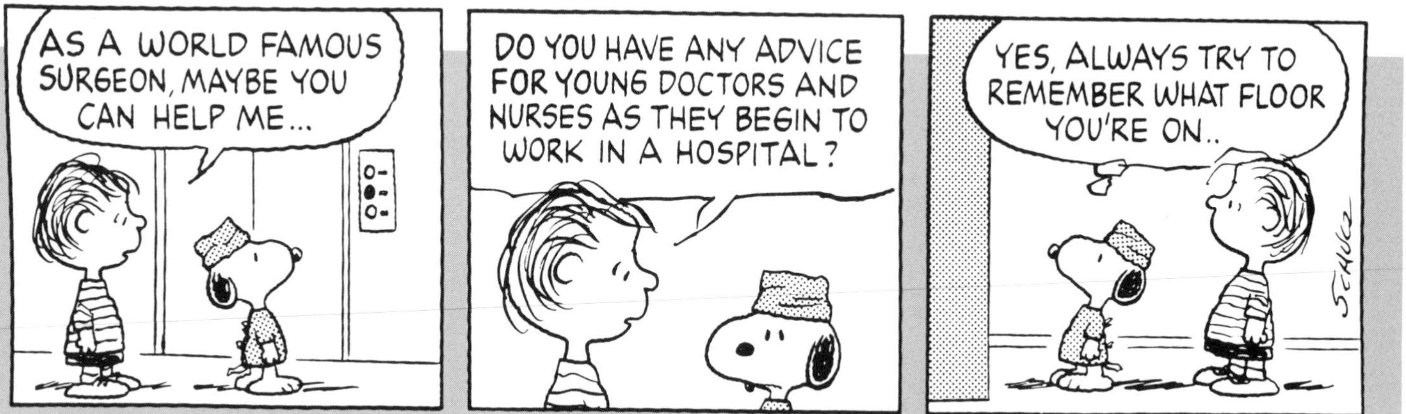
AS A WORLD FAMOUS SURGEON, MAYBE YOU CAN HELP ME...
DO YOU HAVE ANY ADVICE FOR YOUNG DOCTORS AND NURSES AS THEY BEGIN TO WORK IN A HOSPITAL?
YES, ALWAYS TRY TO REMEMBER WHAT FLOOR YOU'RE ON..

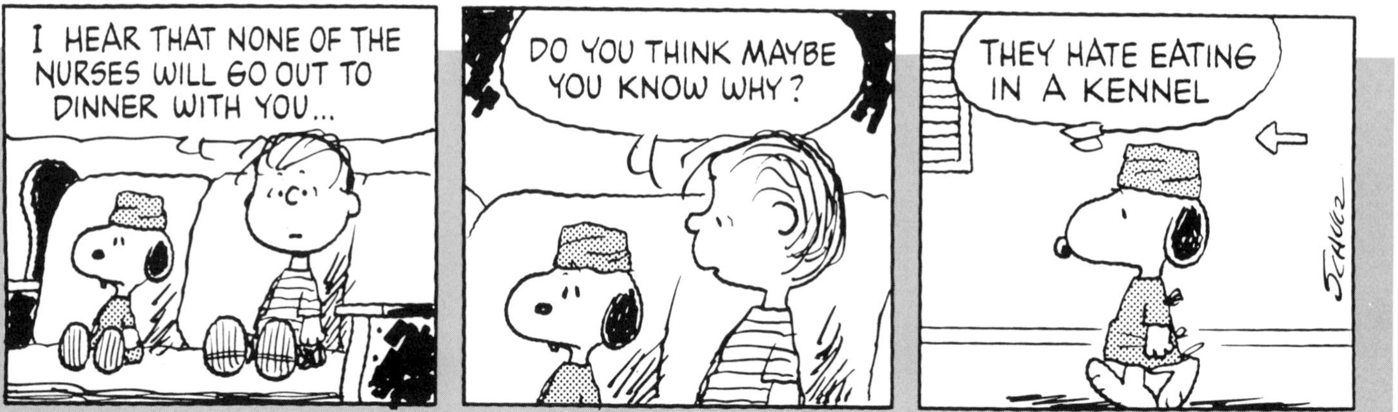
I HEAR THAT NONE OF THE NURSES WILL GO OUT TO DINNER WITH YOU...
DO YOU THINK MAYBE YOU KNOW WHY?
THEY HATE EATING IN A KENNEL

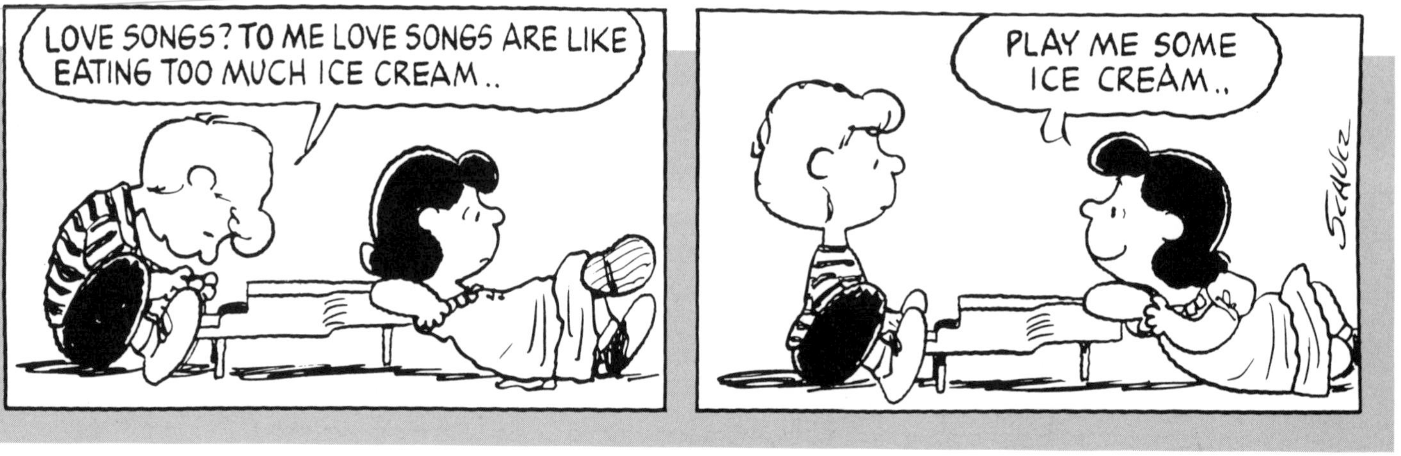
LOVE SONGS? TO ME LOVE SONGS ARE LIKE EATING TOO MUCH ICE CREAM..
PLAY ME SOME ICE CREAM..

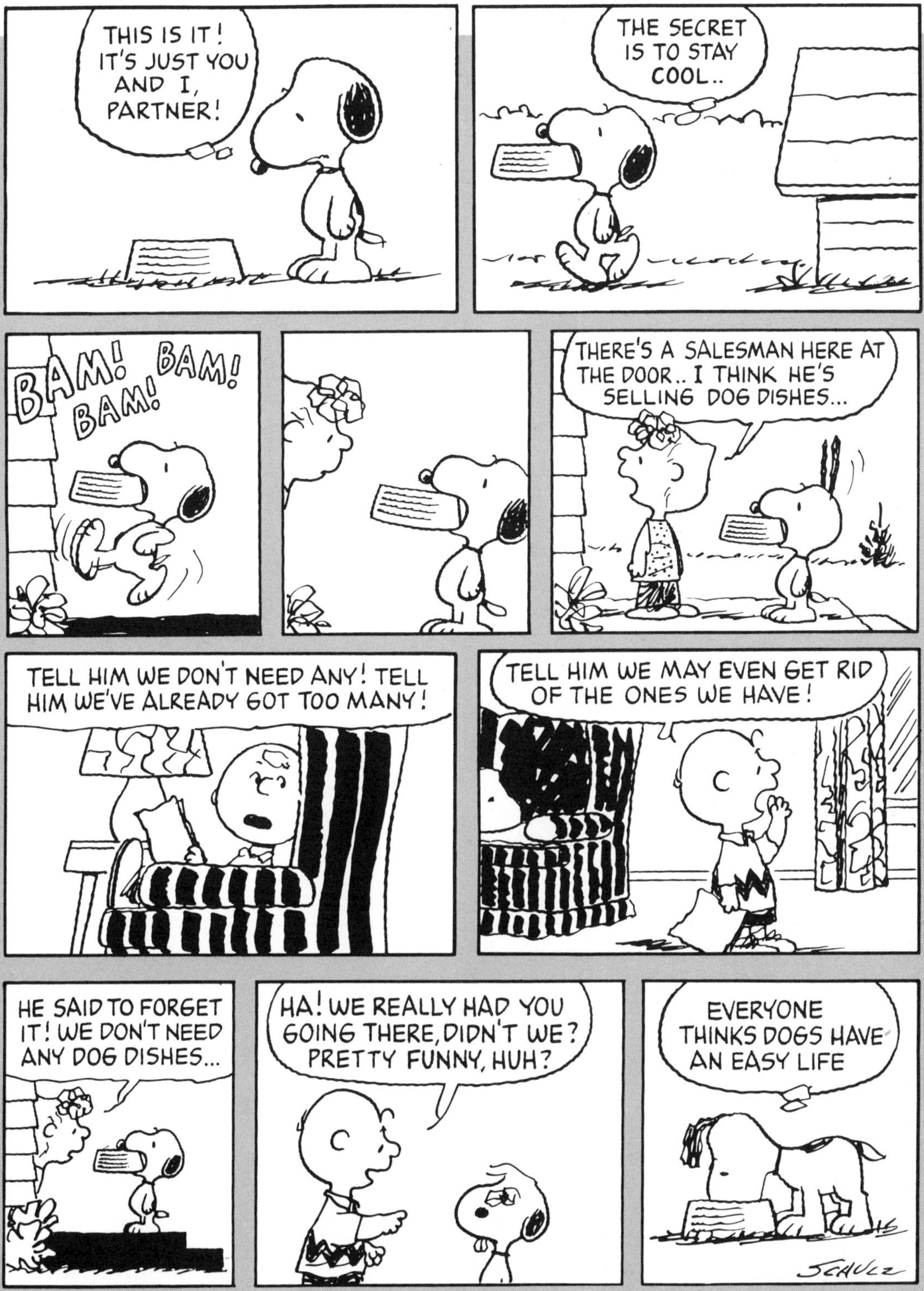
THIS IS IT! IT'S JUST YOU AND I, PARTNER!
THE SECRET IS TO STAY COOL..
BAM! BAM! BAM!
THERE'S A SALESMAN HERE AT THE DOOR.. I THINK HE'S SELLING DOG DISHES...
TELL HIM WE DON'T NEED ANY! TELL HIM WE'VE ALREADY GOT TOO MANY!
TELL HIM WE MAY EVEN GET RID OF THE ONES WE HAVE!
HE SAID TO FORGET IT! WE DON'T NEED ANY DOG DISHES...
HA! WE REALLY HAD YOU GOING THERE, DIDN'T WE? PRETTY FUNNY, HUH?
EVERYONE THINKS DOGS HAVE AN EASY LIFE
SCHULZ

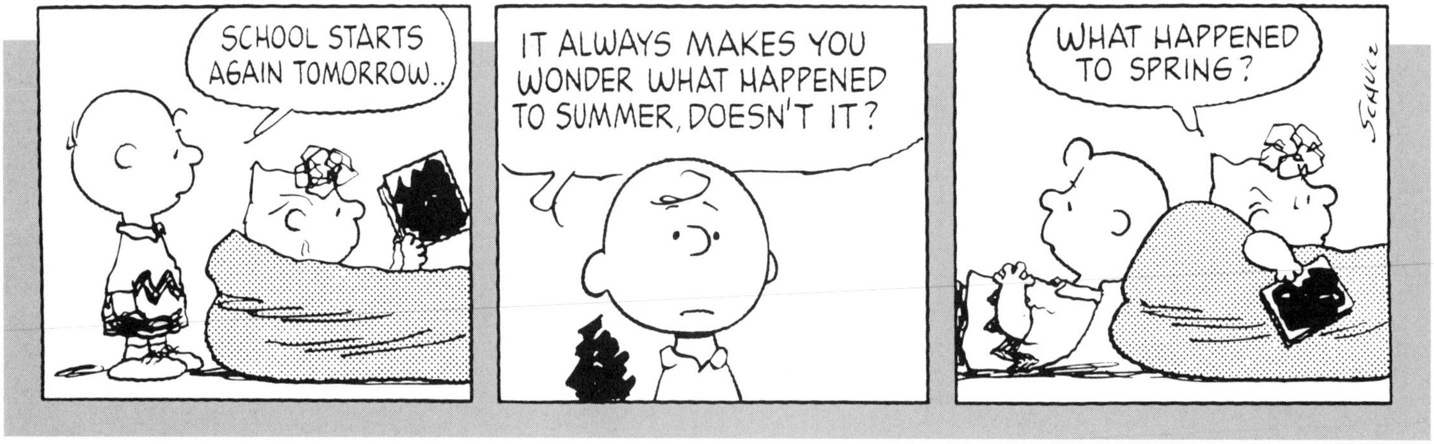
SCHOOL STARTS AGAIN TOMORROW..
IT ALWAYS MAKES YOU WONDER WHAT HAPPENED TO SUMMER, DOESN'T IT?
WHAT HAPPENED TO SPRING?

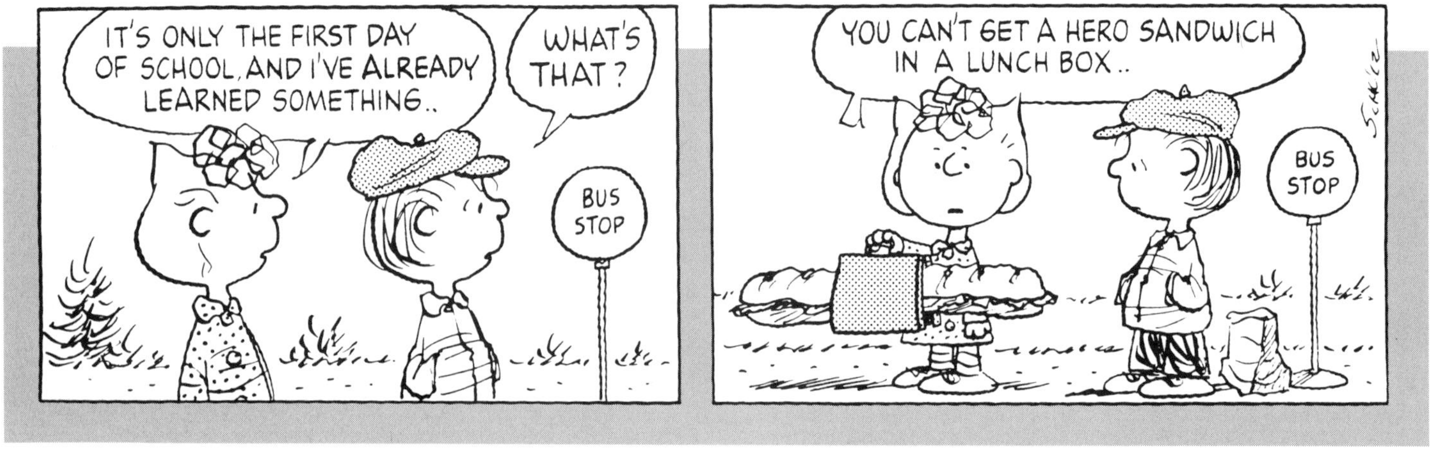
IT'S ONLY THE FIRST DAY OF SCHOOL, AND I'VE ALREADY LEARNED SOMETHING..
WHAT'S THAT?
BUS STOP
YOU CAN'T GET A HERO SANDWICH IN A LUNCH BOX..
BUS STOP

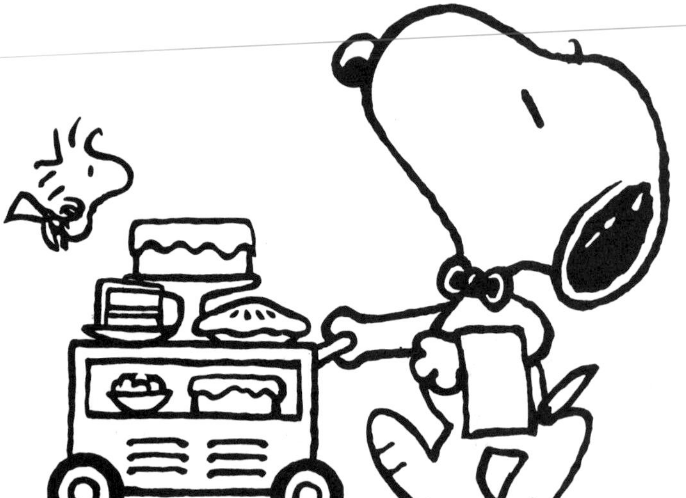

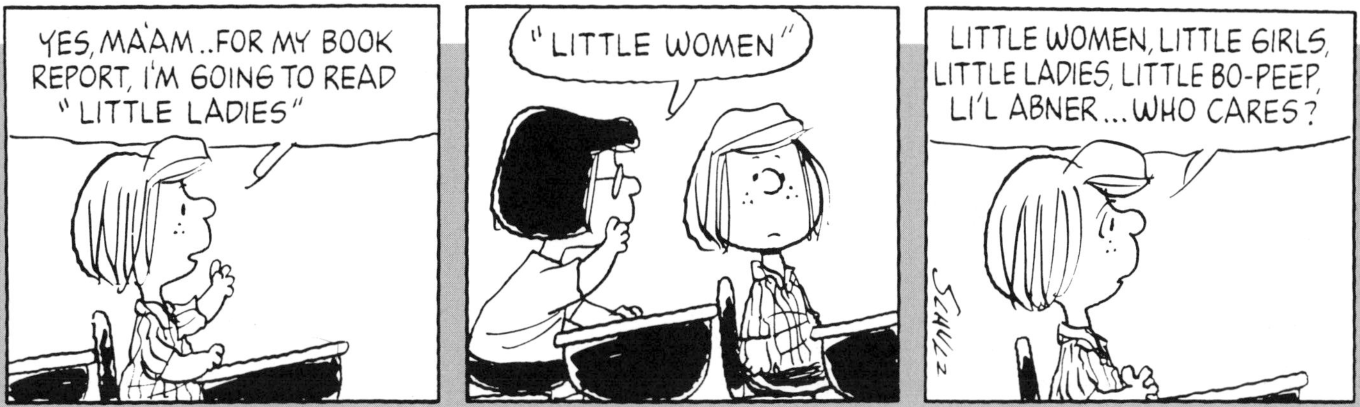
YES, MA'AM..FOR MY BOOK REPORT, I'M GOING TO READ "LITTLE LADIES"
"LITTLE WOMEN"
LITTLE WOMEN, LITTLE GIRLS, LITTLE LADIES, LITTLE BO-PEEP, LI'L ABNER... WHO CARES?

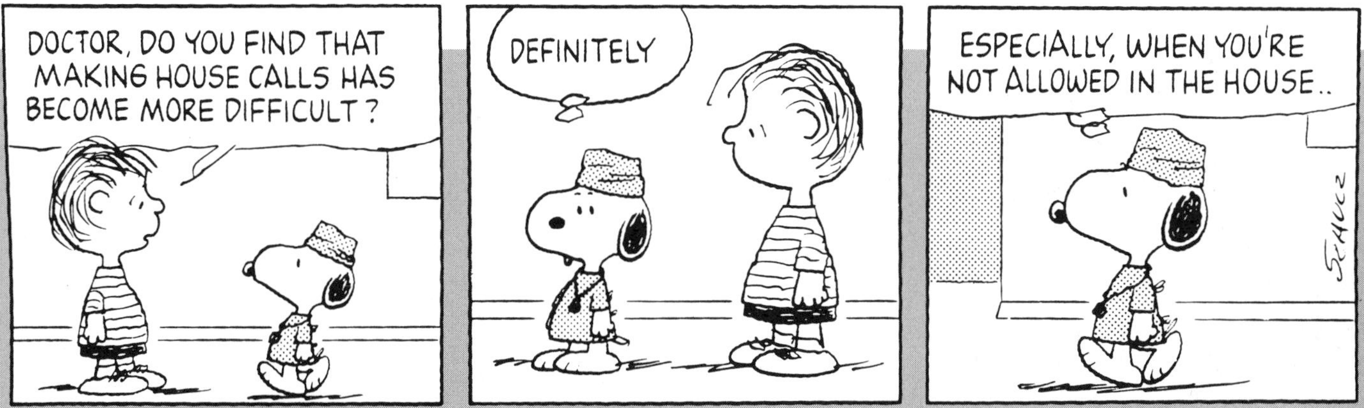
DOCTOR, DO YOU FIND THAT MAKING HOUSE CALLS HAS BECOME MORE DIFFICULT?
DEFINITELY
ESPECIALLY, WHEN YOU'RE NOT ALLOWED IN THE HOUSE..

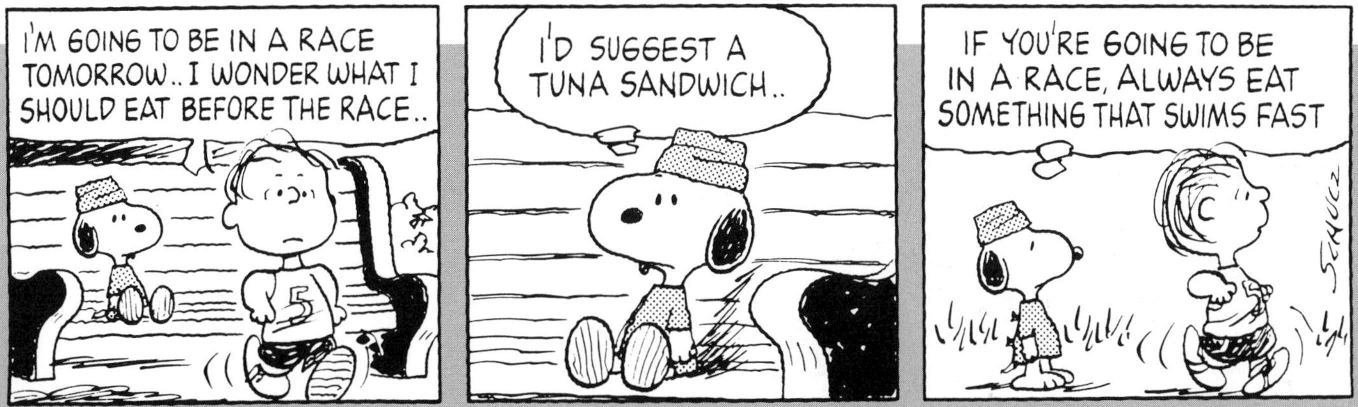
I'M GOING TO BE IN A RACE TOMORROW.. I WONDER WHAT I SHOULD EAT BEFORE THE RACE..
I'D SUGGEST A TUNA SANDWICH..
IF YOU'RE GOING TO BE IN A RACE, ALWAYS EAT SOMETHING THAT SWIMS FAST

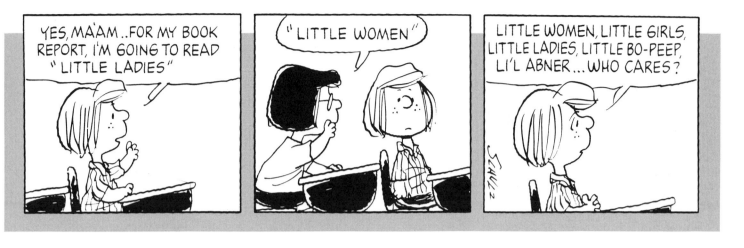

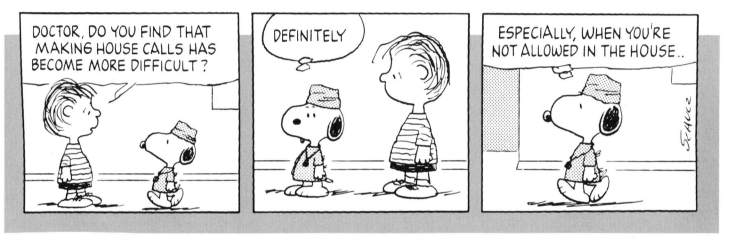

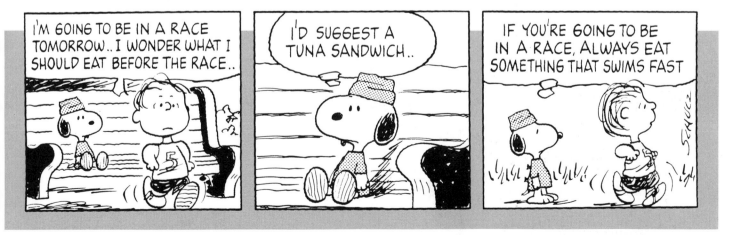

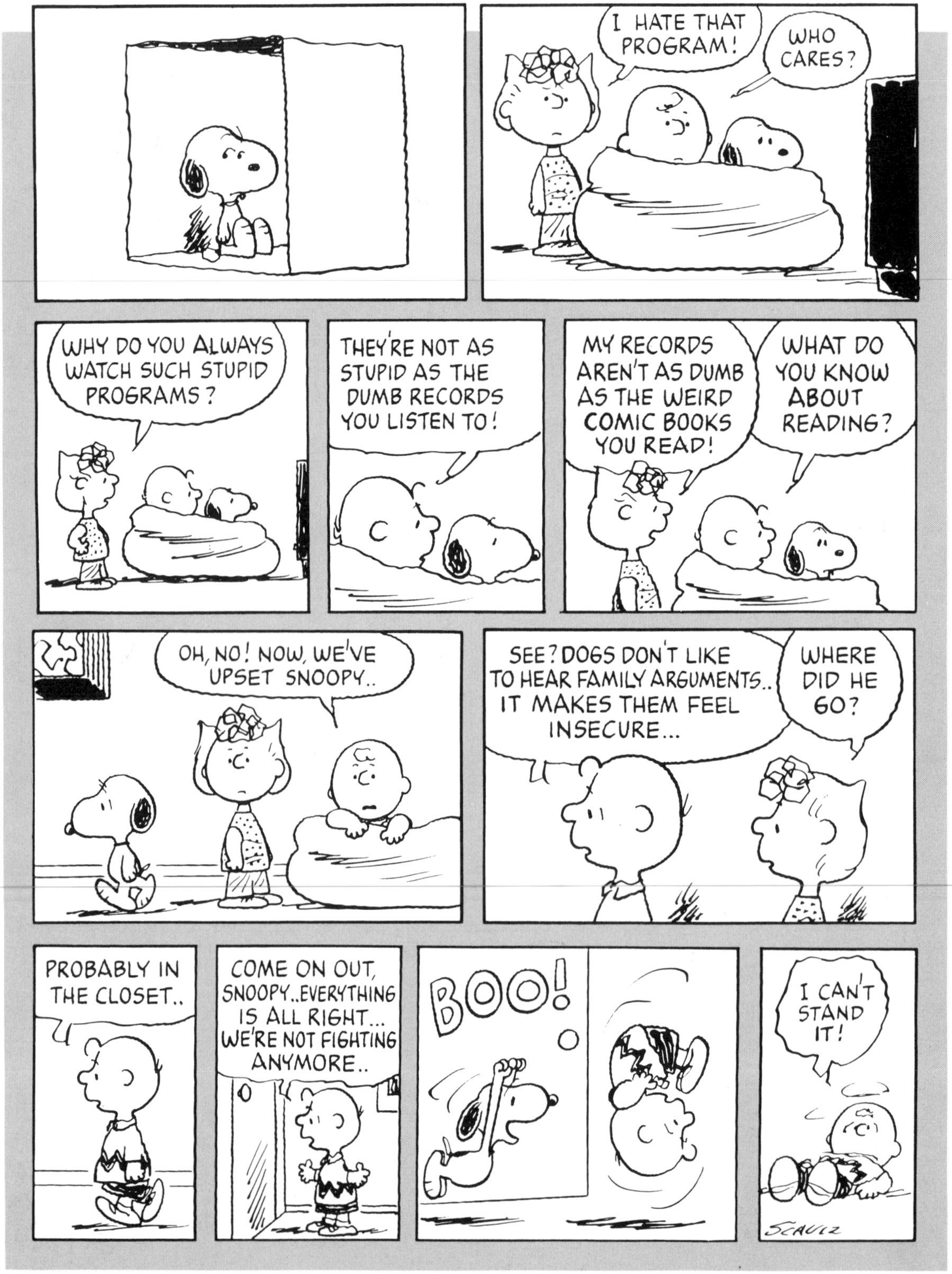
I HATE THAT PROGRAM!
WHO CARES?
WHY DO YOU ALWAYS WATCH SUCH STUPID PROGRAMS?
THEY'RE NOT AS STUPID AS THE DUMB RECORDS YOU LISTEN TO!
MY RECORDS AREN'T AS DUMB AS THE WEIRD COMIC BOOKS YOU READ!
WHAT DO YOU KNOW ABOUT READING?
OH, NO! NOW, WE'VE UPSET SNOOPY..
SEE? DOGS DON'T LIKE TO HEAR FAMILY ARGUMENTS.. IT MAKES THEM FEEL INSECURE...
WHERE DID HE GO?
PROBABLY IN THE CLOSET..
COME ON OUT, SNOOPY..EVERYTHING IS ALL RIGHT... WE'RE NOT FIGHTING ANYMORE..
BOO!
I CAN'T STAND IT!
SCHULZ